*"I feel a strong predilection for the Constitution. I think…she will be a most fortunate Ship; and I am sometimes good in my predictions…"*

*Consul General Tobias Lear*
*16 October 1804*

*Sketch by John Charles Roach for* U.S.S. Constitution *turn-around certificate, Spring 1976.*

# A Most Fortunate Ship

## A Narrative History of "Old Ironsides"

by

Tyrone G. Martin
Captain, USS Constitution
(1974-1978)

The
Globe
Pequot
Press

Chester, Connecticut

*For*
*My Mom and Dad,*
*Proud Americans*

# Preface

It must have seemed a bit odd to the Queen of England. She was standing in the Captain's Day Cabin, looking at the desk that had belonged to Charles Stewart. He commanded *USS Constitution* when "Old Ironsides" defeated British warships *Cyane* and *Levant* in 1815.

But now the year was 1976, with the United States celebrating the Bicentennial of the American Revolution. Queen Elizabeth II understood well that the frigate *Constitution* is the proudest symbol of the maritime history of the Union that emerged from that Revolution.

With me as we hosted the Queen on her Bicentennial ship tour was Ty Martin, Captain of the U.S. Navy's most historic ship. Tall and immaculately dressed in his "old Navy" uniform, including fore and aft hat, Martin was a perfect escort for royalty. An outstanding officer, with a long and distinguished career in the United States Navy, as much an expert on today's Soviety Navy as his predecessors may have been on the British or French squadrons or the Barbary pirates, the skipper knew this ship from the billethead to eagle's crest.

Now Tyrone G. Martin's expert knowledge of *USS Constitution* has been incorporated into a narrative history of the ship that has meant freedom of the seas to generations of Americans. "Old Ironsides," launched in 1797, carrying more than 50 guns and a crew of 450 men, was never defeated in battle and remains today a commissioned unit of the U.S. Navy.

Martin's book fills the need for a comprehensive history of this great ship and provides details of some incidents in her career never before widely known. His volume should be of interest to all those who believe to this day that maritime superiority is essential for the survival of our country.

J. WILLIAM MIDDENDORF II
Secretary of the Navy, 1974-1977

# Foreword

I did not intend to write this book — or any book — on the day I found myself taking command of *Constitution* in accordance with routine Navy orders. I had had 22 years of naval service at that moment, and two previous commands; but this one, I knew, would be different, if for no other reason than the unique character of the ship.

I had no special knowledge of *Constitution* when I took command. Having been a navy history and records buff from boyhood, I suppose I might have known a bit more about her than the average citizen, but I certainly wasn't an "expert" — whatever one of those may be.

Earlier in my career, I had been involved in Naval Intelligence for a number of years. During those years of reading reams of field reports concerning my area of particular responsibility, I developed a habit of periodically taking a sort of sabbatical from the daily routine and writing a paper on some aspect of the subject, seeking to bring together the disparate elements of the reports into some sort of cohesive whole that would help me understand developments and thus better advise my superiors. The habit came with me to *Constitution*, so that when people began showing me treasured family documents from an ancestor who had served aboard "Old Ironsides," and when I had accomplished considerable reading of available authorities, I again turned to the old habit of writing papers as a learning device. From that beginning the present work has come.

In undertaking to write about *Constitution*, I am very sensitive to the fact that many, many have done so before. The broad outline of her story is not new. But, in the course of my initially haphazard study, I discovered that some of the "facts" learned at someone's knee weren't true at all. I also became aware of interesting incidents in her career that apparently never had been made public. Thus, what I have attempted to do in this present volume is to tell *Constitution*'s story just as the records show it, balancing it to provide greater detail to those years **after** the glories of the War of 1812, to record the great events and the doldrums, the noble deeds and the moments of human frailty.

This book never would have **been** without the support and encouragement of a great number of people, most of whom will have to be satisfied with this general acknowledgement of their contribution. Several, however, I want to mention specifically: the artisans of the *USS Constitution* Restoration and Maintenance Facility, who shared their crafts and their love for the ship with me; Edwin Bearss, who parallelled his research for a history of the Boston Navy Yard for the National Park Service with gathering material for me; Virginia Steele Wood, from whose study of the live oak industry I benefitted, and who also regularly turned up new materials; Bill Bass and his late wife, Dilsey, Floridians who, in 1975, began delving into the mysteries of the changes in appearance this fabulous frigate has undergone through the years, and which Bill is continuing with significant success; David F. Long, Professor of History at the University of New Hampshire, who found my early papers historically reputable and who offered valued comment on the manuscript; and W. Davis Taylor, who provided the final encouragement to "make a book of it."

I would be remiss if I did not mention the several hundred young men who composed my crew in *Constitution* during my four years in command. Almost without exception, they were enthusiasts about the ship and believed in her value to us today. **They** were the ones who wanted to "rap" regularly about every aspect of her existence; **they** were interested in learning more facts and stories about her so that they could better show her off to the thousands who visit; **they** continued to ask "When are you going to finish the book?" months after my tour had ended. Well, here it is, lads.

I have appended to the narrative a glossary containing most of the nautical terminology used, so that those less familiar with the sea should be able to navigate with ease. For the serious student, there also is appended a chapter-by-chapter listing of source materials.

Finally, as I have learned historians normally do at the conclusion of their remarks, I take full responsibility for all that's good or bad in this work. It is the labor not of an historian, but of a sailor — a "ship-shover" — who feels as one with this ship and believes hers is a magnificent story that doesn't need embellishment.

Tyrone G. Martin

Cohasset, Massachusetts
1 January 1980

Photo Credits: Unless otherwise noted, all photographs and illustrations are from the author's personal files or were supplied by the U.S. Navy.

# Table of Contents

*Illustration by John Charles Roach.*

# 1 The Quasi-War with France

## SHAKY SHAKEDOWN

"Steady Breezes fine & Pleasant Weather.
"At 8 P.M. Took my departure from Boston Light House bearing W ½ N 3½
Leagues dist."

So begins the operational history of the most famous ship ever to have served in the United States Navy. Captain Samuel Nicholson had her underway at last on the evening of 22 July 1798. If the ship was new, the captain was not. A 55-year-old Marylander, he and his brothers James and John all had seen service in the Continental Navy. Samuel had been a lieutenant under John Paul Jones during the memorable engagement with *HMS Serapis* off England's Flamborough Head in September 1779. Later, he had commanded the frigate *Deane* and had captured three British sloops of war. In the newly created Navy, he was the second senior officer.

Taking a new ship to sea can be a trying experience. The workings of the hull in a seaway can disclose improperly fastened planking, and lines can be stiff and balky. People are still learning their ways about and to work as a team. Equipment and supplies often need restowage. The first problem of note in *Constitution* was the fact that the ship's compasses did not agree. The causes for such a condition are many; in this instance, it was found to be due to the binnacles having been assembled with iron nails — some 3½ pounds of them in each stand. Under the direction of Midshipman James Pity, they were disassembled and refastened with copper nails. His journal for 2 August noted with satisfaction, "... a 6 P.M. ... found our compasses to agree exactly ..."

*Constitution* sailed at this time under orders to defend American merchant ships against depredations by French men-of-war and privateers. During the preceding year, the spreading war between England and Napoleonic France had resulted in a growing series of moves and countermoves by the belligerents to limit the other's access to neutral shipping. America, the largest maritime neutral, was hardest hit.

After four weeks of uneventful patrolling, orders came to Nicholson via Newport to shift his area south: the waters south of Cape Henry to Florida were to be his responsibility. Two cutters from the Revenue Service (a precursor to the modern Coast Guard) would be under his command, and two more might be added at a later date. This was *Constitution*'s first assignment as a flagship. Communications rendezvous would be Cape Henry and Charleston.

During the trip southward, it was found that the ship was trimmed down by

1

*Captain Samuel Nicholson.*

the head. To correct this, Nicholson had two of the forecastle 18-pounders shifted to the quarterdeck and the sheet anchor restowed "abaft the fore Chains." When one pauses to recall that any one of these items weighed in excess of two tons, and that these actions were being accomplished in a ship alive to the sea's motion, one must appreciate the strength, skill, coordination, and danger inherent in the evolution.

The first recorded instance of *Constitution* beating to quarters ("battle stations") for cause was on 31 August. It was a false alarm. That same day also is memorable for including the first instance of flogging in the ship. At 3 P.M. that day, Irish seamen Dennis Carney, John Brown, and Richard Sullivan each received twelve lashes on their bare backs for having given vent to "Mutinious expressions" and fighting with the master at arms.

*Constitution* had almost reached the latitude of Charleston when, at 7 A.M. on 8 September, a masthead lookout reported seeing a ship dead ahead "Looking like a Cruizer." Nicholson crowded on all sail, beat to quarters, and cleared the guns "fore and aft" for action. At 11:30, he hoisted his colors and fired a warning shot from a range of 100 yards. The chase responded by hoisting the Union Jack and firing a gun to leeward, usually the signal of surrender, but she would not heave to. *Constitution* closed to within pistol shot (less than fifty yards) and Nicholson hailed her, saying that if the stranger offered any resistance the American would give no quarter. The chase hove to and sent two boats to *Constitution*, as ordered. As Captain Nicholson later reported it to Secretary Stoddert:

> ... I was convinced they were pirates ... their Capt. now came on board ... they said they were french — Royalists and bound from Jamaica to Philadelphia & had a Commission from the English Government ... which I believe to be Counterfeit ... the Crew is made up of ... about 75 men ... The Ship is called *Niger* ... and ... mounts twenty four nine & twelve pounders ... they have a great deal of money on board & ... the Crew have their pockets full ...

By mid-afternoon, Nicholson had the officers and crew of *Niger* removed to *Constitution* and the latter put in chains. A prize crew was placed aboard the privateer to bring her safely into port in company with the frigate.

In the early evening of the 9th, as the ships were passing Cape Hatteras, a disturbance broke out among the prisoners, some of whom wielded knives. In Nicholson's words:

> ... I ordered them to be search'd & Deprived of their Knives, Money, Watches &c. every one of these People have one or two Trunks American made full of good Cloaths &c which I have no Doubt have been plundered from the Americans ... we are really put on our guard by these people for of all beings I ever beheld in human Shape I declare I never saw so Impudent and darring (sic) a Set of Rascalls, and I have had a great many to take care of in my time. it is my real opinion if they could get an opportunity they would blow our Ship up by way of Revenge. They are fit for and capable of any thing be it ever so Desparate ...

The two ships reached Hampton Roads, Virginia, in the late afternoon of 12 September, when Nicholson wrote this report. Its purple prose makes one wonder if he was not seeking to justify an action which he was realizing probably was an error in judgment. Chaining rather than merely confining fewer than seventy prisoners in the presence of nearly 400 crewmen, including fifty Marines, smacks of "overkill." Depriving them of personal belongings other than weapons was an unjustified act. Indeed, lacking definite evidence of *Niger*'s hostile nature, Nicholson had no grounds for his precipitate actions.

Secretary of the Navy Stoddert did not receive Nicholson's report until the 22nd, well after other correspondence from Norfolk had alerted him to the incident. Perhaps the Captain had not sent it as soon as written in order to reconsider his case. In any event, Stoddert was suspicious of the tale told in what he called "this extraordinary *Official* letter ..."

On board the frigate while Nicholson lingered ashore, perhaps seeking support for his actions, there transpired another event which caused him more immediate, and personal, grief. The ship's log for 21 September noted "Doctor Read and Mr. Nicholson taken very sick." When the Captain returned on the

24th, he found that a Doctor Galt of Williamsburg was on board attending to the sick. Twenty-four hours later, Midshipman Samuel Nicholson, Jr., aged sixteen years, died "of the prevailing epidemic fever." His was the first death entered in *Constitution*'s log. The carpenters quickly made a coffin, and that afternoon he was buried in a Hampton churchyard. Doctor Read died on the 26th.

Nicholson recalled his prize crew from *Niger* on the 28th and 29th, and after a week of waiting for fair winds, sailed south for Charleston waters — just ahead of an angry Secretary's peremptory "proceed instantly to sea." He was joined there on 15 October by sloop of war *Baltimore* (Isaac Phillips, 18 guns), and on the 19th they undertook to convoy eleven merchantmen from Charleston to Havana. All went well for four days, when it was found that the frigate's bowsprit had sprung (split). As Nicholson well knew, in setting up rigging one began at the bowsprit; with it in trouble, the entire "system" was endangered. He decided to let *Baltimore* complete the convoy alone and return to Boston, whither the Secretary had told him to proceed by 20 November, anyway.

Squally weather appeared before the day was out to bedevil the frigate as she sought safety. As the weather worsened, fewer and fewer sails could be set because of the weakness of the top hamper. To add to the problem, it was found that the foremast also was sprung. At times, the bowsprit worked dangerously, threatening to wrench itself and the bows to pieces. The weather moderated somewhat on the 29th, but the squalls returned with the dawn the next day. The carpenters were busy raising the height of the hatch coamings to help reduce the amount of water getting below. Still worsening conditions on the 31st led to the securing of all gun ports. Nicholson resigned himself to heaving to and riding it out, bare poles.

For the next week, the frigate struggled northward. The crew was on constant call, adjusting the rigging to hold the damaged spars in place. Frictions grew. On 7 November, an altercation in the main rigging resulted in James Bates falling to the deck and being mortally injured. At four that afternoon, Robert Sharkey, his assailant, was flogged. Bates was buried at sea.

At noon on 10 November, the ship ended its first cruise back in Nantasket Roads, east of Boston. It had lasted 111 days and had been completely inglorious. The ship badly needed repairs. And the *Niger* affair ended up costing the United States $11,000 in damages for the illegal capture and detention of an English vessel.

## THE WEST INDIES

Following repairs, *Constitution* sailed once more early on 29 December, under orders to report to Commodore Barry on board *United States* at or near Prince Rupert's Bay, the island of Dominica, for operations against French armed vessels "about Guadaloupe." Within a few hours, she was in the midst of a howling gale; driving snow made watch standing wretched. And it soon became evident that her trim still was faulty, for she "plunged and rowled" and shipped great amounts of water. A gun port lid in the captain's cabin was stove in; all the lids leaked. A fire could not be kept in the caboose, so the crew was sustained by bread and cheese. Two gallons of rum were expended in one day just to brace up the "Wheelmen." Life became a wet, lurching misery for all hands and stayed that way until New Year's Day.

Captain Nicholson's string of misfortunes continued to plague him. On the afternoon of 6 January, someone noticed that the foremast tended suspiciously to starboard. Closer inspection revealed it to be sprung fourteen feet above the spar deck. In short order, sail was shortened and everything on that mast sent down. It was stayed so that no further damage could occur before the boatswain's and carpenter's crews could make temporary repairs. Working until late the following morning, they skillfully fished and woolded the injured stick.

Early on the afternoon of the 15th, in fine weather, two sails were sighted to the northwest. Nicholson ordered *Constitution* in chase. As the first dog watch was taking over, one of the strangers was seen to be a warship, but her sole response to both American and English recognition signals was to crowd on more sail. Nicholson accepted the challenge, clearing his ship for action as he went. Rain squalls complicated the chase as the sun set, but intermittent contact was maintained until shortly before midnight.

When Lieutenant Isaac Hull took the deck for the mid watch, *Constitution* still was standing to the north-northwest, reluctant to give over the chase. At twenty minutes into the new day, contact was regained. Nicholson bore up and fired two warning guns, to which the chase responded by wearing around to the south and loosing more sail. Nicholson followed suit, fired two more guns, and soon brought her to heel. She proved to be *Spencer*, an English merchantman that had been on passage from Shields, England, to Barbados when captured by the French frigate *L'Insurgente*. In effect, *Spencer* was a French vessel. Nicholson removed the French prize crew to *Constitution* and sent an officer and nine of his sailors to handle her.

For the second time in five months, Sam Nicholson found himself with an English ship-French crew problem. The last time, he had been wrong in taking it prize. Had he blundered again? He spent a worrisome day assailed by doubts; his mind in a turmoil. At nine that evening, "bro't too and took out of the ship *Spencer* the Officers & Men we Sent on Board her." Nicholson thus gave up a legitimate prize because "it was tho't prudent," and demonstrated for the second time that he understood neither his orders nor the prevailing customs of the sea. His brother officers and American merchants, alike, were appalled by his actions.

*Constitution* arrived at Dominica on 17 January and was immediately assigned a patrol station north and east of the island. She, as well as the other frigates there, really were much too big for the work of trying to catch the swift, small privateers. They were forced to provide the "outer screen" against the advent of similar French units while the brig and schooners pursued their elusive quarry in-

Constitution *getting underway with reefed topsails.*

shore.

The weather turned squally on the 23rd, and it soon became evident that the woolding and fishes on the injured foremast were working loose. Shortly thereafter, "Carried away our Main T. Mast Cross Tree & Main T. Mast Stay." *Constitution*'s whole top hamper was in danger of collapse! Quickly, the topgallant yards were sent down to reduce the strain. At 4 P.M., Commodore Barry was notified, and he ordered his flagship, *United States* to escort her into Prince Rupert's Bay. As she worked into the bay four days later, *Constitution*'s jibboom carried away, leaving her a bedraggled, sorry sight indeed. Enroute to port Ordinary Seaman Cornelius Howard, the only known black "plank owner," had died of "a putrid and nervous fever".

Nicholson returned to patrol duties on 1 February, his worst problems with spars a thing of the past. Week followed quiet week until 1 March, when a night chase resulted in a meeting with *HMS Santa Margaretta* (36), frigate. After, remaining in company through the rest of the night, the two captains agreed to a sailing duel. By mid-morning, the race was on, the two graceful beauties setting and taking in sail hour after hour, sweating sailor's backs glinting in the sunlight as they strove in concert to get the utmost from their ships. *Constitution*'s log proudly but laconically noted the outcome thusly:

> "... at 3 P.M. parted company with the *Santa Margaretta*. Captain Parker after sailing in company 16 hours, and using every Method to out sail us, being sensible of Inability tak'd to the Northward and Shortend Sail."

This appears to have been the race James Fenimore Cooper later credited to Captain Silas Talbot and Lieutenant Isaac Hull. Hull was there, all right, but let's give the devil his due: this was one thing Samuel Nicholson had done right.

Back in Philadelphia, Secretary Stoddert was busy penning two documents that would effect directly Nicholson and *Constitution*. The first was a circular to all commanding officers that must have made the Captain blanch when he saw it. It was intended to clarify and emphasize the authority of commanding officers in making captures. As a preamble to its operative sections, it said point blank:

> A Misconstruction of his authority by Capt Nicholson in relation to a Vessel of friendly Nations, captured by the French renders it necessary that I should make some explanatory observations on the Subject ...

In the second missive, Stoddert wrote directly to Commodore Barry "to order, to Boston without delay, the *Constitution.*" Once the ship was in Boston, the Secretary could remove Nicholson to a less sensitive post.

On patrol, things continued to look up for Nicholson. On 27 March, he recaptured the American sloop *Neutrality* in a four hour chase, removed her French prize crew, and sent her in to "Martinico." A week later, he took the French prize ship *Carteret*, which had been an English packet. She also was sent in to Martinique.

*Constitution* began her voyage homeward on 17 April, escorting a convoy of seventeen merchantmen. The trip was an uneventful one until the convoy broke up on the 29th, feeling free of the threat of French privateers. On the 8th of May, being at that time some seventy-five miles southeast-by-south of Nantucket Shoal, the frigate encountered one more gale. At seven that evening, true to form, "Pitching into a heavy head beat Sea. Sprung our fore Mast in the Wake of the partners on the gun deck ... got the fore runners to aft to support the Mast the crack being abaft..." By the morning of the 10th, the mast had been sufficiently braced to permit the setting of the foresail. The carpenters were busy with their now-familiar routine of fishing and woolding. After two more days of adverse winds, the frigate at last made it around Cape Cod and anchored once more in Nantasket Roads on 14 May. Nicholson went ashore almost immediately, no doubt relieved that the blighted cruise was at an end and yet anxious as to what the future held for him.

## TALBOT TAKES THE HELM

On 15 May 1799, Secretary Stoddert wrote to Silas Talbot informing him he was wanted as the next captain of *Constitution*. Talbot, forty-eight at the time,

*Captain Silas Talbot.*

was a Yankee and an authentic hero of the Revolution. In that conflict, he had served with distinction as a militia captain, a lieutenant colonel in the Continental Army, and a captain in the Continental Navy. He had been wounded thirteen times (and carried five musket balls in his body for life) and was a prisoner of war when peace finally came. When the new Navy was authorized in 1794, Talbot had been the third senior captain appointed, but had his pay stopped on 30 June 1796 when construction of the frigate to which he had been assigned was suspended. He was recalled to active service during the summer of 1798 to oversee the preparation of new warships. Stoddert considered his captaincy to date from that recall, which meant that Talbot would be junior to Thomas Truxtun, who had been sixth on the original list and was the only one of that group who had not seen service in the Revolution. Talbot pointed out that his original commission had never been revoked, nor had he resigned it. The arguments were long and convoluted, but with Presidential intercession and the promise that he would never be subordinated to Truxtun, Talbot agreed to take *Constitution* while the matter was left unresolved.

"Moderate breezes and cloudy" noted the log in the entry for noon, 4 June 1799. At one, Captain Silas Talbot came aboard. All hands were assembled and heard him read his commission as *Constitution*'s new commander. Samuel Nicholson then formally resigned his command. Following these readings, the two captains went below to the cabin, where Nicholson turned over the logs and journals, the magazine keys, and such unexecuted orders as were in his possession. The crew went back to work, the caulkers resuming their tattoo upon the spar deck. At six, Nicholson and Talbot went ashore.

Repairs, resupply, and recruiting a new crew went slowly. A month after her return, *Constitution* had just received a new foremast and the fighting top was put back in place. The caulkers still had the berth deck to finish. Recruiting was being delayed by the fact that the new frigate *Boston* (Captain George Little, 28 guns) also was in the same business. And, of course, Secretary Stoddert was increasingly anxious to get both these ships to the theater of operations.

Beginning on 20 June, and almost daily through the 14th of July, the ship's log recorded the arrival of endless supplies, listed in such arcane units as leaguers, butts, gang casks, firkins, puncheons, tierces, pipes, hogheads, chaldrons, bags, and buckets. Time has blurred the precise amounts (indeed, many never were standardized). But discernable in the inventory are eighteen tons of salt beef and a like quantity of pork, over 37,500 gallons of water, 5880 pounds of flour, almost 3000 gallons of rum (presumably, more would be taken aboard in the West Indies), nearly as much vinegar, 250 gallons of molasses, and — perhaps, startingly — about twenty *tons* of coal (for the caboose).

*Constitution* fired her first national birthday salute in July. The log entry for that day recorded, "At 12 fired a salute of 16 guns in celebration of the glorious forth of July. The 16 guns represented one for each state in the Union, Vermont, Kentucky, and Tennessee have joined the original thirteen."

In July the ship clearly was nearing readiness. All the sails, new and refurbished, were returned aboard. The hull had been painted and tarred, the 'tween-decks bulkheads and ceiling planking whitewashed. The nearly 400 new men kept the lieutenants busy making quartering and station assignments. Finally, on 23 July, Talbot headed seaward, bound for Norfolk and the latest orders from the Secretary. President Adams, at his home in Braintree at the time, saw the frigate go and wrote:.

> After a detention of nine days by contrary winds, the **Constitution** took advantage of a brisk breeze, and went out of the harbor and out of sight this forenoon, making a beautiful and noble figure amidst the joy and good wishes of many thousands of good federalists.

## WEST INDIES FLAGSHIP

The trip to Norfolk required three weeks, thanks to adverse winds. Talbot's orders, which bore the date 27 July, were to:

> ...proceed...by the rout you shall judge most likely to fall in with French Armed Vessels to the vicinity of Cayenne where the French have some large Privateers...Your object must be to protect the Trade by Capturing the French Vessels which depredate upon it or by keeping them in Port, until the 20th of September, when you must...proceed...to the neighborhood of Guadeloupe...and from thence to Cape

Francois in Saint Domingo where you will assume command of all American Vessels on that station...

I will only observe for the present that the Saint Domingo Trade just now opened to us, will employ a very great proportion of our Commercial Vessels, that it will be of the highest importance to give them effectual protection from French Depredations and...to cultivate & preserve a Good Understanding with General Touisant (sic) & the people of the Island...

...It is most probable that you will remain the whole Winter & perhaps longer at Saint Domingo...

Saint Domingue, the French western end of Hispaniola Island, had been in a state of revolt since August 1791. In the intervening years, General Pierre Francois Domingue Toussaint L'Ouverture, a former slave, had emerged as the colony's principal figure in the chaotic politics of the time. Negotiations with him in 1799 had resulted in a reopening of the lucrative American trade with Toussaint's people. West Indies commerce always had been a major part of Yankee overseas business, and with many European ports closed to them because of the wars of the French Revolution, this was a development of great economic importance to the United States. As a result, American naval forces, which previously had operated mainly in the Lesser Antilles, were divided into four squadrons, the two principal ones having their areas of operations extending west and southeast of Puerto Rico, respectively, and the others covering Cuba and the South American coast.

The second leg of the voyage proceeded no more swiftly than the first. On the morning of 15 September, three weeks out from Norfolk and still north of the Leeward Islands, *Constitution* went in chase with "all sails by the wind." In three hours, she brought to the Hamburg ship *Amelia*, which had been made prize by a French corvette ten days earlier. Ten Frenchmen were taken aboard as prisoners, and Acting Lieutenant Nathaniel Bosworth was put aboard with seventeen sailors to take her to New York.

Talbot arrived off the Cayenne coast on 29 September — nine days after his orders specified he was to be on his way to Saint Domingue. After a quick, three-day sweep of the area, he proceeded north, passed Guadeloupe on the 8th, and arrived off Saint Domingue on 15 October, where he rendezvoused with *Boston*, frigate *General Greene* and brig *Norfolk*. The Commodore entertained his captains at dinner, a working affair, and then they dispersed to take up their patrol assignments. *Constitution*'s station generally was the entire north coast of Saint Domingue, but Talbot favored the waters within a 30-mile radius of Cap Francois.

In the seven weeks to follow, life settled into a humdrum of a chase a day, all of which were friendly. On two occasions, at least, Talbot was able to relieve the monotony of the situation by having informal sailing contests with the smaller *Boston*. At 9 A.M. on 1 November, "Wore and Steerd down for her (*Boston*'s) wake allowing her to pass nearly two miles a head, we then Tried on a Bowling which brought us parrallel to her course with an Equal proportion of Canvass we found her far from Equability in sailing, at 11 we Tacked on her weather Bow In order to Give her a fair Tryal at sailing at 12 Shortend sail and brought too the *Boston* a Stern nearly one mile..." And a little more than a day later, "...at 5 wore and came to the wind to the Northward under all plane sail In order to give the U.S. Ship *Boston* another fair Tryal at Sailing at 7 Shortened sail and parted company with the *Boston* this is now the second time we have Given Captain Little a trial at sailing he is now fully satisfied of the *Constitution*'s Superiority..." Not a little pride there.

Toward the end of November, *Constitution* was literally scraping the bottom of the barrel for fresh water, so long had she been underway. Twice in recent days she had received small amounts from *General Greene*, but not enough to sustain her large crew. Talbot thus was forced to leave his station and proceed westward to Mole St. Nicholas, where water could be had and the presence of a U.S. Naval Agent offered the prospect of additional logistic support. A rare squall delayed his progress somewhat, but *Constitution* was towed into port by her boats on 2 December, coming to anchor in twenty-four fathoms just as eight bells struck in the dog watches. Noted the log: "From our last anchorage to this is one hundred days which time we have been at Sea three men we lost overboard and 6 died..."

(Telling time by "bells" resulted from the practice of having the boy assigned to turn the half-hour glass, which measured time, strike the ship's bell each time he turned the glass so the Officer of the Deck would know he was doing his duty regularly: once for the first turning of his watch, twice for the second, etc., until eight had been struck and the four-hour watch was completed. The nautical day began at noon, and the watches changed at 4, 8, and 12 with the striking of eight bells. An exception to this will be noted in due course, but it had no effect on the bell system.)

Watering took just three days, during which time 191 tons (45,840 gallons) had been laboriously funnelled into the ship's casks, rowed out to her anchorage, swayed aboard and stowed. Those members of the crew not so engaged were busy overhauling the rigging or bringing stores from the shore and getting them stowed below.

The routine of October-November was reestablished, with one change: fresh water was strictly controlled. Not long after resuming his patrol station, however, Talbot began experiencing some of the top hamper problems that had plagued his predecessor nearly a year before. The foremast trestletrees were found to be sprung on 14 December, and had to be replaced; this only two days after having to redo the gammoning on a loosened bowsprit. But on the 17th, he became aware of a much more serious problem: "Observed the Mainmast to labour very much about 10 or 12 feet below the Treeletrees." Further observation revealed severe checking in the mast. For the next month, the carpenter strove to insure that the mast would not be lost completely, ultimately fitting it with two 32-foot long oaken fishes woolded in place with 120 fathoms of 6-inch hawser.

## A Most Fortunate Ship

The chartered schooner *Elizabeth* of Philadelphia rendezvoused with *Constitution* on 30 December, laden with stores for the squadron. In an early example of underway replenishment, a technique which is a particular talent in the modern U.S. Navy, Talbot took the merchantman in tow to keep her close by and commenced the transfer by ship's boats. In twelve hours the frigate took aboard 260 barrels of bread, seventy-five each of beef and pork, fifteen of "Indian meal," ten of flour, thirty of potatoes, and eight of cheese, as well as four tierces of rice and one of "pease", another "small cask" of "pease", and six kegs of butter. A heavy swell from the northward brought a halt to the operation until daylight. Ten more hours of heavy labor completed the task, and *Elizabeth* was ordered to rendezvous with *Boston* next.

There exists a tale about *Constitution* wherein she conducts a highly successful six months war cruise, regularly capturing enemy ships and just as regularly relieving them of their stocks of spiritous liquors. The story concludes with the frigate returning to Boston with the same thousands of gallons of water with which she sailed, but totally bereft of the strong stuff. There is the smallest grain of truth in the story, witness the log entry for the afternoon watch on 8 January 1800: "Served half allowance of Spirits to Ships company the Rum being Totally expended." Fortunately for all hands, *Boston* soon rendezvoused with the flagship and early the next afternoon transferred "Thirty gallons of Rum for ships use, served out full allowance of Spirits to ships company."

*Constitution*'s log for this period bears witness to the continuing good health and generally high morale of Talbot's crew. Discipline was exercised for only the second time in the new year on 10 February, when the Commodore suspended from duty Midshipman John Longley and Carpenter Phiny Davidson "for fighting." A week later, only the third death of the year occurred when Ordinary Seaman Dennis Murray went "galley west" and was buried at sea "with the usual custom."

Commodore Talbot had long been vexed by the fact that he had no small, light draft vessels to work in *Constitution*'s patrol area. One of the prizes taken by another unit of the squadron appeared to be just what he was looking for, so he set about fitting out sloop *Amphitheatre* for her new role. It took three days for his carpenters to strengthen her bulwarks and mount the swivels supplied from the frigate's armory. A senior lieutenant in the squadron, David Porter, was detailed to command her. She began her inshore patrol on 3 March, but for weeks her presence seemed to make no difference.

As the month of May opened, Talbot worked to windward to check out any activities going on in or near the ports of Isabella, St. Iago, and Puerto Plata, Santo Domingo, some 90-100 miles east of Cap Francois. Three vessels were seen in the latter port, one of which was found to be Danish when she came out at noon on the 2nd.

Talbot, rendered curious by the activity that three ships in so small a harbor represented, sent in a cutter to reconnoitre. It returned at sunset on the 3rd with the information that the harbor was bounded by reefs to the east and west, and was defended by a small fort on a point of land which apparently mounted four guns. The waters of the harbor were insufficient for the likes of the big frigate. Talbot moved off to consider the situation.

Several days went by, and then, near noon on 8 May, "spyed a sail Close in shore which appeared to be coming to an Anchor In a large Bay to leward of Old cape francois, Tacked and ordered the *Amphitheatre* to stand in and see what that Sail was..." First Lieutenant Isaac Hull, who would soon have occasion to make his mark, recorded what happened next:

> ... at 2 the *Amphitheatre* Returned and Informed Captain Talbot that the strange sail in shore was an American Brig and supposed she was prize to a small schooner and barge which was at Anchor close in shore Sent a Number of Seamen and Marines on board *Amphitheatre* and Manned four boats and sent them in to Engage the Barge and Schooner and bring out the brig Continued standing in till ½ past 2 at which time the *Amphitheatre* fir'd a shot at the Schooner (*Esther*) which she soon returned and a warm Action took place which continued for half an hour, the french Schooner Grounded and a part of the crew swam ashore the remainder to the number of 16 were taken prisoner, our boats boarded the privateer and brought her off with the American brig *Nymph* of Newbury(port) which she had taken the night before and plunder'd of seven thousand Dollars and a quantity of dry Goods, the barge made all sail and made her escape while we were taking the Brig and Schooner...

The ship's log included the information that *Esther* carried three guns and had had a crew of forty-three. Three had been killed and several of the prisoners were "badly wounded." In the brief engagement, *Amphitheatre* had lost her rudder and had had three men wounded. At 7 P.M., "Lieutenant (Isaac) Collins with two armd Boats was order'd in shore to a bay call'd Laragee Salle bay In order to cruize for barge..." *Esther* was taken in tow; a prize master took charge of *Nymph*.

Collins and his little force were nowhere in sight when the sun rose on the 9th. At 1:30 P.M., the large cutter came back, but the midshipman in charge did not know what had become of his senior's craft. Anxiously, Talbot sent *Amphitheatre* and *Esther* looking for it. They returned as night was falling, empty handed. Through the night, an alert watch sought a sign of their missing mates. At seven the next morning (10th), *Herald* joined and Captain Russell reported he had spoke Lieutenant Collins the evening before: he had cut a sloop out of the harbor of St. Iago. At nine, a triumphant Isaac Collins appeared in the 58-ton sloop *Sally*, an American trafficker that recently also had called at Puerto Plata.

Collins' adroit adventure not only brought him the Commodore's compliments, it also gave the squadron commander a means to get at what he knew to be a privateer in Puerto Plata: that one vessel had not come out in the week since seen with two others in there. *Sally* had been one of them; she and her captain, Thomas Sandford, were known there; his ship could call again without suspicion.

13

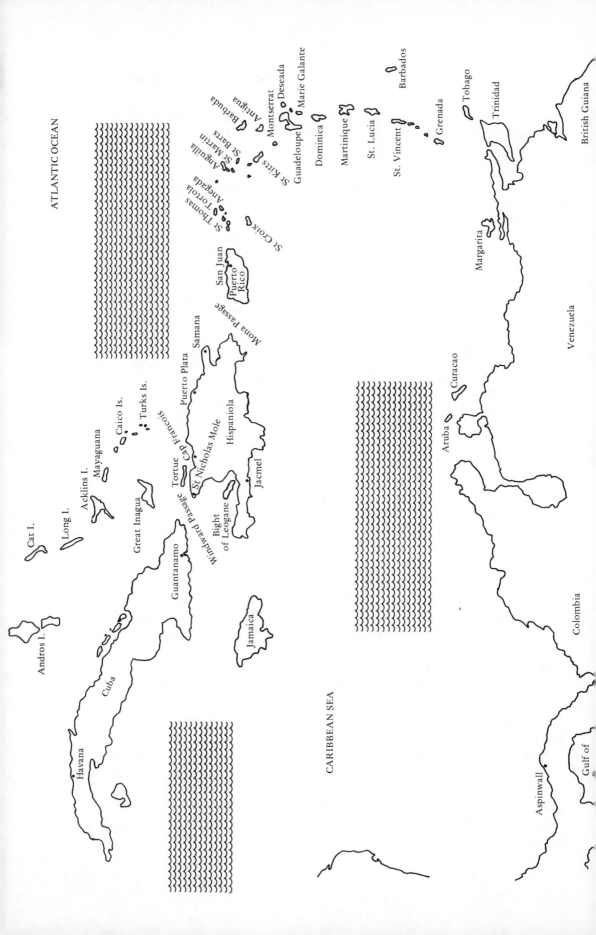

By the evening of the 10th, lying hull-down offshore, *Sally* was ready for her big moment. Talbot ordered First Lieutenant Hull, Marine Captain Daniel Carmick and his Lieutenant, William Amory, together with ninety seamen and Marines to board the sloop as a cutting-out expedition. They were to sail into Puerto Plata with Sandford and only a few *Constitutions* (enough to handle the vessel) visible, innocently making for an anchorage near the French privateer, and then...

At about midnight, not much over an hour after setting out, two shots boomed across *Sally*'s bow. It was *HMS Alarm* (32), frigate. A boat from the Englishman soon came alongside, intent upon discovering the nature of the sloop and her crew. Hull told the startled English lieutenant his orders, and was, in turn, informed that the Britisher had the same operation in mind. The stocky American's response was that if his competitor was not quick about it, he'd find, the next morning, that the Americans had done the job. The Englishman gallantly wished Hull success and returned to his own ship. *Sally* moved on, a fretful wind prolonging the journey.

With the morning sun came a steady breeze. The raiders entered Puerto Plata with no one suspecting *Sally*'s changed character. Hull guided her straight to his objective. A Marine, probably Captain Carmick, wrote what happened next:

> ...We all remained below until we received orders from the officer (Hull), the only one of us who remained on the deck of the sloop, whose business it was to lay us on board, which he did on the starboard bow. The men went on board like devils, and it was as much as the first lieutenant and myself could do to prevent blood being spilt. I believe it was not half an hour before the ship was taken, that I had possession of the fort and all the cannon spiked, and returned again on board the prize before they could get any succours from the city...

Hull's lightning attack had stunned both the privateersmen and the townspeople. And a good thing, too, for he found his prize had had all but its lower masts unshipped and the rigging coiled in the hold. Calmly, he told off gun crews to place the ship's battery in readiness and had the Marines stationed to repel boarders. With the remaining seamen, Hull set about re-rigging the ship. By sunset, the ship was "in every respect ready for service." At midnight, *Sally* and her prize sailed out in perfect order without the loss of a single man. Shortly before noon on the 12th, they rejoined *Constitution* and *Nymph*.

The prize had once been the British packet *Sandwich*, but for the previous three or four years had been a French privateer. She was a fast, copper-bottomed ship mounting 6-pounders and two nines, and laden with coffee and sugar. As events finally turned out, Talbot, Hull, et al, would receive heartiest congratulations from Secretary Stoddert for this daring and skillful operation, but no prize money. The *Sandwich* had been cut out of a Spanish, and therefore neutral, port, and ultimately was returned to the French by the diplomats, with apologies.

Buoyed up by the activity and apparent success of the past several days, Talbot next took *Constitution* on a sweep to Samana Bay at the east end of Hispaniola, after provisioning *Sandwich* and *Sally* and sending them northward. No privateers or traffickers were found in the five-day sweep.

If Talbot had found nothing on the eastward swing, he had been made suspicious about what might be going on at the little village of Baie Citron, about fifteen miles west of Cape Samana. So he went back. On the morning of 3 June, the barge, the pinnace, and a cutter were laden with ninety-five seamen and Marines under Lieutenants Hamilton and Amory, and sent in on a "search and destroy" mission. As they ruefully reported the next morning, when they returned, high surf had pooped their boats and wetted all their powder, causing Hamilton to abort the plan and return to *Constitution* for a fresh supply. He reported, however, seeing what appeared to be a privateer at anchor off the village and two more on stocks being built.

The Commodore decided to try again, but this time he would move his flagship' in to provide gunfire support, the element of surprise probably having been lost. At 2 P.M. on 4 June he had *Constitution* at anchor as close to the village as he could, the boats nearby, awaiting the cover of a bombardment by the batteries of 18- and 24-pounder long guns. But in this, too, was the plan frustrated: a few salvoes soon showed Talbot that the range was too great for an effective cannonade. At five, with the surf still running high, he gave up the attempt, called in the boats, and hauled off shore.

As the ship patrolled slowly westward once more, signs of debilitation and fatigue in ship's company became evident. At 6 P.M. on the 6th, Private Rufus Montor died "of a fever." Hot weather was coming on which would only exacerbate the difficult conditions under which these men lived and worked. Despite the efforts to supply the proper provisions regularly, scurvy became a problem. Tempers grew short as frustrations grew long. Talbot, as any captain would, kept a tight rein and reacted promptly to each infraction. On the morning of June 7th, Seaman Daniel Flynn received twelve lashes for mutinous language and disobedience of orders; that afternoon, Seaman Daniel Freeman got a "dozen o' the cat" for theft and insolence to his superior officer.

Immediately after Freeman's punishment, Talbot ordered out two boats with forty armed men to go with *Amphitheatre* into a bay to the west of Old Cap Francois to cut out a privateer and barge he believed to be lurking there.

At dawn on the 8th, Talbot found *Amphitheatre* in chase of the privateer, heading westward, and the boats pursuing a schooner. He closed the latter, which came to after a volley of small arms fire from the boats and three rounds from the frigate's 18-pounders. Leaving the schooner in the charge of the boats and the redoubtable Lieutenant Hamilton, the Commodore pressed on after the tender and her quarry. The Frenchman, however, was able to gain the safety and protection to be found near the fort at Puerto Plata.

*Constitution* and *Amphitheatre* took up a vigil off the port. At 3 P.M., Hamilton joined with his boats and the schooner, a Danish slaver. Talbot made preparation to go after the privateer, intending to anchor *Constitution* close in shore where her long guns could make a suitable impression on the fort while the boats gained the prize. But soundings by one of the boats proved the impracticability of the scheme, and at seven all were hoisted aboard and the ships headed westward once more. The Dane was sent on his way.

Water was again on the Commodore's mind, so after a brief pause to confer with the patrol off Montechristi, he made for Mole St. Nicholas, arriving on the afternoon of 11 June. What a relief it must have been to all hands to be riding at anchor once more — only the third time in ten months — and not to be constantly alert to the watch officer's hail or the mate's "starter." One, at least, relaxed too much. The next morning, Private Simeon Cook took twelve lashes for neglect of duty and sleeping on post.

Patrolling was resumed again on the 14th, with *Amphitheatre* in company. It was soon apparent that ship and crew alike were coming to the ends of their endurance. Since the preceding August, they had been in port just nine days — and those all too brief periods had involved the back-breaking labor of watering and supplying the ship. The log for the 16th noted thirty sick with fever, and scurvy was becoming prevalent. Many a man's term of enlistment was about done.

For the next several days, *Amphitheatre* was kept close to *Constitution*, systematically being stripped of her war stores and supplies. Talbot had determined that her usefulness as a tender was over, and decided to send her to Philadelphia for adjudication. David Porter would take with him those men whose time already had expired. He parted company from the Commodore on the 24th.

Once more, the crew could begin to measure their patrol time in weeks. Heavy squalls on the 29th must have reminded Talbot that this was the start of the hurricane season in these waters — another worry for a man with a tired ship and weary crew. Two days later, a log entry:

> Our principle sails except a foresail has from actual service become worn out so much as to be totally unserviceable, on a lee shore, or pursuing an enemy under press of sail. We have repeatedly split the fore and main topsails when every effort would have been useless to bend others. Notwithstanding, forty bolts of canvas has been (patched?) on them.

Talbot did his duty relentlessly, although the other ships of his squadron came and went. Real trouble cropped up on the 13th:

> ...at 5 Observed the Main Mast to Incline forward Although various ways has been used in order to Regain its Perpendicular which is not Obtain'd the sprung part of the Mast which I have Mentioned near the Cat Harpin legs Increases and runs downwards and runs In a winding Direction nearly four feet on first Observing a small curve in the Main Mast was the 17th December 1799 — After Chasing to windward under a press of sail...the bolts which rivet through and secure the cheeks of the mast is of little use as they are bent and became loose.

17

## A Most Fortunate Ship

Now a port call was mandatory, and Talbot got *Constitution* into Cap Francois by noon on the 15th. Also present in the harbor were thirty-seven merchantmen and a French armed ship. *Constitution* was in no condition to fight, but the Frenchman apparently was awed by her size.

Repairs began immediately. Having gotten down all the yards and the maintopmast, double runners were rigged fore and aft of the injured mast, and "by Degrees" it was hove straight once more. In three days, "...we compleated the Mainmast by Carrying a fish of 51 feet from the Heel of the Topmast down the main Mast — Which was made from a Sprung Topmast Leaving the full round on the fore part for a Wolding surface..." In another three days, they were ready to go again.

At daylight on 22 July, the big frigate entered the narrow channel, outward bound. A dead calm forced her to anchor in the fairway until seven, when a westerly breeze let her stand along the reef. Suddenly, near the outer fort, she was taken aback by a northerly wind which quickly shifted to the east. Before she could come to anchor, *Constitution* went aground stern first on the reef "which Shock was Sensibly felt and Violently repeated." By shifting guns forward, running out a stream anchor and heaving around, she was brought off and anchored once more in mid-channel. She had been aground only forty-seven minutes. "The ship makes no more Water than Usual..." At five that afternoon, the wind again came fair. Talbot put to sea smartly.

When the sun rose the next morning, the *Constitution*s beheld a marvelous sight: in the offing was *Constellation*, frigate, commanded by Captain Alexander Murray...their successor. Talbot and Murray conferred all day long as merchantmen, notified of *Constitution*'s imminent departure northward, worked their way out of harbor to proceed under her convoy. That afternoon, Murray relieved Talbot as squadron commander and hoisted his broad, blue command pennant. At six, with twelve merchantmen under her wing, *Constitution* headed for Caicos Passage.

It was a long, slow trip for the frigate's worn crew. Merchant ships were a notoriously motley lot as sailors, and generally skippered by men prone to not taking orders. At times, *Constitution* had as many as three of the dullest craft under tow. On one occasion, carpenters had to be sent off to a sloop which had sprung a leak. The convoy finally dispersed for Baltimore and Philadelphia on the 13th and, weather willing, Talbot could take advantage of his ship's speed to gain an early return to Boston. It could be none too soon:

> "...our State of Provisons being as follows Viz. Beef none Pork 14 barrels Rum 60 Gallons put the Ships Company on half Allowance of Spirits..."

Eleven more days were needed to raise Boston Light. It was too long for Seaman Charles Leonard: he died of fever on the 15th. The thirteen-month deployment at last came to an end as *Constitution* anchored in President Roads at 2 P.M. on 24 August 1800. It had been an epic voyage that had demanded the utmost in leadership from Silas Talbot. The President clearly had been right in insisting that he was the man to be *Constitution*'s captain. Secretary of the Navy Stoddert summed up Talbot's achievement accordingly:

> Your feeling as a military man, might have been more gratified had opportunities been afforded you of engaging in scenes of greater brilliancy — but no services you cd. have rendered, could have been more useful & more important to your country than those you have meritoriously performed, in protecting with effect a great portion of our commerce in laying the foundation of a permanent Trade with St. Domingo & in causing the American character to be respected by the just, temperate judicious course by which your conduct has been marked, during the whole time of your command at St. Domingo...

## THE WAR WINDS DOWN

*Constitution* spent less than four months back in her home port. The exhausted crew quickly was paid off; the officers went on leave or were transferred. (Talbot was gone for the latter part of September.) The ship herself received a new mainmast and new sails, and had her rigging thoroughly overhauled.

In Paris, at the end of September, Joseph Bonaparte and Oliver Ellsworth signed "A Convention of Amity and Commerce between the United States and France." When ratified, it would cause each side to return the other's public and private vessels not otherwise disposed of, exchange commercial agents, and guarantee each the freedom of the seas and of trade.

Secretary Stoddert drafted Talbot's new orders on 18 November, at a time when rumors already were circulating in Washington that the treaty had been completed. He was to resume command over the Saint Domingo Squadron and adopt a posture of watchful protectiveness, countering any overt attacks on American property but initiating no offensive actions against the French.

Talbot sailed *Constitution* from Boston on 17 December, two days after President Adams presented the draft treaty to the Senate for its advice and consent. This time the voyage south took a mere twelve days. As 1801 dawned, the Commodore was again on his station off Cap Francois. Other units under him included frigates *Congress* (36) and *Adams* (28), ship *Trumbull* (18), and brigs *Richmond* (18) and *Augusta* (14). Except for the absence of cutting out expeditions, the old routine continued in effect.

The Treaty had rough sledding in the Senate, but with Thomas Jefferson having narrowly won the presidential election, it was ratified as the Adams administration closed its books. All during February, the Secretary of the Navy quietly put the brakes on fitting out ships for further deployments to the West Indies, for the end was in sight. On 3 March, the day after Treaty ratification and the last day in office for the Federalists, the Congress passed the Navy's Peace Establishment Act. It was almost exactly what Stoddert had recommended to the Naval Affairs Committee in January. Only thirteen built-for-the-purpose frigates would be retained by the Service, six of them on active duty, the remainder laid up, each with a caretaker group consisting of the sailing master, three warrant officers, a Marine guard of nine, twelve seamen, and a cook. The Navy's officer corps was to be trimmed to 150, of whom only nine were captains. Talbot's name was not on an early list of those to be retained.

On 4 April, the ship *Herald* (18) sailed from Boston for the West Indies to tell everyone to go home. The orders for Talbot were to take *Constitution* to Boston, pay off the crew, report which of his junior officers were interested in staying in service, and keep the ship otherwise ready for duty.

By this time, Benjamin Stoddert, who had worked hard to create the Navy, had tired of awaiting a successor and resigned the office. Jefferson appointed Samuel Dearborn acting Navy Secretary until one could be found. The correspondence is incomplete in this matter, but in May or early June Talbot was expressing his dissatisfaction over the omission of his name from the list of captains to be retained. On 19 June, Dearborn wrote to Talbot personally to advise him he would be kept on. Talbot then seems to have reopened the entire argument he had had with Stoddert with the new Secretary of the Navy, Robert Smith, who assumed his office on 27 July. Smith's first response was, naturally, that he would familiarize himself with the situation and get back to Talbot. Whatever he learned in the meantime, Talbot submitted his resignation on 8 September 1801 and never again did naval service, a genuine loss. Talbot off Tripoli is an interesting contemplation.

*Constitution* was placed in charge of Lieutenant Hull, with specific orders to get her a thorough overhaul. (Talbot had reported "insufficient Beams and plank", "a subject of great distress", in July.) In October, however, his manpower was reduced by the transfer of the seamen. Months of indecision followed. Hull was detached in April, after turning over responsibility for the ship to the first Commandant of the Boston Navy Yard (Samuel Nicholson), and she finally was laid up in ordinary on 18 June 1802.

The Quasi-War was over; *Constitution* was at rest.

# 2 The Ship and Life Aboard Her

With *Constitution* inactivated for the first time, it seems to be a good time to pause in the narrative and consider her origin, what she looked like in these early days, the make-up and organization of her crew, and the routine of daily life aboard.

## WHERE DID SHE COME FROM?

When the North American colonies were a part of the British Empire, their very large shipping interests had been protected by the Royal Navy. That protection ended when they gained their independence, and the new country was unwilling to maintain a navy of its own. As a result, American merchant ships fell prey to the Barbary pirates in the Mediterranean, who had been pursuing the business of piracy for a millenium. It was not until the last weeks of 1793 that the situation became onerous enough for Congress to take action. After weeks of wrangling, a bill finally cleared both houses of Congress, and President George Washington signed "An act to provide a naval armament" on 27 March 1794. The act authorized the construction of four 44-gun and two 36-gun ships; provided for the officers, seamen, and Marines to man them; established the rates of pay and the rations; and closed with the proviso that "if a peace shall take place between the United States and the Regency of Algiers,...no further proceeding be had under this act."

There having been no Navy Department created upon establishment of the Federal Government under the Constitution in 1789, it fell to the Secretary of War Henry Knox's lot to implement the provisions of the Act. He seems to have foreseen that the task would be his, for he had been conducting correspondence on the subject since 1790 with men experienced in building and fighting warships. Those principally concerned with the design of the ships included John Wharton, Joshua Humphreys, Josiah Fox, and William Doughty.

Humphreys, an American Quaker, and Fox, an expatriate English Quaker, made the major inputs to the designs, incorporating the ideas of others where pertinent. The resultant model for the 44's contained features to be found in both British and French frigates, but it blended them with native ideas to produce a uniquely American man of war. The ships would be very large for their rates, being 175 feet between perpendiculars and with an extreme beam of 44'2". That made them 2-3 feet wider and twenty feet longer than their British contemporaries; thirteen feet longer and a foot wider than the French. The strengthening and widening of the gangways connecting the forecastle and quarterdeck created the "spar deck," capable of accommodating great guns anywhere along its length. The framing of the 44 was so close that the average interval between

21

frame pairs was but 1¼", compared to spacing of a foot and more in some other frigates of the day. And while this great strength of deck and hull permitted the mounting of heavier armament (24-pounders vice 18's), the better length-to-beam ratio and the comparative fineness of the bow resulted in ships capable of sailing with the fastest and most maneuverable in the world.

In Boston, the private yard selected to build one of the 44's was that belonging to Edmund Hartt, which was located near the current Coast Guard Base Boston and which is commemorated in bronze as "Constitution Wharf." Henry Jackson was hired as Naval Agent and charged with assembling the artisans and laborers, purchasing materials not otherwise contracted for, supervising the clerk of the yard, paying wages, and maintaining accounts. The prospective captain of the ship, Captain Nicholson, who had been appointed to that rank on 5 June, was ordered to report as Superintendent, to exercise overall supervision and provide naval expertise to the builders. George Claghorne joined the organization as Constructor, controlling the work force building the ship.

Contracts for materials began to be let in June 1794, but it was nearly a year before actual construction could begin. One of the biggest problems was that of cutting and transporting the live oak wanted for the ship's frames from the sea islands off Georgia. (Tradition has it that the first tree felled for *Constitution* was an immense live oak to be used for her stern post. It was reported to have come from Cannon's Point, at the north end of St. Simon's Island. The stump of this tree was said to have been banded with an iron hoop bearing the inscription "U.S. Frigate Constitution, 1794," and allegedly was on display at the International Cotton Exposition in Atlanta, Georgia, in 1895, but this cannot be substantiated.) *Constitution*'s keel finally was laid some time in the summer of 1795. In the sixteen months which followed, slow but steady progress was made.

Early in 1796, peace was achieved with the Algerine pirates, which should have killed the naval construction program, but President Washington convinced the Congress that the three most nearly built frigates should be completed. The Boston ship was one of them. Work went on slowly and the costs mounted. Ships such as these had never been built in America before; that, together with the requirement to use the finest materials available, was having its effect on the budget.

The 44-gun frigate *United States* was launched in Philadelphia on 10 May 1797; the 38-gun *Constellation*, in Baltimore on 7 September that same year. The Boston frigate was to have been launched on 20 September, but she stuck on the ways after moving just twenty-seven feet. A second attempt two days later moved her another thirty-one feet, but still did not get her floated. A month-long delay became necessary to await the next period of maximum high tides.

A cold, overcast day was 21 October 1797. An east wind swept across the yard. Early that morning, Claghorne caused one of *Constitution*'s cannon, which were not yet on board, to be fired as an announcement to anyone interested that he was ready to try again at high tide. By noon "a very numerous and brilliant col-

*The launching of* Constitution, *21 October 1797.*

lection of citizens assembled at the spectacle." Among those on board for the occasion were Captain Nicholson, prickly as a porcupine and eager to have sole authority over the frigate; Captain James Sever, visiting from his post in Portsmouth, New Hampshire; Mr. Benjamin Russell, newspaper publisher, and his guests, the Duc de Chartres (later King of France), the Duc de Montpensier, and Comte de Beaujolais (all displaced French aristocrats), together with a number of ladies. A few moments later, Claghorne gave the order to knock out the blocks and shores, and this time the large frigate moved promptly and swiftly into the harbor waters. As she went, Captain Sever broke a bottle of Madeira on the heel of her bowsprit, declaring her to be named *"Constitution."* Once anchored, the yard was signalled and *Constitution*'s cannon on shore "announced to the neighboring country that *Constitution* was secure."

At the time *Constitution* was launched, there was an atmosphere of watchful waiting in Philadelphia. Our free trade upon the high seas was being affected by the belligerents in Europe — Britain and France, principally the latter. The country seemed ready to take some defensive measures, but hoped the situation would resolve itself without bloodshed. As talks drifted along in Paris, so, too, did governmental efforts at defense preparations. On 5 March 1798, President John Adams relayed to Congress a letter he had received from his emissaries in France which said, in part: "We can only repeat that there exists no hope...that the objects of our mission will be in any way accomplished." With the need apparent and the way now cleared for a navy, Congress acted to end the War Department's stewardship of the new force. On 27 April, in a bill authorizing expansion of the Navy by not more than twelve vessels carrying no more than twenty-two guns each, and on 30 April, in a second bill establishing the Department of the Navy, the legislators finally had committed themselves to a permanent sea-going armed force.

Meanwhile, *Constitution*'s outfitting went on. On 5 May, Captain Nicholson was directed "to repair on board...and to lose no Time in completing, equipping and manning her for Sea." He was to "open houses of Rendezvous in proper Places" and engage a crew "all certified healthy by the Surgeon, for twelve Months unless sooner discharged." Young Will Bryant, for one, "was in the boat with the first recruits that ever went on board of that ship...no officers on board at that time but petty officers." That was 15 May 1798.

Throughout May, as recruiting went on, stores were arriving in ever-greater quantities for the ship: thousands of musket and pistol balls, nearly 2000 gallons of brandy, the 24-pounder battery, over 500 handspikes, 2143 gallons of rum, carpenter tools, capstan bars, chaldrons of sea coal, a grindstone — the variety and numbers of items necessary to the small, sea-going community staggers the imagination.

On the 28th of that month, President Adams directed the Navy "to seize take and bring into any Port of the United States...any armed Vessel sailing under Authority...from France" off our coasts attacking, or waiting to attack, our merchantmen. The sloop of war *Ganges*, converted from a merchantman and under command of Captain Richard Dale, was the only unit immediately ready to carry out these orders.

June found *Constitution* still largely lacking guns for her spar deck thanks to contractor short-comings. Captain Nicholson approached the Governor of Massachusetts to borrow cannon from Castle Island with which to complete his ship's armament. As a result of his efforts, the big frigate was first armed with fourteen 12-pounder and sixteen 18-pounder long guns on the spar deck, in addition to the thirty 24-pounder log guns on the gun deck — sixty cannon for a frigate (44).

*Constitution* finally was ready for sea on 22 July 1798, as we have seen. It was not an auspicious beginning. Her total cost had been $302,718.84, some 260% greater than originally estimated. Evidence was strong that she was jinxed. It had required three tries to launch her. She had been christened by a man. Her Captain had an abysmal reputation, and the officers were, to say the least, generally an uninspiring lot. The crew was unhappy and demoralized. And as we have seen, her earliest operations seemed only to confirm the jinx.

## WHAT DID SHE LOOK LIKE?

The truth is, we really don't know exactly how *Constitution* looked when first she saw service. Such original draughts as there were to guide her construction

*Sail plan, copied from "Old Ironsides" by James Cruz, circa 1920.*

were taken by Captain Nicholson and not seen again. The earliest known artist's rendering was done about 1803 by Michel Felice Cornè; the earliest model dates from 1812. But if we can not see her directly, we can construct a reasonably good image of her first appearance by extrapolation from existing draughts for her sister and near-sisters, from diary and journal entries, and from newspaper articles of the period.

*Constitution*'s hull originally bore a broad yellow ochre band from the vicinity of the hawse pipes to the quarter galleries, the outer surfaces of the split gun port lids being the same color. This band extended approximately from the level of the channels down to the top of the main wales. Below, in the "bends," the ship was tarred; above it, including the quarterdeck bulwarks, she was painted black. Whether or not there was decorative painting other than this is unknown, but Cornè shows a yellow ochre "pin stripe" on the mouldings at the spar deck sill level.

The bow head area of the frigate originally was constructed with only tail and foot rails, completely free of any weather bulwarks, gratings, or privies. The bowsprit was lashed with 9-inch hempen gammoning passing through a slot in

*An early engraving of* Constitution, *by A. Bowen.*

the cutwater. Topping the cutwater was a figurehead of "an Herculean figure standing on the firm rock of Independence resting one hand on the fasces, which was bound by the Genius of America and the other hand presenting a scroll of paper supposed to be the Constitution of America with proper appendages, the foundation of Legislation." As completed, it also included "his battoon lying beneath him." Presumably, it was painted in "natural" colors. Below and aft of the figurehead on either side were the trail boards. These had carved upon them a curling vine or leaf pattern with no apparent eye-catching feature. Indeed, they may even have been unaccented by paint to make them stand out.

The appearance of the stern is even more dimly seen. Modern students generally feel there originally were six windows in the transom, with pilasters separating them, but anywhere from five to eight have been debated. Be that as it may, the decorations were quite resplendent. High up near the taffrail in the center was the spread eagle. Immediately below was the familiar shield of the United States being "presented" by two nereids, who, in turn, were flanked by pairs of unmounted cannon, one partially resting atop the other. Above each outer window was another nereid, facing the center grouping and holding a wreath in extended hands. On each quarter gallery's aft side were the classical

26

figures of Liberty and Justice. Framing the whole was an entwinement of carved rope. The name was borne below the windows, as it still is, but probably was done in Roman intaglio rather than the modern raised block letters. All of this decoration undoubtedly was picked out in a distinctive color, probably the yellow ochre, but perhaps gilt.

The quarter galleries, those "green houses" on either side of the stern housing the Old Man's privies, also carried the pilaster theme adjacent to their three windows. Likewise, carved bas relief thematically akin to that on the trail boards decorated the panels immediately beneath the windows, with other work forming a radial pattern on the undersides and also "capping" the upper (horizontal) roof line.

The ship was built without the high bulwarks surrounding the forecastle. A simple railing extended aft to the entry ports, with stanchions forming the ports for the forecastle long guns and hammock nettings in the waist. A series of bitts and a knighthead were installed on either side from the forward ends of the rails to the catheads to facilitate anchor handling; there were no anchor ports or billboards, nor were bridle ports present at the gun deck level originally.

The frigate's guns were painted black. Their carriages may also have been black, although red, brown, and green were in common use at the time, as well. Likewise, these colors were equally popular for the deck fittings (coamings, etc.).

No records have been found concerning the first appearance of *Constitution*'s spars and yards. The Corné painting, once again, is the most nearly contemporary. In it, the inner and outer thirds of the bowsprit are black or brown, while the middle third, together with the jib and flying jib booms, are yellow ochre. The masts — lower, top, and topgallant sections — are yellow ochre all the way to the trucks, with blackened doublings. The bands on the fore and main masts are also blackened. The yards are "natural" or black.

Furled on the yards were some of her suit of sails comprising nearly an acre of canvas. When set and seen close aboard they showed the streaky, mottled browns characteristic of woven flax, but at a distance took on the storied whiteness and cloudlike appearance under a bright sun.

The fighting tops, those perches for Marine snipers, were left "natural." Mounted on either side of each was a brass carronade of about 1½-inch bore to be used against the mass of humanity to be found above decks on enemy ships. These "mini-guns" would be removed as excess baggage long before *Constitution* fought her first major action.

A number of boats were carried, but exactly how many is not known; six to eight is the likely range. One was carried in davits astern, one in davits on either quarter, and the remainder nested in chocks on the skid beams spanning the main hatch. While most were painted white (without a different color below the waterline), it was not uncommon to use several colors to ease identification at fair distances. One of the frigate's cutters is believed to have been painted blue at this time.

27

## THE CREW: ITS ORGANIZATION AND DUTIES

The organization into which *Constitution*'s crew was entered was a highly structured yet flexible one that had evolved in the sea-going community largely exclusive of national boundaries through centuries of painful trial and tragic error in the demanding environment of the high seas. It had been a long, slow process, so that there was little change in the system in the life of a single ship — even one whose normal active service spanned more than eighty years.

In the young United States Navy, the most senior man aboard might be an officer of the **rank** of Captain, but who, because he was in charge of a number of ships, was known as the "Commodore." He shared the great cabin with the ship's Captain and took precedence over him in the matter of honors and ceremonies, but left the running of this, his flagship, to the Captain. It frequently was the case early in the nineteenth century that *Constitution*'s Captain also bore the responsibilities of being the squadron commander, as we have seen with both Nicholson and Talbot.

The senior officer directly responsible for the ship was the Captain (which was both his rank and title). Generally in his forties and with fifteen or more years of sea experience behind him, he was totally responsible for everything relating to the ship, and had powers very nearly as unlimited: leave and liberty, promotion and demotion, grog or no grog — life and death. The unforgiving nature of the sea rendered such awesome authority necessary.

Next in line was the First Lieutenant, the senior of the 4-6 lieutenants assigned. The billet today is called the Executive Officer. His duty was to carry out the policies of the Captain, and like the Captain, he stood no watches, but nearly always was "available." He saw to the proper standing of watches, the organization and implementation of daily or periodic routines, insured the cleanliness of the ship and oversaw its maintenance, reporting his activities and findings regularly to the Captain. All others in the ship reported to him, or through him, to the Captain. On special evolutions, such as coming to anchor or getting underway, the First Lieutenant "took the deck" — he was in charge of the event. In battle, he maneuvered the ship in accordance with the Captain's orders. In sum, the comfort and well-being of everyone on board, together with their duty assignments for a wide variety of evolutions, were his responsibility. He was a very busy man. It has been said that an "Exec" who gets a full night's sleep isn't doing his job.

The other lieutenants were the watch standers, relieving one another in an endless rotation at sea and in port, ensuring that the Captain's orders and ship's routine were carried out precisely and punctiliously. The lieutenants also were division officers, responsible for the activities and welfare of the crew, for their direction in battle, as well as for the maintenance of particular sections of the ship and at least one of the ship's boats.

The sailing master was the next in rank; he was the navigator, keeping track of where the ship was and the course necessary to get her where she was going. He taught the art of navigation to the midshipmen. Because he was responsible for the ship's trim (her attitude in the water), he had charge of the stowage of stores in the hold, as well as the water and spirits, and of the anchors and cables.

Because they did not stand watches, the purser, the surgeon and his mates, the chaplain, and the one or two Marine officers aboard were known collectively as "idlers." The purser had charge of the ship's monies and accounts. He purchased and dispensed provisions and other stores, "slops" (clothing), and small stores (sundries). Unlike earlier days when pursers made most of their money by selling their wares at usurious prices, the American purser bore the heavy responsibility for every penny and every item in the ship's account. It behooved him to keep a tight rein on the receipts and disbursements of the myriads of items under his cognizance. Inventories and ledgers very nearly were his whole life. The surgeon and his "mates" (we today might call them "interns") held daily "sick calls" for minor complaints, tended the sick and injured, and advised the Captain and First Lieutenant of appropriate precautionary measures as they pertained to the maintenance of a healthy crew. The surgeon himself lived in the wardroom with the lieutenants, while his mates occupied quarters in the cockpit, where the wounded were tended in battle. The chaplain attended to the spiritual needs of the crew, often as he or the Captain saw them. But besides Sunday services when operations permitted, and burials at sea, the chaplain (especially before the 1820's, when schoolmasters were entered upon the Navy's rolls) frequently taught the three R's to the ship's boys, and perhaps the classics, navigation and a language to the midshipmen. The Marine officer(s), of course, had charge of the functioning of the Marine detachment, which made up about ten percent of the total crew. The Marines were the ship's police force in peace and snipers and assault force in battle. The officer in charge of the detachment, be he Marine captain or lieutenant, occupied an unusual position in that, technically, he coordinated the activities of his group with the ship, but reported directly to the Commandant of the Marine Corps on most matters. This, at other times and in other commands, caused problems.

Junior to the "idlers" (and often cited as being senior only to the "ship's cat") were the midshipmen. Eight to twelve of these teenage student officers were the usual complement for *Constitution*, but in the days following the War of 1812 and prior to the foundation of the Naval Academy at Annapolis in 1845, at times there were as many as two dozen of the "young gentlemen" aboard. They stood watches, practiced navigation with the sailing master, relayed orders from the quarterdeck to their respective stations, and presumably prepared themselves for qualification as lieutenants. They were required to keep journals akin to the ship's log, which the Captain regularly reviewed. Likewise, the sailing master, chaplain, and/or schoolmaster would report on the progress of their young charges in the subjects under their cognizance. In port, midshipmen oftentimes were employed as boat officers, supervisors of watering parties, etc.

## A Most Fortunate Ship

Next in the ship's hierarchy were the warrant officers — the technical specialists: boatswain, gunner, sailmaker, and carpenter. The boatswain was responsible for the rigging and seeing to it everything aloft was properly main-tained; he traditionally carried a silver call (or "pipe") on a lanyard around his neck as his badge of office and, in battle, he took station on the forecastle. The gunner's and carpenter's duties are self-evident. The sailmaker, in addition to caring for several suits of sails, also made the hammocks and sickbay cots. The boatswain, sailmaker, and carpenter together made an inspection aloft daily.

Senior among the enlisted crew were the petty (from "petit") officers. Principal among these was the master-at-arms, who oversaw discipline, commanded prisoners, took charge of clothing and personal items found adrift, ensured decorum on the berth deck, and guarded against liquor smuggling by boat crews and shore parties. The quartermasters were among the most experienced seamen aboard and had charge of signals, keeping a lookout, and steering the ship. Boatswain's mates and gunner's mates assisted their respective warrant officers in the accomplishment of their duties. The boatswain's mates, like their leader, all wore silver calls, which were used to signal particular orders. A gunner's mate was assigned to each deck of guns, and two subordinate quarter gunners to each division.

Beneath this lordly group was the great mass of the crew: ordinary seamen, able seamen, cooks and assistants, armourer, cordwainer, tinker, loblolly boys (sick bay, or hospital attendants), stewards, barber, landsmen, and boys. All told, about 400 souls were in "*Constitution* Town."

Pay in those early years generally was considered adequate. The Captain, with about $75 per month and an allowance for rations, drew slightly over $2000 annually. The lieutenants and the surgeon received about $800 per year; the chaplain, sailing master, and purser, just under $700; surgeon's mates and Marine lieutenants, a bit over $550; the warrant officers got about $450 and the midshipmen were paid about $430. In the crew, petty officers averaged around $19 monthly, and the seamen, boys, etc., from $8 to $17.

Pay could be augmented by "prize money" (although, up to this point, we have seen *Constitution* miss out on it in almost every way possible). In a system that dated back at least 700 years, a victorious crew profited from the capture of enemy ships subsequently brought safely into a friendly port and adjudged a bonafide prize. In the United States, the Federal Government was allocated one-half the assessed value and the crew divided up the rest on a twenty share system. The Captain received three shares (one of which went to the embarked Com-modore, should there have been one at the time the capture was made). The commissioned officers as a body received two shares; warrant officers, two; the various petty officers, six; and the remaining crewmen, seven. Thus, the ship's portion of a $200,000 prize would result in $15,000 for the Captain and, at the other end of the scale, about $100 for each of the seamen, boys, and private Marines in the crew illustrated above. No matter an individual's station in life,

*Engraving from a painting by F. Roux, published in France in the early nineteenth century.*

the prospect of prize money in wartime was a strong inducement to "signing on."

## WATCHES

The officers and petty officers designated to stand watches normally did so on the basis of four hours on and eight hours off (i.e.. 8-12, 12-4, 4-8). The remainder of the crew, other than the "idlers", was divided into larboard and starboard watches, working "four and four." In order to prevent the same people from having to stand the same watches *ad infinitum,* the period between 4 and 8 P.M. daily was divided into two two-hour watches, the "dog" (from "docked") watches. Further variety was provided by dividing each watch section into "quarter watches," which alternated standing their duty in the fighting tops and on the spar deck.

In making watch assignments, the most experienced group as a whole was that assigned to the forecastle, for they were responsible not only for the sails of the foremast and the jibs, but the anchors as well. They were known collectively as the "forecastle" or "sheet anchor" men. The similar group on the quarterdeck was known as the "after guard." Individually, the most knowledgeable and agile men were assigned as fore-, main-, or mizzen-topmen. It was they who worked at the dizzying heights above ship and sea, out on yardarms whose great length magnified the ship's every move so that they were forever in danger of being whipped off to their deaths. Small wonder the rule was "one hand for the ship, and one for self."

31

## BATTLE STATIONS

The crew also was organized into six divisions, based upon the gun batteries. On the gun deck were the First, Second, and Third Divisions, each assigned ten of the 3¼-ton 24-pounder long guns. The Fourth and Fifth Divisions handled the lighter (1½-ton) carronades on the forecastle and quarterdeck. The Sixth Division was composed of the remainder of the crew, which included both skilled persons, such as the carpenter and sailmaker and their mates, who corrected battle damage, and the "waisters," those as yet skilled to do no more than fetch or provide muscle power. This division was commanded by the First Lieutenant; the others, by the remaining lieutenants (the Second Lieutenant had the First Division, etc.). At least one midshipman also was assigned to each division to assist the division officer, ensure the accomplishment of directives, and to relay orders.

The gun crew for a 24-pounder varied from nine to fourteen men, depending upon the size of the ship's company and whether or not one or more members was about on other duty. A "gun crew" actually was responsible for *two* guns: those in the same relative positions on either side of the ship. Thus, several members of the gun crew were supernumeraries assigned to begin to ready the gun on the unengaged side at such time as the Captain might choose to "change sides;" they also would replace men killed, injured, or otherwise reassigned from the engaged crew. A crew typically consisted of a gun captain, sponger, shellman, handspikeman, side-tacklemen, and in-tacklemen. If the ship suffered damage in battle, up to four members of this team might be called away to act as pumpmen, fireman, or wreck clearer, leaving nearly a dozen to handle the gun. Similarly, should boarders be called away in preparation for storming an enemy ship, almost the entire crew had assignments as riflemen or cutlass- and pike-wielding boarders. The gun crews on the spar deck were organized the same way, although the smaller, lighter guns required fewer in each team: four to nine men.

There were a myriad of operations that had to be attended to by the 400 or so crew members over and beyond those associated with battle: weighing and coming to anchor, watering ship, sailing evolutions, man overboard rescue, etc., etc. All these assignments were made by name on the ship's Watch, Quarter, and Station Bill. Maintained by the First Lieutenant, with the assistance of the division officers, it specifically told each crewman what he was to do in each evolution. The crewmen, on pain of the "cat," was expected to have his part memorized thoroughly and to perform the required duty flawlessly under any conditions. Thus, the Watch, Quarter, and Station Bill completely encompassed a man's life so long as he was assigned to the ship.

## AT SEA ROUTINE

The routine aboard *Constitution* at sea logically revolved about her safe navigation through the water. The watch was set on the spar deck and in the rigging, and almost nothing was permitted in those areas that would interfere. The warrant officers' daily inspection of the rigging and repairs that could occur nowhere else were the limit. The watch was to be quiet and alert.

Reveille was held at daylight (i.e., about thirty minutes prior to sunrise) and the hammocks rolled, tied, and stowed in the nettings above the cap rail in less than fifteen minutes. Until breakfast, timed to feed the off-going morning and on-coming forenoon watches, cleaning the ship and readying her for another day was the order of business. The breakfast of tea and bread or hard tack, and the morning ration of grog, required almost an hour to serve, consume, and clean up after. Toward the end of this and all meals, the "smoking lamp" was lighted: those who wished to could smoke in the vicinity of the caboose.

With breakfast over, the cook and his helpers began readying the noon meal — the one hot meal of the day. And elsewhere on the gun deck, the other trades began their work, which continued until 4 P.M. with the noon hour reserved for dinner. Near the cook and his hot caboose, the barber had his chair; the men were required to be shaven twice a week. Forward to starboard, the area typically was reserved as a classroom for midshipmen or the ship's boys; often canvas screens were tacked up to eliminate distractive sights. In the large open deck space beneath the boat skids in the waist, the sailmaker and his mates might be making and mending sails, or the cooper refurbishing barrels. Elsewhere on the starboard side of the gun deck, between the guns, skilled craftsmen such as the cordwainer and a tinker plied their trades. The port side of the gun deck from the main hatch aft was reserved as an officers' promenade, where those worthies, when off duty, might bring folding stools and find relaxation in a brighter and better ventilated area than their wardroom.

Punishment, when it had to be administered, most often was carried out shortly before noon. Because of the unforgiving nature of life at sea, discipline had to be absolute, and the price of disobedience dear. In the U.S. Navy of these early years, flogging was the most frequently imposed form of punishment, although it was closely limited in comparison with the Royal Navy. By the Naval Act of 1799, ship's captains could award no more then twelve lashes for a single offense; courts martial, 100. The limits of an offense, however, were less well defined. If a man were to get drunk, pick a fight with his petty officer, then desert (the three commonest disciplinary problems), he clearly had committed an offense; but his Captain legitimately could find *three* offenses and award him thirty-six lashes.

The flogging was administered with the offender trussed bare-backed to a hatch grating upended for the purpose. It was accomplished by one or more boatswain's mates using the cat-o'-nine-tails — a whip with nine strands, each knotted or weighted at the free end. To ensure a proper "laying on of the lash," the mates would trade off after twelve, or perhaps only six, strokes. Left and right-handed mates, working in company, could wreak particularly frightful havoc. The decreed number of lashes applied, the poor wretch was cut down, his back tended to, and he was returned to duty as soon as possible. His shipmates, who had been required to witness his punishment, returned to resume the day's routine.

Three other forms of punishment were hanging (for crimes like treason or desertion in the face of the enemy), "running the gauntlet," and "starting." Thieves often were made to run the gauntlet, i. e., be made to crawl on all fours or to be hauled atop a small cask slowly through a double line of shipmates equipped with knotted ropes who lashed away merrily at this most reprehensible form of seagoing criminal. "Starting" was the use by petty officers of short lengths of knotted rope, called "starters" or "knouts," to encourage alacrity in their less-eager subordinates. Such use might, or might not, have been specifically directed by one of the officers.

To return to the routine. At about 4 P.M., after a final titivation, the crew's work day ended and it was time for the supper hour. This meal usually was composed of "leftovers" from dinner, together with bread, perhaps some cheese, and tea — and the inevitable grog, and the smoking lamp being lighted.

The officers took their meals in their respective cabin, wardroom, steerage, or warrant officers' mess. The crew was divided into groups of eight or ten men (messes) and ate picnic-style seated around communal pots brought down to the berth deck from the caboose. The senior of each mess was its "president," with absolute powers concerning mess operation. It was he who took the first choice from the pot, and it also was he who decreed the order of serving thereafter. Customarily, one member of the mess was "elected" on a weekly basis to serve as "mess cook." He would have the responsibility for setting out the utensils from the mess chest at each meal, for delivering the meal from the caboose, and for cleaning up afterwards, carefully stowing away any remains as they would constitute a portion of a subsequent meal.

It was at eight bells, too, that the purser and the stewards would go below to break out the foodstuffs for the next day's meals. The ten-pound chunks of salted meat or the salted fish were placed in a "harness cask" near the caboose and soaked in several changes of fresh water through the night to help reduce the saltiness. What food was broken out on which day was a matter of Navy Department regulation which could be varied only on the specific orders of the Captain. In these early days, a man was allowed a pound of bread daily; a pound of pork, a half-pint of peas or beans, and four ounces of cheese thrice weekly; 1½ pounds of beef, a half-pint of rice, 1-1½ pounds of potatoes or turnips, and two ounces of butter twice weekly; a pound of fish once a week; and, of course, the daily ration of a half-pint of "spirits" or a quart of beer. Any spoilage found upon break-out was "surveyed" formally by the First Lieutenant and sailing master, reported to the Captain in writing, and thence to the Navy Department, which oversaw the victualling contracts.

Nothing was wasted unless it was unbelievably foul. The bread (or, more properly, biscuit) oftentimes was weevil-filled. Should the meat offered appear to be the poorer choice, the weevils might not be removed before ingestion. Similarly, the cheese, with age, would become alive with long yellow worms. On "fish" and "butter" days, the ship might smell like an ancient whaler.

A bright spot, to the sailors, in this grim gastronomic picture, was the promise of "duff" on Sundays. Duff was the one "dessert" available to the crew. To make it, the mess cook would beat bisquits into a coarse flour. To this, he would add raisins, water, and "slush" — the residue of beef fat scraped from the coppers of the caboose. The resultant mixture was spooned into a light canvas bag and delivered to the cook, who boiled it into a glutinous consistency in the bag. Not unlike a cannon ball in density, to the crew it was the closest thing to a delicacy.

With a diet such as this, the advent of fresh foods was of great moment. No opportunity was lost, either by individual ships in port or by squadron commanders on station at sea, to provide such benefits to their men. A ship newly at sea from a well-stocked port might present a startling sight and a barnyard aroma: bullocks penned in the manger area of the gun deck; freshly slaughtered halves and quarters hanging from adjacent beams; perhaps pigs and sheep restrained in some of the nested boats, and crated chickens in others; and in the vicinity, the baled hay and bagged corn with which to sustain them for the three or four weeks the luckiest would live.

Besides the official efforts to provide fresh food, all hands could avail themselves of the opportunity to purchase "stores" ashore or from bumboats. The officers, with storerooms set aside for them, could stock up for the next at-sea period. The enlisted men, with no such luxury, oftentimes went on eating orgies, spending their last penny for fruits and vegetables, and gorging themselves until their systems revolted.

With the completion of the evening meal and the final titivation of the ship, the crew was at liberty to relax. Gathering in little groups, endless sea stories would be spun off by the older tars to awe and edify their callow compatriots. "Hammocks" were piped down at sunset, and the ship largely settled in for the night when the darkness was complete. Petty officers, in their portion of the berth deck, might be allowed to have candles or lanterns for an hour; the officers were expected to regulate themselves. The only people allowed to be moving about below decks after "taps" were the midshipman of the watch, the master at arms, and his corporals, who routinely patrolled to ensure the ship's security against fire and flooding, and to discover "skulkers," whose presence might indicate impending desertion or be the herald of mutiny.

## IN PORT ROUTINE

When the ship was in port, a similar routine was in effect. In lieu of the many men engaged in watch-standing, however, there was increased emphasis on and allocations of manpower to maintenance and cleanliness, as well as the need to assign working parties and boat crews to resupply and rewater the ship.

The day began formally at 8 o'clock — after reveille, clean up, and breakfast — with the firing of the morning gun, which announced to all in the harbor that

## A Most Fortunate Ship

*Constitution* was "open for business." On watch on the quarterdeck were a lieutenant, a midshipman, a quartermaster, a boatswain's mate, and one or two boys. This group would monitor the ship's safety, both as to her own anchorage and the activities of other ships in the harbor. They would render or return the "honors" due passing ships and craft, depending upon their relative seniorities. For the arrival and departure of boats, the lieutenant would ensure the timely mustering of the Marine guard and side boys, and the observance of the correct protocol. His was a heavy responsibility, for a ship's — and thereby her Captain's — reputation was made or broken as a result of the promptitude and smartness with which such evolutions were accomplished.

A typical week's cleaning routine was as follows:

**Monday** — scrub clothes; clean hammocks, cots, and windsails; scrub decks with sand and squilgees.

**Tuesday** — pump her out; holystone spar, main, and orlop decks; white wash berthing deck ceiling planking and bulkheads; scrub brightwork.

*The eight-man bilge pump. Just abaft the mainmast the bilge pump is placed over the deepest point of the ship. Water was pumped out of the bilges by a rocking motion of the pump. This bilge water was then allowed to flow across the deck and out the scuppers to help keep the deck moist and prevent it from splitting.*

**Wednesday** — holystone berth deck, combings, and mess chest lids; scrub all paintwork.

**Thursday** — pump her out; exercise at general quarters; scrub spar and main decks; whitewash gun deck ceiling planking; holystone hatches to chain and sand lockers.

**Friday** — scrub clothes; scrub rammers, sponges and handspikes with sand; clean all gun gear; inspect all pumps and associated gear; oil the fire hoses.

**Saturday** — holystone ladders and waterways; air bedding; mending day; clear galley smoke pipe of soot.

**Sunday**—pump her out; holystone around caboose; inspect ship's company.

One journalist concluded a recitation such as this: "God Save Us."

The firing of the evening gun at sunset indicated the end of the public day. Any boats away from the ship began their return trips as soon as it was heard, in order to be back before dark or shortly thereafter. At this time, too, were stationed the Marine sentries with loaded muskets on the forecastle, quarterdeck, and both gangways. They were to ensure that no small craft came alongside the ship unchallenged and that no one attempted desertion. At regular intervals throughout the night their calls of "all's well" carried around the spar deck, while the master-at-arms and his mates maintained their vigil below.

Such was the life at sea and in harbor in *Constitution*: damp, noisy, dangerous, crowded, smelly, too hot or too cold, and in constant motion. Why did anyone ever enlist? To get away from someone or something that, at the time, seemed more disagreeable: creditor; orphanage; irate parents, wife, husband or brother; lack of food and a place to sleep. Some even did it for patriotism or belief that they wanted to go to sea. Why did any ever go back? Many never got clear of creditors or angry males wherever they went. Others went back because, like the astronauts of the twentieth century looking back at the "big blue marble," out on the expanse of the world's oceans they found themselves inexplicably close to understanding their miniscule place in the vastness that is the universe and, at the same time, their oneness with it. They respected the awesome forces of Nature, and the fortunate ones survived them. It is a feeling, a sense, a landsman can never know.

# 3 The Barbary War: September 1795 - July 1804

## BACKGROUND

The depredations of the Barbary pirates and their actions drove the United States to legislate a Navy. But we saw that even this was not a whole-hearted effort, as a peace proviso was a part of the building bill: no piracy, no ships. That "peace" came about, and only Washington's foresightedness had prevented a total scrapping of the small building program. At that point, French actions against our neutral merchantmen caught the country's attention and the Barbary problem slid into the background. Now, with Franco-American relations back on an even keel, we must take a quick look at what had been happening on Africa's northern coast, for the Barbary pirates once again came to center stage.

The 1796 treaty with Algiers — and it had been only with Algiers, most powerful of the Barbary regencies — committed the United States to paying a lump sum of $642,500 to free captive Americans and make a "down payment" for free trade; to an annual tribute in naval stores amounting to $21,600; and to making semi-annual deliveries of "presents" on the same scale as Holland, Sweden, and Denmark. Following the Algerine treaty one was signed with Tripoli in November 1796 (for $58,000) and another with Tunis in August 1797 (for about $107,000, all told). In the great disparity of sums, particularly as regards Tripoli, lay the germ of renewed trouble. The Bey of Tunis, Hamouda Pacha, was cautious in his reaction because the Americans and the Algerines had become friends and he had a common border with the latter. Yusuf Karamanli, the Bashaw of Tripoli, at a distance from his more powerful Moslem brothers, tended to be feistier.

When James Leander Cathcart, the first American Consul following the treaty, arrived in Tripoli in April 1799, he was immediately berated by the Bashaw who claimed he had been promised all sorts of presents by the earlier American negotiators — none of which had been delivered. He would have them or — by Allah — there would be war. Working through the British Consul (because the Bashaw at first refused to see him directly), in four days Cathcart gained a settlement of all grievances, real and imagined, for $22,500. With eighty American merchantmen in and about the Mediterranean at this time, and only the Government's dispatch brig *Sophia* present, it was well to have the pirates mollified.

Threats and peevishness aside, the United States enjoyed about fifteen months without incident in the Mediterranean. Then, in July 1800, a Tripoline polacre captured the New York brig *Catherine*, bound for Leghorn. Cathcart managed to get the Bashaw to disavow the act and release the merchantman and her crew, but only after three months of tough arguing — and with a threat that there would be war if Bashaw Yusuf wasn't made to feel as "loved" as his piratical associates. The Americans had six months in which to prove their affection.

Just as this latest problem with Tripoli was being resolved, the Dey of Algiers decided to flex his muscles by forcing an American warship, the 24-gun frigate *George Washington*, under Captain William Bainbridge, to transport his annual tribute to Constantinople. Bainbridge carried out the onerous task with considerable credit to himself, but it was, nonetheless, an unmitigated affront to American sovereignty and could not be ignored.

## THE FIRST MEDITERRANEAN SQUADRON

Thomas Jefferson became President on 4 March 1801. When he became aware of the Tripoline and Algerine attitudes and actions, he decided to send a "squadron of observation" to the Mediterranean whose purpose, as he wrote in a letter to the Bashaw, was "to superintend the safety of our commerce, and to exercise our seamen in nautical duties," and furthermore, "we mean to rest the safety of our commerce on the resources of our own strength and bravery in every sea." The squadron consisted of frigates *President* (44), *Philadelphia* (36), and *Essex* (32), and the sloop-of-war *Enterprise* (12). To the squadron commander, Commodore Richard Dale, Acting Navy Secretary Samuel Smith wrote several pages of detailed instructions. The squadron units were to fight to win if attacked, but not to seek action. As in the Quasi-War, they also were to defend any American cargo ship being attacked. These elements were to be found in the directives of the earlier war, but there was a surprising new one: should an attacking ship be defeated, it was *not* to be taken prize. Such a ship was to be disarmed and reduced to the barest essentials necessary to make shore safely; if it sank in the engagement, then the survivors were to be put ashore "on some part of the Barbary shore most convenient to you." With these orders, Dale sailed on 2 June 1801. The Bashaw of Tripoli, true to his word, already had cut down the flagpole outside the American Consulate on 14 May, his way of declaring war.

As Dale's units rendezvoused at Gibraltar following a stormy crossing, they found there the two largest vessels of the Tripoline Fleet, the 28-gun *Meshuda* (one-time American brig *Betsey*) and a 14-gun brig, preparing to enter the Atlantic against American shipping. Murad Rais, the Moslem Admiral, denied that there existed a state of war with the United States, but Commodore Dale had heard enough in the diplomatic circles at the Rock to make him suspicious. Upon sailing east, he left *Philadelphia* (Captain Bainbridge) to keep an eye on them and to "take him when he goes out."

Through the summer and fall, Dale kept an intermittent blockade of Tripoli, causing some hardships, but not having sufficient force or logistic support to make it complete. On 1 August, *Enterprise* (Lieutenant Andrew Sterett) encountered the 14-gun Tripoline brig *Tripoli* while enroute to Malta. The pirate attacked. For three hours, the two small vessels blazed away at one another.

39

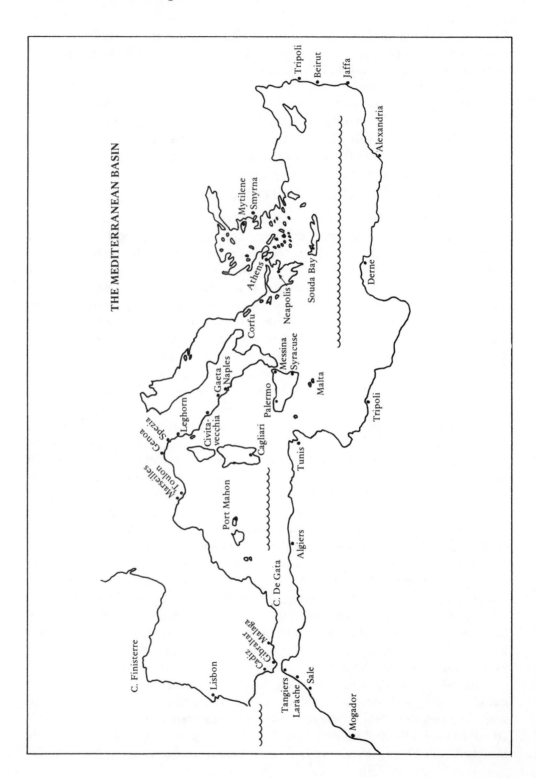

THE MEDITERRANEAN BASIN

Tripoli
Beirut
Jaffa
Alexandria
Mytilene
Smyrna
Derne
Athens
Souda Bay
Neapolis
Corfu
Messina
Syracuse
Malta
Tripoli
Gaeta
Naples
Palermo
Leghorn
Civita-
vecchia
Cagliari
Genoa
Spezia
Tunis
Marseilles
Toulon
Port Mahon
Algiers
C. De Gata
C. Finisterre
Málaga
Gibraltar
Cádiz
Lisbon
Tangiers
Larache
Sale
Mogador

Three times the enemy hauled down his colors and then re-opened fire as Sterett moved to board. Sterett hammered away until the Moslem finally hurled his colors into the sea, then boarded to find a shambles with sixty of the 80-man crew either dead or wounded. Not one American even had been scratched. In keeping with orders, Sterett directed his men to "heave all his Guns Over board Cut away his Masts, & leave him in a situation, that he can just get into some Port." The Bashaw thus received a clear message as to the merits of the Americans as sea fighters.

Back in Gibraltar, Murad Rais gave up waiting for *Philadelphia* to leave the field. With local help, he and his crews acquired small craft and slipped across the Straits to Morocco, thence overland back to Tripoli. *Meshuda* and her consort were left in Gibraltar, and will be heard from again.

With the coming of winter, blockading operations off Tripoli had to be abandoned because of prevailing bad weather. Too, the Navy still was using one-year enlistments, which meant some sort of rotation had to be established and most ships had to return to the United States. *Philadelphia* and *Essex* stayed in the Mediterranean through the winter. *President* and *Enterprise* came home.

## THE SECOND MEDITERRANEAN SQUADRON

In January 1802, Secretary Robert Smith began issuing orders to organize and dispatch a replacement squadron to the Mediterranean. *Enterprise,* the one non-frigate in the Navy — and, in many ways, the type best suited for blockading Tripoli's miniscule port — was to return again. The other units were *Constellation* (38), *Chesapeake* (36), *New York* (36), and *Adams* (28). To command the squadron was ordered Captain Richard Valentine Morris, who requested — and received — permission to take his wife with him. Morris's orders had none of the restrictions in them that had prevented Dale from making a bigger impression.

The ships sailed separately this time, little *Enterprise* returning first. Morris arrived at Gibraltar in *Chesapeake* at the end of May. It was seven weeks before his final ship, *Adams,* put in an appearance. In the meantime, he had gotten on famously with the British and had denied a move by the Emperor of Morocco to secure a release of *Meshuda* and the Tripoline brig. He also sent *Constellation* (Captain Alexander Murray) to blockade Tripoli. When Morris at last sailed from Gibraltar on 22 July, *Adams* (Captain Hugh G. Campbell) remained to watch *Meshuda* and the Emperor.

If ever there was a relaxing way to go to war, Commodore Morris found it. Proceeding at a leisurely pace, he visited ports in Spain, France, Italy, and Sicily before making Malta at year's end. Along the way, his wife announced that there would be a "blessed event." Malta was as close as he had come to Tripoli in seven months.

Morris returned to Malta by way of Leghorn on 1 May following an aborted trip to Tripoli and calls at Tunis and Algiers, ready once more to try for Tripoli. *John Adams* (28), which had arrived in January as a replacement for *Constella-*

*tion,* was sent ahead on 8 May, and on 12 May, off Tripoli, encountered an old acquaintance: *Meshuda* — but now it was *Meshouda,* and by means not now evident, a Moroccan vessel carrying an American safe-passage passport. That passport, however, specified that she could not enter any port blockaded by American forces. Because she was attempting to run the blockade, Captain John Rodgers made her prize and towed her back to Malta.

Morris took his squadron out of Malta again on 20 May and finally appeared off Tripoli. There were alarums and excursions, and fruitless peace negotiations, but the Commodore showed himself slothful and uncertain in everything he did. He was back in Valletta again on 14 June, having missed the birth of a son, his second child, by five days. *John Adams* and *Enterprise,* which had been left off Tripoli, came in per orders on the 30th. Tripoli was wide open. The squadron resumed touring the Mediterranean on 11 July, heading *away* from Tripoli, northward to Naples and Leghorn, then westward to Malaga and Gibraltar.

On 21 June, Secretary Smith had signed orders to Morris directing him to turn over command temporarily to John Rodgers and to return to the United States where a court of inquiry would look into his performance in the Mediterranean. End of the line for Morris. The next squadron commander would have both the resources and the will to take the war to Tripoli.

## PREBLE GETS HIS CHANCE

Edward Preble was a "downeaster," the fifth child of militia General Jedidiah Preble by his second wife. A person of strong feelings and an expert marksman, after three years of formal schooling and two years doing hated farm work, he first went to sea on a privateer shortly after his seventeenth birthday. The next year, 1779, he became an acting midshipman in the Massachusetts frigate *Protector* (26). He was a prisoner of war briefly in 1781 when that ship was taken by two British frigates, but influential friends arranged his exchange in little more than two months. Six months later, he was a lieutenant in the Massachusetts sloop *Winthrop* (12), and served in her on several successful cruises until she was sold out of service in June 1783. For the next fifteen years, he is known to have gone to sea regularly in the merchant service, rather quickly attaining the position of master.

In November 1798, Preble returned from a merchant voyage of some eight months' duration to find that he had been appointed First Lieutenant of *Constitution* six months earlier. Because there were many loose ends attendant upon his most recently completed voyage, he requested and received permission to delay a further six weeks in executing the orders. (He may, in fact, have been seeking to avoid duty under Nicholson.) As things turned out, events caused the Secretary to make further changes, and Preble soon found himself in command of the brig *Pickering* (14). A four month cruise in the West Indies netted him two prizes, and when he returned to Boston in June 1799 he found he had been promoted to the rank of Captain the preceding month. This last development drove

*Captain Edward Preble.*

forever from his mind any last thoughts he may have had to return to the merchant service.

After several months of waiting, Preble was ordered to command the brand new frigate *Essex* (32), which had been launched at Salem, Massachusetts, in September. In January 1800, he sailed from Newport on what proved to be a solo deployment to the Dutch East Indies to protect American merchantmen from the depredations of French privateersmen in the Indian Ocean. Little of note occurred; it was, however, the first time a warship of the United States had operated in those waters.

Preble brought *Essex* back to New York in November 1800. His subordinates recalled that his waspishness to some of them was an unpleasant aspect of the voyage. He had been unmercifully blunt and critical of any performance that did not meet his expectations, and ultimately caused the abrupt end of several budding careers upon their return home. It had become evident during the long trip that the Captain's health was deteriorating. In April 1801, as he was attempting to ready *Essex* for service in Dale's squadron, he had to confess to the Secretary of the Navy that he felt so poorly that relief would be necessary and a leave of absence desireable. Apparently, Preble was suffering from the onset of ulcers. His driving professionalism and choleric temperament were too much for his own system. Relieved in May, he returned to Portland to regain his health.

In January 1802, Secretary Smith wrote to Preble offering command of the frigate *Adams,* which was to be outfitted for Morris' squadron. Preble went to New York and tried to do the job. His sailing master at the time characterized him as being "cross, peevish and ill-tempered, surly and proud." On 13 April, Preble, knowing his health would not permit him to continue, tendered his resignation. Secretary Smith did not accept it, but relieved Preble of the command and placed him on furlough "until your health shall be restored."

In the months that followed, Preble seems to have made a genuine recovery from his debilitating illness. By August, he was writing to the Secretary very confidently that he felt he was on the mend and that it wouldn't be too long before he would be ready to set sail once more. On a trip to Washington in November, Preble met with the President, Secretary of State James Madison, and Robert Smith. It appears that he was given every reason to believe he would soon be ordered to command a frigate, and he seems to have known it would be *Constitution.* What none of the conversants could have known then was that, because both Dale and Captain John Barry would refuse the proffered squadron command, Preble also would hoist the broad blue command pennant as Commodore.

## READYING CONSTITUTION

Preble was in Boston in 19 May 1803 when he received orders from Secretary Smith to "assume the command of the frigate *Constitution* and have her put in a condition to sail at the shortest possible period." Characteristic of the new skipper, the very next day.

> A(t) 10 A.M. Commodore Preble came on board the *Constitution* and took charge as Commodore ... Preble examined every part of the *Constitution*'s Inside & ordered a carpenters caulking stage along side in order to examine the copper on the ships bottom ...

Sailing Master Nathaniel Haraden, who had been the ship's caretaker for her "10 months, 14 days" in ordinary, and who was Preble's "shadow" during those early days, obviously was impressed by this human dynamo who had read himself in as Haraden's superior. On the 21st, a Saturday, the float was in place and Preble and Haraden, using boathooks and rakes, conducted a visual and tactile inspection of the frigate's underwater body. From this Preble decided that recoppering was mandatory — a killing job in the absence of a dry dock. According to Preble, *Constitution* was the largest ship ever to be hove down in the United States.

On Sunday, 22 May, Preble wrote to Secretary Smith that orders already had been issued to return the frigate's guns from Castle Island so their weight could be used to help in the heaving down. By Tuesday, the 24th, Haraden was recording the work regimen for the hired laborers: basically, they worked from 5:15 A.M. until 7 P.M. with an hour off each for breakfast and dinner, and "At 11

*Heaving down* Constitution *at Boston, June 1803.*

A.M. and 4 P.M. They are allowed 15 minutes to Grog." This man Preble was a driver.

The tide being at maximum high, on 28 May *Constitution* was kedged cautiously through a narrow channel to a position off May's (Union) Wharf, where she was anchored fore and aft. It was a 10½-hour job, but only one of the many laborious processes to be accomplished in this herculean process. All the gun deck ports had to be planked up and caulked to ensure the hull's watertight integrity while careened. Guns and ballast — and filled water casks — had to be distributed to assist in the evolution. Gigantic blocks about five feet tall had to be attached individually to the mainmast and foremast, and their two mates to adjacent positions on the wharf. A 140-fathom purchase fall of 10-inch rope was rove through each pair of ship and shore blocks, and led to its own capstan. These would be used to heave her over when the time came. The rudder was unslung and secured to the wharf. Braces were rigged against the fore and main masts on the side toward which the ship would be careened and complementary stays rigged to 18-inch-square wooden outriggers on the outboard side. Relieving tackles also were rigged under the hull to prevent her from capsizing and also to be used if necessary in righting her.

The stage was set by 10 June, when all hands heaved 'round and the heavy frigate was made slowly to roll her port side out of the water. The carpenters then manned their stages and began stripping off the old copper sheets. With them off, seams were caulked with oakum and payed over with a mixture of tallow, tar, and turpentine; then sheathing paper was laid on and new sheets of copper tacked on. At the end of each day, the ship was righted.

By Friday, 17 June, this daily routine had gotten the entire port side of the hull resheathed. Preble and his toilers spent the weekend winding ship and rerigging her in order to do the starboard side. This time, the process went more quickly; at 5 P.M. on 25 June, the last sheet was tacked home, the carpenters hauled off their stages, giving nine cheers, and the caulkers and seamen responded in kind.

About the time Preble was ready to move *Constitution* to May's Wharf, he received some good — unexpectedly good — news from Secretary Smith: Preble would command the new squadron, as well as the frigate. This squadron would consist of *Constitution* and *Philadelphia* (still in the Mediterranean), the 16-gun brigs *Argus* and *Syren,* the 12-gun schooners *Vixen* and *Nautilus* (these four had been recently built as a result of Dale's recommendations), and that old reliable, *Enterprise.* For the first time, the Americans would have a reasonable balance of heavy gun power and swift, light craft able to meet similar pirate vessels on equal terms.

Early in June, Preble received orders to begin recruiting a crew, even as the ship was being rerigged and the jumble of her previously landed stores sorted out and brought aboard. With the Peace of Amiens coming apart, it appeared that England and France would be at each other's throats again shortly, making for profitable days for American merchantmen. This, coupled with the fact that the Navy now was enlisting for two years on a lower pay scale than during the Quasi-War, created severe problems for the Commodore in Boston. It was learned, however, that the war threat also was driving foreign seamen ashore in the United States to avoid impressment. Two of *Constitution*'s lieutenants were dispatched to New York early in July, and in short order filled their quotas. But, Preble lamented on 21 July, "I do not believe that I have twenty native American sailors on board" in the 165 or so men then present. Blacks were not to be enlisted.

Preble also had two problems relating to *Constitution*'s gun batteries, only one of which readily was resolved. The "easy" one had to do with the fact that the new Commodore wanted to put the 12-pounders in the gun ports once occupied by the 18-pounders borrowed from Massachusetts and no longer available. It seems that the gun carriages were incompatible with the gun port dimensions: they had to be landed and altered to fit. The other question had to do with the availability of carronades as replacements for the long guns on the spar deck. The ship had been designed with them in mind, but American industry had not been up to the task. Secretary Smith questioned Preble about putting eight 42-

pounder carronades on the quarterdeck. Preble looked around and answered that none were available, but thought he might be able to get some in Europe. Smith agreed to that, if Preble could manage to make such a purchase within his allocated funds as squadron commander. That, effectively, closed the subject for the moment. *Constitution*'s batteries would consist of the thirty 24-pounders on the gun deck and sixteen 12-pounder long guns on the spar deck, the 18-pounders previously on loan from the Commonwealth of Massachusetts having been returned subsequent to the ship being placed in ordinary.

Preble wanted to get *Constitution* to sea very badly, but she had been allowed to deteriorate markedly since Hull left her in April 1802. The Commodore knew, too, that if he left with a healthy ship he would be that much better able to accomplish his mission. The critical whispers he began hearing in mid-July did nothing to ameliorate the pace at which he drove himself and all those associated with him. He had his orders to bring the Bashaw into line, and was eager to be about it. Finally, everything was "go" on 9 August — except a fair wind. Preble had to chafe and fret for five more days before heading east.

## PREBLE SHOWS THE CUT OF HIS JIB

The transatlantic voyage was made quickly until the frigate arrived in European waters, when the speed of advance slowed to a crawl in light and variable winds. Off Cape St. Vincent on 6 September, Preble met and sent a boarding officer to the 30-gun Moroccan frigate *Maimona,* whose presence in the Atlantic caused his concern about the status of relations between the Emperor and the Americans. At Preble's request, Tobias Lear, our Consul-designate to Algiers, who was going out to his new post with the Commodore, looked over the Moroccan's papers and reported he had seen what he considered to be a valid signature of James Simpson, his counterpart in Tangiers. No one, however, could read the Arabic documents and know precisely what they said. *Maimona* went on her way, but Preble held his suspicions.

*Constitution* still was struggling against fickle winds four days later when she had a nighttime encounter with what was believed to be a man of war. Thinking she might be *Maimona* trying to lure him into a trap, Preble beat to quarters, then hailed the stranger through the darkness:

"What ship is that?"

The stranger echoed the query in return.

"This is the United States frigate *Constitution.* What ship is that?"

The stranger repeated his query and Preble his response, and then the question yet again. At this point, Preble lost patience and called out the warning, "I am now going to hail you for the last time. If a proper answer is not returned, I will fire a shot into you."

"If you fire a shot, I will return a broadside," came back across the water.

For the fourth time, the Commodore asked for identification. This time, the stranger answered, "This is His Britannic Majesty's ship *Donegal,* 84 guns, Sir

Richard Strachan, an English commodore. Send your boat on board."

Preble was almost apoplectic. "This is United States ship *Constitution*, 44 guns, Edward Preble, an American commodore, who will be damned before he sends his boat on board of any vessel!" And to his gun crews: "Blow on your matches, boys!"

Silence followed. Then a boat rowed out of the darkness and a British lieutenant came aboard and presented his Captain's compliments. The stranger was *HMS Maidstone*, a 32-gun frigate, Commander George Elliot. Elliot had been taken by surprise when *Constitution* appeared so close to him; the exchange took place as a stall while he manned his guns. It was a gutty thing to do, as was Preble's willingness to defy a ship of the line. Preble's young officers thereby discovered that the Commodore's terrible temper had its merits. This, perhaps, was the beginning of the deep allegiance that formed about Preble during the coming year, an allegiance of aspiring young officers who would be proud to be known as "Preble's boys," and which would provide most of the successful commanders in the War of 1812, including all three of *Constitution*'s skippers in that conflict.

## MOROCCAN MATTERS

*Constitution* arrived at Gibraltar on the afternoon of 12 September to find *Philadelphia*, the Moroccan ship *Mirboha* (22 guns), and the American brig *Celia* in port. Captain Bainbridge was soon on the flagship informing Preble that on 26 August he had met the other two vessels off Cabo de Gata, Spain, and that the Moroccan's responses to his questions were evasive. Further investigation proved that *Celia* had been captured by *Mirboha* and that the latter was under orders to make such captures by the Alcade of Tangiers. Bainbridge reported further that he had just spent ten days to the west of the Strait looking for *Maimona*, and was told of *Constitution*'s meeting with her.

Over the next few days, American warships gathered at the Rock. *Vixen* from the west and *New York* from the east ("aloft", as they said then) came in on the 13th. Discredited Commodore Morris was in the latter. Commodore *pro tem* John Rodgers arrived in *John Adams* on the 14th, together with *Nautilus* and *Meshouda*. During this period, Preble spent much time with Bainbridge and American Consul John Gavino "coming up to speed" on the political tides and currents.

Morris and Rodgers both were senior to Preble. Morris, however, was under a cloud and not inclined to worry protocol. Rodgers, who was sensitive to such matters as precedence, and told Preble so, magnanimously agreed to cooperate under Preble's leadership in gaining a resolution with the Moroccans. Both recognized that nothing could be done farther east until the intervening line of communication with America was secured. As soon as the matter was settled, Rodgers would go home.

*Constitution* and *John Adams* got underway on the afternoon of 16 September and were anchored in Tangier Bay before the morning gun the next day. It was seen from the ships that, while the flags of Britain, France, Spain, Denmark, Sweden, and Portugal were flying, there was no sign of the Stars and Stripes — something definitely was going on. Eventually, a boat manned by Spaniards came alongside with a note from Consul James Simpson saying only that the boat would bring him any message the commodore might have. Preble sent one advising of the experiences of the squadron, and stating that the captains of *Meshouda* and *Mirboha* were in the frigates. At four that afternoon, several letters came back from Simpson. One reported that neither the Emperor nor the Alcade were in town and so there would be no one available for the consultation or negotiation until possibly the 23rd. A second missive gave the news that the American brig *Hannah* had been detained at Mogador, down on Morocco's Atlantic coast. Preble and Rodgers decided that the latter would proceed off Mogador and the other ports of Larache and Sale and warn off any American shipping making for those ports. Preble intended to return to Gibraltar and issue fresh orders to other units under his command. He planned to be back at Tangiers on the 19th or 20th.

Adverse winds kept Preble from getting back to Tangiers until the 25th, which did nothing to improve his temper. The news from Simpson wasn't too bad. The Consul confirmed that it had been the Alcade who had sent out *Mirboha,* not the Emperor. The taking of *Celia* and *Hannah* had been intended to force the release of *Meshouda,* not declare war, according to the Emperor's Minister, Mohammed Selawy. The Emperor, in fact, was more interested in getting *Mirboha* back than he was *Meshouda.* Simpson suggested that Preble depart for a week, by which time some sort of schedule might be known. The Consul thought the Emperor ought to reach Tangiers from Fez on 3 October.

*Constitution* left the same afternoon and patrolled between Larache and Cape Spartel without sighting a single Moroccan. Bad weather precluded a return to Tangiers so, low on water and provisions, she put in at Gibraltar shortly before midnight, 29 September. Preble had spent the past several days confined to his cabin: frustrations with Moslems and meteorology weren't good for a man prone to ulcers. Since he had last been in Gibraltar, Captain Hugh G. Campbell had arrived in *Adams,* exchanged ships with Commodore Morris, and had sailed for a patrol station off Larache in *New York.* Morris had headed *Adams* for Washington, D.C., on the 26th.

Preble sailed for Tangiers once more late in the evening of 3 October, having in the meantime witnessed the arrival of the last of his squadron — *Syren,* Lieutenant Commandant Charles Stewart — and sent her out on convoy duty with orders to rejoin him at Tangiers. Before leaving, the Moroccan ship's officers were placed under close Marine guard for having attempted sexual relations with the ship's boys.

*Constitution* and *Nautilus* arrived after noon the next day and found the American flag flying once more. Simpson reported that the Emperor was expected on the 5th and suggested Preble ought to fire an appropriate salute as soon as he was in the castle. Preble's response was characteristic of the man: "As you think it will gratify His Imperial Majesty, I shall salute him and dress ship; and, if he is not disposed to be pacific, *I will salute him again.*" And he meant it: *Constitution* was at battle stations with guns primed and matches lighted, and would stay that way until the matter was settled.

After a day of rest, the Emperor looked out of his window on the morning of the 6th to see *New York* and *John Adams* enter port and take anchorages south of *Constitution*'s. Four American warships in view. Simpson came out to the Commodore with a message that only the absence of Minister Selawy was holding up negotiations, and that he was expected momentarily from Tetuan. The *Constitutions* remained living at their guns.

Various delays prevented the negotiations from occurring until the 10th, but the Emperor had sent out fresh meat and fowl to the Americans to make it clear that he was operating in good faith. The largely amicable talks on the 10th were followed by the return of *Mirboha* and later *Meshouda* on the 11th, and the delivery to the Commodore on the 12th of the Emperor's personal letter to President Jefferson reaffirming the friendship treaty his father had signed in 1786. Firing a 13-gun salute, *Constitution* sailed for Gibraltar on the 14th. Preble had gained the security he wanted at the Pillars of Hercules.

## A FALLING OUT

When Preble got back to Gibraltar, he learned of an unpleasant situation that boded ill for the future. It seems that six seamen left as prize crew on *Mirboha* when *Constitution* last sailed had deserted before the Moroccan vessel made for Tangiers. At least three of the deserters were known to be in the British frigate *Medusa* whose Captain, John Gore, had refused earlier American requests to give them up. Preble wrote to the senior British officer in a ship at Gibraltar about the matter:

> SIR, Since I came to this Bay several men have deserted from the ships of the squadron under my command ... They are all Citizens of the United States, and have taken the oath of Allegiance to our Government ...
> Three of those men are detained on board His Britanic Majesty's Ship *Medusa*. In my absence from this, they were demanded of Captain Gore by the commander of the United States Brig *Syren* and refused to be given up ...
> I am informed that John Plover, and William Brown deserters from this ship are on board the *Amphion* now in this Bay. If this information is correct, you will oblige me by directing them to be given up to the Officer who will hand you this.
> The Officers commanding our Ships of War have invariably given up deserters from the British Navy or Army, on the first application and hope I shall not be disappointed in expecting the same liberality on your part.

Preble really was spreading it on thick: remember when he was complaining about how few Americans he had aboard?

Hart replied the next day:

> SIR I had yesterday the honor of receiving your letter respecting the seamen therein mentioned, who you say have deserted from the ships of your Squadron; after receiving your letter I went on board the *Amphion*; Capt. Sutton says that two Seamen did come on board his ship to enter as Volunteers declaring themselves Englishmen, and that he did enter them accordingly, being first convinced of their being Englishmen; the other three you mention that are on board the *Medusa* I can say nothing of till I see Capt. Gore. —
>
> I beg to inform you that it is the Orders & Instructions of our Government, on our meeting with Ships of any foreign Nation whatever to demand all such British Seamen that may happen to be on board them. I am informed there are at present several of that description on board the *Constitution* ...; If ... any British Seamen ... wish to return to their own Service I trust you will Comply as far as in your power with their request; and we on our parts are ready to deliver to you all Seamen of the United States on an Application being made and a promise on your part of a like number of British Seamen in return.

This "tit-for-tat" response completely infuriated the Commodore. His letter to Consul Gavino on the 22nd shows this clearly:

> "Dear Sir You may venture to reserve all the Beef & Pork on hand for this Ship. All the other provisions after the *Nautilus* is supplied, I wish you to send to Syracuse or Malta, as may be most convenient in consequence of the late inhospitable conduct of some of the British Captains towards us here. I have determined on Syracuse for a general rendevous & deposit of Stores ..."

Preble spent the next three weeks at Gibraltar assessing the strategic situation and making plans accordingly. *Enterprise* would escort the stores ship *Traveler* to Syracuse with the first supplies for the new base, and then overhaul her rigging. *Philadelphia* and *Vixen* were off Tripoli. *Syren* was sent to Leghorn to bring some consular presents for Tobias Lear's use at Algiers. Consul Lear and family came back aboard from Gibraltar once the Moroccan affair was settled and the Commodore would drop them off at their new post enroute to his first reconnaissance of Tripoli; *Nautilus* in company. Preble also fired off several letters to Secretary Smith apprising him of the favorable turn of events at Tangiers, and repeatedly citing the need for additional units to guard his long Mediterranean line of communication while operating off Tripoli. He was, in fact, leaving *Argus,* now under Lieutenant Commandant Isaac Hull, in the Straits through the winter for that purpose.

*Constitution* sailed for Algiers on 13 November. Shortly after leaving the Rock, Preble sought to make an impression on his crew about the rewards of desertion. On 15 November, "We punished Edward Madden Marine with forty-eight lashes for refusing duty, contempt of a Commissioned Officer, Insolence to a non-commissioned Officer & attempting to desert. This Marine is a very Notorious character ..." Two others received thirty-six and twenty-four lashes each for drinking, insolence, and neglect of duty. When we recall that no punishments exceeding twelve lashes at a time were awarded under Nicholson and Talbot, it is apparent the severity with which Preble disciplined his crew. Undoubtedly, the presence of so many aliens was a factor, together with the more hostile environment in which he was operating.

## A NEW PROBLEM

In Algiers on the 19th, Tobias Lear and his family were landed amidst gun salutes from the big frigate and batteries ashore. With the Dey absent at his country seat, no diplomacy could be conducted; Preble took advantage of the serenity for a couple of days of relaxation and sightseeing. *Constitution* and *Nautilus* were underway once more on the evening of the 21st.

They were south of Sardinia three days later when a large ship was seen to the northward. It proved to be *HMS Amazon,* frigate (38), and she had some terrible news for the Americans: it was rumored that *Philadelphia* had been taken by the Tripolines. If true, it meant that Tripoline naval power was about to take a quantum jump. Preble's first concern became preventing that so he could get on with inducing the Bashaw to sign a peace treaty. The Moslem certainly never would so long as he had a weapon like that in his hands. Putting aside his anger at the British, Preble headed for Malta where he felt he could gain further intelligence.

*Constitution* lay to off Valletta, Malta, on the 26th as First Lieutenant John Dent was rowed ashore to learn all he could about *Philadelphia.* He returned with letters from Captain Bainbridge himself, detailing the disaster. It seems that Bainbridge had sent *Vixen* off to the neighborhood of Lampedusa on 22 October to look for two Tripoline cruisers said to be at large, leaving only the deep-draft *Philadelphia* to blockade Tripoli, a port largely supplied by coasting craft. On the last day of October, in mid-morning, Bainbridge had seen a Tripoline xebec attempting to make port from the eastward, in shoaling and reef-filled waters. He had pursued until only about three miles from the city, when he realized that he was standing into imminent danger in just seven fathoms of water. It was already too late; as the frigate turned to seaward she struck a sloping sand reef and slid up four or five feet while making eight knots. She was hard aground. Bainbridge tried shifting guns and ballast. He tried jettisoning most of the guns and starting the fresh water from the casks. She wouldn't budge. Nine shallow draft Tripoline gunboats closed in cautiously, gradually increasing the tempo of their attack as it became apparent that the badly listing frigate could do little in her own defense. In consultation with his officers, Bainbridge rather hastily — perhaps precipitately — determined to scuttle his ship and surrender to avoid unnecessary bloodshed. As soon as this was made known to the Tripolines, they swarmed aboard, pillaging and abusing. The Americans (over 300) were led into captivity. The pirates had *Philadelphia* afloat in just forty hours, as the waters were too shallow for proper scuttling. In a few more days, they had stopped the leaks, moved her into the harbor, and salvaged the jettisoned cannon as well.

Come spring, the Bashaw expected to have a bigger frigate than the one the Americans gave the Dey, and that pleased him mightily.

It was a black, black moment for Edward Preble; a time to think and regroup. *Constitution* filled away from Malta and arrived at Syracuse on the 28th. There, he received a warm welcome from the city's Governor and ready assistance in establishing a supply depot ashore in a government armory at no charge. The Governor admitted he was very concerned about the possibility of Tripoline raids on his city, so was delighted to have such stout defenders present. Three weeks were spent in landing stores, spare spars and boats, and other gear, and in overhauling the flagship. Preble busied himself with these things and with sending detailed reports to Washington concerning the disaster and the increased need for reinforcements. *Nautilus* was sent with two sets of letters to Gibraltar and Cadiz for forwarding. *Constitution* and *Enterprise* sailed on 17 December for Tripoli, to reconnoitre the territory and determine the location and condition of *Philadelphia*. The Commodore intended to remain in blockade just as long as the winter weather remained mild and permitted the Tripolines to operate.

There was "instant excitement" on the morning of the 23rd, just as the Tripoline coast was sighted. *Constitution* sighted a sail on the horizon to the southwest and signalled *Enterprise,* who was closer, into chase. Flying English colors, a common ruse of the day, the Americans easily closed in on their prey until *Enterprise* escorted her alongside the frigate. The capture was the 50-ton ketch *Mastico,* which was found to have on board side arms and property known to have belonged to the *Philadelphia*s. There were two Tripoline officers and ten soldiers aboard. It also was learned that the Turkish master had participated in the capture of Bainbridge's command. Preble ordered a prize crew aboard and sent her to Syracuse.

With *Constitution* now off Tripoli for the first time, it seems the proper moment to describe the layout of that port. It is hardly more than an indentation in the Libyan coast, the shoreline shaped somewhat like an ocean wave, cresting from southwest to northeast, the harbor being the front of the wave and the trough. From crest to trough it measures about a mile and a half, and it is perhaps two miles from the front of the wave until open sea is reached. A rocky promontory extending northeastward forms the "blowing spray" from the crest, which trails off in a series of reefs for more than a mile. A manmade mole running southeastward from the promontory forms the inner harbor. Entrance to the larger harbor is gained either from the northeast, between the reefs to starboard and shoal water to port, or through a 250 yard wide opening off the tip of the promontory — the western entrance. In 1804, the town of Tripoli itself ran along the front of the wave for about a half mile and extended inland for about 350 yards. The Bashaw's castle was situated on the shore in the southeastern corner of the town, with the water gate to the inner harbor immediately before it. Aside from the cannon in the castle, there existed the "French fort" (reportedly constructed by French slaves) on a rocky prominence due north of the town, a

53

battery on the rocky promontory at the point where the mole began (covering the western entrance), and the "English fort" (built by English slaves) on a slight knob on the shore about a mile east of the castle. All told, the Bashaw command-ed some 115 guns in these and other lesser batteries. In addition, he commanded a number of gunboats, each mounting a heavy long gun and howitzers, and two row galleys — all of which were kept in the inner harbor and which sallied forth as the occasion demanded to do battle amongst the reef rocks or along the adja-cent coast. All in all, a tough nut to crack with one frigate, five brigs and schooners, and while 4000 miles from home base.

Winter weather soon forced *Constitution* and *Enterprise* off the Tripoline coast. They were back in Syracuse on 29 December. Preble was anxious to know what information the papers captured in *Mastico* contained, but he could find no one locally to translate them for him. As a result, he left *Constitution* in the charge of Lieutenant Dent and sailed for Malta in *Vixen* on 13 January 1804. Arrival the next day was the beginning of a very profitable and pleasant nine-day stay. First, Preble discovered that the British at Malta were far friendlier than those at Gibraltar, and readily offered him the use of the port's facilities in main-taining his vessels, as well as the privilege of enlisting local males to fill out his depleted crews. Second, he was contacted by two representatives of Hamet Karamanli, the rightful Bashaw whose younger brother Yusef had usurped the throne, who were seeking aid and cooperation against a common foe. Preble encouraged their proposals and forwarded them to Washington without making any specific commitments. Third, the Commodore also heard from the "other side:" the Bashaw's representatives made peace proposals that were totally unac-ceptable to Preble, who intended that America never again would pay tribute to the Barbary pirates.

## PROBLEM "SOLVED"

Returning to Syracuse and *Constitution* on the 25th, Preble was ready to take steps to neutralize *Philadelphia*. Her quarantine period over, *Mastico* was hauled into a pier and overhauled with Lieutenant Stephen Decatur, skipper of *Enter-prise*, in charge. When properly outfitted, Decatur would sail *Mastico*, renamed *Intrepid* by Preble, into Tripoli harbor and destroy Bainbridge's former com-mand. Decatur would be assisted by Sicilian Salvatore Catalano, a pilot very familiar with Tripoli. The ketch's crew was made up of sixty-two volunteers from Decatur's command, together with some "gentlemen volunteers" from *Constitu-tion*: Midshipmen Ralph Izard, Jr., Charles Morris, Jr., Alexander Laws, John Davis, and John Rowe. Charles Stewart and *Syren* would sail in support. Exactly who first thought of the operation became a bone of contention in later years, but it was the sort of thing in keeping with the characters of all three. William Bainbridge had written to Preble about it on 5 December. Preble himself had been a party to cutting out operations during the Revolution. And Decatur, of course, avidly sought the means to glory and had proposed using the larger

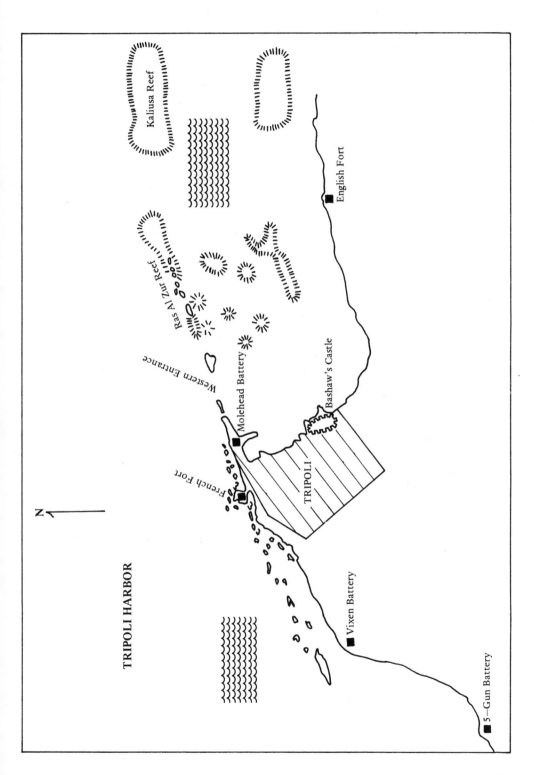

TRIPOLI HARBOR

N

Kaliusa Reef

Ras Al Zur Reef

Western Entrance

Molehead Battery

French Fort

TRIPOLI

Bashaw's Castle

English Fort

Vixen Battery

5-Gun Battery

## A Most Fortunate Ship

*Enterprise* in the same manner. In any event, *Intrepid* and *Syren* set sail from Syracuse at 5 P.M. on 2 February.

There was little for Preble to do until he knew the outcome of Decatur's attack. Anxiety plagued him. On the 12th, when they had been gone ten days, he ordered a watch set at the masthead of his flagship so that he might have the earliest notice of a sail in the offing. An incident on the 14th caused by carelessness added unwelcome stress; the log:

> At 10 the ship was alarmed by the cry of fire occasioned by the ships corporal in fumigating one of the Officer Cabins in the Gun Room. Punished James Wallace Corporal with 36 lashes for attempting to fumigate any part of the ship without regular orders for neglect of duty, and for suffering the rope Yarns to blaze.

Preble obviously had "blazed," as well. He might have recalled that *New York* frigate had been "that close" to being blown to bits because of a similar careless act while the ship was near Malta the preceding April.

The long wait ended on the morning of the 19th, when *Intrepid* and *Syren* were sighted making for the harbor entrance. Anxiously, Preble signalled *Syren* about the mission and received the welcome news that the objective had been achieved. Leaving anchoring to his First Lieutenant, Stewart quickly boarded the flagship to submit his report and tell the Commodore the story in greater detail.

The voyage out had been uneventful and the two had arrived off Tripoli after sunset on the 9th, both rigged and acting like local merchantmen. Decatur had been hopeful of proceeding immediately to the attack, but a rising wind led Stewart, the senior of the two, to demur. As a compromise, Midshipman Morris and Pilot Catalano went closer to the reefs in a cutter to have a good look. Both supported Stewart's belief that the weather was against them. This was soon evident even to the fiery Decatur, as the winds continud to increase and soon had the two small vessels fighting for their existence.

The gale battled them for six days, driving them deep into the Gulf of Sirte, before blowing itself out. Conditions aboard the two ships had been miserable, especially in *Intrepid,* where the discovery of bad beef had reduced them to a diet of bread and water, and where the rats and vermin left by the previous owners provided unwelcome company. Finally, on the 15th, the brig and ketch rendezvoused for the first time in nearly a week and began working their way back toward Tripoli. The plan was that Decatur, sailing a craft familiar to the Tripolines, would proceed in daylight as if he were trying to make port via the eastern entrance before dark. He would, however, anchor just outside the entrance as night fell and wait for reinforcements in the form of boats and men from *Syren* to join him before going on. The united force would then carry out the attack, and the small boats would help get *Intrepid* clear after they had upset the apple cart.

All went according to this plan until Decatur was on the point of anchoring, when he became concerned that the fitful, fickle wind might fail completely before *Syren* could come up. He decided the only thing to do was "go for it." His crew was ready for the task. They had been divided into four parties, first to clear *Philadelphia*'s spar deck, then gain control of the rest of the ship, and then to set the combustibles and fire her. Midshipmen Izard and Rowe would stay with Decatur on the spar deck, while Midshipman Davis of *Constitution* went with Captain Bainbridge's Lieutenant-brother, Joseph, to the wardroom and steerage, and Midshipman Morris had charge of firing the cockpit and after storerooms. The fourth team, with no *Constitutions* in it, was assigned the berth deck and forward storerooms. It was to be cutlasses and tomahawks; firearms were a last resort. The watch word was *"Philadelphia."*

*Philadelphia* was seen in the setting sun, her foremast missing and only the lower main and mizzen masts in place. Her yards were resting on the gunwales. Nearby could be seen two corsairs, the row galleys, and several gunboats. The evening was a mild one for the season, the harbor glassy smooth.

The moon was up by 10 that evening as *Intrepid* passed northward of the English fort, the light airs threatening to disappear completely. If they did, the only motive power remaining to the Americans was the sweeps, and to man them would mean having to reveal more than the odd dozen men then visible about her deck. All was quiet. *Intrepid* was headed straight for *Philadelphia*'s bow. Decatur hung on.

At last, someone hailed from the frigate. Catalano answered that she was a Maltese trader which had lost her anchors and nearly been wrecked in the recent gale, and asked permission to tie up alongside until daylight. Then, just as all seemed well, the wind shifted to the south causing *Intrepid* to be taken aback and *Philadelphia* to swing into the wind. Suddenly, the Americans were in great danger because their ship was very nearly stopped, or perhaps even beginning to drift astern — and they were now looking right into the frigate's full broadside battery, only forty yards away.

Decatur calmly put a small boat in the water and sent out a mooring line to *Philadelphia*'s bow. Just as obliging, the unsuspecting pirates sent out a line from her stern. With both these set, Decatur began breasting the ketch alongside her target, his many crewmen still concealed in the shadows of the low bulwarks adding their muscle to the evolution while lying flat on their backs. Suddenly, something caught the eye of a Tripoline sentinel and he cried a warning about "Americans!" One more pull brought *Intrepid* close aboard and Decatur ordered, "Board!"

Decatur, Morris, and Laws all leaped for the frigate's main chains. Decatur's foot slipped on his first try. Laws got his cutlass hung up trying to enter a gun port. Charles Morris went up over the bulwarks and was first to gain the upper deck. The Tripolines were confused and disorganized. Some jumped overboard; some were killed or wounded. No shots had been fired. No one ashore yet knew what was going on. In less than ten minutes, sixty men had taken the frigate at the expense of one man wounded, in the enemy's harbor.

Control having been gained, the combustibles were ordered aboard and the four teams went to their tasks, all to await Decatur's direct orders before actually lighting the fires. It was another ten minutes before all was in readiness, but so thoroughly had they done their jobs that when fires were lighted the ship literally flashed into flame. Midshipman Morris and his team in the cockpit had to race forward and up those ladders to safety, so quickly had the fire caught in the wardroom over their heads. Most of his mates already were back in *Intrepid* before he got there. Stephen Decatur made it a point to be the last one off, but even he moved rapidly enough to have misplaced the Tripoline flag he had hauled down and had intended to present to the Commodore.

So swiftly did *Philadelphia* go up that *Interpid* nearly was lost. As she blazed "like pine," there was created a fire storm of sufficient intensity almost to draw the small ketch into it. Her main boom became fouled momentarily in one of the frigate's quarter galleries, which threatened to rain fire down upon the American's ammunition stores piled under a tarpaulin on deck. Decatur ordered out the sweeps and managed to get clear, when his men gave three cheers. It was then that all hell broke loose. The shore batteries and enemy war craft in the harbor all opened up at the daring infidels, now fully illuminated in the frigate's funeral pyre. *Philadelphia,* too, joined in: the heat was setting off her long guns, which had been loaded and shotted. But this was the Americans' time of triumph; one ball passing through a sail was all the Moslems could manage.

Elated and pulling swiftly, Decatur made for the eastern entrance once more. There, he met *Syren*'s boats coming to his assistance. Altogether, *Intrepid* and her lesser consorts headed to where *Syren* lay anchored. It was about one in the morning of the 17th when Decatur gave Stewart the good news. The two ships lay there for about an hour, watching the spectacle, then got underway for Syracuse. At 6 A.M., they still could see the fire, forty miles to the south.

The good news was a tonic to Preble, who spent much of the 19th writing about it to many people. In his letter to the Secretary of the Navy, he said of Decatur and company "Their conduct in the performance of the dangerous service assigned them, cannot be sufficiently estimated — it is beyond all praise." Later in the day, he wrote again to Smith about Decatur: "The important service he has rendered ... would in any Navy in Europe insure him instantaneous promotion to the rank of post Captain ... I most earnestly recommend him to the President, that he may be rewarded according to his merit." Decatur was so promoted the following May. England's Lord Nelson, when he heard of the operation, termed it "the most bold and daring act of the age."

## FINAL PREPARATIONS

With the naval balance restored in America's favor — indeed, with the enemy's morale having been delivered a smashing blow — Preble took time to reassess the strategic situation and redeploy his forces. For the nonce, Tripoli was left alone. By 22 February, *Intrepid* was placed in reserve in order that her manpower could be more profitably employed. *Vixen* sailed for Gibraltar with dispatches that day and *Enterprise* went to Messina for repairs on the next. In *Constitution*, Preble had his carpenters improve the protection of his gunners by planking up the waist of the ship from "fore chains to the main mast;" henceforth, no one need be exposed on much of the spar deck. Gun ports were cut in the new bulwarks. *Syren* was sent to Malta and then to resume the station off Tripoli.

*Constitution* began a busy round of port visits when she sailed from Syracuse on 2 March. She arrived in Malta the next day only to find *Syren* still there, forced back by adverse winds. *Nautilus* came in from Syracuse on the 4th. While there, Preble was apprised of rumors that the Bey of Tunis was again making threats — nothing new there, but a worry nonetheless. *Syren* and *Nautilus* sailed in company for Tripoli on the 8th with very specific orders from the Commodore to stay together. The spectre of another *"Philadelphia"* was almost tangible.

Preble wrote a long letter to Secretary Smith on 11 March, reviewing the entire situation and laying out his course of action. He hoped to bring the Bashaw to his knees before the sailing season was out. In particular, "I expect to spend a large quantity of Powder in Fire Ships, and Infernals to blow up the Bashaw's works." Further, he reported that several months of effort seemed about to bear fruit in his quest for the acquisition, by loan, of gun and mortar boats, with which to augment the forthcoming assault. The Commodore closed with his oft-repeated plea for reinforcement — "three frigates" he said this time. The day would dawn when these requests would come to painful fruition.

*Constitution* returned to Syracuse on 17 March to provision for five months. While there, Preble received a letter from Minister to France Robert Livingston informing him that the diplomat, on his own recognizance, had succeeded in getting the French to agree to mediate a treaty between the Tripolines and Americans. Stores aboard, the big frigate headed once more for Tripoli four days later.

Only *Syren* was off the enemy town when *Constitution* arrived on the 26th. She had run into *Nautilus* three days earlier, necessitating the latter's return to Syracuse for repairs. Preble got the French Consul, Bonaventure Beaussier, on board the day after his arrival. The one meeting convinced the Commodore that the Frenchman was so biased in favor of the Bashaw as to preclude his employment as an intermediary.

It was obvious to Preble that the moment for negotiation was not at hand, and as he could see that port activity was nil, he sailed with *Syren* on the 1st for Tunis, where two American warships might have a salutory effect on the blustering Bey.

Each night during the three day stay in Tunis, Preble kept his crew at their guns as a guard against ugly surprises. There were none, however, as the Bey was doing no more than make the same sort of disgruntled noises he had made for years. The Americans sailed on the 6th for Malta and Syracuse. Sailing Master

## A Most Fortunate Ship

Haraden noted in his journal that the Commodore was bedded by fever at this time, a condition made no more comfortable by an ugly gale which slowed their progress for a couple of days.

At Syracuse, when he arrived on the 14th, Preble found the damaged *Nautilus, Argus* (newly relieved of her duties off Gibraltar by the delivery of naval stores which mollified the Moroccan Emperor), and the armed brig *Transfer,* a prize taken by *Syren* off Tripoli prior to the Commodore's arrival. Preble seized this opportunity to augment his forces by outfitting her with sixteen 6-pounder long guns and commissioning her as *Scourge* under the command of his First Lieutenant, John H. Dent, on the 17th. *Vixen* came back from Gibraltar the next day and *Enterprise* from Messina, her repairs completed. Four days later, *Syren* was sent back to Tripoli, *Nautilus* to Messina for further repair, and *Enterprise* to Tunis bearing long-time Barbary negotiator Richard O'Brien. *Scourge,* soon known as a dull sailor, made her way to Tripoli.

*Constitution* was underway on 25 April. She paid quick calls at Malta and Tunis, then headed north around the west end of Sicily, touching at Palermo before anchoring at Naples on 8 May. Knowing from James Cathcart that the King of the Two Sicilies had indicated a willingness to assist Preble in augmenting his forces, Preble on the 10th sent a letter to General Sir John Acton, the Prime Minister provided by England, formally requesting the loan of eight gun boats, two mortar boats, and eight heavy long guns for "floating Batteries," together with all appurtenances and shot and powder. Acton responded three days later, saying His Majesty would be pleased to make six gun boats, two mortar boats (or bomb ketches), and six 24-pounders available — powder, shot, and all. He also would permit the enlistment of his subjects to help man them. The long guns were brought aboard on the 16th, together with 624 shot and 4406 pounds of powder. The Naval Arsenal at Messina would make everything else available.

The flagship headed for Messina, but adverse winds made it a six-day voyage. During the trip, Preble had the six new long guns scaled (cleaned), mounted, and installed in quarterdeck gun ports. He apparently had decided against taking the time to find the necessary hulls for the floating batteries. The displaced 12-pounders probably were relocated forward, but the records are silent on this point. The total battery thus consisted of thirty-six 24-pounders and sixteen 12-pounders — fifty-two guns.

The Commodore inspected the gun boats at Messina on 26 May and found them ready to be manned and sailed. He did this, enlisting ninety-six Sicilians and using most of the crew of the repairing *Nautilus.* An overnight voyage through the Straits of Messina brought them to Syracuse on the last day of the month.

Preble decided to make another swing to the south while waiting for the mortar boats to be overhauled. The one-day trip to Malta nearly ended in disaster on 5 June. The Commodore recorded the incident vividly:

> ... Standing in for the Island of Malta on a wind on the starboard tack all sail sett,
> — at about 20 minutes past 2 PM as I was at dinner, a Midshipman came into the
> Cabbin & informed me we were near the shore, I ordered him to go on deck and tell
> the Officer to tack ship, the helm was immediately put down, & as the ship came to, I
> observed from the Cabbin ports that she was nearly on shore, I sprang on deck and
> found her in stays not a cables length from the shore, and the Rocks to be seen under
> her Bottom, I met the Officer of the Watch Lieutenant Tarbel (l), at the head of the
> Cabbin Gang way and took the Trumpet from him, ordered him below, and took
> charge of the deck, and got the ship on the larboard tack, had she missed stays or shot
> her length further a head in stays she would inevitably have struck the Rocks and prob-
> ably would have been lost, as she was under a press of canvas with a fresh Breeze...

The peppery Preble returned below and penned a letter to the unfortunate
Mr. Tarbell:

> Sir, The imminent danger which you a few moments since ran this ship into, either
> through neglect or want of Judgement obliges me to withdraw my confidence in you,
> so far as to consider it imprudent that you should in future be intrusted with the
> charge of a watch on board her as her loss would involve incalculable consequence to
> the U.S. — You will therefore consider yourself as a supernumerary untill ordered to
> some other Vessel of less consequence —

From an inflexible commander, such a letter could have spelled "finis" to
Joseph Tarbell's career. Preble was not such a leader, and he seems also to have
recognized that his mercurial temper blinded him at times. Three days' perspec-
tive and a petition from the other officers of the wardroom led him to forgive

*Twenty four pound long gun and shot. The long gun, charged with about six pounds of powder
it could fire a 24 pound shot a range of twelve hundred yards.*

Tarbell and restore him to duty, certain that the young man was a good officer
who had learned an unforgettable lesson. The pilot on whom Tarbell had been
relying was fired. It was the sort of outcome that welded Preble's subordinates to
him, for his demands for professionalism were leavened by a willingness to
understand human error.

61

## A Most Fortunate Ship

*Constitution* spent just three days at Malta, and sailed for Tripoli with the peripatetic Richard O'Brien aboard once more. *Argus, Vixen, Enterprise,* and *Scourge* all were there, working in pairs off the eastern and western entrances to the port. The first order of business was to pass supplies to the "small boys" and get an update on the local situation. This was done on the 12th. Looking into the harbor, Preble saw that the Bashaw's gun boat fleet had risen to seventeen units. O'Brien went ashore on the 13th to test the diplomatic waters, but found the Moslem still unready for genuine negotiations. Preble had no doubts now that it would be necessary to thrash him into the proper frame of mind; he knew he was the man to do it. Departing the blockade with *Argus* and *Enterprise,* he was back at Syracuse on the 25th after having "shown the flag" once more at Tunis.

The Commodore moved northward to Messina on the last day of June to press for the completion of the mortar boats. It required another week for him to get them clear of the yard, a week that must have played hell with his ulcer, although no sign of a problem appears in the record. *Constitution* shepherded the two units to Syracuse on 9 July for three days of provisioning. On 13 July 1804, *Constitution* sailed for Tripoli at the head of a column which included *Nautilus, Enterprise,* six gun boats, and two mortar boats. The largest naval force yet seen under the Stars and Stripes was assembling off Tripoli. Edward Preble, as a latter-day Captain of *Constitution* often told school children, was ready to "bash the Bashaw."

# 4 The Barbary War and Aftermath: July 1804 - October 1807

## THE APPROACH

Commodore Preble soon found that transporting the gunboats and bomb ketches from Syracuse to Tripoli was going to be a trying experience. At 7 P.M. on the 13th, after thirteen hours underway, the squadron had covered barely more than half the fifty miles to Cape Passaro, the southernmost point of Sicily. At that point, Preble thought it best to anchor through the night to ensure that all units would be together when morning came. His later letter to Secretary Smith on the subject told the story clearly:

> ... The Bomb Vessels are about thirty Tons, carry a 13 Inch Brass Sea-Mortar and 40 men; the Gun Boats 25 Tons carry a long Iron 24 pounder in the bow, with a complement of 35 Men; They are officered and manned from the squadron, excepting twelve Neapolitans bombardiers, gunners, and sailors, attached to each boat ... The gunboats are constructed for the defence of harbors; they are flat bottomed and heavy, and do not sail or row even tolerably well. They were never intended to go to sea, and, I find, cannot be navigated with safety, unless assisted by tow ropes from larger and better sailing vessels, nor even then, in very bad weather ...

As they got underway again on the 14th, *Constitution* passed towlines to four of the gunboats and both bomb ketches; *Enterprise* and *Nautilus* took the remaining units.

The Americans went first to Malta, where Preble wanted to load some stores he had previously stocked there, as well as drawing some boatswain's, gunner's, and carpenter's stores from the British. With only one large ship in his force, she had to do double duty as heavy bombardment ship and supply ship. Piled in the gun room and between decks were ten tons of cannister shot and about twelve tons of mortar shells. Taken on board at Malta were ninety-two barrels of bread, seven of pork, three of suet, six of flour; twenty kegs of cheese; eleven casks pease; a puncheon (122 gallons) of molasses and a pipe (130 gallons) of vinegar; as well as fifty-seven gang casks of water. Sailing Master Haraden had his hands full stowing all these additional items and getting a decent trim on the heavily laden frigate.

The voyage to Tripoli was resumed on the 21st, after a two-day wait for a fair wind. As they proceeded slowly to the southeast, Preble had his carpenters mounting 4- and 1½-pounder carriage guns in five of *Constitution*'s boats. On the 24th, he spent much of the day replenishing the water casks on the small vessels because they had but a six-day capacity and could be in jeopardy if

63

weather separated them from the flagship.

Edward Preble finally had his force assembled off the enemy's capitol on the morning of 25 July. It consisted of *Constitution* (44), *Syren* (16), *Argus* (16), *Scourge* (14), *Vixen* (12), *Nautilus* (12), and *Enterprise* (12), together with the gunboats and bomb ketches. It was not an ideal force for the job at hand. Only one frigate with heavy long guns limited the bombardment capability, as the remaining units were armed with short-range carronades or light long guns. The small craft were heavy and unwieldy, intended for operations in calm harbor waters, while their opponents (of whom there were nineteen) were built to work both in harbor and along the coastline. As to manpower, there may have been as many as 25,000 Tripolines in and around the city, while just 1060 opponents floated offshore. If the latter had anything going for them, it was discipline, spirit, and a sense of mission.

The weather now took a hand in further delaying an attack on Tripoli. Conditions prevented the Americans from anchoring until the 28th, and shortly after they did that day a gale came up to drive them offshore and endanger the whole enterprise. After three days of battling to keep the boats afloat and together, skies cleared and the Commodore was able to move in once again, arriving on station on 3 August.

## FIRST ATTACK

Wasting no time, Preble rounded to about three miles north of the town shortly after noon and called each ship within hailing distance. Noting that two divisions of Tripoline gunboats had taken stations at the east and west entrances to the harbor, and outside the rocks, he ordered immediate preparations to attack the warcraft and harbor installations. The gunboats and bomb ketches were manned, and in an hour they were ready to go. Conforming to the situation, Preble divided his gunboats into two divisions, under Lieutenants Richard Somers (Gunboats 1, 2, and 3) and Decatur (4, 5, and 6). While they engaged the enemy gunboats, the bomb ketches were to take station about a half mile north of the town and lob their shells into it and the Bashaw's castle. The brigs and schooners would follow the gunboats closely to back them up, while *Constitution* would remain in deep support, providing her muscle where it most was needed.

At 1:30, the American force headed shoreward, and at two the gunboats and bomb ketches dropped their tows to proceed on their own. Preble gave the signal to attack at 2:30, which the bombards promptly opened. The Tripolines just as promptly returned the fire, as the shoreline and warcraft came ablaze with gunfire. Soon, black powder smoke was drifting on the easterly breeze. obscuring all but the easternmost enemy craft.

It was this division of nine vessels that the Americans had selected as the prime target because it was the least supported by shore batteries. Decatur, whose division was the easternmost of the Americans, headed for them, but Somers, who was to support him, found it difficult to maneuver his scow upwind, and finally

*Preble's first attack on Tripoli, 3 August 1804.*

headed for the western Tripoline division — one against five, as one of his other two units managed to close with Decatur. The second (Gunboat 3), seeing an erroneus recall signal fly briefly on *Constitution* hauled off and never became engaged. In Decatur's division, Gunboat 5 (Lieutenant Joseph Bainbridge) had her lateen yard shot away and lost much of whatever maneuverability she had, and although she kept advancing, she ended up having to be pulled off the rocks. As a result of these several mischances, Decatur engaged with Gunboats 2, 4, and 6 (commanded by Lieutenant James Decatur, Stephen Decatur, and Lieutenant John Trippe, respectively).

Advancing into the smoke, Decatur's division attacked with round shot, grape, and cannister, as well as muskets. To the surprise of the much more heavily manned enemy boats, the order went out to close and board. Decatur intended to beat the enemy at his favorite game. It was to be a man to man struggle amidst boat hulls grinding together, yells of challenge and screams of pain, in a swirling smoke that hid events from those in the larger units to seaward.

Decatur, of course, was in the forefront of the action. Laying Number 4 alongside the nearest Tripoline, he boarded with Lieutenant Thorn, Midshipman Macdonough, and all the American sailors he had with him. Sweeping around either side of the long main hatch of the enemy vessel, the Americans soon cornered their enemies, piking and bayonetting those who did not surrender or jump overboard.

This work quickly done, Decatur threw a tow line on his prize and bore down on the next enemy to leeward. This time, he came face to face with his opposite number, who proved to be a large muscular individual with a zest for personal

65

combat. Decatur lunged at him with his short pike, but the Tripoline wrenched it from his hands and very nearly ran him through with it. Decatur tried to cut the head of the pike off with his cutlass, but his blade snapped. The Tripoline's second lunge wounded Decatur in the arm, but the latter pulled it out and sought to wrestle with the man. The two grappled and fell to the deck. Decatur landed on his side, and managed to draw a small pistol from a pocket with one hand as he held the enemy's dagger from his throat with the other. Pressing the pistol into his enemy's back, Decatur fired and ended the match. The ball passed completely through the Moslem and stopped in the folds of Decatur's clothes. Seeing their leader dead, the enemy crew surrendered. Being wounded, and now having two enemy craft in tow, Decatur hauled out and headed to seaward. His slashing attack had cost the enemy two gunboats, fifty-two known killed and wounded, and eight prisoners.

While Stephen Decatur was adding to his laurels, his brother James sought to repeat the pattern. However, as he was driving Gunboat 2 against an enemy, he was struck in the forehead by a musket ball, and died a short while later. The enemy gunboat withdrew behind the rocks.

Gunboat 6, under Lieutenant Trippe, also delivered a withering fire at close range and tried to board an enemy craft. The impact of the two craft colliding was so great, though, that only Trippe, Midshipman Henley, and nine men managed to board before the two craft separated. The odds were better than six to one against the Americans. Trippe soon found himself in personal combat with the enemy commander, a ballet of parry and thrust against a larger man. Trippe received no less than nine scalp wounds and two in the chest before being driven to one knee. As the foe closed in for the death blow, young Trippe called on all his reserve powers to raise a short pike and thrust before the Tripoline's sword descended. He got his man. Once again, the remaining enemy surrendered upon the fall of their leader. There were twenty-one killed and wounded counted, in addition to fifteen prisoners. Trippe's prize was one of the Bashaw's largest gunboats.

While the second division was decimating the enemy to the east, we left Somers in Gunboat 1 advancing against five to the west. His cannonade battered them unmercifully, driving them back through the entrance to the port. His advance, however, brought him under fire of the 12-gun "molehead" battery. It appeared for a time as if he would be destroyed before he could maneuver his clumsy craft clear, but, fortuitously, a shell from one of the bomb ketches exploded in the battery, wrecking the gun platform, and allowing Somers to come off in safety.

While all this fighting had been going on, an enemy reserve division of two row galleys and five gunboats had been standing by just inside the harbor. When their mates began falling back under the American onslaught, these units sought to advance and turn the tide. *Constitution* and her consorts, however, caught sight of their movement and kept them bottled up with a heavy fire.

At 4:30 P.M., the wind veered onshore and caused Preble to signal the withdrawal. The brigs and schooners moved in smartly to get the gunboats and their prizes under tow and out of range, while the big frigate laid down a heavy covering fire on the enemy's batteries. As long as she was firing at them, they remained silent. By 4:45, all were safely to seaward.

Thus ended Preble's first attack on Tripoli. In the main, he had accomplished all he had set out to do. The Tripolines, already impressed with American naval gunnery by the loss of *Tripoli* to *Enterprise,* three years earlier, now knew that the Americans were their betters in hand-to-hand fighting, a form they themselves favored for centuries. Three enemy gunboats had been captured and another three sunk in harbor by the bombardment. Only fourteen Americans had been killed or wounded in the fray, while the Tripolines had suffered more than 100 casualties. Except for the lucky shot at the molehead battery, most of the mortar shells fired landed in the town without exploding

*Constitution* herself, although under fire for two hours, suffered very little. The Tripolines had not been prepared for large warships coming in so close, and as a result spent most of the afternoon firing too high. Thus, the frigate's main royal yard was shot away and a 24-pounder shot was lodged in the mainmast. Another shot, thought to have been a 32-pounder, shattered itself on one of the quarterdeck 24-pounders. A fragment smashed a Marine's elbow, but the Commodore escaped the debris unscathed. Sailing Master Haraden estimated that he saw some 200 shell splashes around the flagship, but he could find evidence of only nine having done any damage.

The squadron lay to two or three miles north of Tripoli until about ten that evening, transferring prisoners and wounded to *Constitution,* restocking supplies, and making repairs. The Americans then bore off to the northeast under easy sail through the night.

At nine the next morning, when twelve miles or so off the city, a lookout spotted a sail coming from the port. Preble ordered *Argus* in chase, and at one in the afternoon she returned with the French privateer *Le Rusé* under escort. Providing the Frenchman with a generous supply of stores, Preble prevailed upon him to return to port with the fourteen most severely wounded prisoners and with a letter for the Bashaw. In the letter, Preble said his offer of $50,000 would remain valid until such time as more American frigates arrived, and when that happened the Bashaw no longer would be offered anything but shot and shell.

*Le Rusé* stood in for Tripoli on the morning of the 5th, while the squadron rested and made repairs. Preble hoped to renew his attack the next day. In the afternoon, *Vixen* was sent in to reconnoitre, which caused several gunboats to move toward the rocks but no shots were exchanged and little of note could be seen. As the sun was setting, the French privateer was seen pulling out of harbor against an onshore breeze. The message, which she delivered the next morning, was that the return of his losing crewmen had angered the Bashaw, and that he saw in Preble's offer not a threat but perhaps a sign of weakness. Said he, "I would rather bury myself under the ruins of my country than basely yield to the wishes of the enemy."

As he waited for this response, and for a favorable wind from the east, Preble took the time to repair and outfit the three captured Tripoline gunboats for service in the United States Navy. The larger two, named Gunboats 7 and 8, were fifty-one feet long and each carried a long 28-pounder in the bow. Preble had them sloop rigged using spare main topgallant and fore topgallant masts from *Constitution*. Number 9, somewhat smaller, carried a long brass 18-pounder, and was rerigged using *Constitution*'s spare mizzen topgallant mast.

## SECOND ATTACK

Preble's next attack, at the urging of Lieutenant Commandant Charles Stewart of *Syren* and others, was to be a bombardment of the city from a shallow bay to the southwest about 1½ miles. With an easterly wind, the Bashaw either would have to endure the bombardment or risk sending his gunboats out of harbor to leeward where the larger American units might cut off their line of retreat. Although there were those who preferred another frontal assault, Preble decided to give it a try.

At midmorning on the 7th, the gunboats began rowing for their assigned station in the bay. The bomb ketches moved behind them to anchorages northwest of the city, while the brigs and schooners maneuvered 2-3 miles to the northeast. *Constitution* remained at anchor farther offshore awaiting a favorable wind (she alone could not be rowed). The first shell was fired by Bomb Ketch 1 at 1 P.M. At 1:30, a breeze sprang up and *Constitution* was able to weigh anchor and move in support.

The gunboats finally attained the eastern end of the bay at about two, and ran right into a fierce cannonade from two new batteries which the Tripolines apparently had erected since Preble's first attack. Although the gunboats were disordered, they returned fire and soon silenced the five-gun battery. But the eight-gun battery, which the Americans nicknamed the "*Vixen* Battery," kept up a steady fire. The nine gunboats steadily worked their way in until they were just 200 yards off, and gradually they shot its walls away and pounded its guns until only one remained active. They also sent their shot into Tripoli itself, but little damage is known to have occurred. On an average, each boat fired about fifty rounds during the course of the afternoon.

Around three, fifteen Tripoline gunboats and galleys were seen sortiing from the western entrance to the harbor and maneuvering as if to attack the American gunboats. Preble signalled for the brigs and schooners to move to the south and east, as if scared off by the few shots the Moslems were sending their way, hoping thereby to encourage the enemy to get farther away from the entrance and then cut them off. Unfortunately, *Argus* and *Vixen* erred and stood instead to the northwest, a position from which the danger of a cutoff clearly was apparent. The pirates kept their boats behind the offshore rocks and worked westward via this "inside passage." Suddenly they charged out to the northwest, seeking to take Bomb Ketch 1 in its unsupported anchorage. Lieutenant Thomas Robinson of *Constitution,* who was her acting skipper, saw the danger and made for the company of the American gunboats, firing his mortar as he went. Preble brought *Constitution* down with all sails spread, an avenging eagle seeking to catch the wily pirates before they could get back to sanctuary. But she was noticed before the range had shortened sufficiently and the Tripolines beat the water to a froth rowing back behind the rocks.

As this was occurring, and as Preble received a lookout's report of a strange sail to the northeast, everyone's attention was arrested by a thunderous explosion in the bay where the gunboats were. There was a stunned silence on both sides as bodies and parts flew up through a roiling, rising pall of smoke: Gunboat 9, the small Tripoline prize, had been destroyed by a hit in her ammunition. Ten of her 28-man crew were killed and six wounded. As the smoke cleared, it could be seen that the entire after section of the boat had been blown away. Up forward, Midshipman Robert T. Spence and his 11-man gun crew calmly finished loading one last round. The bow sank before they could touch a match to it. Spence, who couldn't swim, saved himself by clinging to an oar until picked up.

The Americans reopened fire at a greater rate than before in revenge of their lost comrades. Gunboat 6 had her lateen yard shot away; 4 and 8 both took hits in their hulls, the latter very nearly being holed. As the wind began its diurnal shift onshore, Preble signalled cease fire and withdrew at 5:30. *Vixen, Enterprise,* and *Nautilus* were there to give them a hand getting clear. By 6:45, the entire squadron was standing once more to the northeast to spend the night. It had not been a very profitable day.

As disengagement was going on, *Argus,* which had been sent to check up on the sail to the northeast, signalled it was friendly. Between eight and nine that evening, *John Adams* joined the squadron at anchor, her men giving the hard-fighting old hands three cheers. *John Adams* (28) we have met before, but this time she arrived armed *en flute*; that is, most of her guns had been dismounted and stowed below, so that more deck space was available for the supplies she had carried out to the Mediterranean. The orders given to her commander, Master Commandant Isaac Chauncey, were to deliver the supplies, dispatches, and mail, and, if the Commodore did not otherwise direct, return immediately for another load. Preble sent a boat to bring Chauncey to the flagship, so eager was he for news.

One of the letters Preble received from Secretary Smith would have been hard to swallow at any time, but to arrive just as his program of reducing the Bashaw to agreeability was having an effect, must have made it doubly hard. It was dated 22 May 1804:

> Your Dispatches ... conveying ... the unpleasant information of the accidental Loss of the *Philadelphia,* were not received till late in the month of March last. The president immediately determined to put in commission and to send to the Mediterranean a force which would be able beyond the possibility of a doubt, to coerce the Enemy to a

peace upon Terms compatible with our Honor and our Interest ...

The following Frigates have accordingly been put in Commission ... *President* ... *Congress* ... *Essex* ... *Constellation*.

Your good sense will perceive that we have thus been unavoidably constrained to supersede you in a Command in which you have acquitted yourself in a manner honorable to yourself and useful to your Country ... The only Captains in the Navy now in the U. States junior to yourself are ... James Barron and Campbell, and as the Frigates cannot be commanded but by Captains, we of necessity have been obliged to send out two Gentlemen senior to yourself ...

Be assured, Sir, that no want of confidence in you has been mingled with the Considerations which have imposed upon us the necessity of this measure. You have fulfilled our highest expectations and The President has ... the highest Confidence in your Activity, Judgment and Valour ...

Preble has left us a single sentence to describe the impact of this news upon him: "... how much my feelings are lacerated by this supercedure at the moment of Vicotry (sic) cannot be described and can be felt only by an Officer placed in my mortifying situation ..." This, the Commodore wrote in his journal; not a word of protest appeared in any of his subsequent correspondence with the Secretary. Preble believed in the system, understood its plusses and minuses, and accepted the thorns with the palms.

Preble ordered Chauncey to remain with the squadron and to place his ship in as ready a state as possible. If nothing else, he recognized that the frigate offered a pool of additional personnel for his depleted force.

Now that he knew he was to be superceded by Commodore Samuel Barron, who had sailed from America only a few days after Chauncey, Preble's ambition became the settlement of the dispute by negotiation before Barron arrived. On 8 August, he took Richard O'Brien with him in *Argus* and reconnoitred the city to see if there were any signals flying that would indicate a desire to negotiate. He soon had his answer, for the Tripolines opened up on the lone American and hit her not far from where the Commodore was standing. Fortunately, he was unhurt and the shot failed to penetrate, or he could have had a long swim home.

Preble and O'Brien tried again the next day, with *Vixen* accompanying *Argus*. This time, there was no gunfire. After an exchange of signals, a boat came out from shore to receive the Commodore's message. The letter sent in said nothing about Preble's imminent relief, which might have given the Bashaw hope, and reported the arrival of another frigate, which might discourage him. Wanting to conclude the affair, Preble upped his monetary offer to $90,000.

On the 10th, flags were seen flying in several parts of Tripoli, but it was not until nearly noon that the appropriate signal for parley was seen. Once again, *Argus* and *Vixen* closed the shore with Preble and O'Brien aboard. O'Brien went himself to get the message being relayed via the French Consul. Upon his return late in the afternoon, they found that the Frenchman was proposing that the Americans offer $150,000 to the Bashaw for the release of the *Philadelphias* — a figure half of what the Moslem previously had demanded, but one which Beaussier thought he would be in a frame of mind to accept. Preble very much wanted to bring the Bashaw to peace, but the price was too high. By way of keeping up the dialogue, but knowing the outcome, he responded with a "final offer" amounting to $120,000. There were no signals to parley on 11 August.

## THIRD ATTACK

For the next few days, all was quiet on both sides. After several days of waiting for Barron's arrival, Preble began once more to plan and prepare for further attacks on Tripoli. On the 16th, he sent *Enterprise* to Malta to order supplies and charter shipping to bring it out to the squadron which already was on water rationing. The next night, Preble sent now-Captain Stephen Decatur and Isaac Chauncey in a small boat to learn what was happening in the port. They returned with the information that all the enemy gunboats had been moored in a line across the entrance to the inner harbor with their guns facing east, like a last line of defense. Before Preble could act upon this information, a gale came up which blew the Americans offshore until the 22nd, when Preble's favorite gentle east wind returned. While at sea, the squadron had been joined by *Intrepid* from Syracuse and a charter vessel from Malta, both with welcome supplies and water. *Enterprise* also returned, but had no word of the expected four frigates.

On the night of the 22nd, Preble tried to maneuver for another bombardment of the town but an adverse current and fickle winds aborted the attempt. Two nights later, he tried again. This time, although conditions were poor, the bomb ketches were able to row themselves into range and begin shooting about 2 A.M. Only fifteen or twenty shells had been fired by the time dawn began to break, and Preble ordered them out. The weather frustrated another daylight attack on the 25th. It had been a poor performance, one tending to improve the Bashaw's morale, vacillating as it did with each succeeding development. Perhaps more disturbing than this to the Commodore were the natural signs the old sailor could sense that the season for such operations rapidly was coming to a close. Before long, the winds and waters would make life hazardous for the Neapolitan gunboats, and less livable for the brigs and schooners.

## FOURTH ATTACK

Monday, 27 August, dawned cloudy and overcast with an onshore wind, dead wrong for any attack. By noon, Preble had a feeling that it was going to change for the better and ordered all hands to prepare once more for the fray. Three hours later, his hunch proved to be correct and the squadron got underway for the town on a strong northeasterly wind. As they stood in, the Commodore assembled his captains in *Constitution* to discuss his plans. The frigate anchored some 2½ miles north of the castle at 5:30, and the lesser units remained underway around her, making final preparations. The bomb ketches remained in the outer anchorage with *John Adams* and the supply ships because both had been rendered *hors de combat* by their earlier efforts.

At 1:15 A.M. on the 28th, the wind finally had abated enough to permit the gunboats to operate independently. Preble signalled them into the attack, and they proceeded to positions near the western entrance to the port from whence they could bombard, but where nearby rocks offered them some protection from return fire. Shortly before three, all were anchored with springs on their anchor cables so that they could keep the guns pointed on target. A rocket skyward, a gun fired, and a false fire ignited — all in *Constitution* — was the order to commence firing. At first, the Tripolines did not respond, but then every gun that possibly could bear opened up. The enemy's gunboats fired from their anchored positions off the inner water gate, but made no attempt to close. American fire destroyed a portion of the molehead battery as well as sank a galliot and a galley in the harbor. Torn canvas and cut rigging was the worst the attackers suffered. As the dawn broke, the Tripoline gunboats began to move. One, apparently on picket duty, thrust her bow through the entrance between the rocks to attack the easternmost U.S. boat, only to have its target put two quick loads of shot and grape into it, causing six casualties and a hasty retreat. Thirteen other Tripolines came on to engage the Yankee.

Preble had been watching events carefully. When he saw the enemy gunboats become active, he got *Constitution* underway and began moving in. As she swept in, the friendly gunboats were ordered out. Said one observer, "She had her tompions out, matches lit, and batteries lighted up, all hands at quarters, standing right in under the fort ..." The gunboat sailors cheered. At 400 yards from the rocks, the heavy frigate let go her lethal load at the enemy, driving them back, sinking one and forcing two more to beach. Then broadside after broadside — over 300 rounds — she poured into the fortifications, silencing them. It was a magnificent demonstration of her power. Rigging damage was all she suffered in return, although a fair number of grape shot were found imbedded in her stout sides. As she hauled out of range after her small charges, the Tripolines came to life and fired a final blast of harassing fire for morale purposes.

## FIFTH ATTACK

Negotiations had proven futile. Commodore Barron and his four frigates still had not appeared. The fighting season rapidly was ending. Preble decided on a dramatic act to try and bring things to a head. We saw how he had advised the Navy Secretary in March that he intended to use a lot of powder to blow up the Bashaw's works; now, he thought, was the time for it.

Little *Intrepid*, once *Mastico*, was about to perform her last service to her country of capture. Preble ordered his carpenters to make her over into an "infernal," a gigantic floating bomb. First, they planked in the forward portion of the hold, making it a magazine. Into it was placed about five tons of black powder in bulk. Atop this were laid 100 13-inch mortar shells and fifty 9-inch shells. A trough was run aft to another compartment, which was filled with combustibles. A powder train was laid in the trough, connecting the combustibles to two 11-minute fuses run through musket barrels mounted in the magazine bulkhead and into the powder. *Intrepid* was to be run in amongst the Bashaw's fleet, or even against his castle wall, the combustibles room having been lighted to give her the appearance of a fire ship. The powder train would carry the fire along to the magazine which, if their timing was right, would go off at the right moment with much destruction caused in its vicinity. A small crew would be necessary to guide her in under cover of darkness until she was headed fair for her target, when the combustibles would be lighted, the helm lashed, and the crew depart in attending rowboats.

Preparations in *Intrepid* were completed by 1 September. Master Commandant Richard Somers of *Nautilus* claimed her command as his chance for glory. Newly promoted Lieutenant Henry Wadsworth of *Constitution* was the other officer, while four seamen from *Nautilus* and six from *Constitution* completed her complement. All were volunteers. The officers vowed that the only way the Tripolines would get the powder was in a blast. Everything seemed right that evening for the operation, but, with the *Intrepid* just 400 yards off the western entrance, the wind turned foul and she had to haul off. Nobody in the port seems to have been the wiser.

The next dawning, as was their custom, the Tripoline gunboats left their defensive line deep in the harbor and began moving as if to take up their usual daytime positions inside the rocks adjacent to the western entrance. Soon, however, they moved to new positions under the protection of the English fort and to windward of the normal operating area of the Americans. Preble appreciated the move, seeing that it gave the pirates the weather gage in the event the Americans deployed as they had previously. The Commodore adjusted his plan accordingly, sending the gunboats to duel with their opposite numbers while bomb ketches and frigate worked over the castle and fortifications.

It required the rest of the morning and a part of the afternoon for the brigs and schooners to tow their charges to a position from which they could descend upon the Tripoline flotilla at the eastern end of the harbor. At 2:30, the flagship signalled the attack and the two divisions went forward, one paying particular attention to the gunboats and the other to the English fort and a new fortification slightly to its west, nicknamed by some the "American fort." For the next two hours, the sides flailed away at one another without material result.

To the west, Preble had sent in the bomb ketches to bombard the city. Taking positions more than a mile off, the two craft had their best day since the attack of 7 August. Thirty-three out of forty-one shells fired actually landed in the town. Although both suffered rigging damage from the Tripoline return fire, it was self-inflicted damage that put Number 1 out of action. Repeated firing of the mortar and apparently inadequate repairs a few days earlier resulted in the mortar bed giving way and hull timbers starting. She broke off firing with two feet of water in her hold.

The ever-watchful Preble saw what was happening to the bomb ketches. Once more *Constitution* spread her canvas high and wide and bore down on the offending batteries. Some eighty cannon opened at her as she came, raising spouts of water all around her and sometimes throwing the spray even on the glistening canvas. At 3:30 she came to, her port broadside fair on the town, and there she lay at three cables length for forty minutes, crashing shot after shot into the pirate stronghold — over 200 rounds, this time. As on earlier occasions, the shifting wind necessitated the signal to haul off shore, which all units did without incident.

## THE "INFERNAL"

Following a day of repair and resupply, Preble found the evening of 3 September right for the use of the infernal, *Intrepid*. A light haze covered the surface of the sea, making visibility difficult beyond a couple of hundred yards, although the stars clearly were seen overhead. At 8 P.M., *Intrepid* slipped her cable and headed for the port's western entrance, just inside of which three Tripoline gunboats were known to have taken their regular night stations. She was towing two fast rowing boats, one each from *Constitution* and *Nautilus*, to be used in the escape from the time bomb. *Argus*, *Vixen*, *Nautilus*, and somewhat later, *Syren*, all followed Somers' dangerous craft. They would take up stations off the rocks to pick up the returning adventurers. Acting Lieutenant Joseph Israel, bearing Preble's final words to Somers, pleaded to remain in *Intrepid*. He was allowed to do so — the 13th member of the crew.

Lieutenant George Washington Reed, Somers' next senior officer in *Nautilus*, was the last to speak to Somers as the final escort dropped away. He later reported that the *Intrepid*s were calm, in good order, and determined as they parted company.

Slowly, *Intrepid* moved forward and disappeared into the haze. Some claimed to have seen her throughout what followed, but it seems more likely that her gradual disappearance left them convincing themselves they still could make out her form. After some moments, the Tripoline batteries were seen and heard to open fire, a fire that seemed to be aimed at nothing in particular.

About ten minutes after the shore batteries opened up, at about 9:47 according to Haraden, there was a tremendous explosion and burst of light. In an instant a fiery column flashed skyward. In it, some saw *Intrepid*'s mast rising straight up, trailing its rigging. So swiftly did the fire flash and die that none saw the mast come down. From the point of explosion fountained burning shells, arching across the sky in all directions and raining down on sea and shore alike. And then there was deafening silence, as both sides stopped in awe of what they had seen.

Clearly, something had gone wrong. There had not been time for Somers to have gotten his craft to its destination before the explosion. The haze had prevented a sure knowledge of where *Intrepid* was when she blew up. Still the American units waited off the rocks through the night with waning hope that their shipmates would come rowing out of the gloom as Decatur had done the preceding February. They waited in vain.

*Intrepid*'s mast could be seen resting on the rocks just to the west of the entrance the next morning. Also, there was what appeared to be a portion of her keel or bottom. Coincidentally, three of the enemy gunboats seemed to be missing. Commodore Preble, with so few clues, concluded that Somers had been boarded, or at least cornered, by the picket boats and that, true to his word, he fired the charge so that the Tripolines could not get the powder. However, given the location of the wreckage at or outside the entrance, it does not seem likely that Somers got far enough to engage the gunboats. He probably missed the entrance in the poor visibility and went gently aground on the rocks on the west side of the entrance. In that vulnerable position, he may have been hit by a stray shot from one of the Tripoline guns; or perhaps the jar of grounding set off the powder; or perhaps, in the confusion that must have happened when she struck, someone aboard had an accident or panicked. All thirteen aboard subsequently were found: two bodies still in the wreck, ten floating in various parts of the harbor or washed ashore, and one in *Constitution*'s boat, which drifted ashore farther down the coast to the west. None of the bodies were recognizable; some were not all there. Preble's infernal had done absolutely no damage to the Tripolines. The loss of thirteen Americans in this bizarre mode of attack stunned the squadron. The Commodore felt deeply the loss, himself.

## BARRON SUCCEEDS PREBLE AS COMMODORE

Preparations began anew the next morning for yet another attack, but without quite the drive that had characterized Preble's earlier efforts. The loss of Somers and company and the frustrations with his inability to bring the Bashaw to terms, combined with a spate of bad weather on the 5th, led the Commodore to call off preparations and to make ready the bomb ketches and gunboats for return to Naples. The season, he decided, was too far advanced to risk keeping the unwieldy craft on the open ocean any longer. Late on the 6th, *John Adams*, *Syren*, *Enterprise*, and *Nautilus* towed them offshore, on their way home. *Constitution*, *Argus*, and *Vixen* remained on the blockade, waiting for Commodore Barron to arrive.

Barron and two frigates, *President* and *Constellation*, were sighted at noon on Sunday, 9 September, and when they joined later that afternoon, Edward Preble hauled down his broad command pennant. He surely did not feel it at that moment, but the months to come would prove how very successful he really had been. Indeed, the Congress would vote him a gold medal in March 1805, the first *Constitution* Captain to be decorated for his performance.

Several days were required by Preble to effect a proper transfer of information and orders to his successor. On the 11th, Barron wrote to Preble and told him to take *Constitution* to Malta for repairs, turn her over to Captain Decatur, and proceed home in *John Adams*. That very afternoon, Preble chased and captured two small armed vessels flying the Greek flag attempting to run wheat into

## A Most Fortunate Ship

Tripoli.

The blockaders were milling about some twelve miles northeast of the city as morning twilight was breaking on 12 September. Fitful breezes veered back and forth between the northeast and northwest. *President* was standing to westward under full sail, while *Constitution,* off her port bow, was struggling north- nor-theastward. Suddenly, the latter was taken aback by a wind shift and left unmanageable in the other frigate's path. *Constitution*'s stem struck *President*'s larboard bow, and then she was swung parallel and alongside by *President*'s continued forward motion as anchor fouled anchor and locked both ships together. Quickly, a spring hawser was run from *President*'s lee bow to *Constitution*'s quarterdeck capstan and a strain taken, while others carefully disengaged the tangled lower yards. That done, *Constitution* set sails, and once she had speed enough to relieve the tension on the spring hawser and clear the anchors, cast off and came clear without further incident. *President,* having taken the blow on her bluff bows, suffered no notable damage. But *Constitution* had made contact with one of her most vulnerable parts: flying jib boom, jib boom, and spritsail yard had been carried away; the Hercules figurehead and the upper cutwater and trailboards were a mass of splintered remains; and the bow head area was a shambles. Lieutenant Charles Gordon, the watch officer at the time, was absolved of any dereliction of duty, the vagaries of the wind being acts of God.

*Constitution* departed the blockade late the next afternoon with her two prizes and arrived in Malta's quarantine anchorage on the 16th, where Preble left Lieutenant Gordon in charge of the overhaul and repair program and moved ashore, awaiting transportation to Sicily and Naples in order to settle the squadron's accounts for his time in command.

## REPAIRS AT MALTA

Work began almost immediately to ready the frigate for further service. The six Neapolitan cannon were landed and sent back to their owner. The crew was kept busy taking down and repairing rigging while thirty-seven carpenters and twenty caulkers hired for the purpose began making her a tight ship once more and removing the mass of damaged timbers forward. On the 26th, what was left of Hercules and the trailboards were taken off, the pattern for the new billet head set up, and the timber for the cutwater started fitting. The 27th found the head remnants being dismantled and a 66-foot spar brought aboard to be shaped into a new spritsail yard. Rot was found in the damaged mainmast about eighteen feet above the spar deck. In the week that followed, the yard was finished, guns and carriages overhauled, some boats repaired, and painting begun. By 2 October, the hired labor force had been reduced to twelve carpenters and eight caulkers.

So much painting was going on at this time that it was considered dangerous to light a fire in the caboose. The crew was made to subsist on cold "salt provisions" for two days until the quantities of paint about the ship had been reduced. The paint scheme in use at this time, as Sailing Master Haraden recorded it, was a black hull above a yellow gun stripe, with the hull below that tarred to the waterline. The inner planking of the spar deck bulwarks and the guns were painted *a light yellow*. Twice during October, the efforts to paint out the hull were set back by the weather: heavy rains caused the black to run into the yellow on the hull, requiring it to be scraped and done again.

Elsewhere in the ship, the bow head area was completed and the upper portion planked in to afford more protection to those using the facilities located there. Long, oaken fishes for the mainmast arrived from Syracuse and the tedious work of fitting and woolding them in place began, discovering more rot in the process. The new billet head was bolted in place on 11 October, a very simple affair almost totally devoid of the sculptor's art, as were the new trailboards. All the officers and crew of the ship were herded into the berth deck that same day and "smoked" before the local authorities released the ship from quarantine. All carpenters and caulkers were released a week later, when all boats had been completed and the taffrail, the last piece of light woodwork remaining topside, removed from atop the transom.

The long-awaited supply ship *Alfred* arrived in Malta from America on the 23rd, bringing *Constitution* eight 32-pounder carronades. These were mounted on the spar deck, while the two 12-pounders which had been loaned to *Syren* off Tripoli were stowed below. Commodore Preble returned aboard on the 24th. Stephan Decatur relieved him without fanfare on the 28th, not knowing **his** relief's orders had been dispatched by Commodore Barron two days earlier. He would exchange commands with John Rodgers, then commanding *Congress* (36). Decatur's sole action with *Constitution* was to sail her to Syracuse, where he arrived on 4 November, and where Captain Rodgers succeeded him on the 9th, bringing with him the entire *Congress* officer complement.

## JOHN RODGERS COMMANDS CONSTITUTION

John Rodgers of Maryland was the first *Constitution* skipper not to have served in the Revolution in any capacity. Born in July 1772, he entered the new Navy as Second Lieutenant of *Constellation,* where he gained fame in her victory over the French frigate *L'Insurgente* and his subsequent performance as prize master. He was promoted to Captain a month later, in March 1799, and had commanded both *Maryland* (22) and *John Adams* (28) before commissioning *Congress* for current service.

At the time Rodgers took command of *Constitution* at Syracuse, Commodore Barron had taken up residence ashore there, his health having deteriorated in the two months since he had relieved Edward Preble. His problem was diagnosed as "a complaint of the liver." In a letter on the 13th  he requested Rodgers to take charge and act as commodore with regard to operating the ships at sea. Barron obviously was reluctant to turn over completely his newly acquired command and also felt that his condition in no way reduced his mental capacity. He retain-

*Captain John Rodgers.*

ed primacy, and authority for the day-to-day functions in the diplomatic and political arena involving much correspondence and little physical activity. Rodgers hoisted the broad blue pennant to *Constitution*'s main truck at 1 P.M. on 14 November.

Barron ordered Rodgers to take his frigate to Lisbon, departing on 28 November, where he was to recruit to make up his 80-man deficiency. It was a bad trip. The presence of yellow fever at Gibraltar precluded a call there although, unbeknownst to Rodgers, the supply ship *William and Mary* recently had deposited there the powder and shot for the new carronades, together with a new bowsprit specifically sent out for *Constitution.* And after touching base with our Consul at Tangiers, he ran right into a fierce Atlantic gale that sprung the bowsprit and delayed his arrival at Lisbon until 28 December. In reporting his arrival, he wrote to Secretary Smith that "The *Constitution* is the most laboursome & uneasy Ship I have ever commanded ..." He blamed it, in part, on the way her kentledge (ballast) was stowed. His negative feeling for this particular ship we shall meet again.

Immediately upon his arrival, Rodgers, who failed to understand the poor communications between the distant quarantine anchorage he occupied and the city, wrote to Consul William Jarvis informing him of his needs for recruits and bowsprit repair. He became incensed when a response was not forthcoming in what he considered to be a reasonable time, firing off a very harsh letter, taking Jarvis to task for sloth and indifference, and set the stage for six weeks of exchanged invective between the Marylander and the Bostonian. Despite this, the recruits were found — mostly Danes, Swedes, and Frenchmen — and a new bowsprit fashioned ashore and installed.

Rodgers headed back into the Mediterranean on 9 February 1805, making the usual calls at Tangiers and Gibraltar, which now was reopened. A brief storm off Algeria on the 20th washed the gig off the quarter, but did not delay the ship's arrival at Malta on the 23rd, where Commodore Barron again was ashore and ailing. His hoped-for recovery had not occurred; if anything, he was worse.

At Barron's order, *Constitution* made a brief trip to the blockade on 2 March and arrived three days later. Rodgers, who had not been present for any of the attacks on the city, startled the Moslems at four in the morning on the 10th by firing a single broadside into the town. He returned to Malta on the 19th and remained through the rest of the month.

*Constitution* made a two-day trip to Tripoli and relieved *Constellation* there on 5 April. *Vixen* remained her consort until the 17th, when *President* took her place. The blockade had resumed the rather lackadaisical, informal character it had had under Dale and Morris. The blockaders generally remained more than ten miles to seaward. There was a brief flurry of activity on the 24th, when *Constitution* chased down an 8-gun Tripoline xebec and her two Neapolitan prizes.

Pausing in the flow of our narrative for a moment, it is time to take notice of two events occurring during the winter and spring seasons which shortly would make themselves felt on the course of the war. The first of these was the French offensive which swept down from northern Italy and threatened to engulf the Kingdom of the Two Sicilies. It had the effect of denying the Americans the loan of Neapolitan gunboats for another season's work off Tripoli. The second event had begun in November 1804 when William Eaton, entitled our "Naval Agent for the Barbary Regencies," was sent by Commodore Barron to Egypt with *Argus, Nautilus,* and *Hornet,* and a nucleus force of Marines under Lieutenant Presley N. O'Bannon, to cooperate with the Bashaw's deposed brother, Hamet, in an overland attempt to unseat Yussuf. This ragtag band of American Marines, Greek mercenaries, and Arab tribesmen made an epic march across the desert sands to Derne, capitol of Tripoli's easternmost province, which they captured from numerically superior forces in a single assault on 27 April. From this episode comes the line "... to the shores of Tripoli" in the Marine Corps Hymn. The modern Marine officer's saber is copied from the Mameluke model acquired by Lieutenant O'Bannon at this time.

To return to our narrative. On 5 May, *President* joined Rodgers off Tripoli, bearing a letter from Consul General Tobias Lear, who remained with Commodore Barron. In it, he apprised Rodgers that he had received a letter from the Spanish Consul at Tripoli, written at the behest of the Bashaw, indicating the latter's willingness to negotiate, with $200,000 ransom as a starting point. This, of course, was totally unacceptable to Lear. The consul general also informed Rodgers that, because other squadron units were busy guarding American interests at key points along the Italian boot and pursuing other missions, it was doubtful that any offensive action could be undertaken before the middle of June.

## RODGERS BECOMES SQUADRON COMMANDER

*Essex* joined the blockaders on 26 May and brought with it Consul General Lear and a surprising letter: Samuel Barron was resigning his command to John Rodgers because of his continuing bad health. However, he reserved the right to resume the command if his health improved, and further restricted Rodgers' freedom of action by charging him to begin negotiations for peace without delay. Perhaps it was his poor condition which led him to this position. Or perhaps it was the fact that the Neapolitan gunboats would not be available, and also that the Eaton-Hamet Karamanli expedition had failed to rally a significant portion of the local populace to the latter's banner despite the Derne victory. Whatever the exact motivation, Hamet was to be abandoned and negotiations pressed. Happily, Bashaw Yussuf was in an equally conciliatory mood, brought to that state of mind by the prospect of a renewed onslaught on his capitol and the loss of Derne to his brother.

## PEACE WITH TRIPOLI

*Essex* moved in closer to the city that same afternoon and hoisted the signal for parley, which was immediately answered. From that point on, the diplomats and naval-officers-cum-negotiators moved at an accelerating pace. The Bashaw rejected Lear's first offer, made through the Spanish Consul, on the 30th. On the 31st, Lear offered $60,000 and the return of the Tripoline prisoners in exchange for the American sailors and a treaty of peace and trade. Captain William Bainbridge was released from prison on parole to help work out details. On the 1st, Danish Consul Nicholas C. Nissen replaced the Spaniard as mediator, as it was recognized that both sides had a greater confidence in his fairness to the parties concerned. The draft treaty was completed and initialled on board *Constitution* by Lear and Nissen, representing the Bashaw, on 3 June. Topside, the ship's carpenters were fashioning a new flagpole for the consulate from a spare spar. It was sent ashore and erected that afternoon, while an ensign for it was furnished by *Essex*. At 10:30 the next morning, the Stars and Stripes once more were hoisted over Tripoli, saluted with twenty-one guns from the castle and from *Constitution*. The treaty was presented to the Bashaw in the castle at noon with an American delegation led by Tobias Lear in attendance.

On 5 June, *Constitution, Essex, Vixen,* and the newly arrived *Constellation* all moved in to anchor in Tripoli harbor, the remains of *Philadelphia* still visible on the shore as a reminder of all that had transpired in and around that small body of water during the preceding four years. Captain Bainbridge and some 300 of his crewmen were received aboard *Constitution* that afternoon to the cheers of the squadron.

Commodore Rodgers spent the 6th redeploying his forces in light of the changed political situation. *Vixen* would remain at Tripoli for the time being to support the diplomatic mission. *Constellation* was ordered to Derne to direct the withdrawal of the Eaton force, including Hamet and the mercenaries, and the return of the city to a representative of the Bashaw. *Constitution* and *Essex* sailed that evening for Malta to join *President* (which had been sent thither on 31 May) and the rest of the squadron prior to making for Tunis, where the Bey had, for some time, been threatening war over *Constitution's* capture of his xebec and her prizes the preceding April.

The two-day stop at Malta informed Rodgers that thus far the Bey still was only making noises, and so he decided to wrap up the Tripoline matter himself. Sailing to Syracuse, he landed the *Philadelphia*s on 11 June and then loaded aboard the nearly 100 Tripolines for repatriation. A boat from Malta delivered eight boxes of money (the ransom payment) to the passing frigate on 13 June. Rodgers was back at Tripoli on the 17th, paid two official calls ashore, and returned to Syracuse via Malta ten days later.

Captain Bainbridge, at this point, requested an early Court of Inquiry to take up the matter of the loss of *Philadelphia,* so that the incident could be officially closed. The Court, consisting of Captains James Barron, Stephen Decatur, and Hugh G. Campbell, met on 29 June and cleared Bainbridge of any culpability in short order. The matter was at an end, although its memory would haunt Bainbridge for ever more.

Commodore Rodgers ordered the Fourth of July to be celebrated with all due ceremony. All ships present that morning dressed ship with every flag possessed being flown from some vantage point. At high noon, all fired 16-gun salutes, and that night a gala was held on board the flagship, including many notables from the local area in attendance. The journal entry for the day recorded, "... they (the "respectable" people) took with them 6 silver spoons a number of Glasses and Many other articles too tedious to Mention ..." Souvenirs, it seems, always have been prized.

At the request of Samuel Barron, Commodore Rodgers made *President* (now commanded by James Barron) available to take the ailing sailor home. *President's* crew was exchanged with that of *Constitution,* whose enlistments were expiring, on the 5th. The Barrons headed for America the next day, the first of many reductions in force to be affected in the Mediterranean Squadron in the coming months.

## PEACE WITH TUNIS

The squadron, consisting of *Constitution, Constellation, Essex, John Adams, Enterprise,* and eight gunboats recently arrived from the United States (the latter built as a result of Preble's experience), sailed for Malta on 13 July, and spent eight days at that island, provisioning. While there, Rodgers experienced some of the problems with deserters that had gotten Preble so angry at Gibraltar two years earlier. The British, in greater need of seamen than ever before, were becoming increasingly overt and obnoxious in their practice of acquiring them by any means from any vessel, regardless of nationality. When he sailed, the squadron was increased further by the presence of *Syren, Nautilus,* and stores ship *Franklin.*

This imposing force arrived off Tunis on 30 July, finding sloop *Hornet* already there. Rodgers did not miss the opportunity to make the sort of impression on a landlubber that only the massed presence of warships can. He organized his units into two columns and sailed them into the bay in formation, coming to anchor smartly on signal at intervals calculated to span the width of the entire harbor. It must have been a magnificent and awesome sight to have seen those seventeen white-winged beauties sweep in together, round to, drop anchors, and furl their sails in unison. And below the graceful canvas was the presence of all those gun ports to remind the observer of the power of those vessels. Frigate *Congress* added emphasis by her arrival on the first day of the new month.

After meeting with American Consul George Davis on 2 August, Rodgers sent a letter to the Bey, who had until now refused to see him, demanding an answer within thirty-six hours as to whether or not a state of war existed between Tunis and the United States. Legitimate problems with getting an adequate translation into Arabic led to the Commodore waiving the time limit. The Bey's response, when it came, avoided a direct answer, pointing out that what he really wanted was the return of what he considered to be Tunisian ships wrongly captured by the Americans.

Rodgers held a council of war on the 4th, with Davis and Consul General Lear in attendance. His decision was to send Davis once more to the Bey requiring a guarantee of peace before any negotiations were begun. He accompanied this with a guarantee of his own not to begin any offensive operations unless initiated first by the Tunisians. There followed diplomatic maneuvering involving translations, designation of representatives, and the like, until Rodgers' patience wore thin on the 8th, when he ordered Davis to move himself out to the squadron at four the next afternoon if there still was no definite movement in the exchanges of notes. When this was made known to the Bey, he refused to provide the required written guarantee of peace, and Davis went aboard *Constellation* as ordered — lock, stock, and barrel. The Commodore underscored this move when he ordered units of the squadron out to the mouth of the bay. Their orders were to prevent any Tunisian shipping from leaving harbor and to force into harbor any Tunisian vessels seen in the offing. Perhaps a form of blockade would bring the Bey to negotiate. It did.

Consul General Lear went ashore on 12 August with Chaplain Cruize of *Constellation* to meet with the Bey. In two days, the two sides agreed to maintain peace. Rodgers would make available one of his ships to take an appointed Tunisian ambassador to Washington, where a resolution of the prize question would be worked out. *Congress* was assigned this mission. And finally, Surgeon Dodge of *Constitution* was appointed the new Consul for Tunis, so that the Bey would not be embarrassed by the continued presence of Davis, who had represented the uncommonly hard-nosed Commodore in the recent parley.

## SQUADRON CUTBACKS

Peace had come to the Americans sailing the waters off Barbary, although Algiers would try her old ways once more during the War of 1812. Rodgers spent the next three weeks at anchor, reorganizing his forces and making new officer assignments so that those who had been involved longest could return to the United States. *Constellation* departed for Syracuse and home on the 23rd. *Nautilus* and *Franklin* followed; *Essex* and *Vixen* were sent to Gibraltar, and *Enterprise* to Tripoli. On 1 September, *Syren, Hornet, Argus,* and the gunboats headed for Syracuse. *Constitution* made for the same port on the 4th — as soon as *Congress* and the Tunisian Ambassador had cleared port for Washington.

After nine days at anchor, Rodgers got *Constitution* underway for a tour of a number of Italian ports to assess the fortunes of Americans in the midst of the continental war. From Syracuse, he proceeded to Messina, then Naples and Leghorn, arriving in the latter port on 10 October. He spent a month there, in part because he sought redress for two instances of rudeness he personally had received from guards at the city's gates. But Tobias Lear and his wife, who had been travelling overland from Syracuse, buying the biennial gifts due the Dey of Algiers, rejoined the ship for return to his post and they sailed before the Commodore received any apologies. A two-day gale delayed landing the Lears at Algiers until 19 November. A second gale made the return to Syracuse a miserable six-day trip, ending on the 27th.

Rodgers, like Preble, was a stern disciplinarian. And like Preble, he had to deal with the continuing problem of desertion, particularly since peace had come and so many were anxious to end their service. On the 16th of December, a court martial (there had not been any under Preble) found Seaman John Reeson guilty of desertion and sentenced him to be flogged through the squadron. Rodgers approved the sentence and ordered it executed on the 23rd. The usual procedure was to have the offender trussed up to a section of deck grating mounted upright in one of the ship's boats. Aside from the boat officer and crew, there also would be embarked boatswain's mates to wield the "cat" and a surgeon's mate to ensure the man survived. At the man's ship, the crew would be mustered at the rail to witness the first portion of his punishment. When the proper number of lashes had been laid on, the offender's shirt would be thrown over his back, the boatswain's mates returned to the ship, and the unhappy cargo rowed to the next ship, where her mates would lay on a similar number while that crew watched, and so on until all units present had been visited, or until the surgeon's mate declared the man unfit for further punishment that day. If that were the case, he would be returned to his own ship until sufficiently recovered to resume the evolution until the required number of lashes had been administered. How many lashes Reeson was awarded is not known.

On 28 December, Commodore Rodgers received Secretary Smith's directive of the preceding 5 August to reduce the size of the squadron "after peace with Tripoli shall have been effected." In his response of three days later, he reported that it had been too late to send the gunboats back across the Atlantic safely, and that he had retained the other units until the Tunisian Ambassador returned from the United States with peace assured, a situation about which the Commodore knew the Secretary was unaware when he wrote but felt the Secretary would approve when it became known to him. When the Tunisian returned, Rodgers thought the squadron might to reduced to one frigate, two brigs, and a schooner.

*Constitution* took the Commodore on a brief visit to Malta late in January 1806. While there, he received the Navy Secretary's letter of 12 October, wherein that gentleman ordered home all units except *Constitution* and any two of the "small vessels of war." Rodgers' response reiterated his earlier position and added that the turmoil created by the French conquests in Italy also warranted the presence of American warships in those places where our interests might be jeopardized.

## CAMPBELL RELIEVES RODGERS

Rodgers spent the entire months of February and March in Syracuse, and got underway once more on 3 April with the whole squadron, leaving but a few people behind to close the hospital and others to mind the naval stores. After nearly a month at Malta, he got underway on 5 May, paid a brief call at Algiers, and arrived at Gibraltar on 21 May 1806. There, among the dispatches awaiting him, Rodgers found Secretary Smith's letter of 22 March directing him to turn over command of the frigate and the station to Captain Campbell and to return home, having ordered all other units previously designated to do likewise. The change of command was effected on 29 May. One of Rodgers' last comments concerning *Constitution,* in marked contrast to that made shortly after he assumed command, was that "I have had a fair Trial of the *Constitution,* since the Stowage of her Ballast has been altered ... She sails much better, and from one of the most uneasy Ships I ever was in, is now among the most easy." *Hornet* and durable *Enterprise* were left to make up the rest of the squadron.

Little is known of Hugh George Campbell. He was born in South Carolina, and was in command of the Revenue Cutter *Eagle* when that ship and he were taken into naval service during the Quasi-War. With a number of prizes to his credit, Campbell must be considered one of the more successful commanders of that conflict. Subsequently, he commanded the frigate *Adams* in Morris' squadron, and had commanded *Constellation* and *Essex* since returning to the Mediterranean with Barron.

*Constitution's* service during this period largely was a peaceful round of port visits, mostly in the western Mediterranean: Malaga, Cadiz, and Algiers during Campbell's first four months in command. In September, he took her to Lisbon, where fine naval facilities afforded him the opportunity for a badly needed refit. For three months, the frigate lay there recuperating. Hull and decks were thoroughly recaulked. She was given a wholly new fore mast, new rigging, and new sails.

The wandering life was resumed on 9 December. Subsequent port calls included Gibraltar, Algiers, Tunis, Algiers again, Cagliari, Malta, and finally, Syracuse early in May 1807. The call at Cagliari had been to make preliminary repairs to damages suffered in a vicious gale. The rails and boomkins in the bow head area had been carried away, and the cabin windows stove in. Midshipman William Lewis recalled the humorous side of the event in a letter written to Mrs. Tobias Lear:

> ... In my watch this morning, it fell calm all of a sudden, and the ship of course stopped still; when a great wave struck her astern, demolished the cabin windows, washed the Capt. ... out of ... bed, half drowned; and knocked down the cabin partition on our Moorish passenger (?), who was sleeping just before it. He was terribly alarmed, & began to pray to Allah very fervently ... As for the Capt. ... (he) cut as ludicrous a figure as you can imagine. We who were out of the scrape laughed heartily at their disaster. By the by; I expected to get a scold about it, though it was not my fault; however the old Man proved reasonable enough ...

## *CHESAPEAKE* AND *LEOPARD*

Secretary Smith issued orders on 15 May 1807 directing Captain James Barron to prepare to sail in *Chesapeake* as relief for *Constitution* and Campbell. Outfitting of his flagship at Norfolk was done in a lackadaisical manner. She sailed on 22 June with her decks littered with supplies and her crew not properly assigned stations. As ill luck would have it, there were two British men of war at anchor at Lynnhaven. One of them, *Leopard* (50) got under way and stood out of the bay ahead of *Chesapeake.* Shortly thereafter, the Englishman brought Barron to with a hail that she was carrying dispatches for Barron. The British lieutenant who came aboard showed the Commodore orders from his Flag Officer, North American Station, to all subordinate units to stop and board *Chesapeake* when found in order to retrieve a number of British deserters known to be aboard. Barron rightly refused to allow his crew to be mustered and inspected by them. The lieutenant returned to *Leopard,* which in the meantime had cleared for action, and after a few moments of exchanged hails, the English frigate opened fire on the unready and disorganized Americans. It was perfect carnage. In a few minutes, there were twenty-three casualties about *Chesapeake's* decks. She fired one harmless shot, then hauled down her flag. The British returned and took out four men, but refused Barron's surrender — after all, no state of war existed! All that was left for James Barron was to crawl painfully back to Norfolk where *Chesapeake* could be repaired and where his career would be put in limbo, never entirely to recover. As a footnote to this sad incident in our naval history, the British hanged one of the four sailors taken and later returned two others with apologies, the fourth having died.

Unaware that her relief thus had been delayed, *Constitution* during this time once more was making port calls. Underway from Syracuse on 12 June, she stopped at Messina, Palermo, and Leghorn, in succession. At the last port, she loaded the disassembled 15-ton monument to Somers and other heroes of Tripoli subscribed to earlier by members of the squadron to the tune of $2000. The fifty-one numbered cases were stowed away below for delivery home and assembly at a place to be designated by the Secretary of the Navy. This monument can be seen today on the grounds of the U.S. Naval Academy at Annapolis.

## THE SMELL OF MUTINY

Heading west ("below" in the jargon of the day), *Constitution* met *Hornet* at Alicante and together they sailed to Malaga. There, Campbell read an old Boston newspaper and learned for the first time of the *Chesapeake-Leopard* affair. His reaction was concern for the readiness of his frigate and *Hornet* to fight the British, should there exist a state of war. To improve *Hornet*'s defenses, he had four of his 32-pounder carronades transferred and mounted in the smaller ship, leaving *Constitution* with two each on her forecastle and quarterdeck, in addition to the long 12's.

News of the delay of *Chesapeake* also spread through the crew like wildfire. Already troubled by disaffection and desertion, this latest development moved some to become vocal. It began with a veteran petty officer requesting permission to come to the main mast to state the views of the crew. Lieutenant Charles Ludlow granted permission and heard them out. Respected by ship's company, Ludlow sought to smooth the troubled waters with statements of understanding and appeals to patriotism. But when he reported to Commodore Campbell a short time later, he knew that an ugly mood prevailed. Campbell thought it might help to get to sea and keep the men occupied.

At eight bells of the morning watch the next day, the boatswain's calls piped all hands to quarters for leaving port, but no one moved. They'd get underway only to go home. Campbell ordered all officers to the quarterdeck under arms, and the Marine detachment to be assembled there, as well. Two long 12's were aimed at the larboard gangway. All hands were piped aft, and they complied, falling in as was customary on the larboard gangway. Campbell had his midshipmen load the cannon with grape and cannister, remove the covers from the touch holes, and blow on their matches. The moment of truth had arrived. The mates were ordered to repeat the call to unmoor. Given the choice, the crew manned their stations with alacrity. The crisis had been weathered.

## HOME

On 18 August, Commodore Campbell received the Secretary's orders to shut down all American naval activity in the Mediterranean and return home. The

**Above:** *Oldest-known contemporary portrait of* Constitution, *attributed to Michel Félice Corné.* **Left:** *Josiah Fox, one of* Constitution's *designers.*

Constitution *off Tripoli, 3 August 1804. Note Preble's signal for "general attack" flying at the mizzen truck. (Lithograph of an oil by John Charles Roach, commissioned by the Navy Federal Credit Union.)*

Top left: *Kedging away from the British squadron, July 1812.* Bottom left: *Showing the British her heels.* Top right: Guerriere's *mizzenmast goes by the board.* Bottom left: *. . . and the others follow.*

Top left: Java *blows up.*

Bottom left: Constitution *escapes to Marblehead.*

Below: *A local artist's fanciful depiction of the U.S. Mediterranean Squadron's sortie from Port Mahon.* From left to right: North Carolina, Carolina, Brandywine, Erie and Ontario. *These ships never left Port Mahon together.*

Top: *Celebrating Washington's birthday at Valletta, Malta in 1838.* Bottom: *"Old Ironsides" celebrating the Fourth of July in Naples, Italy.*

threat of war with Great Britain was immediate and grave. Campbell ordered *Hornet* to Malta and Syracuse to arrange for the shipment home of stores remaining at those ports, and to Leghorn to pick up the public monies held there for the squadron. At Algiers on 29 August he met the new sloop *Wasp* (18), just arriving to join the squadron. Keeping her in company, Campbell sailed *Constitution* and *Wasp* for Boston on 8 September. They arrived on 14 October: *Constitution* had been gone four years and two months, the longest time she ever would be absent from the United States.

# 5 Prelude to Glory

## RODGERS IN COMMAND AGAIN

*Constitution* had been in ordinary at the New York Navy Yard barely two months when the Yard Commandant, Commodore John Rodgers, was directed to effect repairs and ready her for further service. Additional units were needed to police coastal waters for violators of the embargo President Jefferson recently had declared against any American shipping being involved in foreign trade.

Between 1 February 1808 and 3 March 1809, the Commodore expended $99,867.76 on *Constitution*'s overhaul. His work program was based largely upon the report made by Captain Campbell when the ship decommissioned:

> ... A thorough caulking above water and bottom examind — A new Main Mast — A Mizinmast doubtfull and Must be taken out to be strictly Examind — one full set of new sails. One fore Top Mast, one Main Do. — One set of Top Gallt. Masts — One fore and Main Top sail yard — One Cross Jack Yard, and Set of studdingsail Booms — One Jibb boom, a Gang of Top Mast and Top Glt. Rigging — Four cables of 21 Inches, and a large proportion of new Water Casks — A set of Boats —
>
> Some alteration should be made In the Magazine And Cockpit, the present Plan in my Opinion being very inconvenient, and am of the opinion that the Quarter deck and forecastle of this ship should be furnished with heavy Carronades, in place of the long light Twelve pounders now on board — the Reason is obvious should we have a Formadable Enemy to contend with it would be Expected that the *Constitution* would be superior to any frigate In the British Navy, when the fact Can be Easily proved to the contrary ...

Rodgers was in complete agreement with Campbell's opinion concerning the spar deck gun battery, for he mounted sixteen 42-pounder carronades on the quarter-deck and two more on the forecastle, together with two 24-pounder chase guns. What is more, he had all guns fitted with firing locks, a more efficient and certain means of firing the cannon than the slow matches formerly used. A curious counterpoint to this improvement in *Constitution*'s firepower is the fact Rodgers apparently decided not to recopper her, or even to conduct an adequate inspection of her bottom.

Rodgers was at home on leave when, in February 1809, he received orders to take command of *Constitution* and a squadron of observation. This he did on the 20th. Preparations for sea proceeded very slowly, partly because the new Administration made some early moves to overturn certain Jeffersonian naval policies. One of these was to put a halt to the employment of a myriad of gunboats to the detriment of high seas operations. Rodgers had to give attention to the retirement of fifty-two of these craft at the same time he was outfitting the frigate.

*Sketch of* Constitution *from John Rodgers' sketchbook. The presence of skyscraper sails above the royals is unique for this ship.*

Although *Constitution* and the squadron — old acquaintances *Syren, Argus, Vixen,* and *Wasp* — were ready for sea by 24 May, sailing orders were lacking until 15 August, when Rodgers got them underway for a short cruise of "instruction and observation" to Newport, Rhode Island, and New London, Connecticut, before returning to New York. On 10 September, two days after sailing with frigate *Essex* and *Argus,* she lost a man killed when several upper masts and yards gave way in light winds. The poor quality of wood used in the recent refit was blamed. Rodgers returned to New York briefly, then took the frigate south to Norfolk for repairs. By the middle of November, *Constitution* was back in New York, snugged down for the winter.

During these early years of the U.S. Navy, there were no schools established ashore to train ship's boys and midshipmen in the skills necessary to their trade. The "school of the ship" was the sole course of study. Some consideration of the deficiency can be found from time to time in the records of these years, with chaplains most frequently being charged with the responsibility. The Navy Regulations of 1802 specifically stated, "He shall perform the duty of a schoolmaster; and to that end he shall instruct the midshipmen and volunteers, in writing, arithmatic, and navigation, and in whatsoever may contribute to render them proficient." Implementation of the regulation was, however, generally impossible: only one or two chaplains were in service during 1801-3 and just one from 1806 until war caused the Navy's expansion once again.

On 6 February 1810, Robert Thompson, the only chaplain continuously in service since 1800, received orders from Secretary of the Navy Paul Hamilton to "repair to N. York and report yourself to Comm. Rodgers. You are to remain on board the Frigate *Constitution* for three months for the purpose of instructing the Young Officers in the theory of navigation and lunar observations. You are thence to proceed to the Frigate *President* — thence to the Frigate *U. States* — thence to the Frigate *Essex,* remaining on board each, for the same purpose, three months."

In May, Rodgers took *Constitution* to sea again, and off Sandy Hook she captured the ships *Golconda* of New York and *Rose* of Philadelphia. Both had violated the 1809 Non-Intercourse Act, which had succeeded the 1808 Embargo and barred trade only with Britain and France by sailing from Liverpool laden with English goods. Late in the month, he brought *Constitution, Argus,* and *Wasp* to Annapolis, whence he proceeded to Washington overland to confer with the Secretary about fleet reorganization and a more aggressive naval policy.

Commodore Rodgers was given the principal command under the new system, that of "the northern division of ships for the protection of the American coast." Permitted to select his own flagship, he chose *President* (44), a "follow-on" to *Constitution*'s design, said to be faster and handier than her older half-sister. Rodgers had been quite dissatisfied with *Constitution* while he had her. Why he failed to perceive the reasons for this, as his successor would, is unfathomable now. It may be that as the Navy's senior operating officer, his principal concerns were external to the ship. Thus it was that the man who would lead *Constitution* to her destiny came to command. On 17 June 1810, at Norfolk, John Rodgers and Isaac Hull exchanged ship commands, each taking his officers and crew with him. Chaplain Thompson went with Rodgers to *President* and died there late in the summer, his teaching tour unfulfilled.

## CAPTAIN ISAAC HULL IN CHARGE

Connecticut Yankee Isaac Hull was no stranger to *Constitution.* He had served in the original wardroom as Fourth Lieutenant, and had risen to be her First Lieutenant under Captain Silas Talbot before succeeding that gentleman in command when he resigned abruptly in September 1801. Hull had remained her caretaker until February 1802. During the Barbary War, Hull first served as First Lieutenant of frigate *Adams,* then commanded the schooner *Enterprise* and the brig *Argus.* In these ships he served with increasing distinction, earning a Congressional silver medal as one of Preble's "boys."

When he returned to *Constitution* in June 1810, Hull was thirty-seven years old and had been a Captain for four years. A serious, thorough-going professional, the short, rotund, bachelor skipper was not so much concerned with the perquisites of rank as with the readiness of his ship and the welfare of his crew, and they returned his allegiance in kind.

*Captain Isaac Hull.*

Hull lost no time in coming to grips with his new command. The very next day, he had the crew drilled at the guns and in the rigging. His carpenters reported finding the caulking very rotten, and on the 19th commenced recaulking. More than a month was spent by Hull in beginning to get the frigate to his liking.

Shortly thereafter, *Constitution* sailed for Boston to take on stores and water. Her sailing qualities proved to be so poor, however, that Hull was forced to write the Secretary that he would be unable to rejoin Commodore Rodgers as expected. He sailed south on 14 July, informing the Secretary: "I have no hopes of her sailing any better than she did coming here. I shall now attend to that particular but I fear she will never sail as she has done until she goes into fresh water."

In Hampton Roads once more, Hull sent divers down on 26 July to check the bottom, which had been last coppered in 1803. They found the hull festooned with marine growth: mussels and oysters growing like bunches of grapes, barnacles, and seaweed by the baskets full. As Captain Hull put it to Secretary Hamilton, "After seeing them and being assured that she has, speaking within bounds, ten waggon loads of them on her bottom you can have no doubts as to the cause of her not sailing." To emphasize his point, samples were sent along, as well.

Knowing now the source of his troubles, Hull sailed from Chesapeake Bay. Enroute, on 9 August, the mizzen royal yard carried away and had to be replaced. The frigate arrived in Wilmington, Delaware, on the 11th, where the fresh water would kill the salt water marine life. Using an iron drag scraper, Hull sought to remove the moribund sea life, but still they hung on. After three days in fresh water, the mussels began to fall away of their own accord. Hull hoped the oysters would soon follow. While waiting, he took a few days leave in Philadelphia.

The 22nd found *Constitution*, in Hull's estimation, ready for sea. Soon underway, he was off Sandy Hook by 4 September. But Hull still was not satisfied with the way the ship sailed, improved as she was. Further examination disclosed that the masses of defunct barnacle shells remained firmly affixed to the copper sheathing. Only heaving down and a thorough scraping could correct the situation. Nonetheless, it must have been a relief to Hull to get to sea and be active again. During the long inport periods, the crew naturally grew restive and got into trouble. The ship's log records the results of boredom and frustration: three men flogged for drunkenness and fighting on 20 July; one man flogged for drunkenness and another for desertion on 8 August; eight midshipmen reported for neglect of duty; and three seamen punished for drunkenness on 1 September.

In mid-September, after two weeks on patrol, Hull was anchored in Nantasket Roads off Boston, his program of ship improvement continuing unabated. Carpenters were caulking the gun deck and, on 17-18 September, some were employed cutting air ports for the berthing deck to improve habitability. Toward the end of the month, crewmen were busy blackening the bends, whitewashing the berth deck and steerage bulkheads, and the spar deck ceiling planking had been painted green, as had one boat.

Hull resumed patrolling between Boston and Hampton Roads early in October, occasionally anchoring off Sandy Hook, a focal point for shipping. While there on 17 October, Midshipmen Richard Rodgers (one of those on report in August), Charles M. Morgan, and Archibald Hamilton, and Doctor Samuel Gilliland requested, and received, permission to go ashore near the lighthouse "to shoot." The shooting turned out to be a duel between Rodgers and Morgan over an unrecorded slight. In the exchange, Rodgers was killed and Morgan wounded. Morgan was arrested and Hamilton and the doctor suspended from duty in an effort to "discourage a practice so much at variance with morality and common law of the country." Public opinion, however, did not support enforcement of the law, and all three soon were restored to duty.

Steerage, the "home" of the midshipmen, received another blow just four days later when Midshipman Sylvanus Sprogell fell overboard from the mizzen channels. "Life buoys were immediately cut away and the boats sent in search of him," but he was not found.

Patrolling for another three weeks, *Constitution* paid a call at Newcastle, Delaware, in mid-November, then headed north for the squadron's winter rendezvous at New London, Connecticut. On the 21st, Seaman Samuel Francis fell from the mizzen rigging and was drowned; the next day Seaman Cable Martin likewise fell overboard and was lost. Thus ended the year's operations on a melancholy note. By mid-December, the entire squadron was snugged down for the winter.

The next three months, not atypically, were ones wherein the Commodore, his Captains, and their officers expended much of their effort in keeping the seamen gainfully employed and out of trouble. *Constitution*'s log shows clearly that the employment was achieved, but that sailors inevitably would get into scrapes. On 11 December, three Marines were punished for drunkenness and a sailor for theft, while the sailmakers made deck awnings, the carpenters more air ports, and the armorers a new Charlie Noble. A week later, the armorers were making a smokestack for the wardroom, and the carpenters overhauled the chain pumps. A court martial was held on board on 20-21 December to try several men belonging "to the U.S. Brig *Argus* & schooner *Revenge*." In January, another court martial was convened, and in February, a third. Two men were drummed out of service. On the positive side, the installation of air ports was completed, and two midshipmen joined the ship.

The rendezvous was broken up on 20 March 1811, with Rodgers taking *President* to New York and Hull heading for Boston. As if to write "finis" to the long winter, all hands were mustered to witness punishment that day. Commencing at 10:30, floggings were carried out on fourteen crewmen. Most of these were for relatively minor offenses, like being drunk and disorderly (nine to twelve lashes), but Seaman Lanson Marks received twenty-four for twice deserting and writing a disrespectful, seditious letter to the Secretary of the Navy "calculated to excite mutiny in the rest of the crew." Marks, one must observe, was fortunate to have been serving under a humane commander.

Early in April, Hull had the gun stripe along the length of the hull painted white. This is the first recorded instance when *Constitution* did not have the dull yellow stripe she bore when commissioned. The use of white paint for this purpose did not become standard practice until after the War of 1812.

## DIPLOMATIC MISSION

Hull had *Constitution* at Annapolis on 24 May, under orders to prepare for foreign service. In response to his letter of that date requesting further details so that preparations would be appropriate, Secretary Hamilton told him he would be sailing to France, Holland, and England, transporting our new minister to France, Joel Barlow, to his post and delivering $28,000 in specie to Holland as interest on our Revolutionary War debt to that country.

Although Hull had had reason to be dissatisfied with his frigate's sailing characteristics in his first year in command, it was during this period at Annapolis that he shipped an additional six 42-pounder carronades on the forecastle. *Constitution*'s battery then consisted of thirty 24- pounder long guns, twenty-four 42-pounder carronades, and two 24- pounder chase guns — an enormous total of fifty-six large caliber guns. While not stated specifically, his reason for this action may have been the increased depredations of Royal Navy cruisers in impressing American seamen on the high seas. During May 1811, *HMS Guerriere* (38) was very active off the Middle Atlantic states, and Commodore Rodgers had defeated the 20-gun ship-sloop *Little Belt* in a night fight stemming from the mistaken belief he had caught up with the larger predator.

As it turned out, *Constitution* idled at Annapolis for more than two months awaiting her illustrious passenger. In addition to increasing his spar deck battery, Hull used the time to insure the ship was ready to voyage into potentially hostile waters. Close attention was paid to overhauling guns, cleaning carriages and slides, repairing elevating screws on the carronades, and filling shot boxes.

If Hull was concerned about combat-readiness, Minister-to-be Barlow was not. On 16 June, while still awaiting his directives from the State Department, the diplomat wrote Hull to say that he would like to have his "chariot" loaded aboard. The Captain's reply was direct and to the point: "I am sorry that it will not be convenient to carry your carriage — we have not one inch of room below and it would be much in the way on deck and very much exposed to salt water and be injured by ropes." Underscoring this latter consideration, he further advised the Barlows to be prepared "for a 60 day passage."

Joel Barlow received his instructions from the State Department on 26 July and he and his suite (including wife, half-sister-in-law, nephew and the U.S. Consul General at Paris, David Bailie Warden) arrived on board *Constitution* on 1 August, whereupon Hull got underway. The Minister sent a final letter to his good friend Robert Fulton the next day from Hampton Roads, which provides a rare outsider's glimpse of life aboard a man of war:

> Here we are, 24 hours from Annapolis — a most delightful passage down the Chesapeake. We are just coming to anchor to give Captain Hull time to receive 100 men from the *Essex*, lying at Norfolk. I will go ashore and stay the night. My wife is in excellent spirits, the captain and all the officers very amiable, the most perfect harmony, discipline, cleanliness, and comfort prevails. Never was a fairer prospect of a good passage ...

The frigate took its departure for France on 5 August. The first days at sea were pleasant ones, during which time the passengers were able to acclimatize themselves somewhat to the alien environment. The ladies, of course, had everyone's attention. Moses Smith, a literate seaman who had signed on just before this voyage, recorded this picture of his rolypoly Captain and his fair guests:

> (Captain Hull was) full of animation ... He had not married and he took delight in showing his gallantry and respect for the ladies on board. He became quite a favorite with them, and appeared familiar with the requirements of polite intercourse, as with the command of our stately frigate. He devised various methods of amusing his gentle guests: and after all, it is not difficult for refined females to dwell upon the deep as would it first appear.

Moses, however, was overly optimistic about the ladies' easy adaptation to the sea, for barely a week out the ship was beset by a gale which lasted for three days

and drove the women out of sight for its duration. *Constitution,* he later wrote,
" ... appeared firm and fearless, like her commander, and it was evident to all
that she was a craft most thoroughly built and prepared to withstand any
disaster."

Consul General Warden noted in his diary for 9 August:

> I dined today with the officers of the Ward Room, with whom I am much pleased.
> The dinner was good ... It is not permitted to smoke a Segar except in the forecastle,
> or on deck near the prow.

One wonders if he found the meals as palatable later in the cruise when the
fresh stores were gone.

The passage, which remained rough after the gale, ended with *Constitution*'s
arrival in the English Channel on 1 September. On the 5th, as Hull was working
his way to Cherbourg, he encountered the blockading British squadron. He beat
to quarters, to be ready for any eventuality, and at 5:30 in the afternoon he
checked his way and spoke a British frigate, the apparent flagship of the
blockaders.

With the recent *President-Little Belt* episode in their minds, the Americans
were tense and expecting the worst. A lieutenant from the Englishman came
aboard with a message that the American Captain was to repair on board the
Britisher. Hull's response was to identify the character of his principal passenger
and indicate his intention to land Mr. Barlow at Cherbourg as directed by his
Government. He would take orders from no other source.

The lieutenant took Hull's message to his Commodore, and soon returned with
a demand that *Constitution* delay her entry into Cherbourg until a specific hour
the following day. Predictably, the American Captain replied that he would
enter as soon as the weather permitted. The British officer left and the tension
continued, but the calm remained unbroken.

*Constitution* anchored in Cherbourg harbor the next morning, having exchanged a salute of fifteen guns with the French batteries. Joel Barlow and his
suite were put ashore with full ceremony, the yards manned and a salute of seventeen guns. Later, when the French Admiral called upon Isaac Hull, a 9-gun
salute thundered out across the waters and was returned by *Courageux* (84).

## ON TO HOLLAND

Hull sailed from Cherbourg on 12 September for Texel to deliver the specie
payment. Adverse winds caused him to put into Deal, England, where he was
wind-bound for two days. When he finally cleared Deal for Texel, he got another
glimpse of the British naval effort against Napoleon: off Flushing, he passed thirteen Royal Navy ships of the line on blockade duty; the USN had *none* at that
time.

*Constitution* arrived off Texel early in the morning of 20 September, and
found there a British blockading squadron of seven ships of the line and a

number of smaller units. In the port could be seen several Dutch men of war flying French flags. On that busy morning, Hull sent a report of his mission to the British admiral in charge of the local blockade, sent Purser Isaac Garretson ashore to proceed to Amsterdam to coordinate delivery of the specie, and received from Den Helder a local pilot. He continued underway offshore throughout the day. The pilot confirmed what Hull had suspected: the frigate's draft of 23'6" was too deep to pass over the bar into Texel.

After a day of waiting, Hull received a letter from the Dutch agents that the French Intendant General and the Director of Douanes (Customs) would not permit the landing of the specie without authorization from Paris. That could take two weeks. Hull fired off three letters on the 21st — to our Consul at Den Helder, the agents in Amsterdam, and Purser Garretson — voicing his concern over the diplomatic complications such a delay could cause with the British blockaders, and stating that bad weather (not unlikely near the Channel at that time of year) could force him to abandon the area.

On the 22nd, Hull wrote to Sylvanus Bourne, Consul at Amsterdam, that "I have determined to leave the Coast immediately." The precise cause for this decision is not known. But Hull evidently had second thoughts about the matter, for after a week of offshore cruising he was once more at Texel. There, he found that authorization had been received from Paris to land the specie. The log for 29 September records:

> ... At Meridian two pilot boats came alongside for the purpose of taking the Money from the Ship ... At ¼ past 1 P.M. the Dutch Pilot boat left the Ship with the Money under charge of Lieut. Swift, — filled away and made sail.

## RETURN TO CHERBOURG

The American frigate returned to Deal, where Hull requisitioned winter clothing for his crew, their usual cold weather garb having proved inadequate for the Channel weather they were experiencing. There, on 3 October, a Judge Thompson of New York, bearer of official dispatches, and a Mr. James Jay came aboard for passage to Cherbourg, as requested by the local American Vice Consul, Edward Iggulden.

*Constitution* sailed for Cherbourg on the 8th, and shortly after midnight on the 9th, a ship was sighted off the weather bow. Without warning, the stranger "fired two Shott at us, one struck under the Quarter and the other under the Weather Beam." Hull cleared for action, then bore up and spoke the other ship. It proved to be *HMS Redpole,* a brig whose captain quickly sent an officer on board to "Apologize for firing at us." There had been no casualties. The brig soon cleared the area.

Off Cherbourg on 12 October, there was another incident. As Hull flew the appropriate signal for the French to allow him to enter port unmolested, one of the English blockaders sailed close aboard him in such a way as to obscure French observance of the flags. Apparently, the British were attempting to create an incident between France and the United States. The French batteries opened up on what appeared to them to be two enemy warships attacking the harbor. The true enemy ship turned away at the first shots, but Hull held steady. The log records:

> ... At ½ past 3 four shots were fired from the French batteries, 2 of which struck the ship, 1 passing through the Starbd. waist nettings, taking off the stern of 2nd cutter and through the lee clew of the main sail. The other struck in the bends just aft the fore chains."

When the British ship was clear, the French saw the prearranged signal and ceased fire.

Once anchored and the misunderstanding resolved, Hull learned that he would be required to wait an indefinite time for Mr. Barlow's dispatches. Thinking he might facilitate things, Hull paid a short visit to Paris, where he visited a number of the famous buildings in the French capitol and was very impressed. Mr. Jonathan Russell, Barlow's predecessor in Paris, accompanied the good captain on his return to Cherbourg.

## INCIDENT IN PORTSMOUTH

*Constitution* sailed for Portsmouth, England, the afternoon of 9 November. In addition to delivering Russell to his new post at the Americn embassy in London, Hull was returning Judge Thompson from his mission to France. Arriving on the 10th, the passengers were landed the next day. Hull went with them to London for a short visit, and his First Lieutenant, Charles Morris, was left in charge.

On the evening tide of 13 November, Seaman Thomas Holland slipped overboard from *Constitution,* perhaps under cover of a passing rain shower, with the intention to desert. At about 8:30, a boat from *HMS Havannah,* frigate, notified Lieutenant Morris that a man, too exhausted to say more than that he was from *Constitution,* had been taken aboard. Morris acknowledged the report and indicated the man would be reclaimed in the morning, presumably when he was somewhat recovered from his exertions.

An officer from *Constitution* appeared as indicated on the 14th to take custody of Holland, but was told that the sailor would not be returned without orders from the Flag Officer, Spithead, as the man had claimed protection as a British subject. Morris, upon hearing this, gained an interview with Admiral Sir Roger Curtis. The meeting was formal and correct, but the Admiral stood firm in protecting the man as an Englishman. He asked Morris if the Americans would return a deserter from one of His Majesty's ships, should such an event occur. The First Lieutenant responded with the belief that Captain Hull probably would accede to any mutually advantageous agreement.

Hull returned aboard on 18 November. His humor, already soured by the discovery that two members of his gig's crew had deserted ashore, was not improved one whit by Morris' report of the Holland affair. He immediately penned a letter to Sir Roger, reviewing the case as reported by his First Lieutenant, and making a formal demand for Holland's return. Curtis refused. It was the "Mediterranean game" all over again.

At this point, the incident took a new twist. That same night, Hull ordered additional Marine sentries posted to prevent further desertions. They were ordered to shoot anything seen floating near the ship.. Around midnight, two or three shots woke Hull, and there soon appeared on deck a dripping figure who told the Captain, "I am an American, your honor." John Burnes (some report him as William Wallace) was sent below for a tot of rum and a warm hammock. Then, as Lieutenant Morris later wrote in his biography:

> ... a boat was immediately sent to the *Havannah* to reciprocate the politeness of the preceding evening, and the next morning we had the satisfaction of assigning the same reason and the same testimony for refusing a demand for his restitution from the captain and admiral.

Soon, rumors abounded concerning punitive action by the British. Hull wrote to Minister Russell:

> ... At this moment it has been hinted to me that they should take him out to sea. I am now getting ready, and hope to be able to give them a fight for him, there can be no doubt but he is an American and belongs to New York, at any rate he is ready to make oath of it and that is more than they asked of the man they detained from me.

Hull sounded his crew out and found that they were ready to a man — even those in irons, whom he ordered released — to take on a British frigate.

Matters grew more tense when two British frigates shifted berths and anchored in close proximity to the American, so close that skilled seamanship would be required to get underway without fouling them. Isaac Hull, whose gunners already were overhauling their guns and "sending up Grape and Round Shott," displayed his skill by shifting his berth a mile closer to open waters smartly and without mishap. One of the British frigates followed.

The potential antagonists eyed each other all day on the 20th. That night, the battle lanterns were hung and lighted, and the ship essentially ready for action. Then, at 3:30 A.M. on 21 November:

> ... Have Short on the Larboard Cable, beat to Quarters and cleared away the Guns, got everything ready for Action. ¼ before 4 Hove up the Anchor, Made Sail and stood out into the Channell ...

The British frigate was soon underway, accompanying *Constitution*. She maintained a respectful distance, however, and once it was clear the American frigate had no belligerent intention, she returned to port. *Constitution* arrived in Cherbourg once more on 22 November and remained there into the new year.

## CHERBOURG, THEN HOME

Three hours after her arrival, First Lieutenant Morris was on his way to Paris to wait upon Minister Barlow and bring his Washington dispatches back to the ship. He remained in the French capitol for six weeks, where he saw Napoleon, and met the aging Lafayette, Tadeusz Kosciuzko, and others remembered for their roles in the American Revolution.

At Cherbourg, the Americans witnessed the ceremonies attendant upon Napoleon's coronation as Emperor on 1 December when "The French, Ships Dressed and fired a 21 Guns ..." Later that month the French, who had been most impressed by *Constitution,* were allowed "to take her dimension ..."

The long wait, with the boredom, the bad weather, and the desire to be homeward bound, was typically difficult for the crew. Acting Carpenter Lewis Crofford died on 14 December and was buried ashore the next morning. Seamen Daniel Bliss and William Cooper were flogged on the 19th for "smuggling rum on board." Midshipman William E. Pearpoint and Boy Abraham Harding both died the next day and were taken ashore on the 21st. The dolorous mission was performed again on the 27th, in falling snow, for James Lornson.

Lieutenant Morris returned on 6 January 1812 and Hull sailed for home on the 9th. On this voyage, he carried some fifty out-of-work American merchant seamen home who had been burdening the local consulates. And in the hold were cases of china being sent to Baltimore by Mrs. Jerome Bonaparte, the former Elizabeth Patterson of that city, and now sister-in-law to the Emperor.

Two hours out, two ships were sighted making for *Constitution.* Hull, as was his custom, cleared for action. *HMS Hotspur,* frigate, was permitted to send an emissary on board. After the merest formalities, the boat left and the ships parted company. The final (peaceful) encounter with the British occurred on the 15th, when Hull spoke *HMS Mars* (74) and passed on. The stormy passage ended at anchor in Chesapeake Bay off Old Point Comfort on 18 February. Hull shifted to an anchorage nearer to Norfolk the next day. A 17-gun salute was fired on the 22nd in memory of George Washington.

## PREPARATIONS FOR WAR

Upon going ashore, Captain Hull soon realized that the temper of the Government was moving toward war. That, coupled with his recent experiences with the Royal Navy, brought home to him the need to be prepared soon, and the importance of taking full advantage of *Constitution*'s scheduled yard overhaul. His orders to Lieutenant Morris were to begin overhauling rigging, recaulking the hull, washing the ballast, and cleaning out the hold — all this at a time when many of the crew were being paid off and officers were taking leaves of absence.

At 4 A.M. on 25 March, *Constitution* got underway for the nation's capitol. Entering the Potomac two days later, she paused for several days to offload a number of her guns, carriages, and shot into an attendant gunboat to reduce her draft for the passage upriver. Underway again on 2 April, she paused once more off Quantico the next day for further offloading, and on the 4th off Fort Washington, where Hull left the ship and went on ahead. Despite lightening efforts, the big frigate grounded on the bar near Alexandria for 4½ hours before finally being warped to a wharf at the Washington Navy Yard at 2 P.M. on the 5th.

Commodore Rodgers had been totally dissatisfied with *Constitution*'s sailing abilities, as was noted earlier. Isaac Hull, upon assuming command, had discovered at least a part of the problem and had done what he could to alleviate it. He knew heaving down and at least bottom cleaning were required, if not an entire recoppering of the underwater body, and he had secured permission to do so. Other areas to be attended to in solving the problem were her rigging and ballasting. With many critical matters to be corrected, it was a happy circumstance that the officer assigned by the Yard to assist Captain Hull was none other than "Jumping Billy" Haraden, who had served in her under Talbot and Preble, and had hove her down before.

Little time was lost in getting the overhaul underway. The first order of business was to clear the ship of stores and equippage. On Monday, the 7th, the magazines were emptied and the water casks unloaded — this despite the fact that the Secretary of the Navy paid a 3-hour visit to the ship, complete with 17-gun salute and attendant protocol. He was back again the next day for another two hours, but still the remaining long guns were landed after he left. Wednesday found the hard-working crew laboriously removing the shingle ballast; then the rest of the week was occupied with stripping the masts. It snowed on Sunday, the 13th, which, coming as it did on the crew's "day of rest," must have done nothing for morale.

As the unrigging resumed on the 14th, carpenters came aboard and began "ripping up planking adjoining the (water)ways": *Constitution* would have new decking. "Time out" was taken on Tuesday: "At 4 P.M. removed the Ship's Company on board the *Gen Greene*, Rec(eivin)g Ship."

Overhauling all the rigging in a loft ashore began with the yard period's third week. Back at the ship, preparations were begun on the 23rd to heave her down. All the spars and upper masts, and fighting tops, had been landed. Gun ports were hammered and caulked shut. Everything loose was put ashore. Lower masts were rigged to take the tremendous stresses of physically pulling the ship over on her side. The hard work and lure of the beach caused another six of the crew to desert.

The evening muster on 2 May disclosed the absence of one Thomas Musto, boatswain's mate. He had been acting peculiarly for at least two days, and it was thought he might have committed suicide by jumping overboard. Musto's body was found floating alongside *Constitution* on the 10th; the inquest decided it was, indeed, suicide due to insanity.

Earlier on the 2nd had begun the process of heaving the heavy frigate down for inspection, first to port and then to starboard. A journal entry reports they found her "bottom better than was Expected." She was hove down "keel out" to port on the 5th and necessary patching done along her very centerline. Early the next morning she was allowed to right the "2nd course" while the remaining copper patching was accomplished on the starboard side. She was righted on the 8th, turned end-for-end ("winded"), and hove down to starboard for the rest of the job. At day's end on the 12th, they were finished; unrigging the heavy tackle required all the next day.

The gathering war clouds continued to give impetus to the work. The foremast was unshipped on 14 May and the bowsprit on the 16th; both were condemned as unfit for further service. New spars began coming back aboard on the 22nd, the new foremast was stepped on the 25th, the main top emplaced the next day and the foretop on 28 May. When all done, *Constitution* would be newly rigged with sky poles (as was Hull's previous command). She would carry more and higher canvas than ever before. And what many today consider to be her "trademark" — the "split" dolphin striker — was installed. Nathaniel Haraden gave his special attention to the ship's ballast, reducing it by a third.

The month of May had seen more than forty new hands and a number of midshipmen join the ship. Offsetting these gains, Seamen John Jeffries and Patrick McDonald died, and William Coombs, Peter Jones, William Weri (?), James Barret, and William Kinney deserted. For Kinney, it was a second try: he had been caught and flogged for an attempt in March.

Early June found the remaining yards being swayed up and installed, while below stores, water casks, and guns — all in limited quantities — were brought aboard. On the 7th, all spars were in place; on the 8th, "got 3d cutter, green boat, and gig" from the boat shed; and on the 9th, at the end of the afternoon watch, the crew returned from *General Greene.*

Wednesday, 10 June, found *Constitution* underway in tow at 8 A.M. She was towed to a position off Greenleaf Point, where she remained at anchor until hove over the bar at eleven the next morning. Anchored once more off Alexandria, she spent the next week taking on stores and water, and having her new gun deck capstan installed. Secretary Hamilton visited her once more on the 13th, but conditions permitted the firing of but fifteen guns in salute. Thus, as the war in which she was to win undying fame was about to break out, the frigate was newly rigged and trimmed, and freshly cleaned; but her gun batteries were wanting and her crew far from complete.

Her Commanding Officer, Captain Isaac Hull, would be equal to the task.

# 6 The Great Chase

## WAR COMES

The seeds of the War of 1812 lay in the American Revolution. Incited by taxation without representation, the Americans had risen up and, with the very great help of monarchical France, had gained their independence from King George III by the Treaty of Paris in 1783. About a decade after that event — and inspired by it — a revolution of "liberté, egalité, fraternité" swept France and ultimately brought Napoleon Bonaparte to power, still trumpeting republican slogans.

The course of events in France inevitably came into collision with England, setting off two decades of almost constant warfare involving most of the principal powers in the world. England, often badly outnumbered in these conflicts, resorted to every gambit her command of the seas afforded her to sustain herself, including commerce control and blockade and, to maintain her ships, the impressment of nominal Englishmen wherever found. These policies necessarily collided with and jeopardized American maritime trade, involving as it did one of the largest merchant fleets in the world.

Repeated incidents over the years exacerbated relations between the two nations, especially since the American view was that they had revolted against these same Englishmen — this same King — to bring an end to such high-handed treatment. The diplomatic negotiations which occurred generally were ineptly conducted and emotionally charged. The English, faced with the realities of a continental war on a grand scale, were in a difficult position, wishing neither an additional enemy nor to appear weak. Public opinion in both countries was divided and disorganized. Even as events were afoot on the diplomatic scene to mollify the Americans, President James Madison sent a message to Congress on 1 June 1812 recounting the grievances — impressment of American seamen, violation of territorial waters, irregular blockades, "illegal" restrictions on neutral trade — and recommending resort to arms to gain redress. After two weeks of debate, the Congress made its decision in a close vote: war was declared on 18 June in the cause of "Free Trade and Sailors' Rights."

Until that very day, *Constitution* had been at Alexandria, Virginia, loading stores. Before the news had been received, she had been gotten underway by her senior officer present, Lieutenant George C. Read, for Annapolis, there to complete her manning. Her commander, Captain Isaac Hull, stayed behind in Washington for a few more days. The First Lieutenant, Charles Morris, likewise was absent from the ship and remained on leave for another week. Thus, it was Lieutenant Read who received, shortly before midnight on the 18th, from the midshipman in charge of the 5th cutter, which had remained behind in Washington for such "last minute" dispatches, this letter from the Secretary of the Navy:

Navy Department
June 18th 1812

Sir,

    This day war has been declared between the United Empire of Great Britain and Ireland and their dependencies and the United States of America and their territories and you are with the force under your command entitled to every belligerent right to attack and capture, and to defend — you will on the utmost dispatch to reach New York after you have made up your compliment of men at Annapolis.- In your way from there you will not fail to notice the British flag should it present itself.- I am informed that the *Belvidera* is on our coast, but you are not to understand me as impelling you to battle, previously to your bearing confidence in your crew unless attacked, or with a reasonable prospect of success, of which you are to be at your discression to judge — you are to reply to this letter and inform me of your progress.

Respectfully yours
Paul Hamilton

Capt Hull
    US Frigate Constitution

The letter is curiously cautious and timid for one announcing the outbreak of war, and reflects the attitude then prevailing among many in high government positions that preserving the small Navy as a "fleet in being" was more important to the successful prosecution of the war than fighting. It was a position that naval officers themselves fought and, to the everlasting glory of the Service, got changed.

At 5 P.M. on 19 June, Lieutenant Read mustered the crew at quarters and read them the declaration of war. In response, the crew requested permission to give three cheers. It was granted. *Constitution* subsequently arrived at Annapolis on the 27th, after pausing off Thomas Creek to backload ammunition and take on her new battery of 32-pounder carronades.

Preparations for sea were pressed. Men were shipped daily and supplies arrived in a steady stream. Powder charges were prepared in thin sheet lead cylinders: about 650 for the carronades and nearly 600 for the long guns. Over 7000 musket and pistol cartridges were made, as well. Time was found for drilling the crew even as it was being assembled; Hull wasted not a moment. The Captain informed Secretary Hamilton that:

    ... The crew are as yet unacquainted with the ship of war, as many have but lately joined and have never been on an armed ship before ... We are doing all that we can to make them acquainted with their duty, and in a few days we shall have nothing to fear from any single-decked ship.

The Secretary wrote to Hull again on 3 July:

    ... If, on your way thither (to New York), you should fall in with an enemy's vessel, you will be guided in your proceeding by your own judgement, bearing in mind, however, that you are not, voluntarily, to encounter a force superior to your own. On your arrival at New York, you will report yourself to Commodore Rodgers. If he should not be in that port, you will remain there till further orders.

These orders further emphasized the "fleet in being" mentality then prevailing at the highest level of the Navy Department. The thought that refusing to fight was condoned must have been repugnant to the likes of Hull, who had "learned the trade" in the close-in work of the Barbary War under Preble. The directive to join Rodgers in New York is questionable, as well, since that officer had sailed his squadron from there on 22 June, and ten days was a more than sufficient period for the report of his departure to reach Washington.

On the 4th, at high noon, a 15-gun salute was fired by *Constitution* in honor of the nation's 36th birthday. Hull sailed from Annapolis on Sunday, 5 July, and eased his way down Chesapeake Bay constantly training his crew (exercised at quarters nine times in seven days) and continuing to gather supplies along the way. He cleared the Virginia Capes and stood northward on the 12th.

## UNFORTUNATE RENDEZVOUS

On the same day *Constitution* departed Annapolis, a British squadron under Captain Sir Philip Bowes Vere Broke, consisting of frigate *Shannon* (flagship, 38), liner *Africa* (64), and frigates *Belvidera* (36) and *Aeolus* (32), sailed from Halifax to intercept Rodgers' squadron, notice of whose sailing had been brought to Vice Admiral Herbert Sawyer at Halifax by *Belvidera*. Four days later, off Nantucket, the squadron was augmented by the addition of the frigate *Guerriere* (38), diverted from a planned repair period in Halifax. The squadron arrived off New York on the 14th.

As Hull later reported:

> ... For several days after we got out the wind was light and ahead which with a strong Southerly current prevented our making much way to the Northward.

On the 15th, he caused one of the carronades to be proof fired five times with double charges and double shot and "Found them to stand very well."

> ... On the 16th, at 2 P.M. being in 22 fathoms water off Egg harbor four sail of Ships were discovered from the Mast-Head to the Northward and in shore of us; apparently Ships of War. The wind being very light all sail was made in chase of them, to ascertain whether they were Enemy's Ships, or our Squadron having got out of New York waiting the arrival of the *Constitution*, the latter of which, I had reason to believe was the case ...

for, as Hull well knew, to have closed on what was believed to be an enemy force was directly contrary to his orders.

> ... At 4 in the afternoon a Ship was seen from the Mast-head bearing about NE. Standing for us under all sail, which she continued to do until Sunset at which time she was too far off to distinguish signals and the Ships in Shore, only to be seen from the

Tops, they were standing off to the Southward and Eastward. As we could not ascertain before dark what the Ship in the offing was, I determined to stand for him and get near enough to make the night signal ...

Ever prudent, Captain Hull beat to quarters and cleared the ship for action at 7:30. With the continuing light airs, the ships closed one another at a crawl as suspense began to mount. At ten, staysails were hauled down and the spanker up. Shortly thereafter, with the lone ship six or eight miles distant, Hull made the private signal of the day. This, he:

...kept up nearly one hour, but finding she would not answer it, I concluded she and the Ships in shore were Enemy. I immediately hauled off to the Southward and Eastward, and made all sail having determined to lay off till day light, to see what they were. The Ship that we had been chasing hauled off after us showing a light, and occasionally making Signals, supposed to be for the Ships in shore.

The chase was on. It was about 11 P.M.

## THE CHASE - DAY 1

Throughout the midwatch of 17 July, *Guerriere*, the solitary pursuer, closed until she was within gunshot to leeward, i.e., to seaward, the miniscule wind during the watch having shifted to the south and west. Approaching four, *Guerriere* launched a signal rocket and fired two guns, and then hauled off to a position northward of the *Constitution.* The signal was intended to inform the others that Captain Dacres was satisfied he had fallen in with an American, but the absence of a response from those he believed to be his squadron mates caused him some confusion and led to his drawing off until the approaching dawn could clarify the situation. Could it be that Commodore Rodgers' squadron somehow had turned up to the westward, trapping him between two *American* forces?

The picture became all too clear with the rising sun. Hull later wrote:

... At day light, or a little before it was quite light, saw two sail under our Lee, which proved to be Frigates of the Enemies (*Belvidera* and *Aeolus*). One Frigate astern within about five or six miles (*Guerriere*), and a Line of Battle Ship, A Frigate, a Brig, and Schooner, about ten or twelve miles directly astern all in chase of us it being nearly calm where we were. Soon after Sunrise the wind entirely left us, and the Ship would not steer it fell round off with her head towards the two Ships under our lee...

What a position to be in: the wind failed and even steerageway lost. In sailor's parlance, the ship was "not under command" — and an overwhelming enemy force still having the wind was closing in. Hull took the most obvious action:

... At ¼ past 5 A.M., it being light and the ship having no steerageway, hoisted out the 1st cutter and out the 2nd ahead to tow ship. Headwind to the Southward. Got a 24 pounder up off the gundeck for a stern gun and the forecastle gun aft, cut away the taffrail to give them room and run two guns out the cabin windows. At 6 A.M. got the ship head round to the Southward and set the top gallant studding sails one of the frigates firing at us (*Shannon*)...

105

*The Great Chase off New Jersey, July 1812.*

This last circumstance only added emphasis to the desperation of the moment. Because she lacked stern ports at the spar deck level, a portion of the stern bulwark had to be cut away so that more guns could fire aft (the space of the Captain's cabin, already routinely dismantled when the ship beat to quarters, was occupied by two 24-pounders run aft through the cabin windows from their normal broadside positions). In addition, the hefty Number 1 (Port) 24-pounder (6300 pounds on carriage) had to be swayed up from the gun deck amidst all the other activity for use at one of the "make do" stern ports because Hull had shipped only one carriage chase gun; all the carronades were mounted on beds that could not be trundled aft along the deck.

It was a half hour before any of the pursuers realized what Hull was doing with his boats, but by the time he had *Constitution* swung southward again Captain Byron of *Belvidera* had boats in the water preparing to tow.

At 6:30, a sounding of twenty-one fathoms was reported routinely to the officers on *Constitution*'s quarterdeck. The situation looked grim. With a wind, there was every possibility that the American frigate could elude her pursuers, or at least outdistance enough of them to improve the odds against her. In the present situation, even though all were equally dependent upon the wind, the greater number of enemy units, with more men and more boats, held most of the trump cards. It was in this period of desperation that Hull's next junior, "that

valuable officer" Lieutenant Morris, his mind jiggled by the leadsman's cry, suggested the possibility of kedging ship. Hull, ready to try anything, instantly saw
the possibilities and ordered it done. The launch and the first cutter were assigned.

"Kedging" involves using long boats to carry a kedge anchor ahead of the ship,
dropping it, and then, by means of the ship's anchor capstan, hauling the ship up
to a position over the anchor. While this is being done, a second anchor is taken
out and dropped, to repeat the process as the original anchor is weighed and
again taken forward by a ship's boat. By stages, a sailing ship could be moved in
a given direction despite adverse winds or currents, or in the absence of a wind,
when the water was sufficiently shallow. It was a procedure more commonly used
in harbor or other confined area.

By seven o'clock, the first kedge anchor was out and the laborious process
started. A cutter would come under the bow and secure the kedge to a belly strap
rigged beneath the boat amidships. Then the oarsmen would bend to their oars
and begin the slow crawl ahead, bearing not only the 4-700 pounds of the
anchor, but an increasing burden of anchor cable twenty-two inches in cir-
cumference. Toiling across the oily swells as the sun rose in the sky (fortunately
cloudy) and the summer temperature climbed apace, they finally came to the
end of the tether and cut the anchor free. Then back it was to the ship's bows,
passing other shipmates taking out the second anchor, to begin the next cycle.

These efforts notwithstanding, the Americans continued to lose ground. At
7:30, Hull hoisted his colors and personally tried a shot at his closest pursuer. It
fell "a little short."

Hull wrote:

> ... At 8 four of the Enemy's Ships nearly within Gun Shot, some of them having six
> or eight boats ahead towing, with all their oars and Sweeps out to row them up with us,
> which they were fast doing. It now appears that we must be taken and that our Escape
> was impossible, four heavy ships nearly within Gun Shot, and coming up fast, and not
> the least hope of a breeze to give us a chance of getting off by out sailing them...

The stress of the moment comes through clearly in these sentences, for Hull
repeats himself on the subject of how close the British were, even in the calm of
his cabin four days after the event.

The British answer to kedging was to concentrate all their boats on the two
closest pursuers, with the result that they again gained on their quarry. At nine:

> ... the Ship nearest us (*Belvidera*) began firing his bow guns, which we instantly
> returned by our stern guns in the cabbin and on the Quarter Deck; All the Shot from
> the Enemy fell short, but we have reason to believe that some of ours went on board
> her, as we could not see them strike the water (only one did, the others went over).
> Soon after 9 a second Frigate (*Guerriere*) passed under our lee, and opened her Broad-
> side, but finding her shot fall short, discontinued her fire, but continued as did all the
> rest of them to make every possible exertion to get up with us...

Shortly thereafter, with the coming of a light breeze, two boats were got in.

*A Most Fortunate Ship*

Through the forenoon watch the contest continued, neither side gaining an advantage. At four bells, Hull ordered drinking water to be pumped overboard in order to lighten ship. More than 2300 gallons were discharged — enough to bring the frigate up about one inch. By this time, the British had concentrated all their boats on moving one frigate, *Shannon. Constitution* held her narrow margin of safety, thanks to the superb efforts of all hands, be they in the boats, manning the capstan, handling sails, or at the guns. By eleven, the breeze was sufficiently great that the big frigate overtook her boats and brought them smartly aboard without any loss of speed.

As the new watch began, the enemy units were ranged inshore of *Constitution,* from a starboard beam to quarter. With the breeze dying again, the first and green cutters were put over to tow once more. Gunfire was exchanged at about two, without apparent result. The hours went by in relentless succession, each side straining for advantage: at 3:30, one of the enemy got dangerously close and then the gap widened again; at 7 P.M., all eight of *Constitution*'s boats were straining at tow lines. Men not actively engaged dropped and napped where they could, as if on some sort of diabolical treadmill, only to rouse out again at the next call of the pipe. It was a performance worthy of a seasoned crew, and exceptional for one so green. Isaac Hull's leadership must have been exemplary.

## THE CHASE - DAY 2

The start of the second day of the chase — 11 P.M. — was marked by the springing up of a welcome breeze; "... boats came alongside, hoisted up the gig and green cutter, and set the fore topmast staysail and main top-gallant studding sail." She was moving on her own, and well. Relief from the physical stress was welcomed, but the tension of the chase remained. Advantage was sought from every breath of air. Thus passed the night.

At dawn on the 18th, Fortune was seen to be smiling on the American frigate. The night-long exertions had gained for her a 2-3 mile lead on her pursuers. Although the breezes remained light, Hull determined to make a break for it, and tacked eastward early in the morning watch. At 5 A.M., he passed close to *HMS Aeolus* without drawing fire, apparently because Captain Townsend feared the concussion of his guns would becalm the Britisher and cost him his close-in position. Instead, he tacked and stood after Hull, the others following suit.

At nine, there was much activity in *Constitution*. The log:

> ... fitted and set Fore and Main skysails saw a ship to windward, supposed to be an American Merchantman standing toward us, the frigates astern hoisted American colors as a decoy, we immediately hoisted English colors, got Royal studding sails and mounts fitted, and shifted the starboard foretopmast studding sail boom which was sprung.

A full dimension of activity as anyone could expect, and with a crew that had been taxed for thirty-four hours, and yet they were setting sail, affecting repairs, seeking to protect a countryman, and trying to elude the enemy — all at once.

Yet the worst was over, and they must have sensed it. By noon, the situation was beginning to be comfortable. The British had not given up, but it was clear that *Constitution* was outsailing them as she headed east-southeast. Dead astern at 3½ miles was *Belvidera, Shannon* was on the port quarter at 4-5 miles, and *Africa* could be seen between the two, back on the horizon. Out abaft the port beam at about five miles were *Aeolus* and *Guerriere*. If they could do nothing else, they could prevent *Constitution* from getting to New York.

The gap continued to widen as the afternoon wore on. At four, the closest pursuer was six miles off and still dropping astern. Hull continued to set and reset sails to gain every advantage. Carefully, he watched wind and sea for clues as to what to expect, minute by minute. This sensitivity and alertness paid him a big dividend when, at about 6:30, he saw a squall ahead. Taking in first his studdingsails and royals, he had his men ready as it came down upon him. Quickly, the skysails, topgallant sails, and flying jib were taken in, and the mizzen topsail and spanker reefed. And just as quickly, as soon as the squall cleared the ship, and obscured him to the British, Hull set topgallants and the main topmast staysail. He was off and running. In another fifteen minutes, she was drawing everything but skysails (which yards were sent down to the tops). For the next hour, the Americans were busy setting all studdingsails. At 10:30, they heard two guns fired from unseen British pursuers on the port quarter. At eleven, as the second full day of the chase ended, only one enemy could be made out, dead astern in *Constitution*'s wake.

## THE CHASE - DAY 3

The Americans were breathing much easier, but continued to seek every advantage, witness the log:

> ... At midnight moderate breeze and pleasant took in the Royal Studding sails ... At 1 A.M. set the skysails. At ½ before 2 A.M. got a pull of the weather brace and set the lower steering (sic, studding) sail. At 3 A.M. set the main topmast studding sail. At ¼ past 4 A.M. hauled up to SE by S.

First light on the 19th showed four pursuers still in sight, but all hull down, the nearest about twelve miles distant. It was Sunday, but Isaac Hull was not ready for a day of rest. He wanted to sail his enemy out of sight, and so,

> ... All hands were set at work wetting the Sails, from the Royals down, with the (Fire) Engine, and Fire buckets, and we soon found that we left the Enemy very fast. At ¼ past 8 the Enemy finding that they were fast dropping astern, gave over the chase, and hauled their wind to the Northward, probably for the station at New York.

Isaac Hull and his crew, who had been together at sea for just five days, had outsailed a numerically superior British squadron in a 57-hour demonstration of endurance, teamwork, and skilled seamanship. It would not be the last time that this combination would embarrass their English cousins.

Constitution *escapes the British squadron, July 1812.*

## HOME SAFE

Two American merchantmen were spoke later that morning, and the 24-pounder at the taffrail was returned below to its normal position. Then Hull, who had been on deck continuously throughout the chase, and his officers and crew stood down as they headed for Boston. On the 20th, life returned to normal. Seaman Henry Gales died and was buried at sea, cause of death not recorded. The next day, Hull penned his report of the affair to Secretary Hamilton as the ship crossed the latitude of Nantucket.

*Constitution* arrived in President Roads off Boston on the morning of 27 July 1812, three weeks after clearing the Virginia Capes. Hull was anxious to replenish his supplies, particularly the water he had pumped overboard, and learn the latest orders from Washington. Dispatches had been sent ashore even before the ship reached the Roads, to alert the local Naval Agent of her unexpected arrival and getting his report to Washington. The frigate's arrival also quashed rumors that had been bruited about for three days that she had been ordered to sea with her magazines empty, a chicken ripe for plucking. As the Monday (27 July) issue of the Boston *Gazette* put it:

> ... We feel additional pleasure in stating the safety of this vessel, as it puts to rest the thousand rumors which have been in circulation respecting her ... she is completely provided with every necessary munition of war, and has a full crew of brave and gallant seamen!

The final observation would be confirmed in full measure just three weeks later.

# 7 "The Americans Were Our Masters"

## PREPARATIONS

When Isaac Hull brought *Constitution* into Nantasket Roads on Sunday, 26 July 1812, he had no intention of remaining long in port. He had come in for water, men, and news, and having satisfied those needs, he intended to be to sea again where he couldn't be trapped by the British squadron he had so narrowly eluded a week earlier. Unbeknownst to Hull, that squadron had dispersed immediately after losing him, and only one frigate had taken up a station off an American port — New York.

The pilot came aboard at 11 that morning, his boat returning to the city with Hull's dispatches to New York for Commodore John Rodgers and to Washington for the Secretary of the Navy, together with Purser Thomas J. Chew, who would arrange for stores, and Acting Sixth Lieutenant Charles W. Morgan, who would begin recruiting more sailors.

Mr. Chew's mission was not an easy one, for his ship was not expected at Boston and no funds had been sent from Washington to the resident Naval Agent, Colonel Amos Binney, to pay for her needs. If that were not problem enough, the declaration of war had been unpopular in New England, and in Boston in particular. And while the local merchants were not averse to making a profit, they weren't eager to grant a line of credit to the Government.

Happily, William Gray, merchant, was a maverick. Only two years in business in Boston from his native Salem, Gray regularly had supported many Federal Government decisions that generally were unpopular among his peers. He was said to be worth three million dollars and to own more ships than even Elias Haskett Derby, another Salemite. It was William Gray, then, who quietly extended a line of credit to Colonel Binney so that Purser Chew could fill his Captain's requisitions.

On Monday morning, using the first, second, and third cutters, Hull moved *Constitution* into President Roads, bringing her to anchor "just below the Fort" (Fort Independence on Castle Island). The frigate *Chesapeake* (36) repairing at the Navy Yard, and two Jeffersonian gunboats, composed the remaining naval force in the city. *Gunboat No. 81* was used to help transport men and supplies to the frigate.

Beginning at 4 A.M. Tuesday morning, the gunboat, schooners, and lighters arrived alongside in an unceasing cycle: "At ½ past 9 A.M. the lighter left the Ship"; "At Meridian ... A schooner came alongside," as did another lighter; "Recvd from the schooner a quantity of Boats'ns stores ..."

Wednesday: "4 A.M. ... Sent a gang on shore to work at a splinter netting;"

"At 7 A.M. a Schooner came alongside with provisions." During the morning, fog and rain set in. "At ½ past 7 P.M. a load of water for the Ship."

The 30th of July had "foggy disagreeable weather," but still the work went on. During a lull in the replenishment operation, "At 6 P.M. beat to Quarters & exercised the guns." Captain Hull continued to stress the training of his crew as he had since the war had been declared six weeks earlier; at least four new seamen had been received that day.

*Constitution*'s arrival in Boston had been greeted with many expressions of relief that she had successfully eluded a pursuing British squadron, and with much approbation for the skill with which Hull had accomplished the feat. As loyal to his officers and men as they to him, he caused a notice to be published directing these accolades to his crew:

> Captain Hull, finding his friends in Boston are correctly informed of his situation when chased by the British squadron off New York, and that they are good enough to give him more credit by escaping them than he ought to claim, takes this opportunity of requesting them to make a transfer of a great part of their good wishes to Lt. Morris, and the other brave officers, and the crew under his command, for their very great exertions and prompt attention to orders while the enemy were in chase. Captain Hull has great pleasure in saying, that notwithstanding the length of the chase, and the officers and crew being deprived of sleep, and allowed but little refreshment during the time, not a murmur was heard to escape them.

Friday, the 31st, passed much as the 30th had: rainy, foggy, and unpleasant. In the evening, Hull once again exercised his crew. By Saturday, *Constitution* was reprovisioned and ready to sail. No orders had come from Washington yet, but Hull received a report from New York that Commodore Rodgers, to whom he was to report, was not present. He had also learned from that city that his younger brother, William, was critically ill there. Locally, the news was that the British frigate *Maidstone* (32) was lurking off Cape Cod and that two others were "in the bay." Being one of those naval officers who believed our few warships could accomplish more at sea than blockaded in port, Hull made the bold decision to sail without orders and almost certainly contrary to the orders he was likely to receive. At this moment, his chances of being a scapegoat were much greater than those of being a hero. Thus it was that at 5:30 A.M. on Sunday, 2 August, in clearing weather, Isaac Hull gave his fateful order to weigh anchor and get underway on a southwest-by-south wind. At 6:45 they passed the lighthouse, and between seven and 11:30 completed taking aboard the ship's boats and making last minute transfers to her tender, *Gunboat No. 81.* At 11:30, the frigate filled away to the northeast. Hull had decided to run down east to attack British shipping in the Halifax-Gulf of St. Lawrence area, with the possibility of proceeding toward Bermuda, the Bahamas, and the West Indies thereafter. He hoped to hit hard in one place and then move to another before superior British numbers could be brought together against him.

## SEARCH

Life aboard quickly settled down into wartime routine. At 1 P.M., Hull had his crew assembled for a reading of the Articles of War, so that everyone understood the rules of the business at hand. At 1:30, they spoke the first of many contacts, the ship *Sally* of Wiscasset, inbound from Ireland with passengers. Later in the afternoon, Hull exercised his crew at quarters; having been together but six weeks, there was much to learn if they were to be a battle-ready team.

Working slowly northeastward, Hull checked out every sail sighted and continued his training program. There was a flurry of excitement at three bells during the midwatch on 3 August, when all hands were shocked into wakefulness by the sound of "beat to quarters" and orders to clear for action. It was a false alarm, however, the lieutenant on watch having been confused by the light of the rising moon into thinking he was seeing signals. On the 5th, the frigate ran into thick fog patches which, alternating with periods of cloudiness or haziness, and oftentimes calms, characterized the next several days.

At noon on 10 August, in clear, pleasant weather, a sail was sighted to the northwest. Hull turned the third reef out of the maintopsail, set the fore and main topgallants, jib, and spanker, and set off after her. At five that afternoon, he fired a gun to bring the chase to, but it was ignored. At 6:15, Hull hoisted an English ensign and fired again, upon which the chase hoisted an English jack and came to. The fifth and green cutters were lowered from *Constitution*'s quarter and stern, and First Lieutenant Morris sent aboard. At seven, the green cutter returned with the information that the prize was the English brig *Lady Warren*, bound from St. John's, Newfoundland, to St. John's Island. She had been in convoy escorted by at least a frigate (*Jason*) and an armed brig, but had become separated from them in thick fog two days earlier. At 7:30, the other cutter returned with Lieutenant Morris, the merchant captain, his supercargo, mate, six crewmen, and their private property. Noted Surgeon Amos Evans:

> ... We set fire to the Brig in different places — and made sail to the NE. She continued to burn for several hours, and presented an appearance after dark awfully beautiful and grand. Such are the dreadful, concomitant evils of a state of war.

The *Lady Warren*'s captain informed Hull that Joshua Barney, an American privateersman, recently had taken several vessels off Newfoundland and had burned some fishing boats, as had the frigate *Essex* (32), under Captain David Porter. He also said that, in St. John's, it was thought that *Constitution* was with Commodore Rodgers' squadron off the English Channel.

After an uneventful and "uncomfortably cold" night, *Constitution* again went in chase at four bells of the forenoon watch. Shortly after noon, Hull sent a party aboard a brig, the English *Adonia* (or *Adiona*), bound from Shedia Harbor, New Brunswick, to Newcastle, England, with "Squar'd Pine Timber." Taking aboard her captain, mate, and nine crewmen and boys, Hull fired her at 2 P.M. and stood westward. Wrote Evans:

> ... At 4 o'clock P.M. her sails took fire and were consumed in a few minutes, directly after which her masts went overboard.

Shortly thereafter, Hull had his crew at gun drill again.

The 12th began with light airs and "thick hazey weather." At meridian, says Midshipman Baury's journal, "Read the Articles of War to our prisoners & gave them each a doz lash for insolence to the Officer of the Deck." The log says nothing of this, but instead records, "At 10 A.M. punished John W. Smith for drunkenness and John Smith the 3rd (i.e., the third person of that name to enter on the ship's rolls) for insolence to his officer on duty." Either way, there was no mistaking that the Captain meant business. Another gun drill ended the working day.

The next two days largely were uneventful except for the regular gun drills and two incidents which Surgeon Evans observed:

> ... Were alarmed about 9 o'clock with the cry of fire in the cockpit — Produced by one of the Surgeon's Mates having left a candle burning in his state room with the door locked. We found considerable difficulty in opening the door, in attempting to force which I had my right hand jammed with a crowbar; in consequence of which I am under the necessity of writing with my left. I have laboured under great pain all day, and am much afraid it will terminate in Tentanus. The cry of fire is dreadful on shore, but ten thousand times more distressing on board a powder ship at sea. It produced much confusion, but was instantly extinguished. The Surgeon's Mate, who is truly a worthy fellow was arrested for his negligence ... At 3 P.M. a sailor (John Lindsy) fell overboard out of the main chains. The topsail was instantly backed and the stern boat lower'd down. The man being (fortunately) an expert swimmer, kept on top of the water, and was pick'd up about 200 yards astern. He said he could have taken off his shoes, but did not wish to lose them! The blood however appeared to have forsaken his cheeks. The tenure of a sailor's existence is certainly more precarious than any other man's, a soldier's not excepted. Who would not be a sailor? I, for one.

August 15th dawned with pleasant weather and light winds. Five sail were seen off the starboard bow, to the southeast, and sail set in chase. By 5:30, it was apparent that one of the contacts was an English sloop of war: *Constitution* had come upon the fox in the chicken coop. The Englishman soon was seen to be in the act of firing a merchant brig. As the big American frigate came up, the Britisher headed first as if to board another of the merchantmen, a Dutch-built barque, but then hauled close to the wind and made all sail westward.

Hull set about determining the identities of the barque, schooner, and two brigs (one afire) he had rescued from the enemy. Sending a party to the barque, he found her to be the prize of the privateer *Dolphin* of Salem, which was the schooner to the southeast. The barque had been retaken by *HMS Avenger* the previous evening, but when *Constitution* appeared she had been left with but three Englishmen aboard. The two brigs were other prizes to *Avenger*. One, they had fired and abandoned, but the second attempted escape. Hull went after her and brought her to by 2 P.M.; she was the *Adelina* of Bath, Maine. A British midshipman and five sailors came aboard as prisoners. Midshipman John R. Madison and five American sailors took over, with orders to proceed to any U.S. port. By this time — about 3 P.M. — *Avenger* was out of sight and Cape Race could be seen forty miles to the northeast.

Interrogation of the prisoners gave Hull reason to believe that he soon would be in action again. According to the captive Englishmen, Royal Navy frigates *Belvidera, Guerriere, Shannon, Spartan, Pomona,* and *Aeolus* generally were in the area to defend against American depredations.

Sunday, the 16th, was rainy and foggy — and except for Hull's usual evening exercises, quiet. Most of Monday passed the same way, although there was momentary interest in the afternoon when what was thought to be a derelict proved to be a dead whale. After the evening gun drill, a sail was discovered ahead, despite "thick & hazey" weather. The chase continued until 11:15, when the brig shortened sail. She was the privateer *Decatur* (14), Captain Nichols and 100 men from Salem. Nichols had jettisoned all but two of his guns in attempting to outrun the big frigate. It was the culmination of a totally disastrous cruise: out just twelve days, the privateer had taken nothing, lost her foretopmast, and had been chased by a British man of war, reportedly *Guerriere*, the previous evening. Nichols told Hull that *HMS Africa* (64) and a war brig were known to be in the area. As for him, he had no intention of giving up: two six-pounders were enough to bring a merchant to heel. The two ships kept company through the night, then *Decatur* headed for Cape Race.

## CONTACT

Hull steered in a generally southwesterly direction throughout the 18th and 19th, occasionally encountering fog and rain, but experiencing fresh breezes from the north and west and cloudiness at noon of that fateful Wednesday. At 2 P.M., a sail was spied to the southward and *Constitution* went in chase. At three, it could be seen to be a full-rigged ship on a starboard tack. Thirty minutes later, Hull knew he had come upon a frigate.

At 4:45, the chase lay her maintopsail to the mast, a clear invitation to duel. But Isaac Hull was not one to rush into things. Though he had been training rigorously, he had a green, untried crew. Ahead, there lay a unit of the most powerful navy in the world — a navy that had been in continuing combat for twenty years. How good was his adversary? It was time to proceed carefully and size him up. He ordered the topgallant sails, stay sails, and flying jib taken in, the courses hauled up, a second reef taken in the topsails, and the royal yards sent down. Upon beating to quarters, his crew gave three cheers — no question about their attitude. According to Moses Smith, the legend *"Not The Little Belt"* could be seen painted on one of the enemy's topsails, a reference to the British war brig which had been shattered by *Constitution*'s half-sister *President* in a night encounter the year before the war broke out.

Ten minutes later, at 4:55, when about two miles separated the opposing frigates, the enemy hoisted three English ensigns and "discharged her Starboard Broadside at us without effect. She immediately wore round, and discharged her Larboard Broadside two shot of which hulled us and the remainder flying over and through our rigging, we then hoisted our Ensigns and Jack, at the Fore and Main Top Gallant Mastheads." The enemy frigate continued alternating broadsides as *Constitution* closed, Hull skillfully maneuvering so as to deny her the opportunity for a raking shot. A British ball struck abaft the larboard knighthead at one point, showering splinters without effect. The American crew fired it back. Another struck the foremast, cutting a fish hoop in two. The American crew, still evincing only an eagerness for combat, fired only when and as individual guns could be brought to bear as Hull continued to evaluate his adversary.

After 45 minutes of fruitless attempts at raking, the Englishman bore up with the wind "rather on his Lab'd Quarter," an invitation to close for a toe-to-toe slugfest that Isaac Hull readily accepted. His enemy was exhibiting a haughty confidence that Hull felt was unwarranted. Setting his maintopgallant sail, he surged in, his gun crews standing silent, readying for a full broadside. Another English ball came aboard, the concussion from which knocked Seaman Isaac Kingman down, but not out. Three times the crew requested permission to open fire, and each time were denied.

## SLUGFEST

Hull was where he wanted to be at 6:05. He hauled down his jib, laid the maintopsail shivering to the mast to slow down. Reportedly at his command, "Now boys, hull her!", the first broadside of round shot and grape crashed out at the Englishman. Blast followed blast. Isaac Hull is said to have split his breeches jumping up and down in the excitement, urging his men on. An average of about thirty rounds per minute was being fired by the Yankee gunners at a range of half a pistol shot. At 6:15, the Englishman's mizzenmast crashed over her starboard side; her main yard shot from its slings. "Huzza, boys! We've made a brig of her! Next time we'll make her a sloop!" The American crew gave three cheers and went on firing.

The return fire from the British frigate generally was high. *Constitution*'s fore royal truck was shot away, together with two halyards — one bearing one of the flags Hull had hoisted. Amidst the cannonade, Seaman Daniel Hogan climbed the rigging and made it fast to the topmast. British shot hitting the hull made little impression  Someone saw a ball hit, make a dent, then fall into the sea, and he cried out, "Huzzah! Her sides are made of iron!" And so was born the famed nickname "Old Ironsides."

The dragging wreckage slowed the Britisher and caused *Constitution* to pull ahead. Seeing this, Hull decided to cross her bow and rake her, "but our braces being shot away and Jib haulyards, we could not effect it." Two broadsides were

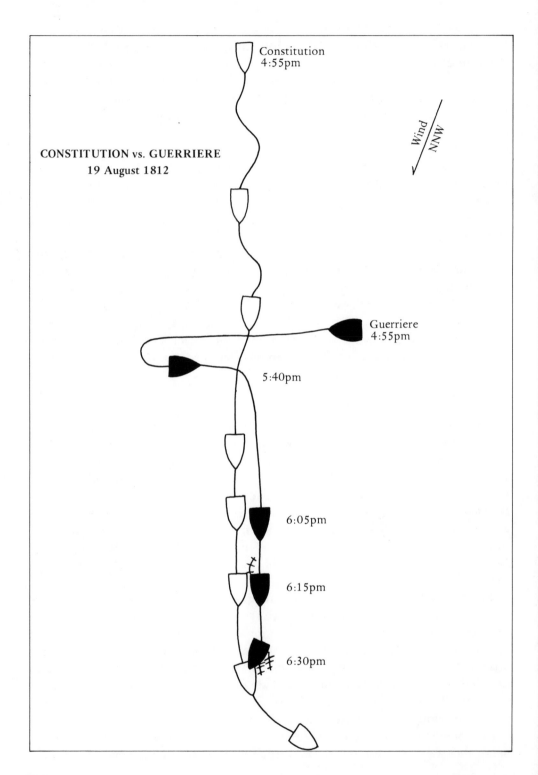

fired into the enemy's starboard bow, tearing a gaping hole. At this same time, the British captain, seeing that the overboard wreckage had come up under his stern in such a way as to cause him to turn to starboard (i.e., toward *Constitution*), put his rudder over to enhance the turn and thus cross behind the American and rake her from astern, where she was most vulnerable. Unfortunately for him, the resulting acceleration of his turn was premature, and he drove his bowsprit into *Constitution*'s larboard mizzen shrouds. The initial shock of the collision momentarily caused the two ships to be at nearly right angles to one another, but the American's headway soon caused the Englishman to swing to a position more nearly parallel to the course of advance. From this position but one of the British guns could bear. Its work killed two and wounded one on *Constitution*'s Number 15 gun, and began a small fire in Hull's cabin area, which quickly was put out.

Meanwhile, topside, both sides were ready to board or to repel boarders. First Lieutenant Charles Morris and Marine Lieutenant William S. Bush both leaped to the taffrail ahead of the boarding party. In the rattle of exchanged musketry, Bush was killed outright, shot in the face; Morris fell, "dangerously wounded" in the abdomen. On the British side, their Second Lieutenant was killed and the Captain, First Lieutenant, and Sailing Master wounded in various degrees. Before a second boarding attempt could be made, *Constitution*'s forward motion exerted sufficient force to pull the antagonists apart. The resultant whipping action in the Englishman's bowsprit was transmitted through the stays to a weakened foremast, which crashed down to starboard, its plunging weight causing the tottering, rotten mainmast to follow it. The time was just 6:30.

## VICTORY

Hull, seeing his enemy thus completely immobilized, stood eastward with fore and main courses and a reef in the topsails. The crew set busily to reeving new braces and halyards, and readying the ship to resume the action. When these immediate repairs were done, he returned to find the shattered Englishman had but the bedraggled remnants of the spritsail remaining. Unseen by Hull were the long guns on the enemy's gundeck that had been torn loose from their tackles and were running amok as the ship rolled deeply in the swells. The British Captain wisely fired a gun to leeward in token of submission as the Yankee frigate came up. Hull made the appropriate response — one gun — and this most decisive single ship engagement was over. Wrote Surgeon Evans:

> ... Our crew behaved very nobly. They fought like heroes, and gave three cheers when the colours were hoisted. They also cheered when each of her masts went over the side, and when her colours were struck.

Third Lieutenant George C. Read was sent to take possession of the vanquished. At 7:30, all the boats were hoisted out to bring prisoners aboard, to take aid to the wounded, and to pass a towing hawser. At eight, a boat returned to *Constitution* with the first of the prisoners. Principal among them was the

119

wounded Captain, James Richard Dacres, to surrender His British Majesty's Frigate *Guerriere.*

## THE LOSER

James Dacres came from a Navy family (his father had commanded *Carleton* in the Battle of Valcour Island against the Americans in 1776) and had entered the service at an early age, attaining the rank of Lieutenant in 1804. In 1805, he was posted to command of the sloop of war *Elk* and the following year to command the frigate *Bacchante* on the Jamaica Station. In this post, he served with distinction. He took command of *Guerriere* about April 1811, and allegedly shortly thereafter first met his conqueror socially. It is said that on that occasion the two Captains made a wager of a hat on the outcome of any future engagement between their commands. Hull reportedly refused Dacres' proffered sword when the battle was done, but said he would have a hat.

Dacres' ship, *Guerriere,* was French-built and had been rated by them at fifty guns. She had been taken by the British off Norway in 1806, and after a two-year refit was commissioned by them as "5th rate, large 38." On 19 August 1812, she was armed with thirty 18-pounders on the gundeck, fourteen 32-pounder carronades and one 12-pounder howitzer on her quarterdeck, and two 12-pounders and two 32-pounder carronades on the forecastle — forty-nine guns, in all. At the time of the engagement, she was due for refit at Halifax. Her hull was foul and there was rot in her masts.

## ASSESSMENT

*Constitution*'s battery at this time consisted of thirty 24-pounders on the gundeck, sixteen 32-pounder carronades on the quarterdeck, one 18-pounder and eight 32-pounder carronades on the forecastle — a total of fifty-five guns. She had completed a thorough refit only two months earlier.

The *Constitution-Guerriere* fight was a straight-forward, toe-to-toe battle between two adversaries each confident in his abilities. *Constitution* was the bigger, heavier, and because of her recent yard period, faster. But as this fight was a slugfest, this last advantage was not a factor. Indeed, with his green crew, Hull may have decided on the direct approach to minimize having to maneuver and fight simultaneously.

In terms of gun power, there was less disparity in the respective broadsides than the simple number of guns and calibers would indicate. The French-made shot used by *Guerriere* generally was somewhat heavier than its stated size — about eight percent, on the average. American shot, on the other hand, ran about seven percent light. Taking this into account, the resultant broadside weights were 581 pounds (British) and 692 pounds (American). But the greater result stemmed from the Americans' higher rate of fire (over 950 shot expended) and their lower aim; *Guerriere*'s wreckage topside was more visible but the damage below irreparable: about thirty American shot had hulled her below the

Guerriere *surrenders.*

waterline, according to Captain Dacres. By contrast, *Constitution*'s hull damage largely was limited to the mess created in the larboard portion of Hull's cabin when the two ships were entangled. Dacres' guns however, **had** done considerable damage to Hull's standing and running rigging. In addition to the shot away braces, which spoiled Hull's plan and very nearly caused him grief, both fore and main masts had been shot through, as was the heel of the foretopgallant mast; the larboard half of the crossjack had been cut away, and the band for the main slings had been broken. The collision had destroyed the gaff and spanker boom, as well. Finally, the Americans' lower point of aim made for the marked difference in personnel casualties: fifteen dead and sixty-three wounded Britishers; seven dead and the same number wounded in the American.

*Constitution* carried a much larger crew than did *Guerriere* — about 450 versus 275-300 (including 4-5 women) — which rendered the superb service of her guns possible. Moreover, as we have seen, Hull had trained his men daily in the handling and firing of their guns. The British, on the other hand, were handicapped by the fact that the interminable war with France had put such a premium on their powder supply as largely to preclude the use of powder merely for training purposes. The morale of the American crew, as well, was superior: even the Englishmen in it were willing to fight. The impressed Americans in *Guerriere*'s crew, on the other hand, protested having to do so, and Dacres

121

gallantly sent them below as noncombatants. Eight surviving crew members subsequently claimed political asylum when landed in Boston, and two signed aboard "Old Ironsides."

Before resuming our narrative, at this point it seems proper to ponder the effect of Fortune in this affair. What would have been the outcome if Dacres had not misjudged his rate of turn and had succeeded in raking *Constitution* from astern? Might he not have downed one or both of the masts already damaged? Might not have *Constitution*'s steering gear been destroyed? And might not Hull then have been in the position, in a largely immobilized ship, of making the difficult decision as to whether or not more blood gainfully could be shed? John Paul Jones abandoned his sinking *Bon Homme Richard* for the newly surrendered *Serapis* in 1779. James Dacres might have stepped from a dying *Guerriere* to *Constitution* if Fortune had been his that day in 1812. The British Captain himself was sensitive to this for he stated subsequently:

> ... I am so aware that the success of my opponent was owing to fortune, that it is my earnest wish, and it would be the happiest period of my life, to be once more opposed to the *Constitution* ... in a frigate of similar force to the *Guerriere*, (with the same crew).

## GUERRIERE'S END

For three hours, the Americans attempted to take their prize in tow. By 11 P.M., however, it was evident that the differing drift rates of the two ships and the difficulties of working in darkness made it an almost impossible task. The hawser was cast off. Hull kept *Constitution* "at a convenient distance" from *Guerriere* through the night, while Lieutenant Read and his prize crew struggled to keep her afloat. In the American frigate, repairs were begun. Both Surgeons, Evans and Irwin (of *Guerriere*), worked to save the wounded. Evans himself did four amputations, so his injured hand had recovered.

At seven on the morning of the 20th, *Constitution*'s foretopgallant yard and the damaged foretopgallant mast were sent down, and a new mast stepped. Elsewhere, the carpenters were preparing fishes for the damaged fore and main masts. As the foretopgallant yard was being sent up at 7:30, Lieutenant Read hailed from *Guerriere* that she had five feet of water in the hold and it was gaining on them. Hull decided to withdraw his prize crew and the remaining prisoners, and destroy the hulk. By 1:30 P.M., everyone was off except for Read and his demolition party. They left for *Constitution* at three.

Moses Smith has described *Guerriere*'s last moments:

> There was something melancholy and grand in the sight. Although the frigate was a wreck, floating about a mastless hulk for the sport of the waves, she bore marks of her former greatness. Much of her ornamental work had been untouched; and her long, high, black sides rose in solitary majesty before us, as we bade her farewell ... her years were now ended; her course was run; she was about to sink into the deep ocean forever.
>
> Captain Dacres stood by our taffrail as we squared away from the *Guerriere* ...
>
> At the distance of about three miles we hove to and awaited the result. Hundreds of

Guerriere *blows up.*

eyes were stretched in that one direction, where the ill-fated *Guerriere* moved heavily on the deep. It was like waiting for the uncapping of a volcano — or the bursting up of a crater. Scarcely a word was spoken on board the *Constitution,* so breathless was the interest felt in the scene.

The first intimation we had that the fire was at work was the discharge of the guns. One after another, as the flame advanced, they came booming toward us. Roar followed roar, flash followed flash, until the whole mass was enveloped in clouds of smoke. We could see but little of the direct progress of the work, and therefore we looked more earnestly for the explosion — not knowing how soon it might occur. Presently there was a dead silence; then followed a vibratory, shuddering motion, and streams of light, like streaks of lightning running along the sides; and the grand crash came! The quarter deck, which was immediately over the magazine, lifted in a mass, broke into fragments, and flew in every direction. The hull, parted in the center by the shock, and loaded with such masses of iron and spars, reeled, staggered, plunged forward a few feet, and sank out of sight.

It was a grand and awful scene. Nearly every floating thing around her went down with the *Guerriere* ... We immediately squared away, and were again under a crowd of sail for our native land.

It was 3:15 P.M., 20 August, and Isaac Hull was eager to broadcast news of his triumph. At six, he beat to quarters and mustered his crew. Lieutenant Bush and one of the British seamen who had failed to survive his wounds were buried with proper ceremony.

## BACK TO BOSTON

At daylight on the 21st, Hull had his crew back at work on repairing battle damage. Rigging was repaired or replaced, new sails bent on, and fishes applied to the fore and main masts. In the afternoon, a new gaff and a new spanker boom were fitted. Rain began to fall after six, but the work was not done until nine. As the day ended, *Constitution* was once again her old self, bowling along on a northwesterly course at eleven knots.

Saturday found the ship a beehive of activity again. The sailmakers were busy mending sails as the boatswain's mates were fitting up two preventer shrouds. And should another engagement be in the offing, the gunner had his mates making up more thin sheet lead cylinders to hold powder charges, and recovering the sponge heads with fresh sheepskin.

Early on Sunday, the 23rd, *Constitution* came up with the brig *Rebecca*, after a three hour chase. The merchant ship was bound from London to Boston under British license. Several days earlier, she had been boarded by *Guerriere*, but Dacres had only put some prisoners on her and had permitted her to continue her voyage. Subsequently, she had been made prize by privateer Joshua Barney, whose prize master now sailed her. After exchanging information, the two ships parted company.

The week that followed passed in relative quiet. Hull exercised his crew at quarters four times in six days. On the 25th, funeral services were held for a second British seaman to die of his wounds. At 6 P.M. on Saturday, the 29th, Boston Lighthouse was sighted four leagues SW by W. A pilot boarded shortly thereafter, and the night was spent working up to the Light against a strong southwest breeze. At 7:30 on the morning of 30 August, Hull anchored *Constitution* with the bower anchor in seven fathoms 1½ miles southeast of the Light — very nearly the same spot he had left exactly four weeks earlier. An hour later, Lieutenant John T. Shubrick was on his way ashore in the third cutter, bound for Washington with Hull's dispatches.

With the battle done and *Constitution* safely in home port, it is an appropriate moment to consider the background of the adulation that shortly was to engulf Hull and his men, and the effect their victory was to have on future events. As has been stated previously, the declaration of war was unpopular in several regions of the country, but particularly so in New England. It was thought that nothing good could come of it. Trade would be interrupted, insurance rates rise, and ships lost through destruction or capture. At sea, the Royal Navy had been well nigh invincible in nearly two decades of war against the might of Napoleon. The miniscule United States Navy (seventeen units) would be swallowed whole — almost without notice.

The nautical negativism was reinforced by a disaster on land: on 16 August, after some indecisive maneuvering, the American forces at Detroit had been surrendered without a fight to an inferior force of British and Indian allies. This news had only recently become known in Boston, just long enough to depress morale further. Ironically, the American general involved was William Hull, Isaac's uncle.

Thus, the stage was set and the nation ready — craving — for good news. *Constitution*'s victory over *Guerriere* was all that. The fight had been short and decisive. *Guerriere* had been destroyed with expedition and with minimal human loss and ship damage. The mighty Royal Navy had been humbled by an upstart. A Son of Liberty had again tweaked George's royal nose. For Hull and his crew, the weeks to follow would be filled with adulation and celebration. Newspapers and magazines published reams on the subject from every angle imaginable. Plays would be written and songs sung. Congress would vote Hull a gold medal and his officers silver ones. For a brief time, New England and the nation were united in the war effort.

Above all, the victory became a bench mark, a touchstone, the symbol of all that was good and right with the American way. Perhaps the most perceptive evaluation ever written on the subject appeared in the London *Times* when the news reached England:

> It is not merely that an English frigate has been taken after, what we are free to confess, may be called a brave resistance, but that it has been taken by a new enemy, an enemy unaccustomed to such triumphs, and likely to be rendered insolent and confident by them. He must be a weak politician who does not see how important the first triumph is in giving a tone and character to the war. Never before in the history of the world did an English frigate strike to an American.

In Boston town, the evaluation made up in verve what it lacked in polish:

> The *Constitution* long shall be
> The glory of our Navy,
> For when she grapples with a foe,
> She send her to old Davy.
> Yankee doodle keep it up,
> Yankee doodle dandy,
> We'll let the British know that we
> At fighting are quite handy.

# 8 Lightning Strikes Twice

## CHANGE OF COMMAND

On 31 August, the morning after his arrival in Boston's outer harbor, Captain Isaac Hull was awakened rudely by the peremptory rapping on his cabin door of one of his lieutenants. Four ships and a brig had been sighted standing toward the frigate from the northeast; from the looks of them, they were men of war. It was 6:30. Hull was on the quarterdeck in short order to see for himself. Warships, they were — but whose? With strong breezes from the eastnortheast, he was cornered, unable to get to the open sea. Was this the British squadron hounding him again? Discretion ever being the better part of valor, he ordered all hands to stand by to get under way. At 6:45, the anchor cable was axed and all sail set to gain the narrows into the inner harbor before that course, too, was closed to him. The strangers were signalling, but were unintelligible. Then, just as *Constitution* swept in through the narrows, the incoming units were recognized as Commodore John Rodgers' squadron, returning from their fruitless sweep all the way to the English Channel. This was the squadron that *Constitution* was to have joined at New York two long months ago — *President, United States, Congress, Hornet,* and *Argus.* They came to anchor in President Roads, off Castle Island, but Hull continued on up the harbor.

> ... We ran up near the Navy Yard and anchored. As we passed Long Wharf were saluted with huzzas by a great concourse of people from that place and the different Merchant vessels. Commodores Decatur and Bainbridge, Capt. Laurence and Sinclair came on board — a number of other officers; and the vessel was crowded all day with citizens — boats surrounded us, huzzaing, &c...

The next few days were distracted by the general euphoria of the occasion, but some work was begun to ready the ship for another trip. *Guerriere's* crew members were landed, as had been the wounded. Painting was begun, covering the scars on the hull, and a party was sent back to the outer harbor to retrieve the abandoned anchor. When Hull went ashore for the first time at 11 A.M. on 1 September, he was met at Long Wharf by the Ancient and Honorable Company of Artillery with a salute, which was answered from "Old Ironsides." The Company then escorted him, amidst hordes of cheering Bostonians, to the Exchange Coffee House, a popular rendezvous of the day.

A sad note was Hull's in this moment of triumph when he learned that his brother in New York had died during his absence, leaving his widow and children at sixes and sevens. Hull confided in Commodore Bainbridge, Commandant of the Navy Yard, that he intended to request a shore assignment in order to settle his brother's affairs and provide for his family. Bainbridge, who

126

had been seeking a seagoing combat command for a long time, promptly wrote to Secretary Hamilton nominating himself for the command and for Hull to succeed him at the Yard.

On a cold, rainy 5th of September,

> ... Were honoured with a superb dinner at Faneuil Hall by the citizens of Boston ... Much order and decorum were preserved on the occasion. Several (17!) excellent Patriotic toasts drank ...
>
> In the Gallery, fronting the President's chair, was a model of the *Constitution* Frigate with her masts fished and the Colours as they flew during the action. The Hall was surrounded with notices of our principal Naval victories ... Several guns were mounted on the Galleries. A wreath of flowers were hung above the head of Capt. Hull ... About 500 persons sat down to the dinner ... A band of musick played in the Gallery, and every toast was honored by several guns from the street ...

The model referred to in this description is believed to be the one presented to Isaac Hull by the crew, and which today may be seen in the Peabody Museum in Salem, Massachusetts.

On 7 September, overhaul work began in earnest. The running rigging was unreeved and sent ashore, together with sails, yards, and water casks. On the 9th, the crosstrees were removed from the topmasts, and by the next afternoon, rigging was being removed from the lower masts preparatory to their being lifted. On 14 September, Bainbridge received the Secretary's response to his request to succeed Hull; it was in the affirmative. Bainbridge moved swiftly and took command at four the next afternoon, hoisting his broad blue pennant as a squadron commander.

## A POOR BEGINNING

William Bainbridge, it will be recalled, had been in command of *Philadelphia* when she grounded and was lost to the Tripoline pirates in October of 1803. A native of New Jersey, and a son of Loyalists during the Revolution, Bainbridge had entered merchant marine service in 1789, at the age of fifteen, and had earned his first command only four years later. With the reestablishment of the Navy in 1798, he was commissioned a Lieutenant and placed in command of the schooner *Retaliation*, the former French privateer *Le Croyable.* He shortly was captured, without firing a shot, by a superior French force, the first officer in the United States Navy to surrender his command to an enemy. Bainbridge was absolved of any blame, promoted to Master Commandant, and given command of the brig *Norfolk,* wherein he had some success in the West Indies. In 1800, then commanding the light frigate *George Washington,* Bainbridge was finessed by the Dey of Algiers into making a trip to Constantinople for him in his ship but under the Algerine flag. This was the first time an American warship had been seen at the Porte, and Bainbridge made a very favorable impression despite the circumstance which had brought him there. Bainbridge subsequently commanded frigate *Essex* in Commodore Dale's squadron before returning to the Mediter-

# A Most Fortunate Ship

*Captain William Bainbridge.*

ranean in *Philadelphia*. Following his release from Tripoli in 1805, he was again cleared of any charges, but requested and received permission to leave service temporarily to return to the merchant marine. In 1808, believing, as a result of the *Chesapeake-Leopard* affair, that war was imminent with Britain, Bainbridge voluntarily returned to active duty in command of *President*. But when war didn't come right away, Bainbridge again became a merchant captain. In February 1812, he had once again presented himself for service to Secretary Hamilton and, in accordance with his wishes, was given a shore command until such time as war broke out, when he would be given a ship. Such was *Constitution*'s new Captain: a man who had somehow survived three incidents which would have written "finis" to many a naval officer's career and whose tremendous ambition was overpowering the Secretary of the Navy into giving him precisely what he wanted.

Surgeon Evans has left a description of the change of command:

> ... The crew expressed publicly much dissatisfaction at the change, in consequence of which the Armourer was put in confinement on board the Gun boat (No. 85) for trial. They gave Capt. H. three hearty cheers as he left the ship. The scene altogether affecting. The whole crew had a great affection for him. They urged him to remain: said they would go out with him and take the *Africa* (the British ship of the line): & finally requested to be transferred on board any other vessel. On being asked by Capt. B., who it was that had ever sailed with him & refused to go again, several persons

spoke — one man said he had sailed with him in the Phila. & had been badly used — that it might be altered now, but he would prefer going with Capt. H., or any of the other commanders. Several others said they had sailed with him before, and did not wish to sail again ...

Obviously, this victorious crew viewed Bainbridge as a three-time loser and wanted no part of him.

After personnel, Bainbridge's main concern in readying the ship for sea was, of course, ensuring that all spar and rigging damage suffered in the recent engagement was repaired or replaced. For the next month, the log records the tedious labor of erecting the shears alongside the mainmast and removing it, and of stepping a new one. Then the process was repeated for the foremast. With that accomplished, the fighting tops had to be set back atop these lower masts, the topmasts fidded home, the trestletrees installed, the topgallant masts set, and all the rigging rereeved. Of course, a new gaff, spanker boom, and crossjack also were put aboard.

One new feature was added to *Constitution*'s appearance at this time: beginning on 21 September, the carpenters cut bridle ports into the hull about midway between the Number 1 gun ports and the stem. These ports would make it easier to moor and unmoor, and to take a towing bridle if that became necessary. Although they looked very much like gun ports, there was insufficient space on the gun deck to accommodate guns in these positions.

At 5 P.M. on the 23rd, George Mitchell was returned aboard ship by a recruiting officer from the Army. George had been allowed ashore on liberty and had tried enlisting in the other Service, taking the $8 bounty in the process. At nine on the 25th, Bainbridge began his day by awarding George twelve lashes for his cavalier act.

Stores began to come back aboard on 4 October, as the crew was busy laying in the ground tier of water casks. This was a three-day job, and was followed by quantities of beef and pork, of rum, firewood, sauerkraut, bread, cheese, cranberries, horseradish (eight barrels), new sails, warrant officers' stores, etc., etc.

At midnight on 13 October, Surgeon Evans recorded a curious incident in his journal:

> ... It is now 12 o'clock at night. A sick man who is delirious insists that he will die at 2 o'clock, & is much disturbed when he hears the **bell** struck, & counts every half hour. He obstinately refuses to have a blister applied behind his neck, saying it may be done at 2 o'clock. I have requested the officer of the deck to omit striking the Bell at ½ after one & two: & intend to sit up till that hour to watch the effect of firm impression on a debilitated frame. He has complete possession of the superstition of his messmates.

And the next day:

> "The sick man mentioned above is still alive, and much improved ..."

On 16 October, Bainbridge moved *Constitution* from the Navy Yard to a position off Long Wharf to complete loading. Five days later, he moved again to an anchorage in President Roads, from whence he could take advantage of a fair wind. *Hornet,* the second unit of his squadron, moved to the same locale on the 24th. Both wind and tide came fair on the 27th, and the two ships stood for the open sea. Bainbridge's orders were to take frigate *Essex* (Captain Porter) and brig *Hornet* (Captain Lawrence) and "to annoy the enemy and to afford protection to our commerce, pursuing that course, which to your best judgment may ... appear to be best." The Commodore already had considered this aspect of his orders and had decided to proceed first to the waters off the Cape Verde Islands, then proceeding in a southwesterly direction to the waters off Brazil, where the British at that time had considerable commerce. After two months on that coast, he intended then to proceed to the vicinity of St. Helena Island, which was a frequented watering stop for rich East Indiamen enroute to England. *Essex,* which sailed a day later from the Delaware, ultimately never rendezvoused with Bainbridge, Porter pursuing instead another option in the squadron's orders: to disrupt British maritime activities in the Pacific, which he accomplished with legendary success before finally being trapped and captured in Valparaiso, Chile.

## SOUTH AWAY

The first days at sea were miserable ones in strong gales and rain, but then the weather settled down and the Commodore began in earnest his training program for the crew. He had them exercised at general quarters about every three days, on the average. The log through this period is replete with such entries as "The Sharp Shooters Exercising at a Mark;" "Exercised the Marines & Riflemen at a Mark;" "exercised the Boarders with Small Arms;" "Beat to Quarters Exercised the Great Guns & manovered with the Hornet."

On the 8th of November, in the mid-Atlantic, Bainbridge stopped the American brig *South Carolina* while *Constitution* and *Hornet* were flying British ensigns. The Yankee skipper, thinking he had outsmarted the English, produced a British license he had purchased. Bainbridge responded by revealing his true nationality and taking the merchant ship prize. The Admiralty Court later repudiated the Commodore's action and it cost him much of the prize money he was to earn to pay the damages awarded the merchant.

Disciplinary problems had been immediately apparent to Bainbridge the day he took command. As the newness of the current voyage wore off, and routine and boredom set in, instances of drunkenness, insolence, and fighting appeared. On 26 November, Captain Lawrence and two of his officers were called to the flagship to be a court martial in the case of Marine Private James Penshaw, who was accused of threatening the life of Midshipman James Delancy. He was found guilty and sentenced to receive fifty lashes. Five others received from six to a dozen lashes for lesser, unrelated infractions.

Landfall was made on the island of Fernando de Noronha, a penal colony for Portugal, on the morning of 2 December. Under the guise of being British, Bainbridge spent two days in the vicinity taking aboard a little more water and a few supplies (pigs, eggs, melons, cocoanuts, cashews, and bananas), and hoping to rendezvous with Porter. With no meeting in the offing, Bainbridge left a letter for Porter and sailed for the Brazilian coast 200 miles distant. Landfall was made on 6 December.

*Constitution* and *Hornet* proceeded southward along the coast, periodically closing enough to catch sight of land. A few native craft were seen, and one Portuguese brig involved in local trade was boarded, before they arrived in the area of Sao Salvador (Bahia, today). Not wishing to reveal his whole strength, on the evening of 13 December Bainbridge ordered Lawrence in to the port to contact the American Consul and gain the latest intelligence.

*Hornet* returned in midafternoon of the 18th, and Lawrence boarded the flagship immediately to report. In harbor, he had found *HMS Bonne Citoyenne*, a war sloop said to be carrying $1,600,000 in specie to England. From Consul Henry Hill, he had learned that there was a British ship of the line, *Montagu* (74), at Rio, and two other lesser units farther south. Only one man of war was said to be near St. Helena. Unfortunately, at the moment *Bonne Citoyenne* was the only Englishman in the harbor.

After receiving the stores brought out by Lawrence, *Constitution* and *Hornet* spent the next few days patrolling to the north and south of the port looking for prizes, without success. On the 23rd, a sail was sighted close inshore making for the port, but Bainbridge's meticulous orders respecting Portuguese sovereignty precluded her capture by Lawrence, who nonetheless followed her into port. While there, he issued a challenge to Captain Pitt Barnaby Greene of *Bonne Citoyenne* to fight him, ship to ship, with *Constitution* pledged to remain aloof regardless of the outcome. Greene steadfastly refused — and rightly so, with all that gold aboard — despite acrimonious assaults on his character by the challenger and Bainbridge. Bainbridge was angered further by a hard-line letter from the Governor of Sao Salvador complaining about the repeated entries into port by *Hornet*. The Portuguese clearly was showing his English bias. Bainbridge ordered *Hornet* to remain guarding *Bonne Citoyenne,* and to take her the minute she left port and cleared territorial waters. He took *Constitution* offshore to cruise for prizes.

## ENEMY MET AND CONQUERED

Between eight and nine on the morning of 29 December, a Tuesday, while some thirty miles off the coast, two strange sails were made out inshore and to windward (i.e., to the northwest). One of these was seen to continue her course along the coast while the other, the larger one, was seen to alter course toward *Constitution*. Bainbridge already had tacked in their direction. The day was pleasant and the sea nearly calm; the wind was light from the eastnortheast.

## A Most Fortunate Ship

By eleven, Commodore Bainbridge was satisfied that the contact was a British frigate. He tacked *Constitution* to the southeast with the intent of drawing his adversary well clear of territorial waters and a safe haven. He *wanted* to fight. The American frigate was sailing close to the wind with her royals set.

At noon, *Constitution* showed her colors, and the opponent shortly thereafter set an English ensign. He then flew a series of signals, the appropriate recognition signals for English, Spanish, and Portuguese warships, but of course got no response from the American.

Bainbridge was satisfied that he was sufficiently offshore at about 1:20, so he tacked toward the enemy, taking in his mainsail and royals. When slightly more than a mile separated them, he tacked again. Both ships now were heading roughly southeast, with the Englishman to windward on Bainbridge's larboard quarter and coming up. Clearly, she had the speed advantage.

At this point, the enemy hauled down her ensign, although her jack remained aloft. The Commodore ordered a shot fired across her bow in an effort to get her to hoist it again. The response was a broadside and the battle was on, both sides firing furiously. The Englishman's first salvoes were the most damaging, *Constitution*'s spars and rigging being well chewed. Bainbridge himself took a musket ball in the left hip. The enemy frigate forged ahead and appeared to be about to cross *Constitution*'s bow for a devastating rake when Bainbridge loosed a broadside, then promptly wore around in the roiling smoke. The enemy followed suit, but was once again left on the windward quarter — this time, to starboard. Once again, the enemy drew alongside and then ahead, seeking to achieve a raking position. And once again Bainbridge fired and wore in the resulting smoke, denying the advantage. The ships once more were heading generally eastward as Bainbridge set fore and main courses and steered closer to his enemy. Yet a third time, the English frigate drove abeam and then began to forereach the American frigate. She then attempted to tack into a raking position, but the loss of her jib boom to American fire caused her to hang up momentarily — long enough for Bainbridge to get in a raking broadside himself from astern before she was once again under control.

During the former of these last two exchanges, a broadside from the Englishman had completely destroyed *Constitution*'s wheel. A severed bolt from it wounded the Commodore again, this time deep in the muscles of his right thigh. He remained completely in command, and quickly issued orders to rig jury steering to the tiller in the wardroom pantry two decks below. A line of midshipmen was established to pass his orders down to the two teams manning the ropes deep in the bowels of the ship. It was a terribly cumbersome and inefficient system, but the inspired American crew strained to make it work.

The two frigates now ran off to the southeast, the Englishman still having the weather gage. But the advantage was seen by both sides to be shifting to the Americans. English gunfire was becoming less accurate than it had been during those first broadsides that had taken the greatest toll in Americans. Her loss of

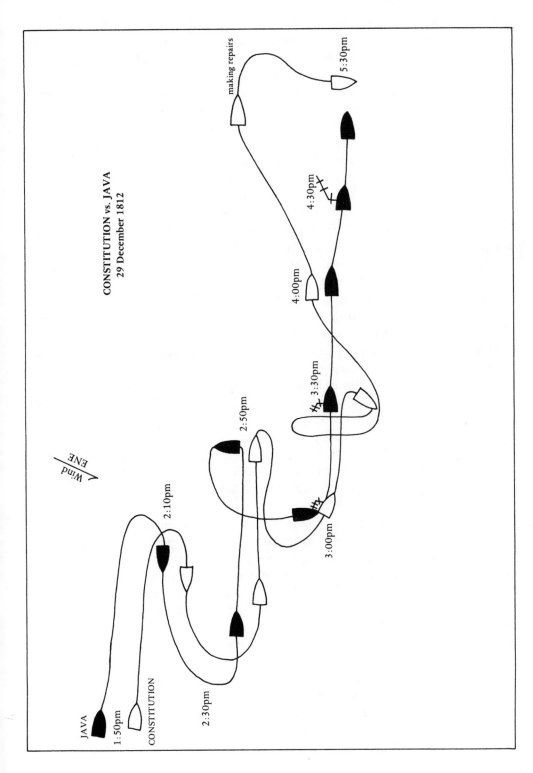

CONSTITUTION *vs.* JAVA
29 December 1812

Wind
ENE

JAVA
1:50pm

CONSTITUTION

2:10pm

2:30pm

2:50pm

3:00pm

3:30pm

4:00pm

4:30pm

making repairs

5:30pm

headsail with the destruction of the jib boom made the English frigate less maneuverable, offsetting in part *Constitution*'s lack of a wheel and slower speed. The English Captain decided his best tactic was to close and take his adversary by boarding. Accordingly, he sought to run down on *Constitution*'s larboard main channel. A misjudgment on his part resulted in the remains of his bowsprit running into the American's mizzen rigging and hanging him up. There, with only one of his guns able to bear, he had to suffer the full weight of *Constitution*'s metal and the hail of musketry from her well-trained snipers. The enemy's foremast was severed just below its fighting top and plunged through two decks; then his maintopmast went, cut off slightly above the cap. The resultant tangle of wreckage further disorganized his gun crews.

As they separated, both ships brought their heads eastward once more. *Constitution*, because of her greater remaining sail area, began forereaching her antagonist. Bainbridge wore once more and brought his ship up under the enemy's stern, where he loosed a blazing raking fire. Crossing northward, he wore still again and unleashed a rake from his larboard batteries. He then drew alongside with his opponent to windward and let fly with everything at close range. The enemy's remaining section of foremast just above the spar deck was shot away. The enemy Captain was dropped by one of the American sharpshooters, Adrian Peterson. The time was about 3:30. In another ten minutes, the enemy had lost his main yard and both gaff and spanker boom, and at about 3:55, "Shott Away his Mizen Mast Nearly to the Deck." All this time, the Englishman attempted to return *Constitution*'s devastating fire, but the tangled wreckage encumbering his starboard side flamed each time he shot. His cannon went still one by one until shortly after 4 P.M., when silence reigned. His colors having disappeared from the main rigging, Commodore Bainbridge assumed his opponent had surrendered, and he took his ship off to windward a short distance to effect necessary repairs before closing and taking possession.

But the fact was that the Englishman had not surrendered. First Lieutenant Henry Ducie Chads, himself wounded, had assumed command upon the fall of his Captain, and strove mightily to prepare for further fighting. A staysail was rigged between a spare spar jury rigged to replace the foremast and the bowsprit, in an effort to bring the ship under some control. As this was being done, the damaged mainmast — at least, what was left of it — tottered and fell. When *Constitution* began to close once more, an hour later, the British had rehoisted an ensign to the mizzen stump and were trying to set more sail. Seeing that the American was taking an unassailable raking position across his bow, the British lieutenant wisely hauled down his flag, only just in time to prevent another American broadside. It was about 5:30. In *Constitution*, recalling the fight against *Guerriere*, the "crew gave 3 hearty cheers, as they had done when we first beat to quarters & several times during the action." Bainbridge had his victory, at last.

Java *loses her foremast.*

Java *surrenders.*

## AFTERMATH

At six, First Lieutenant George Parker, who had succeeded the recuperating Charles Morris, boarded the defeated enemy from *Constitution*'s one remaining undamaged boat (out of eight) to find a shambles. Four of her forecastle guns were upended, and so were six more on the quarterdeck. Tangled rigging was everywhere. The wounded and dying made it a grisly scene, which condition also existed on the gun deck below. The defeated frigate was *HMS Java* (38), the former French frigate *Renomée,* commissioned in the Royal Navy only the previous August. She had sailed from England for India on 12 November and had detoured to Sao Salvador because of a shortage of water. Quite similar to *Guerriere,* she carried twenty-eight 18-pounder long guns below, and two long 9-pounders, sixteen 32-pounders and one 18-pounder carronades on her forecastle and quarterdeck, a total of forty-seven guns. (Bainbridge had made a small substitution in his ship's armament since her last fight, adding an 18-pounder chase gun and removing two carronades — leaving fifty-four guns, in all.) Her gunfire, devastating in its opening broadsides, had diminished steadily in accuracy and volume as the fight progressed, symptomatic not only of damage received but the presence of a new crew that had been allowed to fire but six blank charges in practice.

*Constitution* suffered nine killed and twenty-five wounded (three mortally) out of her crew of 480 men. Conflicting reports by several present make it impossible to be as precise concerning *Java.* She had somewhere between 373 and 426 people aboard at the time of the fight. Deaths were reported as totalling between twenty-two and sixty, while the wounded were numbered at either 101 or 102. In any event, the disparate ratio of four or five to one in casualties between the two ships is indicative of the volume and accuracy of the American fire when compared to her enemy's. The unusually large number of people in *Java* stems from the fact that she was carrying nearly 100 passengers out to their new duty assignments in and around India, including the Governor General-designate of Bombay, Lieutenant General Sir Thomas Hislop.

The wrecked condition of *Java* already has been noted. On the American side, *Constitution* once again had come through without crippling damage but had not escaped entirely unscathed, Commodore Bainbridge's report notwithstanding. Careful scrutiny of the ship's log for the succeeding days discloses that both the fore and mizzen masts were "wounded" severely enough to require fishes, as were certain of the yards. Additionally, the maintopmast had to be taken down and replaced. Thus, it would seem that the slightly larger dimensions of "Old Ironsides' " masts had saved her — narrowly — from the fate suffered by her two opponents to date.

Considering his personal "damaged" condition, the weakened state of his ship's rigging, the fact that he was thousands of miles away from home in waters infested with the enemy, Bainbridge reluctantly determined to destroy *Java* rather than attempt to tow her home. Slowly — very slowly with only one boat available — the prisoners and their belongings were brought aboard and distributed about the spar and gun decks of *Constitution* under guard of American Marines, the enlisted men manacled to preclude an uprising. Last to be transferred was *Java's* mortally wounded Captain, Henry Lambert, one of England's finest frigate captains, whose green, nondescript crew had not been equal to his tactical skill. It was a terribly painful move across choppy waters, but was made with all the care and tenderness possible. By noon on the last day of 1812, all were clear and the demolition fires set. At three, she blew up. Noted Surgeon Evans: "The explosion was not so grand as that of the *Guerriere*, as her small Magazine only took fire." This was at least the fourth scuttling he had witnessed; he was becoming an expert on the subject. Bainbridge made sail for Sao Salvador.

At 8:30 on New Year's morning, land and a sail were sighted ahead. On the chance it might be *Montagu* or another enemy warship, the prisoners were herded below and confined in the hold, and the ship beat to quarters. In the heat and closeness of their confinement, the British suffered considerable discomfort — particularly the wounded. This act was to bring the wrath of some English observers down on Bainbridge's head, with charges of cruelty and malice, despite the obvious military requirement to ready his ship for battle that the situation generated.

The number of contacts grew from one to three as the distance between them closed. Soon, it was seen to be *Hornet* with two prizes: the salt-laden American merchant ship *William*, once prize to *Java*, and the British schooner *Eleanor* (or *Ellen*), which was carrying a cargo valued at $150,000. Lawrence had been just off the port when *Java* and *William* first were sighted on the 29th, and had remained hovering off the entrance ever since, keeping *Bonne Citoyenne* covered and yet being in a position to evade should *Constitution* be defeated or additional enemy units appear. Bainbridge came to anchor offshore and *Hornet* ran alongside, her tops manned and the crew bellowing out three lusty cheers. Lawrence came aboard and updated the Commodore concerning events in the port; then the frigate got underway and entered Sao Salvador at one that afternoon to find a friendlier Governor. *Hornet* remained offshore to nab *Bonne Citoyenne* should the Britisher choose to cut and run while *Constitution* was busy offloading prisoners and making repairs.

Offloading of prisoners began at 2 P.M. on 2 January 1813. The Commodore had arranged a parole for all of them with General Hislop and Lieutenant Chads whereby they would return to England, not to fight in this war again prior to formal exchange. Among the last to leave was poor Captain Lambert, in dreadful pain from the musket ball that had broken a rib, punctured a lung, and had come to rest near his spine. As he waited on a couch under an awning on the quarterdeck, a limping Bainbridge, suffering himself and supported by two of his officers, came to Lambert and returned his sword, saying, "I return your sword, my dear sir, with the sincere wish that you will recover, and wear it as you have hitherto done, with honour to yourself and your country." Lambert died on the evening of the 3rd, but this one act of Bainbridge's ameliorated any animosities existing between victors and vanquished and, in fact, General Hislop and the Commodore remained corresponding friends to the end of their days. Lieutenant Chads, in his initial report of *Java*'s loss to the Admiralty, expressed his "grateful acknowledgements, thus publically, for the generous treatment Captain Lambert and his officers experienced from our gallant enemy, Commodore Bainbridge and his officers."

Ten carpenters were hired in Sao Salvador to assist ship's company in repairing *Constitution*'s battle damage. Fishes were got out for the masts and spars. Bulwarks were repaired. The problem of the shattered wheel had already been attended to: *Java*'s had been removed and installed in *Constitution* before she was scuttled. Water and stores were shipped. Seaman Stephen Welsh died of his wounds and was buried.

Bainbridge had now to consider his next course of action. There still was no sign of *Essex* (she already was farther south, at the rendezvous off Cabo Frio at this time). *Constitution* had been mauled in the fight and really was unfit for extended cruising far from home. British forces in the area would be rallying to his presence soon, and would be bent on revenge. And there was *Bonne Citoyenne,* the spectacularly rich potential prize. Weighing all these factors, the Commodore decided to head back home, taking with him *Hornet*'s two prizes. *Hornet* he ordered to remain off Sao Salvador until *Bonne Citoyenne* sailed, or superior British forces appeared, or until about the 25th of the month, when she was to head for home, reconnoitering Dutch Surinam and British Guiana along the way. (*Montagu* subsequently forced *Hornet* off and she came home after other adventures.) The two ships departed Sao Salvador on the afternoon of the 5th, and after remaining in company for a day, went their separate ways. Ordinary Seaman Reuben Sanderling died of his wounds late on the 6th and was buried at sea.

## HOME TO BOSTON

The trip northward was uneventful and, in the main, pleasant. Ordinary Seaman John Cheevers, whose brother James had been killed outright in the *Java* fight, died of his wounds, and Lieutenant John Aylwin followed him on the 29th. Aylwin had been *Constitution*'s Sailing Master during the engagement with *Guerriere* and had been wounded in the same place on that occasion. His lieutenancy had come as a reward for his gallantry then.

Commodore Bainbridge undoubtedly spent a considerable amount of time during this peaceful period savoring the hero's return he must have expected after having witnessed what transpired when Hull came in. *His* would be the second such victory and would prove that beating the Royal Navy had not been a fluke. Unhappily for this unhappy man, a chance meeting with an American brig on 12 February did much to diminish his hopes. From *Sarah,* he learned that Stephen Decatur, in *United States,* had defeated soundly the British frigate *Macedonian* south of the Canary Islands just as Bainbridge had been about to sail from Boston. *Java* was the *third* Britisher to fall. Making it worse, from Bainbridge's point of view, was the news that Decatur had succeeded in bringing his prize home and that his casualties in the engagement were even lighter than Hull's had been. Other news included the facts that *Wasp* had taken the British sloop of war *Frolic,* that President Madison had been reelected, and that William Jones had succeeded Paul Hamilton as Secretary of the Navy. This last item was good news to Bainbridge, who had known Jones for years and with whom the Commodore had corresponded when determining his plan for this cruise. He also was warned that there was a powerful British squadron blockading New York and that frigate *Acasta* was said to be in Massachusetts Bay.

During the homeward trip, Bainbridge engaged in considerable official and personal correspondence. One of the latter that has come down to us indicates that even before receiving news of Decatur's victory, the Commodore was not a totally happy man. In a letter to John Bullus, then Naval Agent at New York, he made a much more open assessment of the damage his ship had suffered, and then made the surprising statement that, "... My Crew owing to the constant Exercise we give them, are very active & clever at their Guns, but in all other respects they are inferior to any Crew I ever had ..." Was it the crew that had steered the wheelless ship and handled her sails in a maneuvering contest against a faster-sailing enemy that he was criticizing? Did he really mean it? His reports to the Secretary of the Navy say nothing of the sort. Was he laying the groundwork for defending himself against criticisms of the casualties incurred or the damage received? Or unfavorable comparison with Hull's achievement? (He hadn't yet learned of Decatur's victory when the letter was written.) Perhaps because of his Tory parentage and early misfortunes in the Navy, Bainbridge seems almost unable to enjoy the fruits of victory when they finally were his.

When *Constitution* appeared off Boston Light on 15 February, the city had been aware of Bainbridge's victory for nearly a week. First public notice of it had been given during a performance of "Hamlet" at the Boston Theater. In the audience that night were Commodore John Rodgers, Captain Isaac Hull with his wife of five weeks, and some other officers.

Adverse winds prevented the ship from entering harbor immediately. When Bainbridge finally was able to come ashore at Long Wharf on the 18th, the city was ready for him. The route from there to the Exchange Coffee House (really a hotel and restaurant) was decorated with flags and streamers. A procession was formed at Faneuil Hall which included the Ancient and Honorable Artillery Company, the Boston Light Infantry, and the Wilson Blues. The tall Commodore was escorted by John Rodgers and the stumpy Hull, as well as other notables. Two bands played. And for the next two months Boston and the country gave themselves over to honouring the latest naval heroes. Congress again voted a gold medal to a skipper of *Constitution,* and silver medals for the junior officers, and finally voted $100,000 in lieu of prize money to reward the *Constitution* for both *Guerriere* and *Java*. Hull and Bainbridge each realized $7500 from this largesse; the average seaman received about $60 per fight.

The loss of *Java*, their third frigate to be defeated in 4½ months, stirred the Admiralty into action. Henceforth, detailed loss reports would not be made public in order to limit public outcry. (*Java*'s and all later ones during the War of 1812 still cannot be seen.) Gunnery training was to be revitalized. Small ships of the line were to be razed and larger frigates built to counter these American champions. And, effective immediately, no frigate of the Royal Navy was to engage an American 44 one-to-one; only when in squadron strength was the Royal Navy to take on an American heavy frigate. Thus, fifteen years after she was launched, *Constitution* had proved conclusively the correctness of her designers' work.

# 9 Overhaul, Change of Command — and a Sea Story

## OVERHAUL

*Constitution* began her overhaul a few days after her return to the Navy Yard. Because of the Yard's limited facilities and ongoing work, much of the frigate's work had to be contracted out to civilian concerns. Wharfage for her had to be rented, as did storage space for her rigging and sails. Commodore Bainbridge's first report to the new Secretary of the Navy, William Jones, of the material condition of his command indicated she would need new beams, waterways, decks, ceilings, and knees. The beams of the gun and spar decks had been there since 1803, and had seen rough duty in the Barbary War and now in the present war. Her copper, although patched by Hull, ought to be completely replaced. He believed her frame and planking to be sound. Jones was disappointed that so much seemed necessary.

Ripping into the decks showed Bainbridge's estimate to have been quite accurate. By 14 March, he was able to report that two-thirds of the beams needed to be replaced, saying that some were so rotten he was surprised they hadn't given way. Poor weather was slowing the course of the overhaul, but the Commodore, who shortly after writing this letter resumed duties of Yard Commandant, as well, was optimistic that it could be accomplished in a reasonable time. A shortage of materials, especially southern long leaf yellow pine, particularly concerned him. The British blockade of the East Coast below New England largely had eliminated coastwise traffic, the major carrier of bulky goods. Overland drayage was tortuous, slow, and very expensive.

James Lawrence returned to the United States during this period in *Hornet*, bringing news of his decisive victory over the British war-brig *Peacock* off Guiana. As a part of his reward for this action, he was promoted to the rank of Captain and scheduled to be Commodore Bainbridge's relief in *Constitution*. However, when it became known that Captain Samuel Evans of *Chesapeake* was ailing and required replacement, Lawrence was reassigned because *Chesapeake* was ready for a cruise and *Constitution* had just begun her overhaul. It is said that Lawrence was not pleased with this turn of events. *Chesapeake* was considered to be one of the unlucky ships of the Navy at that time, the complete antithesis of *Constitution,* whose popularity was unparalleled. But being the newest Captain in the Navy, having achieved that position ahead of some of his contemporaries, Lawrence could not very well refuse. Thus it was that he went to his death in June, leaving the country shocked at the swiftness of his defeat by *HMS*

*Shannon,* and with a ringing watch-phrase that lives in the Navy today: "Don't give up the ship!"

Repairs to *Constitution* went on very slowly because of the supply problems and because of demands being made by the naval force growing on the Great Lakes. General Hull's defeat at Detroit the previous summer had made it quite apparent that the United States was in great danger of invasion from Canada, and that control of Lakes Ontario and Erie, in particular, was vital to the country's security. The British, for their part, recognized the situation as well. Thus, there came to be a naval building race along the wooded shores of those fresh water lakes hundreds of miles from the sea. For the Americans, it meant trans-shipment of naval stores over incredibly difficult trails to Sackett's Harbor, New York, and Erie, Pennsylvania, for the development of this force. Only the timber was available in the immediate vicinity. Because the Navy suffered from a shortage of men and materials at this time (indeed, it did throughout the war), stringent measures had to be taken to provide the needed resources. Men and materials were diverted from the salt water units to do the job. Frigate *John Adams,* being rebuilt at New York, was laid up and her entire crew and allocated stocks were sent thither. "Ninety-four men from Boston," mostly *Constitutions,* were ordered there in April. (In Oliver Hazard Perry's flagship, *Lawrence,* in his victory at the Battle of Lake Erie the subsequent September, some of his gun crews were from the big frigate. One of these gun captains was killed by a 24-pound ball passing right through him. Midshipman Dulaney Forrest was stunned by a grape shot and fell near Perry. Perry helped him to his feet and asked as to his condition. Forrest responded with, "I'm not hurt, sir, but this is my shot," and pocketed the lump of iron from the folds of his coat. What a souvenir — the one with your number on it. In this same engagement, now-Lieutenant John H. Packett commanded schooner *Ariel* (4) and very ably supported the flagship. Both Packett and Forrest had been with Bainbridge in the *Java* fight.)

*Constitution* had to wait until the third week of May before suitable deck timbers were received and her work could proceed. By the middle of June, much of the work had been accomplished. Some joiner work remained, but the one big job to be done was recoppering. Along the way, Bainbridge made two major changes to the ship. In rebuilding the upper bulwarks, he caused three gun ports to be built into the stern at the spar deck level, no doubt as a result of Hull's experience when chased the previous summer. He also raised the level of the gun deck between the fore and main masts by approximately six inches. Why he did so — other than he thought it was a better arrangement — is not clear. This "stepping" of the deck rendered it difficult to move large objects the full length of the gun deck and, more importantly, it reduced the overhead clearance in the vicinity of most of the 24-pounder battery to about 5'6", a figure slightly less than the average height of his men. The only positive element in this alteration is that it raised the headroom for much of the berth deck to six feet, making it easier to move about the living space, especially when hammocks were slung. "Habitabili-

*Captain Charles Stewart.*

ty," however, was not a major consideration in the Navy until this century.

Thus matters stood when Captain Charles Stewart arrived from Norfolk on 23 June 1813. He formally took command of *Constitution* on 18 July.

## A NEW CAPTAIN

Charles Stewart came of Irish stock, red-headed, and was a couple of inches above average in height. He had been born in Philadelphia, the youngest of eight children of a merchant captain who died when Charles was two. His step-father arranged a billet as cabin boy for him at the age of thirteen, when his limited formal education ended. Nearing his twentieth birthday, and already a qualified skipper, Stewart accepted a lieutenancy in the new Navy in March 1798. He served in *United States* (44) and commanded *Enterprise* (12), and emerged from the Quasi-War as the senior lieutenant in the Navy. Stewart was first commander of *Syren* (16) and was second in command to Preble in the Mediterranean Squadron (1803-4), participating in all the major actions during those years. He achieved his Captaincy in 1806, but, like Bainbridge, obtained leave to reenter the merchant service. Again like Bainbridge, he was back in Washington late in 1811 to pursue a combat command in the imminent war. Not until December 1812 did he get one: *Constellation.* Unfortunately, before he could get his frigate to sea, a large British blockading force, including four ships of the line, trapped him in Norfolk. He eagerly accepted orders to *Constitution* five months later, anxious to have the opportunity for glory many of his peers already had enjoyed. Stewart was a literate, just, thorough-going professional.

The first six months in command were frustrating ones for Captain Stewart. Boston was not yet blockaded, because the British retained hope that the early anti-war sentiment of the region might thereby be encouraged into secessionist or other activity favoring them. On that score, he could get to sea. But, on the other hand, the Department's proper emphasis on the fair weather operations on the strategically more important Great Lakes was draining much material and most available manpower in that direction. This led to little work and no recruiting being done for *Constitution*. However, with the coming of fall, operations on the Lakes dwindled into the winter doldrums. The pace on the seaboard picked up. Stewart got the ship completely recoppered and rerigged, and began recruiting a crew. By Christmastime, when she was ready to go, the British had begun an informal, intermittent blockade of Boston. In addition to requiring a fair wind and tide to go to sea, Stewart also had to watch for an absent enemy.

## A SEA STORY

Let us pause in our narrative for a moment or two to consider a fable involving *Constitution*. A favorite theme with authors of sea stories has been that of the female in an unusual role — the woman captain, the lady pirate. There was, in fact, a woman in the Royal Marines in the mid-18th century who was wounded twelve times in action against the French in India. *Constitution* was the setting for the exploits of a fictitious lady Marine during the War of 1812. The slim volume in which it appeared was entitled "An Affecting Narrative of Louisa Baker, A Native of Massachusetts ... enlisted, in disguise, on board an American Frigate As A Marine." Louisa's story of disgrace and subsequent return to Goodness and Family was guaranteed to hold romantically inclined readers of the day enthralled.

Louisa, she informs us, lived with her family some forty miles west of Boston. In 1809, at the tender age of sixteen, she is seduced by a dastardly suitor and subsequently is ordered out of the house by her shamed parents. She thereupon decides to go to Boston and begin life anew where her past would not hound her. After two days of diligent but fruitless job hunting, Louisa decides that her life is forever blighted and that there is only one profession open to her. With hardly more than a slight flicker of an eyelash, she joins the "staff" of a bordello in West Boston.

The years and the "business" are not unkind to the enduring Louisa. Indeed, we find her in 1812 in a rather permanent association with the "Lieutenant of a privateer." One day late in July, the two are talking about the month-old war with England and how young men are leaving in droves for the fields of glory. Louisa bemoans the fact that women, who are every bit as patriotic, are not allowed to participate in the noble cause. Her worthy lieutenant, tongue in cheek, allows as how it would be easy for a woman to disguise herself in a loose-fitting sailor's rig and sign on. Predictably, but to the lieutenant's surprise, Louisa decides to do just that.

At a rendezvous in a house on Fish Street, our heroine enlists as a Marine for "one of the frigates then lying in harbor." Louisa never names her ship, but the course of events leaves no doubt that it is *Constitution.* Collecting an advance on her pay, and her uniform, she returns to her house to get ready for her adventure.

Early the next morning, her femininity subdued through the use of "bands," Miss Baker reports for duty. Shortly thereafter, in the opening days of August, the ship sails. Louisa records a bout with seasickness, but nonetheless is able to establish herself as a good shot and is assigned to one of the fighting tops as a sniper. Her Captain, she notes, is "humane and experienced." She is known to her shipmates as "George."

In mid-month, the frigate encounters a British counterpart (Louisa doesn't say it is *Guerriere*) and a fierce, if short, fight ensues. "George" is busily engaged in shooting at enemy blue jackets through the smoke, and miraculously escapes injury when the butt of her rifled musket is shattered by a grape shot. But the battle is soon over, and the victorious Americans head back to Boston. Louisa carefully notes that seven of her shipmates have died and seven others wounded.

*Constitution* is in Boston for six weeks. Louisa returns to the bordello on liberty to compare notes with her former associates, all of whom are highly titilated by our gallant heroine's bold activity. Needless to say, our "Marine" is once again on board when next the frigate sails.

Two months are glossed over quickly, and *Constitution* is in battle (with *Java*). Louisa's reporting of times and of casualties is exactly as reported in the local newspapers of the day, as she relates her role as a sniper. She says she fired nineteen times at enemy crewmen with uncertain effect.

With the battle won, Louisa is almost "discovered." In climbing down from the fighting top, she slips and falls overboard, very nearly drowning before she can be picked up. Then, in her semi-conscious state, she realizes her shipmates have begun to remove some of her clothing. In the nick of time, she regains her faculties and halts the proceedings just before being disbanded.

At this point Louisa condenses her story. In short order, we learn of the ship's return to Boston, the subsequent blockade, and her reenlistment. "Two more successful" cruises are given short shrift, as is another sea battle. Suddenly, the war is over and Louisa is discharged, nicely recompensed with pay and prize money.

Having purged herself of sin in the cauldron of battle, Louisa resolves to return to her family and seek reconciliation. She purchases herself a new feminine wardrobe in the Cornhill district of Boston and sets out for home. Arriving when the family is at dinner, she is not immediately recognized. But soon her identity is established and the prodigal is welcomed back into the fold with an effusiveness typical of the day.

## A Most Fortunate Ship

This narrative made such a hit that it went through three editions during 1815-16. Louisa Baker was, in fact, Lucy Brewer, who experienced nothing more than a vivid imagination. In 1816, she married a Mr. West and continued writing: "The Awful Beacon" was next, a moral dissertation of exceeding dullness was published the same year.

But despite her fictional character, Louisa Baker had been a thorn in the collective side of the U.S. Marine Corps, appearing and reappearing to harass their publicists and historians. During the Bicentennial, she was the heroine of a paperback retelling the story and having added many, many details not previously reported.

# 10 Stewart's Trials and Triumph

## TO SEA, AT LAST

Captain Charles Stewart finally got the opportunity to make his contribution to the war effort on 31 December 1813 when, at three in the afternoon, and with no enemy in the offing, he weighed anchor and cleared Boston Light on his first war cruise. Striking out to the south and southeastward, he sought out British merchantmen engaged in the West Indies trade, heavily laden, homeward bound cargo ships lightly convoyed by escorts involving but one or two frigates.

The first action to occur was when *Constitution* went in chase shortly after dawn on 13 January 1814. After firing three warning shots, she brought to a schooner which proved to be an American, the *Regulator.* A few hours later, she was in chase again; but both foretopmast stunsail booms sprung at about four and the chase was lost with the coming of night.

More uneventful days followed as Stewart directed his command out into the central Atlantic at the latitude of Cuba, then slanted back down to the southwest toward the South American continent. Except for overhauling the Portuguese *Adrianna* (20) on the 15th, the sea was bare. On the 28th, Stewart set all sails and ran dead before the wind to see what kind of speed he could get out of *Constitution,* but the winds were such that only an unspectacular ten knots was achieved.

On the 30th, Stewart held his third practice at general quarters, and during it there occurred a bizarre accident: "Boatswain's Mate Richard Ormerod's pistol going off half cocked in his belt wounded him severely in the thigh." Ormerod survived. They then were about 300 miles due north of the mouth of the Amazon River.

Hoping to be like the fox in the chicken coop, as Talbot had been nearly fifteen years earlier, Stewart slipped quietly westward, just barely maintaining contact with the shore. A chase eluded him in the shoal waters close to the Guiana beach on 1 February. In chase again at dawn's early light on the 3rd, Stewart soon identified his quarry as a Royal Navy war brig. Harassed by the big frigate all day long, the Britisher finally was seen to go aground amongst the shoals, her masts shivering at the shock of contact. Knowing that he could not get at her, Stewart hauled off. The next day, he was "... Standing Nwd. windward of Barbadoes, thinking it best to change our cruising ground as the brig chased yesterday will no doubt give the alarm on this Coast."

All was quiet until the 8th, when, in the afternoon, *Constitution* went in chase of what was identified as an English packet. Unfortunately, she was lost in the darkness. Actually, she was the brig *HMS Columbine* (20), and she shortly alerted Rear Admiral Durham's squadron off Barbados to the big American's presence. Stewart must have had the same thought which caused him to leave the Guianian coast, but here he had no fear of being cornered in shoal waters and merely made his identity less clear by repainting the gun stripe yellow, in the British style. That was on the 11th.

The heavy frigate again went in chase during the waning moments of the evening watch on 13 February. This time, there were two contacts. The first she overhauled at 2 A.M. She proved to be the British armed merchant ship *Lovely Ann* (10), laden with lumber, fish, and flour. Taking out the Englishmen and putting aboard a prize crew, Stewart resumed the chase of the second contact at three. Nearly six hours later, a shot through her sails brought H.M. schooner *Pictou* (14) to a halt. *Pictou* had been convoying *Lovely Ann* from Bermuda to Surinam. Placing a prize crew aboard, Stewart returned with his prize to the *Lovely Ann.* There, he caused the merchantman to be emptied of her cargo (most of it into the sea) and readied it to carry the Englishmen to Barbados under a flag of truce. Midshipman P.M. Whipple was placed in charge, and *Pictou's* Captain Stevens having given his parole for his crew, the 60-odd prisoners were placed aboard and *Lovely Ann* sent on her way. *Pictou* was scuttled, recognizing that the odds were against her making an American port through the many British blockaders.

Moving west toward Tobago, Stewart came across another British merchant on the 17th, and in a chase lasting little more than an hour had the schooner *Phoenix* in his bag. Loaded with lumber and official dispatches, the prize had been enroute from Demerara to Barbados. After taking out the crew and passengers, Stewart scuttled her. Among the dispatches, the Captain found a petition from the merchants of Demerara pleading for escort ships to convoy fifty-one cargomen which had been waiting there for many weeks, fearful of being taken by American privateers and naval units. This paralysis of British shipping by the mere threat of American activity was, certainly, every bit as important to the progress of the war at sea as the captures themselves.

Passing into the Caribbean between Tobago and Grenada, Stewart next turned northward. An hour's chase after first light on the 19th rewarded him with the capture of the brig *Catharine,* bound from Grenada to St. Thomas. As before, the prize was scuttled after removal of all persons. Moving westward, he encountered a Swedish brig southeast of Puerto Rico, bound for St. Barthelemy, and passed all of his English prisoners to her for setting ashore.

A chase early in the morning of the 23rd proved to be another Swede. As her identity was being established, another contact was sighted heading northward into the Mona Passage, just east of Puerto Rico. Off in pursuit at 6:30, *Constitution* "gained slowly" on her quarry through the day as they beat against headwinds. By four that afternoon, it was clear the contact was a frigate. At least fourteen gun ports could be made out in the gun stripe. Thinking it might be *President* (which actually had arrived in New York from the West Indies on the 18th), at 5:30 Stewart had the appropriate day signal displayed. In response, the stranger hoisted a British ensign and fired a gun to windward — a recognized signal of challenge. Stewart shaped his course for his becalmed adversary's larboard quarter, setting the foresail in the prevailing light wind, while sending down the royals and clearing for action. Through long glasses, *Constitution*'s officers thought they could make out similar activity in the Englishman. At 5:45, *Constitution* lost the wind and went dead in the water, still out of range. Shortly thereafter, a fickle breeze allowed the quarry to set all sail and move away. She was hull down on the horizon by 7:30, when *Constitution* finally was able to get underway again. Nightfall, and gusty weather which tore three of *Constitution*'s sails, permitted the enemy to escape.

The "one that got away" had been *HMS Pique* (36, Captain Maitland), once the French frigate *Pallas.* It appears that her Captain was perfectly willing to engage an American warship — he fired a challenging shot, after all — but when he finally realized he was up against one of the fearsome 44's he quite properly carried out the year-old Admiralty order not to engage one of that ilk alone.

Back in the Atlantic once more, *Constitution* headed northwest to pass along the Bahamas and have a look at traffic in the Gulf Stream. On the 24th, an American privateer was spoke. On 1 March, she overhauled a Swedish ship and a Spanish brig, and on the 7th, in the Gulf Stream at the latitude of today's Daytona Beach, she spoke the Russian ship *Independence.* After checking the coastal waters around Charleston for two days, she moved back out to sea where, on the 14th, "John Goss seaman fell from the Mizen Topsail Yard and struck his head on a carronade and was immediately killed."

Stewart returned to the Gulf Stream, then worked his way eastward to a position southwest of Bermuda where "... The Mainmast appeared to work in the neck rather too much." He continued on a course counterclockwise around Bermuda until the 26th when he "Observed the Mainmast work very much and discovered a considerable Crack extending from the neck of the mast nearly down to the fife rail." Clearly, it was time to seek refuge in a friendly port — without encountering enemy warships. Stewart headed toward Boston, which deep water port alone had not yet felt the full brunt of the British blockade and where, the winter only now beinning to wane, they would not yet be present in numbers, in any event. A heavy squall on the 27th gave the crew fits as the mainmast persisted in bending forward despite the slack in the stays.

*Constitution* made landfall in the vicinity of Cape Ann and turned southwestward toward Boston. At eight that morning, 3 April, two ships were sighted to the eastsoutheast standing toward her with a fresh breeze from the east. In a half-hour, it was clear they were warships, and by 9:15 there was no mistaking the fact that they were gaining with every possibility of being able to cut off *Constitution* from her home port. Stewart set skysails and royal stunsails in the near calm, trusting that the mainmast would not fail him. The British clearly were closing by ten, when the Americans began pumping fresh water overboard in order to lighten ship. Spare spars and casks of beef followed, and then the "spirits." The breeze began to come steady for the big American about this time, so that by 10:30 it was apparent she was opening the range on her pursuers — but not dramatically. Captain Stewart was too much a seaman to trust to the momentary good wind so that when he came abeam of Halfway Rock at noon, he rounded to the north and entered Marblehead harbor, dropping anchor at 12:30. The two British frigates, *Junon* (38) and *Tenedos* (38), on their way to blockade Boston, rounded to about six miles offshore, unwilling to chance unknown waters leading to what might be a fortified port (it wasn't). A few hours later, when he was satisfied that an attack was not in the offing, Stewart shifted his berth to an anchorage abreast the fort in the adjacent town of Salem. The two Britishers shortly resumed their blockade duties, perhaps expecting to have another crack at this most famous of the American frigates when next she sortied.

This chase of *Constitution* took place on a Sunday, and it is said that as the word that "Old Ironsides" was being hard-pressed spread, all the able-bodied turned out to do what they could in her defense. Ministers stopped their sermons in mid-harangue and cancelled the remainder of services with hasty benedictions in the common cause. Militia artillerymen manned their guns in the Salem fort while others wheeled their field pieces into positions on likely promontories. It took time for the report to get to Boston, but by seven that evening the New England Guards had mustered at their armory and were setting out, albeit without ammunition. Commodore Bainbridge, the Yard Commandant, halted them with a request that they take charge of the heavy artillery to be sent thither, so they returned to the gun house then on Boston Common. They were about to start again when a second report was received that *Constitution* was safe in Salem so, after much sound and little fury, the Guards returned their equipment and went home.

Two weeks later, in the absence of the lurking British, Stewart brought his ship back to Boston for a new mainmast and new sails. He was hopeful still of making his mark in a memorable way.

## BLOCKADED

The advent of British warships off Boston, clearly and regularly visible to the populace of the surrounding shores, was completely disquieting to the local government. Fears of raids and invasion were rampant. While Stewart toiled to get his ship back in operating condition, *Junon* and *Tenedos* continued their vigil, watching not only *Constitution* but frigate *Congress* (36) in Portsmouth, New Hampshire, as well. On 7 May, HMS *Nymphe* (38) arrived on the scene and replaced *Tenedos,* which went to Halifax for upkeep. On the 9th, *Nymphe* "made all sail towards Boston to make a reconnaissance" while *Junon* did the same towards Portsmouth. The next day, "... Stood close in to the little town of Cape Ann or Gloucester, and regulated our watches by the town clock, which wanted ten minutes to eleven;" and later, "The ship within one mile of Boston

Lighthouse. Saw the *Constitution* nearly unrigged. No other man-of-war in the harbour." Unchallenged, *Nymphe* moved offshore once more to prey on shipping rounding the head of Cape Cod while *Junon* took station off Cape Ann. On 22 May, the British blockaders were augmented by the arrival of *HMS Ramillies* (74), wearing the flag of Rear Admiral Thomas Masterman Hardy, who had been Lord Horatio Nelson's Flag Captain at the Battle of Trafalgar.

The augmentation of the British squadron only served to increase tensions in and around Boston. For Captain Stewart, it must have been a difficult time, to find himself once more trapped in harbor just when he felt on the verge of a memorable cruise. And it was a bad time for the senior American naval officer, as well: Commodore Bainbridge was worried about the ship of the line *Independence* (74), which was then nearing launch in the Navy Yard. Every time one or more units of the British squadron closed Boston Light to ascertain the status of the two warships, there was another outbreak of invasion jitters.

*Nymphe* came back off the light on 4 June to check on *Constitution* "who, we heard, was ready to sail." Not against the prevailing odds. And they got worse on the 7th when *HMS Bulwark,* another 74, arrived on the scene.

The 18th of June was to be the launching day of *Independence,* first ship of the line for the United States Navy, from its covered launch way inside Shiphouse #1. By eleven that day large crowds had gathered to witness the important event, both from the grounds near the shiphouse and from more remote spots like the Charlestown Bridge and Copp's Hill, across the Charles River in Boston. The liner moved down the ways only 70-75 feet and came to a stop. Somehow, the tallow had been removed from a section of the ways. Bainbridge tried a second time on Sunday, the 19th, but he could not force her farther. One man was killed in the attempt. The British almost immediately were aware of the schedule and of the failure — even to the distance she moved on the ways — so good were their lines of communication with the disaffected elements of the populace. This letter to the editor of the *United States Gazette* clearly reflects the attitude of these people:

> ... it was no wonder she *stuck,* as they undertook to launch her upon the anniversary of the declaration of war. The war itself *sticks;* the recruiting *sticks;* the loan *sticks;* in short everything connected with the transaction of that ill-fated day *sticks;* and no wonder the 74 *sticks*...

In the small hours of 21 June, the British blockading force sent its worst scare yet into the city of Boston. Master's Mate Charles Goullet daringly took a large ship's boat into Boston Harbor to within a mile of where *Constitution* lay and burned a sloop, sending the following note to the *Boston Patriot* newspaper by a passing fisherman:

> Sir — As you may probably wish to be accurately informed of the particulars of a fire, which no doubt was sufficiently visible to the eyes of the Bostonians this morning, I transmit you by the bearer, the following true statement. Not being a sufficiently

good pilot to navigate as far as the *Navy Yard*, the tender which I have the honor to command; I proceeded in my boat, at 2 A.M. and after reconnoitring the *Harbor of Boston*, boarded a pleasure boat, where I refreshed my men. At 6, having made myself sufficiently acquainted with the strength and navigation of your port, I thought proper to burn a sloop, in order to deter others from running ashore.

I strongly recommend Com. Bainbridge to place the *Constitution* in the best possible state of defense, not only for her own protection, but that of his *unfledged Independence.*

Publication of this note by the *Patriot* spurred more than a week of verbal sniping between it and the politically opposed *Columbian Centinel;* sniping which ended only with the publication by the former of sworn statements from the captain and crew of the fishing boat which had delivered it in the first place.

The 22nd of June was, at last, the launch day of *Independence,* much to Bainbridge's relief. At three that afternoon she slid into the Charles, welcomed by 21-gun salutes from *Constitution* and the Half Moon Battery. Perhaps "Old Ironsides" felt a sense of kinship with this first ship of the line, as well: it had needed three tries to launch her, too, seventeen years earlier.

On 3 July, *Bulwark* and *Nymphe* closed on Boston Light to check up on the two American men of war. "Observed United States ship *Constitution* ... ready for her." *Nymphe* checked in again on the 19th and "...observed *Constitution* ready for sea. There are various reports concerning her and none to be depended upon." Another 74 joined the watchers on the next day, the *Spencer;* on the 23rd, *HMS Leander* (50), reported for duty. According to a squadron officer, "She is one of the large new fir frigates, mounting fifty guns, twenty-four pounders and forty-two pounders, 500 men. I think her a great deal more than a match for the *Constitution.*"

All during the month of July, the Commodore was in constant conflict with the local governments. Early in the month, representatives of both Governor Caleb Strong and the Town Council called upon him to suggest the removal of *Independence* and *Constitution* to anchorages east of Forts Warren and Independence. In other words, put the ships out where the British could get at them without having to get anywhere near their businesses. Obviously, "Old Ironsides" was not universally loved; the euphoria of her victories had ended. Bainbridge responded angrily but quite reasonably in the negative, pointing out that the proposal not only would cause the loss of the ships, but, while they were there, would mask the guns of the forts if the British had something in mind other than just finishing the ships.

Later, some of the local authorities proposed the sinking of block ships in the harbor entrance to deny the enemy access. Bainbridge stated his belief that such an action would not guarantee denying the British access to Boston because of the many routes available around the harbor islands and via the long, exposed coastline. He also pointed out that the blockships would limit the ease with which either *Constitution* or *Independence* could sortie, thus causing them to remain in Boston longer than might otherwise be the case.

The British strikes against Washington and Maine raised local fears to new heights — and also put an end to much of the political foolishness. Suddenly, cooperation between the Navy and local governments became the plan of the day. The Commodore laid out a series of recommended actions to fortify or otherwise defend the various approaches to Boston and Charlestown. The militia was called out and the work begun as the summer waned. As a sop to those who continued to believe in the blockship concept, some hulks were moved and anchored in positions from which they would be readily available if a given emergency should render them useful. At the Yard, Bainbridge had *Independence,* still incomplete, and *Constitution* moored in the stream so that their guns covered the water approaches. Because he had been unable to get *Independence*'s planned gun batteries from the foundries, he borrowed six 32-pounders from the Commonwealth and five 24-pounders from *Constitution* and, together with the two 24-pounders from the gunboats, gave the liner some firepower. He also enlisted 150 men for a term of two months with which to man her.

So passed summer into fall. The British squadron was augmented further by the arrival of *Newcastle,* a sister to *Leander,* and *Acasta,* a 44-gun frigate. As the weeks went by, Stewart, knowing that the normally worsening weather conditions on the New England coast would make life more difficult for the British, enlisted additional seamen to bring his crew up to full strength and waited for his opportunity.

## OFF AND AWAY

By mid-December, the blockaders had been reduced to *Newcastle* and *Acasta,* and the brig-sloop *Arab* (18). All of the others had been reassigned or were, as in the case of *Leander* at Halifax, in upkeep. Sunday, the 18th, dawned fair and clear, with a fresh breeze from the westnorthwest. To seaward, there was no enemy in sight. At two that afternoon, Stewart set sail and his longed-for moment was at hand. Cheered by people massed on Long Wharf and by the privateer *Prince De Neufchatel* (18), "Old Ironsides" glided swiftly down the harbor and out to the open sea.

*Arab* returned the next day to find the quarry had escaped and promptly sailed for Provincetown, where *Newcastle* and *Acasta* were anchored in protected waters. She reported the news on the 19th, the same day *Leander* sailed from Halifax for Boston. The three ships were united once more on Christmas Eve and the senior officer, Captain Sir George Collier of *Leander,* had to decide their course of action. Learning from the other skippers stories, all false, that *Constitution* was joining up with *Congress* from Portsmouth and *President* from the Delaware for a major strike against British shipping in home waters, Sir George got underway in pursuit of the imagined threat toward the English Channel, leaving *Arab* as the sole blockader.

In the meantime, Stewart was heading for Bermudian waters alone. By dawn of the first day at sea, the clear skies had given way to a gray overcast and the seas were making up. Soon, *Constitution* was buffeting into head seas and shipping water through leaky gun port lids. Life became a wet misery for the crew, compounded by the fact that the fast getaway had left the ship short of fresh rations. Within four days, such fresh meat as there had been was expended. Tea and sugar were gone, as well.

The officer of the deck reported hearing a gun as dawn broke on Christmas Eve, surmising that it might be a signal gun of a convoy or a man of war. An especially sharp lookout was kept in that direction for a couple of hours before a sail was sighted. Immediately, Stewart went in chase. At ten, he came up on a brig showing the Union Jack upside down, a signal of distress. A ship's boat soon returned with papers identifying the prize as the *Lord Nelson,* which had been a part of a convoy from St. Johns, Newfoundland, to Bermuda, until parted from it by the same gale that had bedeviled "Old Ironsides." The smaller ship had been much damaged. Stewart placed a prize crew aboard and set off in pursuit of the convoy, knowing it was guarded by but one frigate, of which he had no fear.

The next morning, Stewart took *Lord Nelson* in tow and sent working parties aboard to avail himself of her cargo as the two continued on under easy sail. She proved to be a "perfect slop ship and grocery store, very opportunely sent to furnish a good rig and bountiful cheer for Christmas." There soon was flowing aboard the frigate generous quantities of tongues, corned beef, smoked salmon, dried beef, codfish, pineapple, cheeses, barrels of loaf sugar, brandy, gin, port wine, tea, flour, and hams "inferior not even to Smithfield Virginia." The next afternoon, Sixth Lieutenant William V. Taylor was sent aboard the prize to cut away her masts so that the now-empty hull would ride better, but he misunderstood his orders and zealously scuttled her before anyone could stop him.

Moving to the southeast, Stewart hoped yet to come upon the convoy, by now bound onward for Barbados. On the last day of the year, a chase brought him up with a Spanish brig which had no useful intelligence. At nightfall of 3 January 1815, he gave over the chase, deciding to remain in the area of his present position in hopes of intercepting Europe-bound Englishmen entering the Atlantic via the Windward or Mona Passages from the Caribbean. He was then about 150 miles northnortheast of Puerto Rico; apparently he had decided not to go any farther south lest he encounter one of the British squadrons known to be operating in the Antillies, and about which he had expressed concern on his previous cruise. Four days of patrolling brought him nothing but a brief conversation with an American schooner. He headed east to get into the shipping lanes from the Southern Hemisphere.

On 9 January, he ran into another gale which left *Constitution* rolling heavily in the trough, shipping water through every opening and wetting even the berth deck. To help her ride better and to preclude their loss, Stewart had the topgallant yards landed and those uppermost masts sent down. Life got no better until the storm finally passed them by on the 14th. Inspection of the ship for damage found that some guns had had their tompions washed out of their muzzles and the shot rolled out of them. On the 18th, Seaman William Herrington fell overboard from the fore channels. Despite the fact that they were then in chase, Stewart paused to rescue him. The chase, a brig, could not be come up with before sunset and was given over. Stewart turned northeastward.

By 20 January, *Constitution* was in the sea lanes some 300 miles westnorthwest of the Canary Islands. Life became more interesting. On the 21st, she chased and spoke a Portuguese ship and a French brig. She brought to the French brig *Cassimere* three days later, and placed most of the crew of *Lord Nelson* aboard her for delivery ashore. A Portuguese brig was stopped on the 25th. Another storm from the 29th to the 31st made life a trial once more. Stewart shaped his course northward on the latter date, and after speaking a Portuguese ship four days later, on the 6th he turned eastward for the waters off Cape Finisterre.

On 8 February:

> At 7h. 30m. A.M. spoke and boarded the barque *Julia* under Hamburg colours from Cork bound to Lisbon out 15 days, informed us that the news at Cork when they left was, that peace had been signed at Ghent between the British and American Commissioners.

And at four that afternoon, an officer boarded a Russian brig from Kinsale, and from her:

> ...Two American masters of vessels, passengers, came on board and brought papers which confirmed the report of peace having been concluded...

Thus did Stewart learn that peace was imminent, after two years of negotiations. The initialling at Ghent, which had taken place on 24 December, only made peace likely; until ratified by Parliament and Congress, the state of war would continue to exist.

*Constitution* remained patrolling an area off Cape Finisterre for the next several days, sometimes coming within fifteen miles of the shore. Only a Swedish merchantman was spoke until late the afternoon of the 12th, when, in squally weather, what appeared to be a frigate was sighted on the weather beam. As the contact passed astern of the American at some distance, Stewart wore ship in chase, clearing for action. At seven, he beat to quarters and slowly ranged alongside as heavy seas rolled the guns under. The first hail, at eight, got no answer. Stewart fired a carronade shot over her and hailed again, determined that nothing would put him off. To his disappointment, the stranger proved to be the Portuguese frigate *Amazon*. Securing his guns, Stewart tended slowly southward.

Dawn of the 16th found him within sight of the Rock of Lisbon at the mouth of the Tagus River. Also in sight were sails dead ahead and on the starboard quarter; Stewart chose to chase the latter, flying an English ensign to confuse his quarry. At 7:30, the chase was found to be Portuguese, so Stewart came about and made for the other contact which, at long range, was thought to be a privateer. This ship was, in fact *HMS Elizabeth* (74), which shortly thereafter went in to Lisbon, learned that "Old Ironsides" was in the area, and promptly got underway again in pursuit. Unbeknownst to Stewart, also in the area was *Tiber* (38), commanded by James Richard Dacres, who had lost *Guerriere* to *Constitution* 2½ years earlier and who wanted another chance. He, too, became a hunter when he learned of his old adversary's presence. At nine, before he could come up with the presumed privateer, Stewart spotted a fat merchantman ripe for plucking and shifted the chase to what promised greater profit. A few hours chase brought into his bag the British *Susanna*, bound from Buenos Aires to Liverpool with a cargo of hides, tallow, vicuna wool, and nutria pelts, valued at $75,000. She also carried two "tiger" cubs (probably jaguars), which Stewart had chained in one of *Constitution*'s boats stowed on the skid beams.

Continuing to move southward for the next two days, Stewart prepared to defy the odds and get *Susanna* back to an American port. At daylight on the 19th, *Constitution* went in chase for the first time since taking the Englishman, but it proved to be a Russian ship: *Joseph.* A second chase that day turned out to be another Portuguese. Late that afternoon, Stewart ordered *Susanna* to head across the Atlantic. She made it.

## A TACTICAL TRIUMPH

The 20th of February 1815 dawned cloudy and hazy with a cold, damp northeast wind propelling *Constitution* in a southwesterly direction under short canvas on a course roughly paralleling the African coast. Madeira was about 180 miles to the westsouthwest. All was quiet, but Stewart was keeping an alert watch because his activities of the preceding ten days certainly must have stirred up a hornet's nest off Gibraltar, a major Royal Navy base. At one that afternoon, a ship was spied on the larboard bow, heading toward the American. In a half hour, a second contact was sighted beyond the first and somewhat to the westward, "both standing close hauled towards us under a press of sail ..." It was clear that the first unit was a full-rigged ship and presumably a combatant. So matters stood until four, when the nearest contact signalled to the other and turned southward, apparently so the two could join forces. Stewart instantly crowded on sail in pursuit, setting his stunsails as the big frigate gathered way. He was certain he had two Englishmen before him and thought their maneuvering meant they intended to keep away from him until nightfall when they could elude him. In fact, they intended to keep him from discovering a West Indies-bound convoy over the horizon to the southwest. Every stitch of canvas was set in *Constitution,* alow and aloft. At 4:30 a sickening cracking sound gave warning to those below that the main royal mast was giving way. Slowing his pursuit, Stewart quickly sent men aloft to cut away the wreckage while others prepared a spare spar. In a half hour, it was aloft and the main royal drawing smartly once more.

With the range closing again, *Constitution* "fired on the chase from the first gun 1st division and the chase gun on the forecastle ..." The range was too great. It was apparent that the enemy would be able to combine forces before Stewart could come up on the nearest one, so at 5:30 he cleared for action and made deliberate preparations for battle. Shot was gotten up and powder charges made ready. The decks were wetted and sanded. Personal weapons for the boarding party were broken out and positioned in tubs about the decks, ready to hand. And Surgeon John A. Kearney and his mates made their preparations down in the cockpit for the grim work they knew lay ahead of them.

At 5:40, the enemy "passed within hail of each other, shortened sail, hauled up their courses, and appeared to be making preparations to receive us." Stewart knew now he had his sought-after fight before him — two against one. After briefly trying to get the weather gage and not succeeding, the Englishmen "formed on a line of wind at half a cables length from each other." That is, they formed a column heading roughly westward with about 100 yards between them. The smaller of the two was in the lead.

At six, in the setting sun, *Constitution* broke the Stars and Stripes as she came ranging up on the windward side of the enemy column. They responded by hoisting Red Ensigns. Five minutes later, "Old Ironsides" was alongside the aftermost ship at about 200 yards with her sails lifting gently, her momentum carrying her forward until she was in a position at the apex of an equilateral triangle, her opponents' column forming the baseline. From this ideal position, Stewart "invited the action by firing a shot between the two ships which immediately commenced with an exchange of broadsides." An English ball killed two men in the waist and continued on to smash one of the ship's boats, putting an end to the "tigers." Firing continued hot and heavy for about fifteen minutes, when enemy fire slackened markedly. By this time, the sea and the combatants were smothered in smoke. Stewart ordered a cease fire to give it time to drift clear and to determine the condition of his opponents. It took about three minutes for it to blow away ahead, and then he saw that he was now abeam of the leading ship, while the other one was luffing to cross under his stern and rake. Blasting a final broadside into the antagonist abeam, Stewart threw his main and mizzen topsails flat aback, with topgallants still set, shook all forward, let fly his jib sheet, backed swiftly astern, and unleashed a heavy fire. The rear enemy thus was forced to fill again on his original heading in order to avoid being raked from ahead. At this point, the leading enemy adroitly attempted to tack across *Constitution*'s bow and rake *her* from ahead; but Stewart once again filled his sails, boarded his fore-tack, and shot ahead. When the enemy wore to avoid collision, Stewart rewarded him with two raking broadsides in the stern, at which time the Englishman ran off to leeward to escape the heavy fire. He had divided his enemies.

Looking back, Stewart saw that his larger antagonist also was wearing to get between *Constitution* and his cohort, and himself wore short, crossed her stern,

Constitution *backs down as* Cyane
*attempts to rake from astern.*

and gave her a rake from the larboard battery. He then luffed back across her wake to a position on her larboard (windward) quarter, and was about to give the starboard battery an opportunity from a range of just fifty yards, when the enemy struck his colors and fired a gun to leeward. The time was 6:45. In short order, Second Lieutenant Beekman V. Hoffman was aboard with fifteen Marines to take possession of *HMS Cyane* (24), a light frigate under the command of Captain Gordon Thomas Falcon.

During this early part of the engagement, there occurred an incident to give sailors pause: A man at one of the forecastle carronades collapsed just as a shot entered through his gun port. The gun captain thinking him dead, ordered the body passed across the deck and thrown overboard on the unengaged side. As one of the men, standing in the fore channel, was wrestling the body through the

port, he thought he saw some facial muscles twitch. Pulling the body back on deck, his mates sent him below to the cockpit to be checked by the surgeon. He revived and was back at his gun in time for what is about to be recounted. He had, it seems, suffered an epileptic seizure; his mates had not been aware of his condition.

An hour later, having taken the enemy officers into *Constitution* and assured himself that his prize crew could control *Cyane,* Stewart set off after the other enemy. That ship had not, in fact, run away, but had, instead, drawn off to effect repairs to her sails and rigging, and was returning to the fray. Thus it was that, within fifteen minutes of setting sail, Stewart found himself bearing down on an enemy which, in turn, was heading for him. At 8:40 the two passed each other at fifty yards going in opposite directions and exchanged broadsides.

159

Stewart adroitly wore short and got in a stern rake before his enemy was out of range. Realizing her mate had struck, the latter then made all sail before the wind, seeking escape. Stewart quickly was in chase, and at 9:30 began picking away at him with two bow guns, every shot being carefully sighted, and few missing. The range steadily decreased until the American seamen could hear planking being ripped up as their shots told. Some of these sounds may have been those of the wheel being shot away. A short-coming in her design prevented the enemy from using stern chasers in her own defense. At ten, recognizing there could be no escape, the enemy came by the wind and also fired a leeward gun. Third Lieutenant William B. Shubrick went over to accept the surrender of *HMS Levant,* a new 18-gun corvette commanded by Captain George Douglass, the senior of the two British captains.

*Cyane,* the larger of *Constitution*'s opponents, carried thirty-four guns into this fight: twenty-two 32-pounder carronades, ten 18-pounder carronades, and two long 9-pounder chase guns. *Levant* carried eighteen 32-pounder carronades, one 12-pounder carronade, and, again, two long 9-pounder chase guns. Whatever their aggregate weight of metal, their strength lay in short range weapons whose maximum effective range was on the order of 400 yards. In contrast, *Constitution* carried the batteries that had served her so well in this war: thirty 24-pounder great guns, 22-24 32-pounder carronades, and a long 24-pounder chase gun. The maximum effective range of her long guns was about 1200 yards — three times greater than that of the carronades — and gave Stewart the option of fighting at longer ranges when it was advantageous to do so.

The withholding or absence of records makes it difficult to assess crew sizes and casualties with precision. *Constitution* appears to have had 451 officers and men aboard at the time of the engagement, while, in round numbers, *Cyane* had 180 and *Levant,* 140. *Constitution*'s log states that she suffered four dead and fourteen wounded that evening, although most authors have noted three dead and twelve wounded. A list of these crewmen, alluded to in Stewart's report of the action, is missing. It is known that none were officers. As regards the British losses, estimates by Americans on the scene place the death toll in *Cyane* at twelve and in *Levant,* twenty-three; they counted twenty-six wounded in the former and sixteen in the latter. The bulk of these undoubtedly occurred as a result of the repeated rakes "Old Ironsides" poured into both ships; being a night action, Marine snipers did not make the sort of contribution they had in previous engagements.

British gunners in this fight appear to have concentrated more on the American frigate's hull than they had in previous encounters. Aside from a few lines cut in the opening blasts of grape shot, *Constitution* suffered no rigging or spar damage; her hull, on the other hand, was found to have about a dozen 32-pounder balls imbedded in it — none of which had opened a serious wound. *Constitution*'s heavy batteries, on the other hand, had wreaked havoc in her

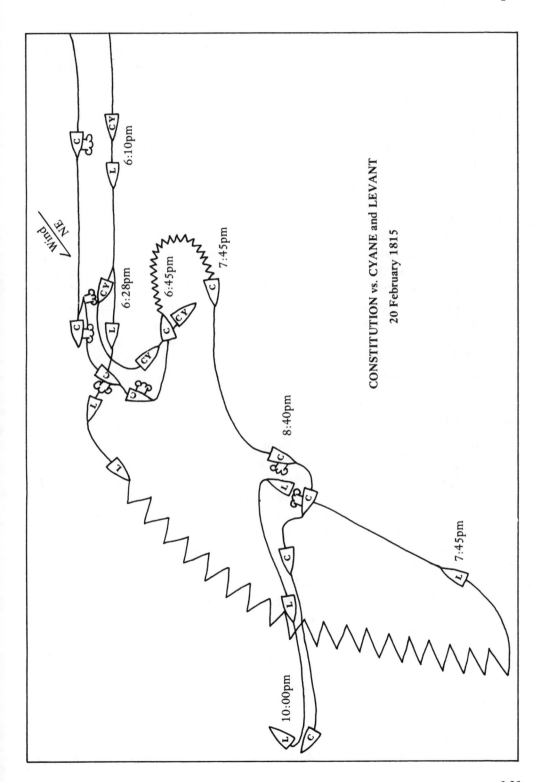

CONSTITUTION vs. CYANE and LEVANT
20 February 1815

more lightly built opponents. *Cyane*'s main and mizzen masts were tottering and ready to fall, and every bowline and brace had been shot away; other spars were wounded, as well. Five of her carronades had been dismounted as her thinner sides could not stop the American's weight of metal. She had been hit nine or ten times between wind and water and had five feet of water in her hold. *Levant*, as has been noted, had her wheel shot away and her bulwarks shattered. Her rigging, too, had been decimated and her mizzen mast was threatening to fall.

In summary, Charles Stewart and *Constitution* had everything going for them in this fight: heavier gun batteries (although he could only suspect that might be so beforehand); a tough hull better able to resist damage — with spars and rigging to match; and, because the British blockade had put so many American sailors on the beach, Stewart had been able to ship what was perhaps the most experienced crew "Old Ironsides" ever would have. Captain Stewart proved himself to be a superb tactician and ship handler, who took advantage of every break he got and acted decisively to deny the enemy any. He fought at ranges which insured his gunners rarely would miss while his enemies were working at close to their maximum effective range or with most of their guns masked. His experienced crew, in which he had the greatest confidence, was able to respond with alacrity to his demanding orders for swift and certain sailhandling. If his adversaries can be said to have done anything wrong, it would have to be having had the temerity to challenge him in the first place. On *that* day, in *those* circumstances, Stewart, *Constitution,* and the crew were simply unbeatable.

## AFTERMATH

It required but three hours to put *Constitution* back in condition for further action, but the same could not be said of her prizes. After laying to through the night, the trio got underway under easy sail the next morning, heading southward to put more distance between themselves and the centers of British naval power. Boats plied regularly back and forth between the captor and captives as American working parties sought to repair the results of their recent handiwork, and as prisoners, prize crews, and baggage were redistributed. On the 23rd, a gang was sent to *Levant* which took out her mizzenmast and floated it to *Constitution* for repairs; it was back in place before sunset the same day.

Within twenty-four hours of his victory, Captain Stewart began to get complaints from his prisoners that they were missing many personal articles, alleging that the Americans were stealing from them. A search by his officers on the 22nd failed to turn up any of the missing items. When the complaints persisted, on the 24th he caused searches of all his people, their baggage, and every space in the ship, but found nothing of consequence. He had all British baggage stowed in a locked bread room and placed the key in the personal custody of his First Lieutenant.

The British officers proved to be every bit as quarrelsome as the tars. *Constitution*'s log contains this entry for the 25th: "The prisoners orderly except some of the British Officers of whom this ship's ward room officers complained, that they did not conduct themselves, below, like gentlemen, being in their language indecent, vulgar, and abusive to each other." So unpleasant was their company that Chaplain A. Y. Humphreys, upon learning that he was being reassigned to the prize crew in *Levant*, wrote in his journal, "A reprieve to any condemned malefactor was never hailed with sincerer gratulation."

Captains Falcon and Douglass were not above conducting themselves with similar pettishness. On one occasion, Falcon observed to First Lieutenant Ballard that the toilet facilities in "Old Ironsides" were substandard when compared to those he had enjoyed in his own ship. Ballard is reported to have responded that the Americans were not so concerned about such matters "provided our guns tell well, and you can be a competent judge of how far that end has been obtained." On another occasion, Stewart is said to have returned to his cabin from attending to some business on the quarterdeck only to find Captains Falcon and Douglass in a heated argument. At contention was which of them had been most at fault for their collective defeat. Stewart listened to the acrimony for a few minutes, then reportedly told them, "Gentlemen, there is no use in getting warm about it; it would have been all the same whatever you might have done. If you doubt that, I will put you all on board again and you can try it over." The offer was not accepted.

The ships continued slowly southward as repairs went on in *Cyane*. Stewart had decided to head for the Cape Verde Islands, where he would parole the troublesome Englishmen and take on fresh stores before returning across the Atlantic. Continuing British complaints caused still another thorough search for missing articles on 2 March, as well as a close examination of just what had transpired in the first hours after the battle. The log tells the result:

> ... It appeared that after the ships had struck their colours that their men broke into the Spirit and Slop rooms, and Officers apartments, and pillaged all they could. Found much new Slop clothing among their men which their Officers affirmed had been served out to them the day prior to the action, but when they were shown that they had no numbers on it was admitted that they could not have been served out but were plundered.

As for the missing officers' possessions, evidently their sailors stole them and then pitched the loot over the side before individuals could be apprehended. A sorry lot. Waxing eloquent over this apparent disintegration of the character of the vaunted British tar, Chaplain Humphreys declared, "The sun of Britain's naval glory is set."

Repairs to *Cyane* were completed two days later. Stewart promptly placed his small force in a scouting line, the ships separated at maximum signalling distance on a line perpendicular to the direction of advance. By this means, he intended to minimize being surprised by the enemy men of war he knew were looking for him. When they ran into fog on the 6th, he brought them back into a tight little group. At four that afternoon, still in thick fog and with little wind, a

Cyane (left) *and* Levant (right) *follow* Constitution *into Porto Praya.*

lookout in *Levant* caught sight of land. In another two days, the group anchored off the island of Maio, one of the smaller Cape Verdes some twenty-five miles northeast of the principal island of Sao Tiago. Because the anchorage was very exposed, Stewart lay there only twenty-four hours for the fog to lift. When it did not, he got underway anyway at three the next afternoon, feeling he could navigate safely the short distance to Porto Praya on the big island.

*Constitution* and her prizes anchored in the harbor of Porto Praya at 11 A.M. on 10 March, after *Levant* narrowly had avoided running aground as they entered. Stewart was suspicious of Portuguese neutrality, but received assurances from the Governor on that score and a promise that the countryside would provide him with the fresh provisions he desired. It was Stewart's intention to capitalize on the presence of a British brig in harbor by chartering it as a cartel to take his paroled prisoners home. He sent Captains Douglass and Falcon ashore to make these arrangements, and when they returned to report success he permitted two of their officers and twelve seamen to go aboard the brig to insure that it did not try to sneak away in the night.

## CHASED

The next morning, Stewart began shifting prisoners to the British brig, and had sent a working party ashore to load stores. About noontime, Third Lieutenant Shubrick had just assumed the watch when he was attracted by the stifled exclamation of a British midshipman and the apparent whispered reprimand he was receiving from his lieutenant. As he was trying to determine what had caused the little byplay, his quartermaster called his attention to the harbor entrance, where a low, heavy fog covered the sea. Visible above it were the upper masts and sails of a large ship. That must have been what had startled the midshipman. Captain Stewart was called immediately. By the time he reached the deck, two more sets of upper sails came into view, obviously the rigs of warships; all three were bound into the harbor. No doubt recalling that the American frigate *Essex* had been taken by the British in the neutral port of Valparaiso in 1814, Stewart took instant action to get his ships to sea, where he would have maneuvering room. Quickly, his crew was called to their stations. Just four minutes after sighting the last two contacts, he cut his anchor cable, set topsails, and stood out of the bay on a course calculated to give him the weather gage for whatever was to follow. Signals to *Cyane* and *Levant* ordered them to follow suit, which they did with an alacrity that testifies to the competence of their prize masters and small crews. Realizing what was happening, some of the British prisoners already ashore for transfer to the cartel rushed to the Portuguese fort and began firing at the escaping Americans.

*Constitution* and her consorts just cleared East Point, marking the northern limit of the harbor, as their pursuers came into long cannon range from the south. The enemy crowded on sail. "Old Ironsides" crossed her topgallant yards, and set main and fore courses, spanker, flying jib, and her topgallants, and headed eastward, the wind coming from the northnortheast. The gig and first cutter, which had been moored astern, were cut adrift. *Cyane* and *Levant* followed the motions of their leader smartly. Now it was going to be decided on the ships' sailing abilities. Stewart thought his pursuers were two ships of the line and a frigate.

What Charles Stewart did not learn until much later was that his pursuers were *Leander, Newcastle,* and *Acasta,* those three nemeses which had held her blockaded for eight long months in Boston. After learning of her escape, as we have seen, Commodore Collier headed for the English Channel with this group. Failing to find his quarry there, he had patrolled southward until the trail became warm off Portugal. It grew red hot when he encountered the Russian ship *Joseph* on the same day *Constitution* met *Cyane* and *Levant.* Despite the fact that *Constitution* had posed as a British man of war when she met the Russian on 19 February, she had been correctly identified and so reported to Collier. After that, it became only a matter of time before the two would meet again.

The chase was continuing at a smart ten knots. Gradually, it was seen that *Acasta* was weathering on both *Cyane* and *Levant,* but not on *Constitution,* which slowly was pulling away from her consorts. Seeing that that particular enemy, whatever her specific rate, was bigger and faster than *Cyane,* whom she shortly would have under her guns, at 1:10 Stewart signalled Lieutenant Hoffman to tack to the northwest. This Hoffman promptly did — without drawing a single enemy after him. Now the hunted were on the short side of a three-on-two situation. The British Commodore evidently, at this point, intended solely to "get

*Constitution*." Hoffman subsequently idled awhile in the fog to the northwest, assuming that if he were pursued the British most likely would look for him to run with the wind. When he felt they must have passed safely ahead and away from him, he shaped a course for New York, where he arrived on 10 April. *Cyane* was taken into the U.S. Navy as a ship sloop and served actively until 1827. She finally was broken up in 1836.

At 2:30, one of the pursuers tried firing at *Constitution,* but the range was too great. By three o'clock, it was seen that *Levant* soon would be endangered as *Cyane* had been. Once again hoping to improve the odds, at 3:12, Stewart signalled to Ballard to tack to the northwest. This time, unaccountably, *all* three pursuers followed suit. *Constitution* quickly sailed over the horizon and out of danger, discretion being the better part of valor.

Lieutenant Ballard, seeing he had become the center of attention, made the one desperate move he could: he went back to Porto Praya because it technically was a neutral port. The British squadron, as Stewart had feared earlier, moved in without a pause and began bombarding the hapless *Levant,* and after fifteen minutes of enduring what must be reported as haphazard fire (not one man was wounded), Ballard hauled down his colors. Commodore George Collier never was able to provide a satisfactory explanation for his actions on this occasion; the fact that he had allowed *Constitution* to escape his force of ships especially built to get her is said to have contributed to his suicide after the war.

## HOMEWARD BOUND, BUT NOT DIRECTLY

*Constitution* stood south until she reached the latitude of Guinea, then turned west. Despite the fact that he had lost one-third of his crew through the manning of prizes and casualties — including First and Second Lieutenants, sailing master, at least four midshipmen, chaplain, sailmaker, and a surgeon's mate — Stewart was not quite ready to return home. In a letter taken from *Susanna* he found a report that *HMS Inconstant* was due to bring bullion to England from Rio de la Plata. He intended to make a leisurely pass across the Atlantic Narrows trade routes in the hope that *Inconstant* would be met. What a rewarding way to end the last war cruise it would be!

Idling through tropic waters, the big frigate headed southwest in solitude. Stewart knew that the warmer clime could have an adverse effect on the prisoners confined below and, recognizing the risk arising from having a crew barely in the majority, set up a system of exercise for his involuntary dependents. Each morning, one third of the captives were permitted on the spar deck, while another third passed their time on the gun deck and the remainder stayed in the hold. Each noontime, the groups were rotated. At the end of the first dog watch, all returned to the hold. On the 18th, Stewart required all the prisoners to bathe in tubs set up in the channels. This was repeated on the 24th, by which time *Constitution* had passed south of the Equator.

Cabo de Sao Roque, the northeast corner of Brazil, was sighted on 26 March.

Stewart turned northwest. When, four days later, he received the morning report noting but 6000 gallons of "fresh" water remaining, he decided to put in at "Maranham" (Maranhao, today Sao Luis), at the mouth of the Itapecuru River. Prior to entering port on 2 April, Stewart had all the enlisted prisoners put in irons so there could be no "surprises" during the normal confusion attending the start of a port call.

Fourth Lieutenant William M. Hunter was sent ashore to make contact with local government officials and learn the latest news. He returned shortly saying that it would be all right to land the prisoners and arrange for their return to England, but that no one yet knew whether peace had become a fact. A local ship chandler of British origin refused to furnish them with supplies.

Prisoner offloading began at eight on the morning of the 4th. Once again Stewart received complaints from the Britishers about thievery. This time, the Captain composed a search party of his officers and the British officers to search the ship and the crew from keelson to main truck — and even into the empty water casks — for the supposedly purloined goods. Nothing was found. One wonders, at this point, whether these complaints hadn't become practical jokes by the British, recognizing the sensitivity in this regard on the part of their conqueror. All of the *Constitution*s must have been glad to see the last of their enemies.

Stewart got underway for home on the 13th, but foul winds prevented him from completing negotiation of the tortuous channel until the 15th, when he finally reached the open sea. Moving to the northwest, toward the Antillies where British squadrons roamed, Stewart ran daily exercises at battle stations to whip his diminished crew into some fighting trim for what might lay ahead. Ten days later, *Constitution* went in chase at daylight. By 8:30, then some four miles on the contact's weather beam, Stewart saw she was a two-decker. A short while later, it was seen that *Constitution*'s foretopmast was badly sprung, so Stewart prudently kept his distance until repairs could be made. The liner, whatever her nationality, showed no curiosity in her smaller neighbor and continued on her way.

*Constitution* arrived off San Juan, Puerto Rico, on the morning of 28 April, and Stewart sent Lieutenant Hunter ashore for the latest intelligence. Late that afternoon he returned with confirmation that the peace treaty had been ratified. In fact, America had ratified the Treaty of Ghent on 17 February, but because there was a 30-day "time late" clause built into it to provide time to communicate that fact to the farflung naval units on both sides *Constitution*'s capture of *Cyane* and *Levant* stood as valid wartime conquests.

Stewart took his departure from Puerto Rico late the next morning, bound for New York, where he arrived off the Battery on the afternoon of 15 May. He marked his return with a 15-gun salute and went ashore to the plaudits of his fellow countrymen, enjoying much the same reception as Hull and Bainbridge had received in Boston. Congress could do no less than vote him a gold medal for

167

his classic action, making him the third successive skipper of "Old Ironsides" to be so recognized and his ship the only one that could boast of having had all her captains in that war decorated.

Following the festivities in New York, Stewart returned *Constitution* to Boston, where some of her crew were transferred to duty in *Lynx* (6), then being readied for duty with Commodore Bainbridge's squadron in the Mediterranean, while the remainder stripped her of guns and equipage with which to outfit *Independence* as that ambitious gentleman's flagship. Stewart was ordered detached on 25 June, but the ship remained in First Lieutenant William B. Shubrick's charge until ordered laid up on 25 January 1816.

Objective analysis of the War of 1812 must conclude that the victories of *Constitution* and *United States,* together with those of *Essex* and the war-brigs, had no direct effect on the course of the war. The losses suffered by the Royal Navy were no more than pin pricks to that great fleet: they neither impaired its battle readiness nor disrupted the blockade of American ports. By comparison, Oliver Hazard Perry's fresh-water victory on Lake Erie in 1813 and Thomas Macdonough's on Lake Champlain a year later prevented the overland invasion of the United States and determined the course of the war. What *Constitution* and her sister did accomplish was to uplift American morale spectacularly and, in the process, end forever the myth that the Royal Navy was invincible. They demonstrated unmistakeably that the American man-of-warsman was every bit as good as his British cousin and that his ship could stand with the best. The big frigates made Americans proud to be Americans, proven equals to any other nation in the world.

As we now know, *Constitution*'s days of daring battles and stirring victories were at an end. She and her men had accomplished far more than any other single ship in our naval history. But, as we know, too, she still had many miles to sail and duties to perform under the Stars and Stripes.

# 11 Mediterranean Sojourn

## PREPARATIONS

On 28 June 1815, *Constitution* was surveyed to determine her true condition. It was found that she was sound in her hull, but that the decks required caulking. The standing rigging, much patched, was passable, but the running rigging needed total replacement. Three yards and the foretopmast also had to be replaced, but, other than a repairable wound in the head of the foremast which could be done in place, all other masts were fit for further service. One suit of sails still was usable.

Upon receipt of this report, the Board of Naval Commissioners, created in February of that year to assist the Secretary in running the larger Navy, ordered that she be prepared for duty in the Mediterranean. Reports soon were received, however, that Commodore Decatur had defeated the Algerines at sea and had brought an end to the renewed problem with the Barbary pirates which had arisen during the war with England. As a result of this unexpected turn of events, *Constitution* was laid up, to languish for nearly five years.

In April 1820, Isaac Hull, now Commandant of the Navy Yard, received orders from the Board to take *Constitution* out of ordinary and put her back in shape. He was to replank the hull with oak, not pine; make the internal arrangements in accordance with the layout used in the newest 44's; and return the gun deck to its flush (single-level) condition.

As the work began, and the decayed outer planks were ripped away, Hull was encouraged by what he found. Everything below the berth deck appeared sound and he even had hopes of saving it. Spar and gun deck planking would have to be replaced, but many of the beams and knees "may answer again." As the repair monies were limited, efforts were made to draw the iron spikes carefully so that as many as possible could be used once more. Hull thought perhaps two-thirds could.

During the warm summer months, the ship was a beehive of activity. By early July, outer hull planking had been replaced up to the lower gun ports, and above them to the plank sheer. In mid-July, two 32-pound shot — undoubtedly from *Cyane* and *Levant* — were taken out of the hull planking and sent to the Commissioners, where they were displayed in the Washington office. On 25 July, the Board told Hull to get *Constitution*'s guns back from *Independence*, which was in ordinary in Boston.

In September, Hull began to fret about the Board's intentions concerning "Old Ironsides' " future employment, about which he had been told nothing. Winter wasn't too far away, and she still had to be hove down, rigged, and fitted with sails. The Board ignored all of his questions.

October came in foul, slowing work markedly. Unfortunately, it was out in the weather where most of the work was: laying and caulking the spar deck and putting up the quarterdeck bulwarks. On the last day of the month, the Board bombed Hull with orders to copper the ship and "in all respects equipped for service with all practicable dispatch." What the good Yard Commandant felt about this turn of events is unrecorded, but it certainly couldn't have been complimentary of the Commissioners. Immediately, he began preparations for heaving her out. He told Washington, however, that he expected "such severe weather before we can be ready, that we shall have a disagreeable time in doing it."

In mid-November, Commodore John Rodgers, head of the Board, provided Hull with an inventory of the furniture to be provided in the frigate. It states most eloquently the spartan conditions under which ship's company lived:

Captain's cabin — 1 sideboard, 1 secretary, 2 sofas, 1 set of curtains, 1 clerk's desk, 1 set of tables, 18 chairs, and cooking utensils.

Wardroom — 1 dining table, 1 small table for each stateroom, 2 dozen chairs, 1 walnut sideboard, 1 green cloth cover for dining table, and cooking utensils.

Steerage — 1 mess chest, 3 camp stools, 1 frying pan, 1 iron tea-kettle, 1 tin coffee pot, 1 coffee mill, and 2 tin pitchers for each six-man mess.

Gun Room — same as for a Steerage mess.

Crew — 1 mess chest, 2 kids, and 2 cans for each six-man mess.

*Constitution* was heaved down and out on Saturday, 25 November and five strakes of copper put on before the day was out. It was seen, too, that the lowest part of the cutwater and the forwardmost section of the shoe were missing; repairs were effected by the 28th. The coppering job was completed on 8 December, the old sheets being shipped to the Washington Navy Yard per the Board's orders. Despite Hull's fears about the weather, the whole operation had taken about the same amount of time as when it had been done in 1803 and 1812.

With the coppering finished, Hull pressed on with the overhaul. During the next two weeks, he manufactured and installed a new foremast, inspected and returned the mainmast, positioned the fighting tops, and was busy setting up the lower rigging. By nightfall of 22 December, all 150 tons of iron kentledge was aboard and he had begun paring back his work force. As of Christmas Eve, 40,000 gallons of water had been sent aboard and, Hull told the Board, she could be ready for sea even before a crew could be recruited.

In completing the sparring and rigging of *Constitution*, Hull incorporated a development which hitherto had not been employed in large men of war: sliding gunters. The sliding gunters were, in effect, "mast extenders," with an iron hoop at one end to fit over the uppermost mast section, and raised into position by a halyard affixed about one-third the spar length from the hoop and passing through the truck at the top of the mast. It was handled from the fighting top.

170

These Hull had fitted apparently so that skysails could be employed when desired without having to carry the more conventional "sky poles" permanently in place more than 200 feet above the water — at times, unwanted top hamper. In another "first" for the ship, he also provided a ringtail — a sort of stunsail — for the spanker.

After all the pressure it had exerted on Isaac Hull to complete *Constitution's* overhaul, the Board once again lapsed into a curious silence after Christmas. Except for telling him, on 15 January 1821, that the frigate would be fitted one hemp and one iron anchor "cable" (actually, chain), there was no interchange.

Early in February, rendezvous were opened to ship a crew for "Old Ironsides." Hull set about ordering the necessary clothing (for 430), hammocks, powder and provisions for the ship — all this without any guidance from Washington as to the locale or duration of her forthcoming employment. Rodgers finally wrote on the 22nd to say the ship would be going to the Mediterranean.

During that same month, Secretary of the Navy Smith Thompson ordered Sailing Master Briscoe S. Doxey from the Washington Navy Yard to Boston, there to conduct an experiment using *Constitution* as his test vehicle. Doxey was to construct and demonstrate the practicability of the "propello marino," a device "invented by him for propelling becalmed ships."

Doxey arrived early in March, and for the next five weeks or so, he, with the assistance of Master Builder Josiah Barker and his men, set about erecting his machine and installing it in *Constitution.* In essence, it was a "portable" set of paddle wheels installed on a cranked axle (probably through Number Six gun ports on the gun deck) and powered by a team of seamen. No sketches of the device have been found. The first tests, during mid-April, failed because the paddles were too short and they couldn't "take proper hold of the water." Following modifications, successful tests were made in Boston Harbor on 23 April, when the ship, tethered to an anchor by "Two hausers lengths" as a precautionary measure, was propelled at a stately three knots. "The paddles revolved five times a minute on a circle of 23½ feet diameter and the effect was such as to move the ship against a strong wind and tide." *Constitution* with *paddle wheels* — what a sight!

## A NEW CAPTAIN

Captain Jacob Jones had hoisted his broad command pennant as next commander of the Mediterranean Squadron and *Constitution's* Captain on 1 April. He was a man of somewhat above average height, lantern-jawed and, as naval officers of the day went, of easy temperament. Born in Delaware in 1768, he truly was one of the "old men" of the Navy, having been thirty-one years old before becoming a midshipman in 1799. He had been trained in medicine, and had tried his hand at both doctoring and court clerking before turning to the sea. He served first in *United States* under Commodore Barry and then in *Ganges*, a 24-gun converted merchantman, during the Quasi-War. It had been his misfortune

171

*Captain Jacob Jones.*

to be Bainbridge's Second Lieutenant in *Philadelphia* when that frigate was lost to the Tripoline pirates, and Jones had spent nineteen months as a prisoner of war on that occasion. Following duty in New Orleans, in 1810 he was promoted to the rank of Master Commandant and given command of the brig *Argus* (18), and the following year commissioned the ship-sloop *Wasp* (18). In that command, he earned fame and a Congressional gold medal by defeating the British sloop of war *Frolic* (18) in a vicious action that left both combatants disabled. Promoted to Captain, he was given command of the captured frigate *Macedonian* (38), but the British kept him bottled up in New London for the duration of the war. *Macedonian* later was a unit of Bainbridge's squadron in the Mediterranean immediately after war's end.

Jones, who seems to have made up for his late entry into service by pursuing a career with an unusually high proportion of sea time, was anxious to shake out *Constitution* s sails. The receipt of defective supplies in response to earlier orders by Hull caused some delay. Doxey's "marvel" was another which, the test completed, he dismounted and stowed below, ostensibly to test further during the cruise. Letters home from young Midshipman Samuel F. Dupont provide some idea of the new Captain:

> ... Our captain, or rather our commodore, is an excellent man, but he has his crotchets...
>
> ... The *Constitution* is the most beautiful frigate I have seen; but we shall be extremely plain, for the commodore is far from disposed to make a display. Therefore though we shall be very comfortable, we shall be very far from being a dashing ship. The captain is in a great hurry to be off, but we are not half ready yet and will need three weeks more...
>
> ... The captain has the rheumatism, and I believe that hurries him as much as anything, that he may reach a warmer climate...
>
> ... The captain is about the most extraordinary man I have ever seen. In an argument, the other day, he said the greatest curse to this country was the trial by jury; and that Nelson was not a brave man! but all this is only to appear singular...

In these waning days of outfitting, *Constitution* was visited by a ranking member of the Royal Navy. He was received with all due honor by Commodore Jones, wined and dined, and shown about the ship. He was most complimentary in his remarks and every inch the perfect guest. As he was about to depart, however, he turned to the Commodore and said, "You know, I think for my professional honor I must be critical about *something* in this ship: that is, without a doubt, the *ugliest* ship's wheel I think I've ever seen!" The American responded, "I quite agree with you, sir, but you see, we took that from *Java* after defeating her, and keep it as a memento."

## OFF TO THE MED

*Constitution* was underway from her anchorage off Hancock's Wharf at 7 A.M. on 13 May, bound for the Mediterranean, scene of her early greatness.

The voyage across the Atlantic was made quickly and was one of the most peaceful she ever experienced. In twenty-one days she was at the Rock of Gibraltar. There, she found *Columbus* (74), wearing the broad pennant of Commodore Charles Stewart, and the brig *Spark* (14). The area was much different, politically speaking, since Jones and his ship last had been there with Preble. The Barbary pirates, insofar as the Americans were concerned, no longer were an active problem. Napoleon was out of power and coming to the end of his days on a remote island in the South Atlantic; much of Europe still was recovering from the two decades of warfare induced by the French upheaval. The American naval depot at Port Mahon, Minorca, under consideration five years before the War of 1812, had come into existence. Stewart briefed Jones as to the relatively quiet political climate and "who was who." There were no crises to make combat a possibility. Stewart and his two ships headed home on 6 June, three days after Jones had come in.

## DOLDRUM DUTY

If the area was quiescent in the aftermath of an exhausting war, Jacob Jones, in his 53rd year, was equally willing to let things drift. Even before leaving

Gibraltar, one of his midshipmen (who basically was an admirer) was writing home that, "The ship is not, and will not be in any kind of discipline." Underway on 11 June, Jones wended his way to Port Mahon, arriving on the 20th, where liberty was granted to the crew by watches — a new development since the coming of peace. A three-day trip brought them to Genoa on the last day of the month. *Constitution* was the first American frigate to visit that port. The Fourth of July observance in the ship consisted of 24-gun salutes at noon and sunset, and on oration by the chaplain. Commodore Jones seems to have liked this city particularly well and spent much time ashore. His officers regularly took the opportunity to ride out into the hinterlands to escape the *ennui* of shipboard routine. Some went to Coletta and were shown the house reputed to be that in which Christopher Columbus was born, but thought it very possible that the great navigator never saw it. Jones took Midshipman Dupont and two others and spent some time in Florence.

*Constitution* sailed from Genoa to Leghorn between 18 and 20 July, and there found the ship-sloop *Ontario* (18), the sole other unit of the U.S. Mediterranean Squadron. The two lay in harbor until the 30th, when Jones got them underway for Gibraltar. Shiphandling drill was conducted for the junior officers on 2 August as the two ships lazed along under gentle breezes. On the 7th, *Constitution*'s main topgallant stunsail boom "accidentally fell from aloft" and struck Gunner's Yeoman George Willard on the head; he lingered in agony for nearly three hours. Burial was the next morning.

Strong gales buffeted the ships on 11 and 12 August, and as the storm abated on the 13th, an American ship in distress was sighted. She had lost both her main and mizzen topmasts in the storm. *Constitution* kept her in tow all that day while her carpenters manufactured new masts from spare spars the big frigate carried. Late that evening, the ship *Hazard* was whole again and on her own. *Constitution* and *Ontario* arrived at Gibraltar on the 17th, where they lay until 5 September.

Commodore Jones brought both of his ships back to Port Mahon for nearly a month's upkeep beginning on 12 September. The day after his arrival, he off-loaded Briscoe Doxey's "propello marino" into a warehouse ashore, determined to have nothing more to do with that clumsy contraption during these lazy days in the Mediterranean. The crew enjoyed regular liberty runs ashore where the incredible poverty of most of the people allowed the tars' meager monies to cover legendary debaucheries. While there, Captain Benjamin W. Booth was detached to return home to his ailing family. Booth had been Jones' "Flag Captain," a combination Chief of Staff and sometime Flagship Commanding Officer. First Lieutenant Foxhall A. Parker acquired whatever special duties Booth may have had, although a two-ship squadron hardly could be considered a very demanding organization.

When they got underway again on 9 October, the Commodore planned to survey a somewhat greater portion of his area of responsibility than heretofore,

Constitution *in the Mediterranean in an 1823 painting. Her consort is thought to be* Nonsuch.

and somewhat more energetically. Proceeding first off Genoa, he detached *Ontario* to pay a call there while he continued on toward Tripoli, going the long way around the west end of Sicily rather than through the Straits of Messina. *Ontario* once again was in company when the two arrived off the Bashaw's capitol on the last day of the month. The American Consul came out to confer and dine with the Commodore, then the two ships turned westward once more. There was a similar touch at Algiers on 14 November before dropping the hook again at Gibraltar. They had been underway for forty-four days, shaking out a few of the cobwebs engendered by the long port visits. But after twenty- six days in Gibraltar, Jones moved the squadron back to Port Mahon for the winter. Arriving on 21 December, they found there the schooner *Nonsuch* (6), which would serve as Jones' dispatch boat. She was welcomed most for the mail she had brought with her for both ships.

*Constitution* was moved into the "navy yard" on 2 January 1822 for an overhaul. On the 10th, Seamen Samuel Oakly and William Tailor were punished for drunkenness — the only instance of a flogging recorded during Jones' entire tenure. On the other side of the "ledger," the chaplain christened a child on board with the name Constitution Jones Nelson on Sunday, the 13th. How this came to be is not recorded. Neither is it known whether this log entry for the 28th is somehow related: "A Carpenter employed making a Coffin for Charles Nelson, eldest son to one of the Seamen." It appears that *Constitution* was in an unaccustomed "family way" on this trip, in any event.

The curse of the early Navy — duelling — once more afflicted *Constitution*'s officers on 4 February, when Midshipman John S. Paine shot Midshipman Thomas B. Worthington through the body, killing him instantly. Midshipman Dupont, later a Rear Admiral during the Civil War, also was involved and wrote of it to his brother thusly:

> Charges of a most disgraceful nature were brought by three of the midshipmen of this ship against a fourth one belonging to this ship. (N.B. There were about 19 on board at this time, in all.) The commodore investigated these charges himself, and was under the impression that they were false, and sent for us all, and told us that he hoped we would treat the accused as a gentleman, for he did not consider him guilty of the charges alleged against him. The accused procured a warm and staunch friend in the squadron, and challenged the three gentlemen. They refused to give him satisfaction under the plea that he was not a gentleman. His friend urged the thing as much as possible, but nothing would induce the gentlemen to give him satisfaction. The friend then called for the opinion of the midshipmen of this ship, and wished to know if we were in the place of the accusers, if we should not feel ourselves bound to give the accused any satisfaction he might require. Seven of us, the oldest in the steerage, signed a letter to that effect. Some days after, Midshipman Thomas B. Worthington, and myself, received each of us a challenge from two of the gentlemen, for having signed a letter with the intention, as they said, of establishing the character of the midshipman they had accused. The reason they gave for selecting us two was that they considered us the most important signers... I procured immediately in Midshipman (John) Marston, a warm, sincere, and firm friend, and accepted the challenge without hesitation... Midshipman Worthington did the same... We went out, and Worthington was to fight first — he did so — and... he fell. I waited till he was removed from the ground, and took my station to meet my gentleman. Everything was ready, and the word was about to be given, when my friend stepped forward... and repeated verbatim what he had told the gentleman when he delivered him my acceptance; and to my astonishment... they accepted what they had refused to Worthington and myself before we came out. My antagonist fired his pistol in the air and came and offered me his hand, which I felt bound to take, and everything was settled... The commodore, as you may suppose, soon became acquainted with the affair; he approved in the very highest terms of the conduct of my second, and only regretted he had not stood such to both of us...

As for those of whom the Commodore must have disapproved, a court martial was convened on 13 February to try Midshipman John S. Paine for his part in the affair. It found him guilty in findings published on the 28th, and sentenced him to be suspended from service for six months. He was detached that afternoon. Midshipman Samuel Gaillard, the other duellist, received no formal punishment, but resigned his warrant in the following year and later went mad. Paine returned to the service at the end of his suspension and retired as a Commander in 1855.

Washington's Birthday at Mahon was the occasion of a 22-gun salute at high noon and the day chosen by *Constitution*'s midshipmen to host a dinner for their opposite numbers in a visiting Dutch squadron, the mids from *Ontario* and *Nonsuch,* and their own lieutenants.

> ... sixty sat down to the table. We had three courses without counting the dessert. We had... turkeys, chickens, partridges, woodcocks, rabbits, beef, pork, pasties, in-

numerable, etc., etc., etc., all of which was quite difficult to get... they drank five dozen bottles of white wine, and whiskey in proportion. There were but two or three who were in the least intoxicated...

One of the hosts grumped that it was "a stupid dinner that cost me four dollars."

"Making the rounds" recommenced on 12 March, when *Constitution* and *Ontario* headed west, and *Nonsuch* southeast. After a week at Gibraltar, Jones sailed for Cadiz for a two-week stay before returning to Gibraltar once more on 11 April. A few days later, *Nonsuch* came in, and then the whole squadron reentered the Mediterranean on 18 April. It was a difficult time for Commodore Jones, for while at Gibraltar he had received news from home that a new baby had died and his third wife, whom he had married early in 1821, was not well. And to compound his pain, he had also received official notice that it was planned to leave him on station for yet another two years.

The squadron reached Leghorn on 2 May after looking in briefly at Port Mahon in search of expected mail. The log for 6 May contains the notation, "Carpenters scaffing skysail mast on the royal mast." Evidently, the sliding gunters had not proven successful and Jones was having the royal masts extended to provide fixed skypoles. The extreme range of motion present at the trucks of the three great masts rising more than 175 feet in the air no doubt was too much for a "stick" held in place by a ring and a halyard, and expected to sustain a sail, no matter how small.

The last few days of the Leghorn stay was one of repeated honors and ceremonies — side boys, salutes, mock drills, and lots of spit and polish for the visiting dignitaries. The Duke of Wurtemburgh was so entertained on the 18th; Lord George Byron, the romantic poet, on the 21st; and the Prince of Borghese on the 23rd. For a while, it was thought that the Prince's wife, Napoleon's sister, would sail with them to Naples because "The commodore is very accommodating in that way," but she apparently had no such plan. The squadron cleared for Naples late that afternoon.

Commodore Jones now was headed for the Eastern Mediterranean, which area he, until this time, had neglected. Greece was the reason for his interest. For many years, brigands known as "Klephts" had roamed the Grecian mountains in Robin Hood fashion practicing brigandage against their Turkish overlords; similarly, Grecian pirates long had infested the island-studded waters of the Aegean Sea. The example of the French Revolution and the blood-stirring events of the Napoleonic Wars had aroused these activist elements of the native Greek populace to seek their own sovereignty. During 1821, these two groups had risen up and coalesced to provide the spearhead of an independence movement against the Turks. The moribund Ottoman Empire reacted predictably but inadequately to the uprisings, and it appeared that the rebels would be successful. For the United States and other maritime nations trading in the area, there was concern that their neutrality be respected by both sides, both ashore and afloat. That was what Commodore Jones was setting out to do: ensure that American people and property were not being victimized in the ofttimes brutal actions of the conflict. After brief stops at Naples and Messina, the three Americans headed for the hot spot.

*Constitution* and the rest of the squadron passed north of Milos on 17 June and stood on through the Cyclades to the northeast. They received quite a surprise as dawn broke on the 21st, as they approached the strait between Lesbos and Chios: a Turkish fleet of some thirty units. After the first thrill, it was seen that the force was headed for Mytilene, on the east side of Tenedos. A Greek sloop was seen heading northwest. Neither Turk nor Greek appeared to take notice of the other, although one suspects the latter was very much aware of the former. Tacking to the southeast, the little American group navigated for Smyrna (Izmir), reaching port at sunset the next afternoon. It was the first time American warships had been there.

Jones spent only two days at Smyrna. His consultations with the U.S. Consul and local American business interests indicated no problems worthy of the Commodore's attention. Passing back the way he came, Jones paused off Milos on the 29th, then reconnoitered the sea lanes between there and Hydra before returning westward once more. A two-day call at Malta and one of just 20 minutes at Malaga to deliver a message to the local American Consul broke up the run to Gibraltar which ended on 1 August. The "round" ended at Port Mahon once more on the 12th, where the ships spent two weeks in upkeep, overhauling boats, painting hulls, and taking on stores — and the crew had daily liberty.

The next round was more or less done "counterclockwise:" underway on 26 August, the squadron touched at Gibraltar, Algiers, and Leghorn before *Constitution* returned alone to Port Mahon on the last day of October. *Ontario* had been left to idle in Leghorn while *Nonsuch* was busy running errands. Jones made still another trip to Gibraltar beginning on 12 November. On 6 December, the day after leaving port, *Ontario* was spoke as she headed for the Rock. Late that afternoon, an American brig was sighted with its ensign flying upside down. She proved to be the *Sultana,* out of Boston. A collision the night before had cost her her bowsprit and had fouled up much of her rigging. Taken in tow like the *Hazard,* she was restored by "Old Ironsides' " carpenters in a couple of hours and cast off. The two ships parted thirty-six hours later, separated by strong gales which continued for three days. Repeated storminess caused the big frigate to beat back and forth off the entrance for two days before she finally was able to enter Port Mahon on 20 December and snug down for the winter.

As had been the case in 1822, the winter season of 1823 was spent in overhaul. New lower stunsail booms, which doubled as boat booms when in port, were made by the carpenters, the ship was scrubbed and painted inside and out, the masts and boats refinished, and the rigging worked over. A new feature of the ship's routine was a weekly exercise at general quarters, apparently in an effort to reduce a little the very great boredom of the duty. Sail drills were held late in March to get the topmen back in harness for the coming cruising season. That season began with the squadron getting underway on 9 April.

On the 11th, as they were heading on a southerly course:

> At 2h 15' discovered a sail on the weather bow which in a few minutes struck us about the fore chains & passed astern backed the mn Topsail & made signals to the squadron. At 2h 30' wore ship; got the boats ready to send to the wreck. But had lost sight of her, wore ship frequently in search of her. At 4 fresh gales squadron in Company.
>
> At 5 discovered a sail to Leeward. Wore ship & stood for her... At 6 rounded to & up foresail & sent a boat to board the strange sail. but in the act of boarding she went down. Crew all saved except the Captain, who was knocked over-board when she struck us. The Mate informs us that she was the schooner *Becton* of St. Joes (England) from Leghorn. bound to Plymouth laden with Government Timber...

The squadron continued its voyage to Algiers, where it lay to for a day while *Nonsuch* carried a communications to the Consul. *Constitution*'s rotten flying jib boom carried away in light breezes while there, and was replaced a couple of days later as the squadron was making for Gibraltar where, on 23 April, a 24-gun salute was fired in honor of the coronation of King George IV.

Following 18 days in Gibraltar, Jones made for Tunis (a 5-day stay), Syracuse (six days), Malta (six days), and Leghorn (fifteen days) before touching base once more at Port Mahon on 26 July. Needless to say, nothing had occurred to disturb the tranquility. The Commodore moved out again with *Ontario* in company on 6 August, bound for Gibralter. A heavy gale enroute cost *Constitution* her cross-jack, but the carpenters readily replaced it while at the Rock.

The U.S. Minister to Spain, Hugh Nelson, came aboard with a suite on 20 August, intending to make a leisurely "familiarization tour" of some Spanish cities while enjoying the variety of a cruise in a man of war. Setting sail on 8 September, *Constitution* and *Ontario* went first to Malaga, then to their base at Port Mahon. While in that port, a heavy northwest squall "blew away" *Constitution*'s main and mizzen skysail masts. She, herself, dragged her anchor and had to drop another to keep from grounding. The ever-ready carpenters had new skypoles in place within three days. And hoping that this might be his last call at Mahon, on the 6th of October Jones had Doxey's paddlewheel rig returned aboard and stowed below for transport to the United States.

All three units of the squadron sortied on 10 October and made Gibraltar eleven days later. *Constitution* and *Nonsuch* left that port on 2 November for the quick trip to Cadiz, where Ambassador Nelson debarked and returned to Madrid. The two ships returned to Gibraltar on the 16th. Jones knew, at this point, that he was to be relieved. His had not been a successful tour. Whether because of the man or the situation, the American squadron had become something of an embarrassment to the Government. The lack of discipline and many unseeming incidents ashore caused by sailors and officers on liberty led the Department to take positive action. A new Commodore of the right stripe soon would straighten out the disciplinary problem. And there was an additional reason for wanting a strong leader in the Mediterranean at this time: the Greek independence movement, after initial successes, was falling apart through the stresses of internal disagreement and external pressures brought on by the threat of Egyptian forces supporting the Ottoman Turks in the efforts at suppression. This, in turn, gained the attention of the nations represented in the Congress of Vienna who were concerned that what had been a small scale local conflict might boil over uncontrollably. England, France, and Russia were moving to limit the war. The United States, with large trading interests in the area, had to be prepared to defend those interests.

The "changing of the watch" began on 4 December with the arrival of the ship-sloop *Erie* (18). *Ontario* headed back into the Mediterranean four days later to take up an Aegean vigil, firing a parting seven-gun salute to Commodore Jones. *Erie* was sent "above" on the 13th, while *Constitution* swung somnolently at her anchor, waiting for the moment when she could head home. As it turned out, she would do so for more than four months. The log on 9 April 1824 says, "At 5" 20' saw a sail with American colours — & made her number which proved to be the *Cyane,* our *Relief* (the log keeper's emphasis)..." This was, of course, the same *Cyane* captured by "Old Ironsides" in 1815. At 8:30, *Cyane*'s skipper, Captain John O. Creighton, came on board *Constitution* and, after being briefed, succeeded Jacob Jones as Acting Commodore, awaiting the arrival of the man specifically picked for the position. Jones got *Constitution* underway at 9:20 the next morning and made a 40-day passage to New York. Her arrival at the Navy Yard on 20 May 1824 somehow symbolizes the entire deployment: the larboard anchor was dropped and parted its cable; the starboard anchor likewise was dropped and parted its cable; the ship drifted aground, where she remained for nine hours before floating free and being safely anchored. Jones hauled down his pennant on 31 May, leaving *Constitution* to be readied for a return to the Middle Sea under a new commander.

## OVERHAUL

Little is known about the overhaul *Constitution* received at New York during the summer and fall of 1824. It is possible that the principal reason for bringing her back at all was to effect the complete turnover of officers and crew. She was not recoppered at this time, and there is no evidence that any major structural work was done. Aloft, her rigging was modified somewhat with the addition of spencers, an alteration then being made to several units of the Navy. Spencers were fore and aft sails similar to the spanker, but which were used on other than the mizzen mast and which had a gaff supporting the upper edge, but no boom below. Installed on both the fore and main masts, they would allow "Old Ironsides" to be sailed closer to the wind than her square rig alone permitted — in effect, making her somewhat like a schooner as regards the capability. In addition, the spencers were handled from the spar deck by fewer men than the square sails, making it possible to reduce the demands on the watch on deck at any given time. Upon completion of the overhaul, *Constitution* was armed with her usual

*Captain Thomas Macdonough.*

thirty long 24s on the gun deck and two 24s as chase guns, but her carronade battery contained only eighteen 32-pounders.

## A NEW SKIPPER

Thomas Macdonough was to be *Constitution*'s next Captain. Born in Delaware in 1783, he obtained his warrant as a midshipman during the Quasi-War with France. He was attached to the frigate *Philadelphia* under Bainbridge, but was on detached duty when that ship was lost to the Tripolines and so escaped imprisonment. Being familiar with that ship, he was one of those in Stephen Decatur's band which destroyed her in February 1804. A tall, commanding figure, young Macdonough also was in the thick of it next to Decatur in the first battle of gunboats in August of that year, making a material contribution to the capture of two of them. For these deeds, he received a silver medal from Congress. In the War of 1812, then-Lieutenant Commanding Macdonough had been placed in charge of the naval defense of Lake Champlain. On 11 September 1814, his small squadron of locally-built craft defeated a similar British force, thereby aborting almost before it had begun a planned British invasion down the Hudson River valley — one of the most important victories of that war. For this action, he was promoted to Captain and awarded a gold medal by Congress. His post-war duties had included three years as Commandant of the Portsmouth

Navy Yard and command of the frigate *Guerriere* (44) in the Mediterranean. Exactly when he took command of *Constitution* is unknown as log-keeping was not resumed until the date of her sailing: 29 October 1824.

## SAME OLD BUSINESS — BUT UNDER NEW MANAGEMENT

Captain Macdonough took *Constitution* across the Atlantic in twenty-five days, a most respectable passage. Awaiting him at Gibraltar was *Cyane*. Macdonough, being senior, took over as acting squadron commander pending the arrival of Commodore John Rodgers, the stern disciplinarian and respected senior officer of the Navy whom the Secretary had selected as the man to set things to rights once more. Still, Macdonough — and undoubtedly Creighton before him — knew where the winds were blowing and already was tightening up. For starters, the days of free and easy liberty parties were over.

The two warships got underway and headed into the Mediterranean, Macdonough having decided that Gibraltar was too far removed from likely areas of interest to be the proper place to winter over. On 2 December, *Ontario* replaced *Cyane* as *Constitution*'s companion. They lay to off Algiers for two days while communicating with the shore, then proceeded to Tunis, anchoring there on the 11th. Outgoing Consul Coxe and his family were taken aboard *Ontario* for transportation to Syracuse, from whence they could continue their journey. The two units reached the Sicilian city shortly after noon on the 21st, and were joined soon thereafter by *Erie*.

A first order of business in *Constitution* was to attend to her main mast, where evidence of rotting had been discovered in its head. Into the new year the carpenters worked, excising bad wood until they were sure none remained, then fashioning a replacement piece, and finally scarphing it in place and replacing the hoops. By 13 January 1825, the mast was being rerigged. The very next day, as the two ships swung out of phase at their anchors, *Ontario* fouled *Constitution*, carrying away her jib boom. More work for the carpenters.

*Constitution* and *Erie* got underway on 5 February, the former having on board the American Consul for Syracuse, who wished transport to Messina. The 75-mile trip into the Straits of Messina required five days as adverse winds caused the ships to sail miles latitudinally for every mile gained to the north. Once there, the two settled down once more into the winter routine of overhaul. Midshipman Augustus Barnhouse was required to resign on 8 March for "ungentlemanly and unofficerlike conduct," a sure sign that the "good old days" were no more. He left the ship immediately.

Back in the United States, Commodore Rodgers was receiving his orders at about this time. His primary mission was to make contact with the Turkish Minister of Marine, the Capudan Pasha, in order that a treaty might be drawn up placing relations between the two countries on a formal basis. Naval officers had become involved in what otherwise might properly be expected to be the province of the Foreign Service because European diplomats in Constantinople were maneuvering actively to prevent such talks between our Minister and the Turkish Foreign Minister. The Sultan had let it be known that his naval commander in chief would be an acceptable line of communication, and since the two representatives could meet without suspicion at sea, the secrecy of the proceedings could be preserved and alien meddling avoided. The Commodore's second mission, as mentioned earlier, was to restore good order and discipline in the squadron. For his flagship, Rodgers was given the ship of the line *North Carolina* (74), a warship new to the Mediterranean. They sailed on 27 March.

*Constitution* and *Erie* continued at Messina as Rodgers beat a stormy passage across the Atlantic. *Cyane* joined them there on 6 April and *Ontario* on 9 May, the latter having gone to Gibraltar from Syracuse. Finally, no doubt wondering why he hadn't heard any more about Commodore Rodgers, Macdonough got the entire squadron underway on 29 May and headed for Gibraltar to see if there was any news there.

Rodgers and *North Carolina* reached Gibraltar on 30 May. The Commodore was surprised and disappointed not to find his squadron waiting for him. The more he thought about it, the angrier he got — so much so that, as he wrote Secretary of the Navy Samuel Southard, "...I shall feel it my duty to remove him from the command of the *Constitution,* for not meeting me here or apprising me where I might find him." This was to cause some harsh words to be delivered to Macdonough later when he first met Rodgers, but the latter quickly changed his attitude when he learned that his junior had been operating completely in the dark, and the two subsequently were on the best of terms. While waiting for his other ships to arrive, Rodgers provisioned for five months and then left to show the flag at Malaga, Algeciras, and Tangiers.

Macdonough and the squadron sailed into Gibraltar on 12 June, learning for the first time that Rodgers was in the area and that he soon should be back. The Commodore came in at 2:30 in the morning of the 17th and took over the command. For nearly a month they lay there as he inspected each ship and saw to it they were brought to his standards. *North Carolina* led them eastward from the Rock on 9 July.

Stopping but briefly at Tunis, the squadron proceeded directly to the Aegean and anchored off the island of Paros early on 9 August. Watering the ships and "examining the relicks of antiquity" were the order of the day. During the voyage to Paros, *Constitution*'s log had been filled with entries like "took in sail to maintain station on the flagship" and "lay to waiting for the squadron to come up." She was like an Arabian stallion in a herd of Percherons, getting ahead of them almost without effort. What a frustrating time it must have been for her watch officers, harnessed with the responsibility of staying with a plodding liner.

The squadron was underway once more on the 14th, bound for Smyrna, where Commodore Rodgers hoped to learn from American Consul David Offley the whereabouts of the Capudan Pasha, Khosrew. They arrived on the afternoon of the 19th. Rodgers was disappointed to learn that Offley had no knowledge of where Khosrew might be. But if the Commodore was frustrated in the pursuit of his mission, the reputation of the American squadron was raised immeasurably when many officers and men from the ships helped fight a major fire in the city and undoubtedly saved many lives. Rodgers received a testimonial letter from the merchants commending these unselfish efforts.

On 30 August, near midnight, the squadron stood out from Smyrna, making sail for Vourla, some twenty miles to the westward, where fresh water could be readily obtained. This was the sultry month of August, when temperatures of ninety-five in the shade were recorded, and because of it and perhaps partly as a result of their exertions in Smyrna, a considerable number of men came down sick. *Constitution* had at least ten percent of her crew on the binnacle list. A temporary hospital was established on a small island, variously called Round or Uras Island, where it was hoped better ventilation and cooling sea breezes would correct the situation. In the week that followed, *Constitution* lost Marine Privates William Sawyer, David Lockhart, and James W. Swords, and Ordinary Seaman John Sloan to the malaise.

The squadron got underway shortly before noon on 8 September, Rodgers intending to make for Napoli de Romania (today Nauplia), the current capital of the Greek revolutionary government. However, in rounding north of Uras Island, *Constitution* went aground. Commodore Rodgers signalled the remaining ships to reanchor and then came on board the frigate to learn first hand the seriousness of the accident. Happily, there was no important damage; the ship was refloated at nine that evening and all were underway once more early the following morning.

Napoli de Romania is located at the head of the Gulf of Argos on the east coast of Morea, a craggy town of great natural defenses. It was to here the Greek revolutionaries had retreated, forced back by the unremitting pressure of the Egyptian army which had entered the fray seven month earlier. So long as they could maintain their link with the sea, the Greeks could not be ousted from this stronghold. When the American squadron arrived on the afternoon of the 12th, it was well received by the struggling revolutionary leadership. They could not, however, enlighten the Commodore as to the current location of the Capudan Pasha. Rodgers sailed on the 18th, having decided to give over his attempt to make contact with the Turk during that sailing season, and made directly for Gibraltar. *Ontario* was left in the Aegean to represent American interests at sea during the winter: It apparently was during this trip that *Constitution* initiated use of her spencer rig, for it appears in the log for the first time.

## A NEW COMMANDER

By the time Gibraltar was reached on 9 October, Thomas Macdonough was in a bad way. He had been suffering for years from consumption, and it was apparent that his condition had grown markedly worse in recent weeks. In response to his request, Commodore Rodgers directed Flag Captain Daniel T. Patterson

*Captain Daniel Todd Patterson.*

to proceed to *Constitution* and relieve the ailing hero of Lake Champlain. Patterson reported aboard on the 14th and took command about two days later. Five days after, attended by Surgeon William Turk, Commodore Macdonough left "Old Ironsides" as a passenger in the merchant brig *Edwin,* bound for Philadelphia. He died just as the capes of Delaware were sighted some three weeks later.

New Yorker Daniel Todd Patterson was a little more than two years younger than his predecessor and like him had become a midshipman during the Quasi-War. He had been shipmates with both Macdonough and Jones in *Philadelphia* and, with Jones, had gone into captivity when that unfortunate ship was lost. Subsequently, he had served on the Gulf Coast and had spent all of the War of 1812 in Louisiana, making significant contributions to the defense of New Orleans. For these actions, he was highly commended by General Andrew Jackson and the Congress, and promoted to Captain in February 1815. He had remained in the South until selected as Flag Captain by Commodore Rodgers.

While the squadron was at Gibraltar, it was joined by the frigate *Brandywine* (44), on her maiden voyage. This "grand child" of *Constitution* had just returned the Marquis de Lafayette to France following his memorable grand tour of America, and arrived without either Commodore Charles Morris or Captain

185

*George Campbell Read in later life
as a Rear Admiral.*

George C. Read, both of whom had escorted the Marquis to Paris.

Following a stay of more than five weeks, Rodgers left Gibraltar for Port Mahon with the squadron — *North Carolina, Constitution, Brandywine,* and *Erie.* The 13-day voyage was completed on 29 November. *Erie* was sent on to relieve *Ontario* in the Aegean.

*Constitution,* the grand old lady of the squadron, was assigned an overhaul at the Navy Yard in Mahon, whence she moved on 3 December. Two days later, amidst the hustle and bustle of stripping ship, Captain Patterson was ordered by the Commodore to assume command of *Brandywine,* so that that active ship would have a fully qualified skipper should her services be needed. First Lieutenant Elie A.F. LaVallette became "Old Ironsides' " "commanding officer." (In those days, a full-fledged Captain of a ship might also be known as her "commander," but the senior man with more restricted powers — what we might term an "officer in charge" today — was called the "commanding officer." Thus, LaVallette was to be the frigate's lord and master while she was in overhaul. The problem of a "commander" would be addressed when she was ready again for sea.) Through the remainder of December and most of January 1826, *Constitution* lay pierside with her stores, ammunition, and rigging ashore. Her guns were shifted back and forth about the decks as gangs of caulkers made her tight once more. The work schedule ran dawn to dusk, with no mention of liberty parties nor duels. Colors were lowered to halfmast on 22 January when the squadron learned of Macdonough's death; *Brandywine* fired nine minute-guns. The next day, Captain George Campbell Read, newly arrived from France, relieved Lieutenant LaVallette and became *Constitution*'s Captain. Work virtually was completed by the end of the month; the frigate moved back out to anchorage on 3 February.

The schooner *Porpoise* (12) arrived in port on the 16th bearing orders for *Brandywine* to return to the United States. Being senior to Read, and not wishing to pass up any opportunity for notable service, Captain Patterson requested and got Commodore Rodgers' permission to exchange commands with his junior, just as Rodgers himself had done with Isaac Hull in 1810 in another trade involving *Constitution*. The official interchange was made on 21 February, although further personnel exchanges and transfers went on for several days. Two notable additions to *Constitution*'s officer personnel were Schoolmaster George Jones, who subsequently wrote sketches of life aboard as he found it, and Midshipman David Dixon Porter, son of Captain David Porter and much later to be the Navy's second Admiral. *Brandywine* sailed on the 26th.

Rodgers got his squadron underway for the sailing season on 10 April. He paid the usual call at Gibraltar — more than three weeks — and made stops at Algiers (three days) and Tunis (another three) before setting sail for the Aegean and a hoped-for rendezvous with Capudan Pasha Khosrew. Pauses at Milos and Paros further delayed his arrival at Vourla until 19 June. There, the squadron watered; *Constitution* took on 35,150 gallons. From thence, on 30 June, the Americans proceeded to Mytilene on the island of Tenedos, arriving on 2 July. The local Governor provided Commodore Rodgers with the certain information that Khosrew was at the Dardanelles with his whole fleet, and offered to provide guides for an overland journey hence should the American leader wish to pay him a visit. Having offered Rodgers guided access to his country, the official then asked what country was represented by the flag with red and white stripes. The Commodore was well aware that William Bainbridge had visited Turkey a quarter century earlier, but the Turk said it was the first time he ever had seen that flag. The Capudan Pasha himself, on a later occasion, also would express ignorance of where the United States might be.

On the 4th, just when some of the American officers were hoping to celebrate their national birthday with an excursion ashore, the calm of the morning was broken by the distant sighting of ships coming up over the northern horizon:

> ... Others succeeded, and then others, and then the whole horizon was covered with them, the foremost now coming into full view, and displaying the outlines of large men of war. It was the Turkish fleet, just from the Dardanelles, breathing ruin to the Greeks; still it was a beautiful sight. They first ran out into the sea, and, then changing their course, bore right down upon us; the foremost... shewing herself a seventy-four, with the Commodore's flag; the next a large frigate, and the rest sloops and frigates all of the first class, a few schooners excepted. A midshipman now reported that the *North Carolina* had beaten to quarters; our drums were ordered up; a short tapping

succeeded, in which the words 'to quarters, to quarters, to quarters, to quarters,' could almost be heard; and when the music, which, at first, was rather slow, had quickened, until only a roll could be heard, every man was in his place, and ready for battle... divisions were reported, and then preparations were made for fight: gun tackle was thrown loose; shot racks filled; matches placed by the guns; cutlasses and boarding caps brought on deck; pikes prepared; carronade slides greased; cartridge boxes buckled on; grape passed up; and all being in readiness, the bustle was succeeded by an almost painful silence... On they came, in gallant style: the flag ship still led the van: she had just passed the *North Carolina,* when a volume of smoke shot from the latter, and the thunder of one of her forty-two's succeeded. Another followed, and another; the firing soon passed through the squadron, and was promptly returned by the Turk... The firing was no more than our 4th of July salute, given at noon, our usual time; which the Turk, mistaking for himself, returned, highly tickled, no doubt, to find himself saluted by the whole American squadron...

This Turkish squadron consisted of two liners, four frigates, and seventeen corvettes and brigs. It was commanded by the Capudan Bey, Khosrew's immediate junior. As it swept into anchorage off Mytilene, one of the frigates ran aground, but came off a few hours later, much as *Constitution* herself had done at Vourla the year before. Nonetheless, the report of this grounding caused the Capudan Pasha himself to come to Tenedos to investigate the incident, which speaks volumes about the level of competence in the Turkish Navy of the day, thereby saving Commodore Rodgers his planned journey overland. On 6 and 7 July, the American and the Turk exchanged calls and conducted the long-awaited preliminary negotiations. Although no treaty was forthcoming immediately, the stage was set for what would be the completion of the desired pact four years later.

On the 9th, Rodgers took his ships north to reconnoiter the Dardanelles. When the ships bearing the strange striped flag appeared off the entrance forts, paroxysms of alarm shook their commanders, who sent off alerts and requests for support to repel the enemy. The Capudan Pasha, having been made the wiser by his recent meetings with Rodgers, is said merely to have laughed at the fears of his subordinates and enhanced his reputation with the depth of his knowledge. The Americans returned to their anchorage off Mytilene.

A second division of Turkish warships appeared on the 14th, this time including Khosrew in his flagship, bearing his "ensign...of silk; a pure red, and so long as to reach the water, when the breeze declines..." The next day, the two leaders exchanged salutes and visits, followed by a further exchange of visits and gifts by ships' captains and officers. All considered a very successful day — except, perhaps, the enlisted men who had been kept at their stations and performing, largely from dawn to dusk. None is known to have left a memorial of how the day went for him.

By Monday, 17 July, all were exhausted by these expressions of friendship and amity, and ready to get on to other things. Rodgers got *North Carolina* and *Constitution* underway late that afternoon. *Ontario, Erie,* and *Porpoise* all had been sent on other duties during the preceding days. They beat to windward (north) and then, with all sails set, came down on the Turkish fleet:

> ...We ran close by the starboard of the Pasha, and each ship manned her shrouds, and cheered him as she passed. His spars, and guns, and bulwarks, were covered with men and officers: he shewed himself in the quarter gallery, and answered the honours with many bows. Steering sails were then set, and we shot to the Southward...
>
> Cheering is a handsome operation, when the man are in clean dress, as they were to-day. The Summer uniform is white canvass shoes; white trowsers, frock (a shirt with blue collar, set off with white fancy work), hat covered with white canvass, and blue belt with white stars. All hands are called on such occasions: at the order, they mount rapidly, and take station in the shrouds, so as to form three pyramids, rising one above another, to each mast; their faces are turned outward and, at the order, all simultaneously take off their hats, wave them and cheer: the officers usually joining with them.

The two big ships came to at Vourla the next morning, where they remained until 11 August, watering and doing routine maintenance. From there, they went to Athens, but remained only a few hours on the 13th because a sudden storm threatened them at anchorage. Next, at Milos, they were rejoined by *Ontario*. Sailing thence on the 21st, Rodgers left *Ontario* behind on her now-familiar commerce protection patrol and returned down the Mediterranean to Port Mahon, dropping the hook in those frequented waters on 10 September.

While the remainder of the squadron continued active in representing American interests around the Middle Sea, *Constitution* remained at Port Mahon for the rest of the year and beyond. Evidently her thirty years of service were beginning to tell markedly. In March 1827, her decayed mainmast was sent ashore for repairs that required more than two weeks of fulltime effort by the carpenter's gang. On 30 March, she got underway for the East, under orders to take up the duties previously assigned to *Erie*, which had returned to the United States, and *Ontario*. The repairs effected during her long stay must have been superlative, for she made the run to the vicinity of Malta in just two days — a run of some 500 miles.

Patterson made the routine calls at Milos and Vourla before arriving at Smyrna on 25 April for briefing by the steadfast Mr. Offley. He sailed on 3 May for the short trip to Scia (Chios) where, in 1822, the Turks had massacred 80-90,000 Greeks and destroyed the city. Moving south and east from there, *Constitution* sailed past Samos and came to anchor not far from the ruins of the city of Ephesus, which had been founded by the Greeks in the 11th century B.C. and once had been a Roman provincial capital. The Captain and his officers made a brief sortie ashore to see the Temple of Diana, the Arcadian Way, and the church where St. Paul had preached.

Having satisfied his curiosity, Patterson got underway again on the 7th, heading west. Passing between Tinos and Andros, then past Kea, he came to the island of Aeginia (Aiyina) on the 10th. "Admiral" Canaris of the Greek revolutionary navy paid a call the next day. A short sail on the 14th brought the big frigate off Athens, which city was then being besieged by the Turks.

*A Most Fortunate Ship*

Patterson next decided to check up on the situation at the centers of revolutionary power, so he headed south on the 17th and after calling at Paros for four days went on to Napoli de Romania. On 1 June, the Captain had to go ashore to settle a problem arising over the handling of some supplies brought in by the American ship *Chanticleer* which, it appeared, were going in to the wrong hands. In conjunction with the authorities, things were soon straightened out. "General" Colocotroni paid an official call to the ship later in the day. Clearing the port the next morning, *Constitution* returned to Smyrna, where she arrived on the 8th.

The 4th of July was spent at Smyrna. *Constitution* fired a 21-gun salute at high noon, in accordance with the custom, and received in response the same salute from the men of war of England, France, Holland, and Austria then in port. Two days later, she shifted to Vourla for water, and then on the 12th made for Athens once more. On her arrival on the 13th, it was learned that the Turks were in essential control of the city. The frigate moved to Salamis on the 18th, and there there occurred a curious incident of which a participant has left us a record:

> ...four or five emaciated Greeks ventured down to the beach, and made a signal to our ship. They were soon brought on board, and two of them returned to the shore, loaded with provisions for their starving families in the mountains — the others offered to sell a statue of great value that was buried on shore, some distance up the gulf. The captain, regarding the purchase as an act of charity, readily agreed to give the stipulated sum. The ship was forthwith got underway, and anchored within ten miles of the nearest landing. Everything was got in readiness for the expedition to start next morning at daylight — officers were appointed, men selected, a rude carriage constructed — boats provisioned and armed. Our party consisted of twenty-five men... We soon arrived at the landing, and found the statue about three miles from the beach, buried some six or seven feet underground. It was no easy task to place it on the carriage: it could not have weighed less than five tons; and to transport it down to the boat, was a work of great labor and fatigue; the sun was oppressively hot, and the wheels sunk deep into the sand every roll. We reached the boat about an hour before sunset, wearied, and fatigued beyond imagination... the launch... pushed off from the shore, spread its wings to the evening breeze, and was soon 'walking the waters like a thing of life'...

Whatever the rationale put forth to justify the act, *Constitution* thus became a party to the pirating of an antiquity out of Greece, a sadly frequent occurrence during this troubled decade. The statue borne back to the United States was a headless one of Demeter or the Roman Ceres, goddess of harvests. Commodore Patterson ultimately presented it to the Pennsylvania Academy of Fine Arts in Philadelphia, where it was installed over the entrance.

*Constitution* met *Porpoise* at Milos on 2 August. The latter brought Patterson the news that he was now the commander of the American squadron in the Mediterranean, Commodore Rodgers having sailed from Gibraltar in *North Carolina* the previous 31 May. Knowing that English, French and Russian intervention in the revolution rapidly was bringing things to a climax, Commodore

Patterson decided that the place for him to be was Smyrna, where, through the Consul, he could gain the most information available in diplomatic channels, and where resided the largest American business community in the region. There he anchored on 7 August to await developments.

August became September, and then October, and still nothing decisive had happened. Late in the month, as the Commodore had decided to patrol the war zone and was about to weigh anchor, a French steamer came in with the stunning news that a combined British-French-Russian naval force had destroyed completely the Turkish fleet at a place called Navarino on 20 October. The news, of course, caused a sensation. Most feared was the reaction of the Turks, who already in this civil strife had made a reputation for awful and fearful decimation of civilian and alien populations. The extensive foreign business community at Smyrna was apprehensive about what the Turks might do for vengeance. Foreign warships then in port, other than *Constitution,* moved close inshore where their guns could fire into the city, and began outloading their nationals. Patterson made all preparations to fight quietly but kept his flagship in her normal anchorage, a gesture appreciated by the local Pasha, who swore to keep any rioters out of the foreign quarter. For days, rumors ran rampant, but there continued to be silence from Constantinople and relative calm in Smyrna. Only the American Consulate continued to fly its flag, the sure sign that the Consul still was in residence. November came, and with it a lessening of tensions and a growing confidence that the situation was as stable as could be expected. Satisfied that he had done his duty, Patterson got *Constitution* underway down the Mediterranean on 15 November and arrived in Mahon exactly a month later, having stopped for but two days at Tunis enroute.

As had become her routine, *Constitution* moved into the Yard for winter refit on 9 January 1828, where she remained until 3 April. On the 28th of the month, fully provisioned, she turned her bow again westward, heading for home. She made the expected stop at Gibraltar, but adverse winds — fickle winds — kept her in port much longer than any of her crew wished. And during this unwanted stay there occurred as fanciful an incident as one ever could expect to encounter. Marine Private William Fleming recorded it in his journal thusly:

> ... this day a most singular circumstance occurred. About a week ago there arrived here a large black brig mounting 6 brass guns... The next day, the captain of her was taking sick, and fearing that his end was approaching, sent for Mr. Henry, the American Consul, to whom he told that the brig he commanded, and said belonged to him, was not his, but was owned in Boston by two brothers and a sister, that he sailed from Boston about nine years ago, on a trading voyage round the Horn, and that one of the brothers went out as supercargo. The vessel and cargo were valued at 70,000 dollars, on which there had been no insurance. After doubling Cape Horn, the supercargo died; where the captain disposed of the cargo to great advantage. From here he proceeded to Jamaica, in the West Indies, where he procured a new set of papers, and sailing under English colors, he called the vessel, the Mary of Jamaica. From here, he proceeded up the Straits, where he has been trading for the last three years. No intelligence of the vessel never having been received by the brother and sister in

Boston, they concluded of course that she was lost — by which they were reduced to poverty — the sister living in the capacity of a servant and the brother, unable to withstand his adverse fortune, finally entered the U.S. Service as a Sailor. Mr. Henry having communicated this information to Capt. Patterson, it became a topic of conversation throughout the ship. A sailor, on board, by the name of R having heard the circumstances, went to Capt. Patterson, and stated to him that the vessel belonged to him and his sister... Capt. Patterson sent him on shore to the American Consul, with whom he went to see the captain of the brig, whom he recognized... The Captain acknowledged everything to him, and begged his forgiveness for the great injustice he had done him... The vessel was immediately taken possession of by the American Consul, and a guard of soldiers put on board. A large amount of property was found on board, and spices to the amount of 60,000 dollars, was found secreted in her sails. The Captain has been since put in prison; and sailor R returned home with us to communicate the joyful intelligence to his sister; leaving the American Consul the settlement of his affairs.

This romantic, happy tale is a fine way to end a cruise. *Constitution* sailed at last from Gibraltar on 23 May, after three years and eight months humdrum duty in the Mediterranean, and arrived back in Boston on the Fourth of July 1828, just in time to fire the traditional salute at high noon. The task of laying her up required until the 19th, when Patterson hauled down his broad command pennant. And none were sure that another ever would be hoisted over the veteran frigate.

# 12 Rebirth and Brouhaha

## A TIME OF UNCERTAINTY

As *Constitution* lay at Boston, she was nearing her thirty-first birthday, a very old age for an active wooden warship. They typically had service lives of ten to fifteen years; indeed, the ship of the line *America,* built at Portsmouth, New Hampshire, and given to France at the end of the Revolution, was broken up after just three years. There were no orders forthcoming for further employment of the gallant frigate. If one were to judge her future by her appearance — shorn of all spars and housed over — one would have had to be pessimistic.

In the fall, the ship was routinely surveyed at the direction of the Board of Commissioners. It was found that her frame was sound, but that she would need

> ...new plank from lower edge of wales to the rail, new ceiling in the hold, new orlop and berth decks and beams — magazine, platforms and spar deck planked, new quarter galleries and channels — knight head, stem and head to be repaired, and to be coppered and caulked throughout.

It was also reported to the Board that she would need all new masts, yards, rigging, and anchor cables, as well as sails, awnings, and five new boats. In his estimate, septuagenarian Naval Constructor Josiah Barker tallied all these items up and found their accomplishment would require more than $104,000. A few months later, he revised that figure upward to over $112,000.

On 17 August 1830, Secretary John Branch requested that the Commissioners provide him with data on "all works which are now in progress for repair of vessels, also a list of all such as are deemed to require repairs." Statements were to be appended to this latter list detailing the conditions of these vessels as disclosed by formal survey (inspection), the cost of effecting repairs, and the value of each unit when repaired.

As a result of this directive, Yard Commandant Charles Morris, once "Old Ironsides' " First Lieutenant, was called upon to provide the requisite information on ship of the line *Columbus, Constitution,* and razee *Independence,* all then in ordinary in Boston. Barker conducted the actual surveys and, in *Constitution*'s case, again noted a sound frame. In essence, all but the live oak frame and her stout white oak keel was in need of replacement or very extensive repairs. And in the normal way of human events, the projected cost had risen — to $157,903. If done, the resultant ship, it was thought, would "be worth about eighty percent of a new ship of the same class." By comparison, repairs to 16-year-old *Independence* would cost over forty percent more while those to the 14-year-old *Columbus* would be thirty-five percent less. Morris sent these estimates to the Board on 28 August 1830.

Before this report reached him, Secretary Branch again wrote to several Yard Commandants asking for reports on specific ships, among them, *Constitution.* The fact of this request, together with the more general one calling for information on all ships, soon became public knowledge, and, just as quickly, was misinterpreted. On 14 September, in the Boston *Advertiser,* there appeared an article erroneously reporting the Navy's decision condemning the frigate to the shipbreakers. It said, in part:

> ...Such a national object of interest, so endeared to our national pride as Old Ironsides is, should never by any act of our government cease to belong to the Navy, so long as our country is to be found upon the map of nations.

## ENTER OLIVER WENDELL HOLMES, SR.

Two days later, again in the *Advertiser,* there appeared a poem by a young student, inspired by the article, that would preclude any course of action by the Navy other than total restoration. Oliver Wendell Holmes had written the stirring stanzas of "Old Ironsides:"

> Ay, tear her tattered ensign down!
>   Long has it waved on high,
> And many an eye has dance to see
>   That banner in the sky;
> Beneath it rung the battle shout,
>   And burst the cannon's roar; —
> The meteor of the ocean air
>   Shall sweep the clouds no more.
>
> Her decks, once red with heroes' blood
>   Where knelt the vanquished foe,
> When winds were hurrying o'er the flood,
>   And waves were white below,
> No more shall feel the victor's tread,
>   Or know the conquered knee; —
> The harpies of the shore shall pluck
>   The eagle of the sea!

Published by other newspapers around the country, and distributed by handbill in some cities, these lines aroused a public clamor.

Largely ignored in the outcry was the 18 September edition of the highly respected *Niles' Weekly Register* which noted the alarmist report, but doubted that "those having superior authority" would ever "permit a proceeding so repugnant to the best feelings of all the people." If, indeed, wrote the editor, the *Constitution* were too far gone, "let her be hauled upon the land, and have a house built over her, to remain so long as her wood and iron will hold together."

While the noise ebbed and flowed across the land, the Commissioners received the survey report and passed it to the Secretary on the 20th. In two days, the directive was enroute to Boston to repair *Constitution* "with as little delay as practicable." The public interest seems to have caused Mr. Branch to "expedite" things — at least on paper.

During the fall and early winter, Commodore Morris proceeded with a determination of his supply needs. His main requirement, he found, was for pine not in stock: 59,000 feet of white pine would be needed, together with thirty-four yellow pine beams for the berth and orlop decks.

On 24 February 1831, Morris recommended to Commodore Rodgers, head of the Board, that repairs to the ship be delayed until the drydock then under construction at the Yard was available, if there was no "urgent necessity for her services." He noted that, because of her "age and frequent repairs," she was considerably hogged; "her original lines ... altered and injured." These defects, he felt, could best be corrected by placing her in the dock. Should they heave her down, as had been done in the past, "the defect will be still further increased, and besides the risk (of heaving down) ... the repairs cannot be so advantageously or so thoroughly made as in a dock."

The decision to retain "Old Ironsides" in service had been heartily endorsed by the American people. It took little consideration on the part of the Commissioners to await the availability of a drydock for the best job possible. Some preparatory work was done in and for the ship as she waited. By early 1831, all of her bulkheads had been taken down to ease the passage of workers and materials within her hull. By spring 1832, all articles and fittings had been removed.

Commodore William Bainbridge returned as Commandant of the Yard in the summer of 1832. On 15 September, the Board directed that, when the frigate was in dock, a sample of her live oak was to be taken for comparison with docked timbers at the Yard. "Docked timbers" were those maintained in storage submerged in a large wet dock or "cobb wharf" constructed especially for the purpose. If the docked timbers did not compare favorably, use of this expensive means of stockpiling wood would be reevaluated.

Construction of the drydock proceeded without any major interruptions. The Board wrote to Bainbridge on 7 November that he was to have *Constitution* ready for docking "as early in the Spring as the weather will justify." On 4 December, they inquired when the ship could be docked and how soon she would be ready for sea. The answers, dated 28 December, were "April 1" and "four months."

By April 1833, Commodore Bainbridge had submitted a letter resigning command of the Yard because of failing health. While awaiting a successor, he continued to oversee preparation for *Constitution*'s docking. Mid-month found the protective roof removed and the ballast being taken out. During this same period, Commodore Rodgers wrote him directing that *Constitution* was to have bulwarks of yellow pine at the gangways and to plan for guns to be installed there, as well. On 28 April, Bainbridge reported the ship "in readiness to be placed in the dock."

In May, Commodore Jesse Duncan Elliott appeared as Bainbridge's replacement. A cantankerous and unpredictable individual amid equally feisty peers,

Elliott, as will be related, was the cause of the most ludicrous episode in the ship's history.

Late in the month, the Board directed that *Constitution*'s docking be held in readiness as President Andrew Jackson had indicated a desire to "witness the ceremony." It was expected that he would be in Boston some time between 25 June and 1 July.

On 23 June, Commodore Rodgers wrote to Elliott ordering him to let *Constitution* "stand upon her blocks so as to straiten her." The ship was to be stripped of hull planking as far as necessary to determine the extent of repairs needed, but since the Board expected to be in Boston about 10 July, more "particular directions in relation to her repairs" would await that event, as "Great care must be taken to preserve the original form and dimensions."

## FIRST DOCKING

At 5:30 the next morning, 24 June 1833, shorn of masts and ornamentation, but with Vice President Martin Van Buren, Navy Secretary Levi Woodbury, War Secretary Lewis Cass, and Massachusetts Governor Levi Lincoln in attendance, *Constitution* was drydocked. President Jackson earlier had cancelled his attendance due to illness. In command once again, especially for the occasion, was Commodore Isaac Hull, up from his post as Commandant of the Washington Navy Yard. By 1 P.M., she was safely "shored and secured." Scrapings from her barnacle-encrusted bottom became much sought-after mementoes of the occasion.

It was during this month of June 1833 that Jesse Elliott began a project that would bring controversy swirling about his head and the taint of unpredictable behavior to his memory: he ordered from a local woodcarver named Laben S. Beecher a figurehead of Andrew Jackson which he planned to install in *Constitution*. He took this action apparently with the expectation of currying favor with the President and despite existing regulations which limited use of figureheads to ships of the line.

The Board of Commissioners were more than a month late in making their inspection of the Yard and the ship, not arriving until 15 August. The very next day, however, a letter was sent to Commodore Elliott, giving priority to the restoration of *Constitution* over other Yard works. It further directed him to conform to "her former internal arrangements, as reflects the position of her decks — accommodation for officers — store rooms and similar objects, taking great care to preserve the original form of the bottom." Upon docking, the keel was found not only to be badly hogged, but thirty inches out of line, as well.

Commodore Hull, evincing his continuing love of and interest in the ship, wrote to Elliott at about this time inviting him to make requisition on the Washington Yard for all iron and composition castings needed for her repair. Earlier, Elliott had been told to ship all copper sheathing to Hull for recycling. The latter subsequently had canes, snuff boxes, and many other articles made

*Phaeton made for President Jackson from* Constitution *wood. (Courtesy of Historic Hermitage Properties Collections, The Ladies Hermitage Association.)*

from the wood and metal removed from the ship and sent to "notable persons" around the country. The Commissioners arranged to have picture frames made for their offices. President Jackson even received a small phaeton made from *Constitution* wood, in which he rode during the inaugural of his successor.

In September, the Board reversed its decision of the previous April and told Elliott the waist "is not to be timbered and planked up, but to be left open as it was formerly." Work proceeded apace, and by late November outside planking had been completed below the wales and the clamps were in for the berth deck. Beams for that deck were being put in as December began, and the ship planked up to her "thick-strake." Elliott noted that if the mild weather then being experienced continued through the winter, the ship repairs would be completed by early spring.

The weather continued unseasonably mild into the new year. On 8 January 1834, the Board was advised that the berth deck had been laid, outside planking completed to the lower port sills, and the ports themselves being formed. The gun deck beams soon would be in place; the ceiling planking had almost reached that level. It might even be possible to undock her by 15 March, Elliott reported.

In the next five weeks, work progressed to the point where the spar deck planking was about to be laid. Naval Constructor Josiah Barker, in immediate charge of the restoration, recommended to the Board, with Elliott's concurrence, the installation of more modern bilge pumps on the gun deck and hoped for a quick

197

answer so that the spar deck work would not be delayed. The response, dated 24 February, specified continuance of the ship's previous pump system.

The Board, in the same letter, took up some matters concerning external decoration. When finishing the stern some "slight carved work of the scroll or wreath character may be adopted to guide the painter and relieve the flatness." The billet head and curve of the cutwater were to be restored as they had been, but the bow head area was to be protected by "close woodwork as was recently done with *United States.*"

From the foregoing, it would appear that the powers in Washington were unaware of Commodore Elliott's project to place a figurehead of the President on *Constitution*. If that was the case, the cat shortly would be out of the bag, for the word was out in Boston. Because of Jackson's western background and his stand against the United States Bank, he was a most unpopular figure in that city. How the local people viewed the "desecration" of "their" beloved frigate with his image is clearly evident in this handbill of the day:

> FREEMEN AWAKE!
> OR THE CONSTITUTION WILL SINK.
>
> It is a fact that the old 'Glory President,' has issued his special orders for a Colossean Figure of his *Royal Self* in Roman Costume, to be placed as a figure head on *Old Iron-sides!!!* Where is the spirit of '76? — Where the brave *Tars* who fought and conquered in the glorious ship, where the Mechanics, and where the Bostonians who have rejoiced in her achievements? Will they see the Figure of a Land Lubber at her bow? No, let the cry be 'all hands on deck' and save the ship by a timely remonstrance expressing our indignation in a voice of thunder!
>
> "Let us assemble in the 'Cradle of Liberty,' all hands up for the Constitution — let the figure head (if mortal man be worthy) be that of the brave HULL, the immortal DECATUR, or the valiant PORTER, and not that of a Tyrant. Let us not give up the ship...
>
> North-enders! shall this Boston built ship be thus disgraced without remonstrance. Let this *Wooden God*, this Old Roman, building at the expense of 300 dollars of the People's money, be presented to the *Office Holders* who glory in such worship, but for God's sake SAVE THE SHIP from this foul disgrace.
>
> A NORTH-ENDER

With inflammatory sheets such as this in circulation, and with Beecher telling him of being approached by irate citizens, Elliott was forced to surface his project. On 1 March, he wrote the Commissioners that the figurehead nearly was finished and bore a "remarkable strong resemblance" to the President. He said he would await their decision as to what was to be done with the now-controversial piece and offered as the lame excuse for having gotten into the predicament that "on an examination of the papers on file in my office I could find nothing which had offered as a guide to my predecessors but what left the ornamentation of public vessels built or repairing at this yard entirely to their discretion."

The Board responded to Elliott's surprising report by calling his attention to published regulations, which required a Commandant, in making repairs, "to act in strict conformity to the instructions from the Board... or to the report of the officers of survey, and no additional repairs, or alterations, of any moment are to be made, without instructions from the Navy Commissioners." The Board felt that this had "been adverted to" with the long-established usage of substituting billets for figureheads in vessels less than "Ships of the Line," and should have led Elliott to consult with the Board before giving the order. However, since the figurehead was nearly finished, Elliott either could put it aboard *Constitution,* or hold it for installation on either *Vermont* or *Virginia,* ships of the line then under construction.

There is evidence that Commodore Elliott also had had Beecher carve bas relief busts of Isaac Hull, William Bainbridge, and Charles Stewart, her "big war" commanders, and had them installed on the stern of the ship. It is said they outlived the original Jackson figurehead and remained on board for nearly forty years.

About 21 March, Beecher came to Elliott with a report that "three highly respectable citizens had offered him $1500 for permission to carry the image away in the night." The artist thought he might be able to realize as much as $20,000 if he chose to bargain, according to one account.

Elliott's immediate response to this threat was to order a party of seamen to Beecher's studio to bring the Jackson figurehead to the Yard and safety. The statue, roughed out only to the shoulders, was placed in the machinery house near the drydock, where Beecher subsequently worked. Later on the 21st, upon hearing of rumors that a raid might be attempted by local citizenry, the Commandant directed Master Commandant John Percival of the receiving ship *Columbus* to take aboard a supply of cutlasses and boarding pikes with which to arm the Yard's seamen should the need arise. There was no raid.

Despite the principal distraction of the day, Elliott found time to write a letter to the Board about another element of *Constitution*'s restoration. Work on the ship had progressed to the point where the joiners soon would be put to work erecting bulkheads and otherwise rendering the ship more habitable. The Commodore sought the Board's guidance as to the kind of wood to be used in the bulkheads and whether or not "the Bulwarks and stern part of the cabin be ceiled" (i.e., sheathed), and what with. Three days later, the Board directed that the after cabin be fitted with hardwood. The forward bulkhead of the main cabin, together with those for the wardroom, steerage, and all others were to be made of pine. The stern and sides of the cabin were not to be covered, but the overhead could be ceiled with pine and painted. This decision did not satisfy Elliott. He wanted a more sumptuous cabin than they called for, and on 5 April he wrote again, pleading that "a slight ceiling be put upon the stern and sides and painted." The Board, however, remained adamant on the grounds that ceiling those areas would "injure the durability of the planking."

The Jackson figurehead, which was causing such a storm outside the Yard's gates, was put firmly in place on *Constitution*'s bow during April. By the latter

199

*Captain Jesse Duncan Elliott.*

part of the month, all of the outer hull work was done, and the ship ready for caulking and a first coat of paint. Recoppering was completed a week or so into May. The Board, curious to know how successful the restorers had been in straightening *Constitution* and reducing her hog, on 7 May ordered Commandant Elliott to plan on taking appropriate measurements before and after undocking so that a comparison could be made.

All the while *Constitution*'s restoration progressed, the local press pursued Elliott. Some, the most kindly, referred to him as "Mr. Elliott," the others, as "an enemy to your country," a "political partizan," "sycophant," and "Coward." He was threatened with tar and feathers, and assassination. Through it all, Elliott stuck to his avowed purpose of honoring the President.

## A PLOT IS HATCHED

Sometime during May or early June, there arrived in Boston from the West Indies a merchant captain with a cargo of sugar. While idling in the offices of his employers, Henry and William Lincoln, his cargo and vessel sold, the conversation turned to the figurehead controversy that had Boston so embroiled. The skipper, Samuel Worthington Dewey, later cousin to the then-unborn "Hero of Manila Bay," George Dewey, off-handedly stated he would get rid of the offend-

Constitution *moored between* Columbus *and* Independence *following undocking. The controversial figurehead of President Jackson is clearly visible.*

ing Jackson on the smallest of wagers. The younger Lincoln jokingly offered a hundred dollars and Dewey, with a reputation for daring, quickly took it up. The conversation passed on to other subjects, and the Lincolns forgot about it.

On Saturday, 21 June 1834, almost exactly a year since she had entered Drydock #1, *Constitution* was undocked with the stumpy figurehead of Andrew Jackson, in draped cloak and baggy trousers, and with top hat, prominent at her bow. Commodore Elliott had her moored between *Columbus* and *Independence.* To watch over his pride and joy, a guard was placed forward in *Columbus,* in a position from whence he could view the figure; a second was stationed on the forecastle of *Constitution;* and a third on the wharf nearby. The moorings were so arranged that, at night, light from a forward gunport in *Columbus* would illuminate Jackson. And in the "immense crowd" watching the undocking and mooring evolution was young Sam Dewey.

Two days later, the Yard Commandant submitted to the Board his report on the "before and after" sights taken as the ship was undocked. Differences, he wrote, could be noted at only three of the eight stations used, and these were so small as to be of no concern. *Constitution* had, indeed, been "straightened."

## ANDREW JACKSON BEHEADED

July 2nd was a day of infamy as far as Commodore Elliott was concerned. By nightfall, a thunderstorm "of unusual violence" rapidly was enveloping Boston. The thick blackness was broken intermittently by crashing lightning bolts in whose flashes might have been seen a small boat with a lone occupant pull away from Gray's Wharf and head for the Navy Yard on the other side of the Charles

## A Most Fortunate Ship

River. The occupant was 28-year-old Sam Dewey, bent on accomplishing the dare so lightly issued by William Lincoln some weeks before. He was soon below the tumblehome of *Independence*. Slowly, silently, he sculled forward around her bow and slipped beneath the cutwater of "Old Ironsides."

Dewey climbed up the manropes and worked his way in the shadows along the spar deck to the bow head. Evidently, the forecastle sentry was huddled in some lee from the weather. Fortuitously, the planking of the bow head area had been completed earlier that day, offering Sam a perfect shield from observation by any sentry. Leaning over the side, he began by starting a cut through the neck of the figurehead, but the screech of metal on metal shortly told him he had hit a bolt. Looking to see if anyone had heard the noise, he spotted the wharf sentry peering intently in his general direction. Dewey remained stock still, until the torrential rain overcame the guard's curiosity and sent him scurrying back to his shack. Young Sam began his next cut between chin and lower lip, and this time met no obstacle. In a moment or two the deed was done; "Old Hickory's" pine pate rested securely in the headsman's burlap bag.

Returning to his boat the way he came, Dewey found that it had swung in close to *Constitution* in the meantime and very nearly had been swamped by water draining from the frigate's deck. Gingerly, he got aboard and carefully worked his way clear of the moored ship. He succeeded in getting his craft safely back to Boston's friendly shore. Soaking wet and triumphant, he went immediately to his mother's house on School Street and hid his trophy in the woodshed.

With the clear dawning of 3 July, Dewey's handiwork became known to Lieutenant James Armstrong, whose unhappy duty it was to report the decapitation to Commodore Elliott. It must have been a memorable moment. Elliott lost little time in penning a long report to the Secretary of the Navy, now Mahlon Dickerson, and requesting instructions:

> Sir, — I herewith enclose a communication...relating to outrage committed upon the frigate *Constitution*...by some person or persons unknown.
> This insult to the Government appears to have been long premeditated...
> Suspicion rested at first upon the marine on post, and the ship keeper; but it seems to me at present more than probable that some persons from outside the yard... accomplished his work and made his escape...

Bostonians in the main were delighted by the big joke that had been played on the cantankerous Commodore. The severed head made the rounds of a number of club meetings and parties in the area, including one at which forty-four prominent Whigs honored Nicholas Biddle, president of the United States Bank.

At the Yard, Commandant Elliott promptly had increased the security forces around "Old Ironsides," with a naval officer and a Marine posted at night specifically to defend the remains of the figurehead from any further depredations. A wise move. A second attempt, by persons unknown, was made on the evening of 5 July. Soon discovered, one of the infiltrators escaped over the Yard wall. A second man was thought to have drowned. The rowboat they had used in their approach became Elliott's prize.

Some time later, Dewey took his trophy to Washington, intending to deliver it to President Jackson himself. But the President was seriously ill when Sam arrived and so, after apprising Vice President Van Buren of his mission, he was directed to deliver the remains to the Secretary of the Navy. Dickerson's first reaction to the sight was to threaten legal action; but, recognizing that the suit would have to be tried in Boston, he acknowledged Dewey's immunity and allowed him to leave after telling his story in detail. The Secretary already had written to Elliott and told him to do nothing further concerning the figurehead for the time being, but to cover the raw cut with a tarpaulin. Let the public forget about the incident.

On 15 August, the Commissioners were in Boston once more. They directed that *Constitution*'s channels be installed in a new fashion then being tested. These were to be so located that their undersides would be placed on "the lower part of the second strake above the spar deck port sill...so far from the seam only as will allow for caulking." The effect of this would result in the channels being some 16-17 inches higher than the spar deck, and would require them actually to be a series of short platforms between the spar deck gun ports. The Board also directed that the ship's hammock nettings be enlarged, as they did not appear sufficient to stow the allowance prescribed for the ship.

Elliott was not convinced of the need for changing the hammock stanchions and caused those on one side to be stowed. He found, as he reported to the Board on 1 September, that he could put thirty-seven on the forecastle, 128 in the waist, and seventy-eight on the quarterdeck; doubling that figure for total capacity provided an excess of eighteen over the 468 in allowance. The Board withdrew the requirement.

On 26 October, Elliott reported that *Constitution*'s channels had been install-ed in the new higher position. At the same time, he noted that all who had seen the result agreed that she would lose "the workings of the whole of her spar deck with the exception of two guns on each side." He also felt that, without the chan-nels to block it, the concussion of the lower guns soon would enervate spar deck crews. It was his desire that the matter be referred to a board of naval architects.

Commodore Rodgers ordered Elliott, on 15 December, to ready *Constitution* for active service. Life aboard took on a more familiar tempo. On the 19th Elliott was told to embark guns from stores as follows: 24-pounders lettered "A" and numbered 33, 34, 56 through 70, and 78 through 85; twenty 32-pounder car-ronades lettered "O" and numbered 1 through 18, and 21 and 22; and two Congreve 24-pounders as chase guns. Elevating screws for the guns were to be taken from sloop *Boston,* then in ordinary at the Yard. On Christmas Eve, Josiah Barker reported to the Commandant that the bowsprit was in, rigging going on, all but one sail finished, and water casks ready. These last were in addition to the eighty-eight new iron tanks installed when the ship still was in drydock.

The new year, 1835, marked its arrival in an end to the mild weather. The mercury plunged below freezing and stayed there for twelve days. Boston Harbor became sheeted with ice as far as Fort Independence, often steaming in the pale winter sunshine. Ship's work stayed on schedule, but it looked as if she'd be ice-bound.

Rodgers, perhaps concerned by all that had been accomplished in Boston since 15 December, wrote Elliott on 8 January cautioning him not to proceed so rapidly with *Constitution*'s outfitting that the rigging was not given "a proper stretch" and readied to withstand the North Atlantic gales prevalent at that time of year. Elliott was ahead of the Board in this matter: no rigging was being cut until it had been "on the stretch with heavy weights" for forty-eight hours.

After two weeks of freezing weather, it turned unseasonably mild and Elliott moved quickly. *Constitution*'s lower rigging was "overhead" by the 13th and the topmasts up on the 15th. Rigging continued apace and the top-gallant masts were up by the 28th. By this time, too, all water and provisions had been stowed, and anchors selected (two of 55-60 hundredweight and five of 50-55 hundredweight). Elliott was hopeful that she would be ready for sea on 5 February, if the chain from the Washington Yard arrived on time.

*Constitution* was ready to receive her officers and crew on 9 February, and shortly thereafter Elliott wrote to Rodgers advising him that the chain pumps "gave satisfaction" but that the channels were most unsatisfactory. He enclosed some damaged chain plates, hoping they would convince the Board of "the insecurity of trusting to them, or the bolts, when fitted, in that manner." In setting up the rigging, the bolts had been drawn into the wood, twisting and fracturing plates. The Board wouldn't budge.

As Bainbridge had done before him, Jesse Elliott had himself relieved as Navy Yard Commandant and assigned as "Old Ironsides'" Captain. On 2 March, *Constitution* sailed for New York with the entire Elliott family aboard, her spars once more standing tall and her black hull accented by a white gun stripe now carried all the way around the enclosed bows and cutwater. Astern, the regal decorations of her youth had given way to a memorial to past glories. And up forward, just beneath the bowsprit, was the incomplete figurehead of Andrew Jackson, shrouded in canvas. Happily, Bostonians did not carry out their threats to bombard the frigate in the Narrows if the hated statue were still on board — this, despite Commodore Elliott's final gesture: painting the canvas with five stripes, recalling a five-striped flag raised in Massachusetts at the outset of the War of 1812 to protest the war and foster the embryonic and short-lived secessionist movement by the same parties who were, in 1835, anti-Jackson.

# 13 The Mediterranean, Pacific, and Home Squadrons

## QUICK TRIP TO FRANCE

We have seen how Elliott left Boston the center of controversy because of the Jackson figurehead. In a small way, the problem also preceded him to New York in March of 1835, for he had taken the trouble to arrange for restoration of the damaged piece during his stay there without having had the courtesy to work through Commandant of the New York Yard, Commodore Charles G. Ridgely. The latter complained about it to the Secretary of the Navy on 9 March, the very day *Constitution* arrived in New York. In addition to taking umbrage at Elliott's "end run," Ridgely wondered if the work was authorized and was concerned that the carvers, Dodge and Son, wanted six weeks in which to remake the entire figurehead. Secretary Dickerson reassured him that the figurehead was authorized, but only so much work as was necessary to restore the head was to be allowed. This was completed on the 14th.

While these repairs were being made, Elliott received on board Edward Livingston, former Secretary of State and currently our Minister to France. For twelve years, the two countries had been negotiating claims resulting from the American Revolution and the Napoleonic Wars. We were demanding $25 million in payment for French depredations against American ships and property, and the French wanted a much smaller amount to pay for supplies provided in 1776. In 1831, a treaty had been ratified to settle the question, but when the first French payment fell due, their Chamber of Deputies failed to appropriate the money. The matter dragged on for several years. In his annual message to Congress in December 1834, President Jackson recommended that the Congress pass "a law authorizing reprisals upon French property," if the debt were not paid promptly. Understandable French reaction to this resulted in the recalling of ministers, although the French legislature voted the money and authorized its payment once the Americans gave a "satisfactory explanation" of the President's remarks to King Louis Philippe. *Constitution* was assigned to hurry Livingston back to France with Jackson's response.

Underway on 16 March, the voyage ran into difficulties the first night out when the frigate slammed into a gale. Deadlights were shut and guns housed. Upper yards were taken down and storm sails set, and still the ship scudded along at better than ten knots. A cold rain made the watch miserable as the wind lashed it about them. The storm worsened through the night, the masts straining and her canvas threatening to rip clear of the bolt ropes. The bow dug repeatedly into walls of rushing water. The sea came by the hogshead into the wardroom past the rudder casing.

As often happens at such times, there occurred a moment of peace — long enough to let the crew think that, perhaps, the worst was over. Then came a warning cry of "Look out to windward!" as a monstrous wave was sighted rushing out of the darkness at them with the force of a careening freight train. With a sickening lurch, *Constitution* rolled into the trough ahead of the wave and then was hit by the towering wall of water. A thunderous roar blotted out all sound as it cascaded across and into the ship. It was gone almost as quickly as it had come. In the relative silence that followed, a series of heavy, jarring thumps was felt and heard forward. Number 16 Starboard gun, a Congreve 24-pounder, had leapt from its carriage and been propelled through its port by the heavy water. It was dangling outside the ship by its breeching tackle, its more than two tons of cast iron threatening to beat in the bow.

The jib boom snapped off and was blown away at about this time, causing some ship control to be lost. A tremendous sea pooped her and threatened to wash everyone and everything off the spar deck. Elliott's gig was smashed to smithereens. A second wave followed, but the ship withstood it. Seizing the moment, an axman hacked at the breeching tackle and succeeded in dropping the errant chase gun into the sea. That danger past, and recognizing that the severity of the storm precluded his continuing to carry any press of sail, the Commodore hove to until the next afternoon, when the storm abated.

The remainder of the voyage passed uneventfully, and the anchor was dropped at Le Havre on 10 April, a passage of twenty-five days. Because of the uncertainty of the diplomatic situation, *Constitution* remained in France while Livingston went to Paris with the President's message. The Minister informed the King that Jackson had meant no insult to the French, but he refused to "explain" his threat of reprisal. As might be expected, this was unsatisfactory to the French; Livingston returned with his retinue to the frigate, expecting that war would be formally declared before he reached home. As it turned out, the English Foreign Minister, Lord Palmerston, stepped in as mediator and brought about a peaceful resolution of the difficulty.

*Constitution* sailed from France on 16 May, and after a 5-day stop in Plymouth, England, headed for home. It required five days to beat to the western end of the Channel against head winds, and then it became apparent that there was a gale somewhere to the southwest, beating the Bay of Biscay to a froth. That night, because the Officer of the Deck reduced sail in accordance with general orders to adjust them at his discretion that the ship might ride safely and comfortably, the high winds drove her to leeward so far that she was in danger of being wrecked on the Scilly Isles. When apprised of the situation, Elliott daringly ordered all possible sail set in an attempt to drive her clear to westward of the land before the winds could drive her onto it to leeward. It was a chancy thing. His new rig, with the raised channels, very nearly did him in. The drawing sails placed such a strain on the shrouds that the chain bolts at their lower ends actually were being drawn out, as a claw hammer pulls a nail. Luffs were placed on the weather shrouds to help take up the strain, but still more came free. It was touch and go; the race in doubt. Rocks covered with spray were seen all around as the ship continued to career through the sea at nine knots and better. At last, she came through and was safely in the Atlantic. Dame Fortune had seen her thread a gurnet probably known only to the local fishermen — and probably even they used it only in fair weather.

New York was reached on 23 June. It had been a trip to remember.

## A "HAUNT"

*Constitution* sailed once more on 19 August 1835 — probably with her channels restored to their former positions — to proceed to the Mediterranean as flagship of that squadron. Shortly after entering the Gulf Stream a couple of days later, she encountered a squall and had one of her lieutenants washed overboard from the port gangway entry port. Heavy seas, high winds, and the fact that the ship was making twelve knots at the time determined Commodore Elliott not to lower a boat. It was a hard decision, but the right one — to hazard more lives when it was doubtful they could even reestablish the point where the man went in was irresponsible. By nightfall, the high winds had passed but a chilling rain seemed a suitable companion to the saddened crewmen standing the night watch. Maintaining the routine was one of the best means to overcome the depression. Every half hour, the Midshipman of the Watch went aft and hove the log, making a record of his reading on the slate at the binnacle.

At seven bells, just a half hour before midnight, the Mid again returned to the taffrail with a couple of sailors to heave the log. Suddenly, he screamed. Faintly, rising above the gunwale of the Commodore's gig in the stern davits, could be seen a pale face — the face of the missing lieutenant. Overcoming their initial fright, the watch realized it really *was* he, and assisted him back aboard ship. Revived by a tot of brandy, he told how he had managed to grasp a trailing line as he first hit the water. The ship's speed quickly swept him aft to the vicinity of the rudder chains, to which he made himself fast with the line. Because the ship was going so fast, and plunging so much, he had been barely able to get enough breath, let alone call for help. Subsequently, he discovered that one of the Jacob's ladders triced at the stern had become freed and was hanging down near him. Tortuously, he managed to get on it and struggle up to the gig, where, with all the remaining strength he had, he was able to tumble himself over the gunwale and into its bottom, where exhaustion had overcome him. He had only just come to and was beginning to orient himself when he had been espied.

## HURRICANE

On 30 August, Elliott began to see Nature's signs that he was in for another bout of weather. The wind veered unexpectedly five and six points. Long, stringy cirrus clouds were followed by their lower, denser stratus cousins. The sea began to roll. And the sun, on setting, was blood red. The barometer was plunging. No doubt about it, they were in for a "blow."

Once again, the light spars and upper masts were sent down. Boats and other topside equipment were thoroughly lashed down. Inboard lifelines were rigged so that the men could move about the spar deck in greater safety. The hatches were battened down. And relieving tackles were rigged in the wardroom so that emergency steering would be available in the event the wheel was carried away.

The sky was obscured completely by dense, black clouds when dawn came dimly, and the waves had grown huge. *Constitution* rode under close-reefed maintopsail and a storm staysail on a starboard tack as the winds came to her from the southeast. She was in the so-called "dangerous semi-circle" of a hurricane — the worst place to be.

In no time at all, the frigate's world had become one of mountainous waves spuming great tendrils of spray ahead of them; of driving, lashing rain; of rolling, dark cloud cover alive with Nature's energy. The main topsail though close reefed, tattered with a thunderous clap. All hands were called to the spar deck with the ominous call "All hands save ship" to be ready for any emergency. Orders were best transmitted with hand signals. For twenty-four hours, they were battered, clinging to the lifelines, and existing on cold "salt stuff."

There was a sudden silence at seven the next morning. *Constitution* was in the "eye" of the hurricane, an area of seeming calm and silence in the midst of so much turmoil. The sailors knew it would be a short respite; none at all, in fact, for advantage was taken of these moments to check ship's security.

First, the darkness returned, and then the seas, stoving in ports and crushing boats. Finally, the winds returned in a terrible blast, threatening to take the masts right out of her. This was the worst the storm could offer, and having survived the onslaught, *Constitution* and her crew had merely to hang on as the hurricane swept on by.

But another surprise awaited them: later in the morning, as the weather improved, a huge iceberg was sighted ahead. It floated majestically in the still- stormy sea, seemingly unmoved by the forces around it. Elliott wisely gave it a wide berth, recognizing there was more of it below the surface than above. So large was it that the frigate sailed in relatively calm waters with peaceful breezes while in its lee for an estimated two miles. As she passed into the clear once more, the foresail was shredded in the renewed blast of wind.

By late in the day, life was able to return more nearly to normal. A hearty meal was served, as was a proper ration of grog. Normal watches were set; the men allowed to rest. Double lookout watches, however, were kept because of the possibility of meeting more icebergs. That night, a thermometer was watched closely so that any sudden drop in water temperature might warn them of an icy presence.

At the start of the forenoon watch on 2 September, a lookout reported a ship, fine on the lee bow. Closer investigation showed it to be an American in distress, her foremast gone and her ensign flying upside down at half mast. She was wallowing terribly. Elliott hailed and learned she was sinking. The seas still were heavy, so he decided to stand by until it was safe enough to launch boats. The rescue began two hours later and was accomplished without injury. Saved were sixty passengers and crew, fifteen of them females. Shortly after all were aboard *Constitution* and her boats stored, the hulk rolled over and went down. That she had managed to last long enough for the rescue was attributed to her cargo of cotton, which had helped keep her afloat.

## IN THE MIDDLE SEA

*Constitution* spent but a day at Gibraltar before proceeding to Port Mahon. She arrived there on 19 September and remained in port three weeks making voyage repairs and reprovisioning.

Dueling had been a problem in the Navy from the outset, as was noted earlier. Following the War of 1812, perhaps because of the boredom of endless peacetime duty in distant waters, the practice had become more prevalent, especially among midshipmen, often for reasons of trifling consequence. While *Constitution* was in Mahon two of her midshipmen demonstrated the extreme to which the practice had sunk.

It seems that a midshipman about to go on liberty, and planning to ride horseback to the top of the island's Mount Toro, exchanged his cloak for the reefer (pea coat) of another Mid in the duty section. When the latter arose for the morning watch on a cold, rainy day, he found the cloak lying on a stool, already soaking wet. One of his messmates had used it during the midwatch without having had the courtesy to say anything. Words followed, and by the time the cloak's owner, Midshipman John Maffitt, returned aboard, the challenge had been made and accepted. The subsequent duel took place the next day near a grave yard. The midshipman who had appropriated Maffitt's cloak was mortally wounded; his conqueror was sentenced to court martial by the Commodore. He later relented and allowed the young man to return to the United States and resign his warrant.

On 1 November, the big frigate began what had been for so long the routine of the American Mediterranean Squadron in peacetime: a series of roughly annual tours of the Sea, making diplomatic visits and checking up on the welfare of American interests on the littoral. From Mahon, she went east to Athens and was visited by the Greek King, Otho, and his Queen, hosting them to a day-long gala on board. Port calls followed at the island of Chios and at Vourla, Turkey, in November; Smyrna, Turkey, in January 1836; and Gibraltar and Tangiers briefly in February. Two months were spent using the facilities at Lisbon for overhaul before returning to Mahon in the middle of April.

On 23 May 1836, *Constitution* sailed for Toulon to pick up mail and funds from the American Consul, then headed for her first visits to Italian ports on this cruise: five days in Genoa and ten in Leghorn. While at the latter port, there occurred an incident at the regular Saturday personnel and ship inspections that indicates the Commodore could, on occasion, share a joke. According to Midshipman Maffitt, the Commodore came to the galley division in the course of his inspection. The division consisted of fourteen black cooks and the caboose, and also a goat the Commodore had aboard for milk. He found that the overhead above the ship's coppers had turned yellow from the constant heat. Turning to the midshipman in charge of the division, he pointed to the defect and charged that young worthy with neglect of duty, threatening him with court martial if he didn't square away. *Everything* was to be perfectly white — *perfectly white*, sir! At the next inspection, the Commodore found his desires followed to the letter: the overhead was white, the caboose was white, the blacks were white, and so was the goat — thanks to a liberal application of whitewash! Elliott was about to explode with his renowned wrath when he realized that his orders had been carried out to the letter. He called off the rest of the inspection and retired to his cabin — hopefully, for a good laugh.

*Constitution* followed her visit to Leghorn with a stop at Civitavecchia, port of the Papal States, and at Naples. While there, one of the ship's lieutenants married a Spanish lady in what is the first recorded wedding in the ship. The ship's chaplain performed the ceremony beneath awnings over the spar deck amidst red and white bunting, near the boat skids which had been made over into an artificial woodland grove with false trees and flowers, and even stuffed birds. The dancing which followed was interrupted for a few minutes by the advent of "King Neptune" and his full retinue, all costumed members of the crew. With all due pomp and circumstance — and tomfoolery — that worthy blessed the new couple and delivered presents from all the crew. The lieutenant-bridegroom responded with a well-filled purse to be distributed to the "King's minions." Dancing was resumed following the departure of the Sea Lord and continued until "small hours."

The odyssey resumed on 11 July. Heading down Italy's boot, the flagship made calls at Palermo and Messina in Sicily before crossing the Ionian Sea to Corfu on the 30th. Athens was regained on 19 August after calls at Milos and Napoli de Romania. King Otho and his Queen visited the ship once more. *Constitution* was joined here by her sister ship, *United States*, for duty in the squadron — two of the three original ships in the Navy working together once more thirty-nine years after they were launched.

Souda Bay, Crete, and Sidon and Beirut, Lebanon, were visited before Elliott came to anchor in Tripoli (then Syria), amidst the Egyptian Fleet. During an exchange of visits, Elliott was subjected to some boasting by the Capudan Pasha, who extolled the speed and handiness of his flagship. The Commodore never was one to ignore a challenge, and this time was no exception: in the trip to Jaffa (Tel Aviv), a distance of less than 100 miles, he sailed "Old Ironsides" completely *around* the Turk *twice* while beating him handily. It became one of Elliott's favorite stories in later years.

Constitution *rounding Elba in a gale in 1837.*

The Viceroy of Egypt paid an official visit to the ship while she subsequently was in Alexandria, and then she paid a call at Tripoli, Libya — her first since those memorable days more than thirty years earlier. The year was rounded out by visits to Tunis, Mahon for stores, and Cadiz, before starting the new year at Lisbon once more, on 4 January 1837.

For more than a year, Commodore Elliott had besieged Secretary Dickerson with urgings that the dignity of his position and the demands of his office were such as to require a Flag Captain to act as his principal staff assistant and to handle the routine of his flagship. The Secretary stood firm that he did not, as the area was peaceful and the squadron miniscule in force. Elliott persisted. Finally, in December 1836, he wrote to Dickerson and advised him that some time previously, perhaps as early as October, he had appointed Lieutenant William Boerum, his First Lieutenant, as the ship's commanding officer. From the limited evidence available, it appears that both Elliott and Boerum pursued the fiction that the latter was the legitimate Captain of the ship. The Secretary appears not even to have commented on the Commodore's December letter.

After three weeks at Lisbon, *Constitution* returned once more to Mahon for her annual two-month stand-down period, after a stop at Gibraltar. By the time she sailed again on 23 April, her First Lieutenant had been promoted to the newly-titled rank of Commander (formerly Master Commandant).

Elliott's second, and final, tour of the Mediterranean began on 23 April 1837 and had all the appearance of an avid artifacts collector making the rounds of antique shops and flea markets. Paying calls at nearly all of the ports visited during the previous year, as well as additional ports in Cyprus and Turkey, the Commodore amassed a curious collection of ancient memorabilia which he subsequently delivered to a number of colleges upon his return to the United States. Stowed away in *Constitution*'s hold — and, eventually, in every safe corner — were a stuffed ibis, two marble eagles, a marble head, a limb from a cedar of Lebanon, two Roman sarcophagi, a half-dozen marble columns, a set of casts of papal busts, two paintings, a dozen miscellaneous pieces of ancient worked marble, a mummy, myriads of coins, a vase brought up from the sea bottom at the site of the Battle of Actium (31 B.C.), and a variety of "antiquities" from Palestine, Syria, Greece, and Crete. Thus laden, he returned to Mahon in October and remained there into the new year.

Most of the month of February 1838 was spent at Malta. While there, Washington's Birthday was celebrated in exemplary style. *Constitution* was *fully* dressed with every signal and national flag available, and at noon a 21-gun salute was fired. Every British man of war in the harbor — all 14 of them — responded in kind. The paintings of this event, by J.G. Evans, misdated "1837", reposes at the Naval Academy.

During these waning weeks of the cruise, Commodore Elliot was busy rounding up a second collection for return to the United States: live stock. For himself and others, he installed on the berth deck a menagerie consisting of five jackasses, one jenny, an Arabian bay horse, five Arabian mares, three Arabian colts, one Andalusian colt, three Andalusian hogs, two Syrian broad-tailed sheep, and some Minorcan chickens, together with an assortment of grass, grain, and garden seeds. The displaced crew had to sling hammocks on the gun deck, but the warrant officers, midshipmen, and other officers remained in their quarters on that same deck.

*Constitution* — Elliott's ark — began her homeward voyage from Mahon on 15 June 1838. With the Commodore's typical luck in this regard, the heavily laden frigate ran into a gale as soon as she entered the Atlantic. Elliott headed southwest to pick up the prevailing trade winds, but before crossing paused at Madeira for a week to refresh the stock. The odyssey came to an end at Norfolk on the last day of July. The frigate was placed out of commission on 18 August.

Elliott's unauthorized use of *Constitution* to carry livestock proved to be a final straw. This, together with many other complaints concerning his performance while in command, resulted in his being suspended from duty for four years. In 1844, he was appointed to be Commandant of the Philadelphia Navy Yard, where he served one year before his death in December 1845.

## ON TO THE PACIFIC

*Constitution* did not linger long in the back waters of Norfolk. On 1 March 1839, she was back in commission once more under Captain Daniel Turner, who had served in the ship as a midshipman under John Rodgers in 1809 and 1810. During the War of 1812, he had served on the Great Lakes under Perry, earning a silver Congressional medal for his part in the Battle of Lake Erie. and subsequently had seen duty in the Mediterranean and the West Indies.

For this cruise, *Constitution* would be flagship for Commodore Alexander Claxton, the new commander of the Pacific Squadron. He would be relieving Commodore Henry E. Ballard in the liner *North Carolina*. His orders were to protect the American commerce on the west coast of South America as far north as Panama, to cruise to California occasionally, and to "look in" at the Sandwich and Society Islands as conditions warranted. He would have from two to four smaller units to assist him in policing this vast area.

"Old Ironsides" was in her 41st year, very long in the tooth for any warship, but despite her age she continued to command the love of her crewmen. One, who joined her just before this cruise, has left a description of his first sight of her:

> ... I perceived the old *Constitution* lying in the river, with her neat and faultless hull, and elegant tapering spars; she certainly was an object which the criticising eye of a sailor would wish to gaze ardently upon; she is at any time a superb looking frigate...

Her first port of call was New York, where she arrived on 20 April, to complete her crew and receive Powhatan Ellis, Minister to Mexico, and his suite for transportation south. That worthy came aboard on 19 May; Turner got underway the next day and soon had studdingsails set under fair skies. As the sailors put it, "Our old frigate was...walking off under a crowd of sail,... quick on the heel as ever."

Vera Cruz was reached on 16 June after twenty-seven days at sea. Ambassador Ellis, retinue, and baggage, were landed with all due ceremony on the 19th:

> ... It was a beautiful morning; our tars were dressed in their mustering suits of snowy white; they laid aloft with orderly and graceful motion, remaining in the slings of the several yards, until the signal for laying out. As soon as the boat containing the Minister shoved off from the ship's side, the thunder of our ponderous twenty-four pounders on the main deck boomed along the silent waters and reverberated amongst the distant hills. At the sound our watchful tars spread themselves along the several yards, with extended arms, a regular distance from each other, and as the smoke cleared away, and each parallel line of living beings, neatly and uniformly dressed, stationary as chiseled statues, broke upon the sight, they formed a *tout ensemble* scarcely to be equalled.

*Constitution* departed early the next morning, and after a brief call at Havana, was on her way to Rio. The 33-day voyage was a pleasant one for ship's company, but showed signs of growing problems between the Commodore and the Captain. Claxton and Turner were longtime friends in the Service, one considering the other something of a protege. In fact, Claxton particularly had requested the younger man for his Flag Captain. It seemed that the cruise would be made on the happiest of terms for all concerned. Boredom, however, is a condition very much to be avoided at sea, and the means to do so are limited. Claxton had no other ships in company; neither could he possibly spend all his days corresponding — particularly since weeks would pass before his letters could be sent. As a result, he began injecting himself into the ship's routines with every intent of being helpful to Turner and in no way meaning to imply any shortcoming in that officer. One day, Turner found out that the purser had issued some clothing to the crew from slops without his permission. The purser reported that the Commodore had ordered him to do so. When confronted by Turner, Claxton said merely that he thought it was a minor, but necessary, action and that he hadn't wanted to trouble his friend with it. Other instances where the Commodore had inserted himself into the ship's routine in small ways led to Turner telling his senior directly that it wasn't his place to become involved unless he felt the Captain wasn't doing his job. Friendship carried the day, and all seemed to be settled.

*Constitution* spent just two weeks in Rio, her sailors enjoying the sights and liberty, and then it was away for the Horn on 9 September. Two days out, shortly before noon, Seaman William Johnson fell overboard from the mizzen top. A boat was lowered immediately, but all it found when it reached the spot where the man was last seen was his hat.

After passing south of the Falkland Islands, another tragedy struck the ship: through miscalculation, an insufficient quantity of whiskey had been shipped, and "Old Ironsides" had run dry. Silas Talbot had been able to borrow from a squadron mate when that had happened to him forty years before, but Captain Turner had no such recourse. Not until they rounded the Horn and reached Valparaiso could any relief be expected. If ever a blow could be struck at a ship's morale, this was it. And the fierce waters of the Horn had yet to be faced. Some of the sailors turned to an expedient available to them in small stores: they bought up all the eau de cologne the purser had stocked and mixed it with a little hot water and sugar. These enterprising businessmen then sold it to their mates for a dollar a bottle. It took the officers three or four days to uncover the operation.

*Constitution* sighted Staten Island on 27 September and Cape Horn itself two days later, having up until that time had remarkably pleasant weather. Her good fortune was not to last, however, for by the next morning she was laboring under almost bare poles "against the tempestuous elements." Wrote a participant later:

> ...The gale continued without intermission for sixteen or seventeen days, buffeting which 'Old Ironsides' proved herself the sturdy and efficient sea-boat she was always celebrated for: no ship was ever more comfortably secured against the bitter blasts and drenching billows than was ours on this occasion...

Lest, however, one get the mistaken impression that it was a pleasant experience, witness a meal time during this period:

> ... our frigate... labored dreadfully, rolling almost her spardeck guns under — dinner was piped, and our lads... huddled together around their several messes, endeavoring... to transmit... bean-soup to the inner man. Each one... placed himself

in some solid and secure position to commence his meal, taking advantage of the interval between every roll of the ship to bring a portion... to his... lips; a fellow on the forward part of the deck, sung out lustily, 'look out for your beans;' the words were scarcely uttered than, before any body could make a second preparation, she gave one of the most tremendous rolls I think I ever experienced;...my eyes, what a scene now presented itself — away went simultaneously with one movement — on one confused mass, kettle of hot-water — baskets of small biscuit — pans of soup — pots — kettles — frying pans — gridirons — and all the *etceteras* of the galley; here might be seen a poor fellow struggling... to regain his feet, which the well-greased deck almost rendered an impossibility;... though many lost their dinners — and several got sore heads and pummeled ribs..., yet all... joined in laughter that this affair occasioned.

Once clear of the gale, *Constitution* made steady progress northward. On the evening of 28 October, Third Lieutenant R.R. Pinkham died of an "abcess of the left lung" which had become apparent shortly after leaving Rio. The next day, at noon, sail was shortened and the ship hove to. All hands were mustered aft to bury the dead. The band played the "Dead March" from "Saul" as the six gun captains of Pinkham's division bore his remains, boxed in what had been his cot and covered by the Stars and Stripes, to the lee gangway. Following a reading of the burial service by the First Lieutenant, the body was committed to the deep as the Marine detachment fired three volleys. Sail was set; Valparaiso raised on 2 November.

## ON STATION

The sloop of war *St. Louis* (18) was found waiting in port. She had beaten the big frigate by two days from Rio. It was soon apparent, however, that only rarely did anything happen with alacrity on this station. Thirteen days were spent watering and provisioning (and, presumably, "whiskeying"), and another eleven in a leisurely sail up the coast to Callao, Peru, the principal American rendezvous on this coast of South America. She remained at anchor there for a full three months, while readiness was forgotten and the crew found pursuits more to their liking in runs on the beach.

During this time, too, Commodore Claxton's boredom again led him to take an increasing hand in the ship's affairs in order to pass the time. Incident followed incident until Claxton and Turner grew increasingly frigid toward one another. The matter came to a head on 2 February 1840 when Turner sent a letter to the Commodore requesting permission to return to the United States. Claxton responded that he hadn't the authority to grant such permission. Turner sent in a second request: to be allowed to move ashore until such time as the Secretary of the Navy (now James K. Paulding) could make his pleasure known in the matter. Claxton again turned Turner down, this time on the grounds that there was no Captain present who could relieve him. The Commodore, of course, considered it beneath his station to command his own flagship, although such was more often the rule rather than the exception. From this time onward, the Commodore and the Captain apparently communicated with one another only by formal letters.

**SOUTH AMERICAN PORTS OF CALL**

Given the fine state of affairs in the "high command," it was a good thing it was such a somnolent station. Between late February and early June, *Constitution* made visits to Talcahuano, Chile, and Payta, Peru, with a month's "rest" at Callao in between. She then settled down for another three months at Callao.

Not all of the sailors' amusement came from the beach, although there were runs ashore that became legendary. While in New York, ship's company had chipped in and purchased a library of three to four hundred volumes. This was placed under the charge of the ship's yeoman, who kept the books stowed in the fore passage near the armory. Time was set aside on Sundays for the exchange of books; reportedly, there were many avid readers. Authors included Scott, Marryat, Cooper, Irving, and Bulwer-Lytton.

In Rio, the crew had subscribed about 250 dollars to be used for the purchase of theatrical equipment: a wardrobe of varied costume parts and a full range of paints with which to paint scenery on old canvas. "Damon and Pythias" was the first production attempted, at Callao, and was well received not only by ship's company, but by visiting British and French officers, as well. Something called "Ruffian Boy" and a farce entitled "Lying Valet" were two other works in the repertoire. So taken were the thespians with their success that the crew contributed an additional two or three hundred dollars for more equipment. At least two pieces were composed on board: "Life in Peru" and, inevitably, "Old Ironsides." A song from the latter shows how the crew felt about their ship:

> She's a craft that has weathered the gale and the fight,
>     And is ready to brave 'em once more;
> She is quick on the heel, and that hundreds can prove,
>     Since she last left Columbia's shore;
> And tho' she is old, she's as sound as a *roach*,
>     If she has any fault none can twig it;
> So push round the jorum, let's drink once again
>     Success to our trim noble Frigate.

*Constitution* sluiced the mud of Callao harbor from her anchors once more in the middle of September 1840 and proceeded north again. A quick stop was made at Payta, "celebrated for its cloudless skies, agreeable women, profusion of onions and scarcity of water," before heading for Puna, Ecuador, for a two week stay where one could find "relentless mosquitos, trees loaded with delicious oysters and guanas, paroquets and alligators in no small quantity." It is small wonder that the *Constitution*s were happy to return to Callao on 11 October for two more months of swinging with the tide.

The seasons in the Southern Hemisphere are reversed from those in the northern, and so on 2 December *Constitution* left Callao for the higher, cooler latitudes farther south. She made Valparaiso nine days later and remained for most of January 1841.

Talcahuano, Chile, was visited from 4 February until 8 March, and was always thought of as a place of death by the crew thereafter. On 2 March, a seaman by the name of Gibbs slipped and fell into the water from the starboard boat boom and never came to the surface. Two days later, Quarter Gunner William Leeds died of dysentery, a malady that had spread to others in the ship. Dysentery also precluded the need for a Court of Inquiry at cruise's end concerning the adversary relationship between the Commodore and the Captain by bringing the former to his death shortly before the breakfast pipe on 7 March. Captain Turner assumed the command of the squadron in accordance with Navy Regulations, but chose not to assume the title of Commodore. He lowered Claxton's broad command pennant and resumed flying the coach whip commissioning pennant.

The decision was made to inter the late Commodore in Valparaiso instead of the detested Talcahuano. The frigate got underway on the 8th and arrived there three days later, her ensign at half mast. The funeral began at eleven the next day. In the procession, besides the officers from "Old Ironsides" and 250 crewmen, were officers from *HMS President,* the French frigate *Thetis,* the Danish frigate *Bellona,* the Chilean frigate *Chilia,* and the French war sloop *Camille,* as well as a detachment of Royal Marines, and the masters and supercargoes of every merchantman in harbor. As they made their way to the cemetery, the mourners were accompanied by *Constitution*'s band. Sixty-one minute guns were fired by the frigate. Following the graveside service, both the U.S. Marines and the Royal Marines fired three volleys.

Returning to Callao on 26 March for her final visit, *Constitution* remained at anchor for more than three months, preparing for the voyage home and awaiting her replacement.

The Fourth of July was a memorable one during which the crew not only celebrated the nation's birthday but their imminent departure for home, as well. A double tot of rum from official sources, coupled with liberal amounts of smuggled goods, turned the frigate into a scene of drunken revels, with singing, drinking, and fighting all going on simultaneously in various parts of the ship. Twenty-six months of tedium were swilled away in herculean fashion. Fortunately, nothing worse than many bad hangovers were suffered as a result, and no enemy chose that moment to attack.

Perhaps the absence of an enemy on the 4th was fortuitous, because on the 10th both Captain Turner and the commander of *HMS President* received official reports of an incident in November 1840 when a drunken, braggert Canadian named Alexander McLeod had been arrested for announcing publicly in New York that he had killed an American named Durfee three years earlier in an incident on the Niagara River involving Canadian dissidents. The British Foreign Minister demanded his release and warned that if McLeod were executed there would be "war, immediate and frightful." Such was the extent of the information both Captains received.

Captain Turner ordered the ship prepared for action, quietly, while a wary eye was kept on *President.* Bulkheads were struck and furniture sent below. Battle lanterns were hung. Extra powder cartridges were made up and distributed evenly between the magazines. Round, grape, and canister shot were broken out and placed in their ready racks and boxes. Long out of the habit, it took the crew two hours to complete this task.

While these preparations were going forward, *HMS President* and her smaller consort, sloop *Acteon*, gave the Americans a thrill by suddenly getting underway and maneuvering about the harbor. It brought to the Yankee minds a remembrance of *Essex* being cornered and defeated in Valparaiso thirty-seven years earlier. They wondered if it would happen again, but vowed to fight to the end. Eventually, the British returned to anchor. Turner stood down from battle stations. Both sides eyed the other with suspicion and waited.

## GOING HOME

As it turned out, no shooting resulted from the war scare. *Constitution* got underway later in the day, 11 July, to begin her voyage home. One result of the incident, however, burst upon the *Constitutions* a few nights later when Captain Turner beat to quarters during the midwatch to make his point about readiness.

The depletion of the whiskey supply on the outbound voyage already has been mentioned. On the homeward trip, the provision of hot water for evening tea was stopped. Water wasn't in short supply, fire wood was; and Captain Turner, mindful of the possibility of war with Britain, was husbanding his supply early, in case it became necessary to run all the way home without another port call. Ship's company grumbled at first, but when informed of the reason, put a good face on it.

The voyage was a swift one, free of head winds and ice. The big frigate flew around the Horn, passed the Falkland Islands and the Rio de la Plata, as fast as anyone on board could hope. On 24 August, they sighted their first sail since the Pacific and from a Brazilian brig learned that war between Britain and the United States continued to be just a threat. Four days later, off Rio, they encountered our sloop of war *Marion,* which confirmed the good news. *Constitution* dropped anchor in the beautiful harbor of Rio at nine that evening, and the crew had their hot tea.

Captain Turner found the frigate *Potomac,* bearing the broad pennant of Commodore Ridgely, whom Elliott had upset at the outset of this chapter, and schooner *Enterprise* already in harbor. On the morning of the 29th, he saluted the Commodore with thirteen guns. A few days later, Dom Pedro II, 17-year-old Emperor of Brazil, made a grand tour of the harbor and was greeted by salutes from all warships present. And, on another evening, the *Constitutions* again got roaring drunk. Wrote a participant:

> ... this...affair is one of so common and every-day a nature on board a man-of-war as to be scarcely worth adverting to; for no person who is at all conversant with the character of a sailor, would for one moment imagine that four or five hundred tars, their hearts elate at the prospect of soon reaching home, would be in the vicinity of

> such stuff as whiskey at night, and the decks but dimly lit with one or two lanterns, and not try every scheme to test its quality.

That man obviously knew whereof he spoke!

Commodore Ridgely boarded *Constitution* on the 14th, a sick man. He, together with his clerk, a chaplain, two or three midshipmen, and about twenty seamen, all invalided or with their time expired, would ride her home. The frigate got underway the next morning to three cheers from the other American warships. On her way down harbor, she clipped *HMS Queen Victoria,* ketch, which had failed to veer her anchor chain and clear the channel. The Britisher lost her flying jib and jib booms for her lack of good sea manners, while *Constitution* had a davit arm ripped from her larboard quarter.

The last leg of the voyage home was almost perfect. Except for a brief, severe squall on 21 October, the winds were fair and fresh. Twelve knots was not uncommonly found upon tossing the log. So swiftly was *Constitution* proceeding that, on 23 October, she overhauled the barque *Sarah,* which had left Rio eleven days ahead of her. Then, the winds largely failed her until the 29th, when they came fair once more. Two days later, she saluted ship of the line *Delaware* (Commodore Morris) and dropped anchor in Hampton Roads at six in the evening. A day or so later, the steamer *Poinsett* towed her to an anchorage below the Navy Yard. The commission ended when Captain Turner went ashore on 8 November, the crew paid off and the ship in the hands of the Yard.

## THE HOME SQUADRON

Slightly more than seven months elapsed before *Constitution* returned to active duty, commissioned on 22 June 1842 with Lieutenant Charles W. Chauncey as "commanding officer," and scheduled to become a unit of the new Home Squadron, a sort of "ready reserve" unit, which had been established during the preceding year.

On 14 July, the ship received from the schooner *Martin Smith* four 68-pounder Paixhans cannons. These were monster shell-firing weapons which were located, two on either side of the gun deck, in the midship ports. Named for their inventor, French General Henri Joseph Paixhans, these medium-range guns could fire exploding shells and so constituted a new capability for the old frigate.

The "commander" of *Constitution* came aboard on 15 July. He was Captain Foxhall Alexander Parker, who had been Jacob Jones' First Lieutenant-cum-Flag Captain in the early 1820's.

For months, *Constitution* lay swinging at her anchors, some of her crew finding little else to do but fight, drink, or attempt desertion. A deranged Marine private jumped overboard and drowned. The carpenter's gang was kept busy for a while closing off a portion of the storeroom abaft the well and below the cockpit to become the shell filling room for the new guns. The gunner's gang was equally busy, learning to fill and handle the new-fangled ammunition that had the potential of exploding in one's hands. Parker finally put to sea on 10 November

*Captain Foxhall Alexander Parker.*

and spent the next three weeks in basic seamanship and gunnery exercises off the coast. He came back to Norfolk on 2 December.

Despite rumors to the effect that she was to become flagship of the Brazilian Squadron, *Constitution* instead was designated to go back into ordinary and be replaced by *Brandywine*. On the last day of December, she was shifted to a berth off the Navy Yard. In the weeks that followed, the sails were landed, the lower and topsail yards were transferred to *Brandywine* together with the gun deck gun battery, and then all the stores were shifted to the other ship. At 9 A.M. on 16 February, Parker placed her out of commission and immediately transferred the crew and himself to *Brandywine*.

# 14 Around the World

## GETTING READY

The inactive *Constitution* was used as headquarters for all the ships in ordinary or laid up at Norfolk. Lieutenant Gabriel G. Williamson was in charge of the shipkeepers, and he and his men had quarters aboard the old frigate. She had been thus used for about six months when the Department wrote the Norfolk Navy Yard to request an estimate of the cost to ready her for "special service" of three years duration. Naval Constructor Foster Rhodes responded that $70,000 would be needed, an amount so great that there were unsufficient funds available to do the job. Captain John Percival was ordered to conduct an independent survey for himself and report the findings. He said he could ready her for a trip around the world for no more than $10,000. Commodore Lewis Warrington, Chief of the new Bureau of Construction and Repair, confirmed Percival's estimate. He got the green light to "make it so."

Shipkeepers began transferring their gear to the sloop *Ontario* on 9 November 1843, as preparations were begun to overhaul "Old Ironsides." With the advent of the first increment of crew from the receiving ship *Pennsylvania* on the 21st, Williamson himself moved over to his new headquarters. All the familiar details of an overhaul were repeated again. First, Percival docked her and completely recaulked and recoppered the bottom. She had been taking on about a foot of water per hour in the well during her last outing the previous fall. Next, her masts and spars were worked over and the rigging rereeved. The gun batteries placed aboard consisted of twenty-six long 24s and the four 68-pounder Paixhans on the gun deck, and twenty 32-pounder carronades above.

Orders came for the ship to be completely ready for sea as of 1 April 1844. From the 18th of March, she began loading stores and receiving additional drafts of seamen from the "guardo." By 11 April, however, "Old Ironsides" still was short of men and it had become apparent that her complement could not be completed soon in Norfolk. Captain Percival, who formally had taken command and placed *Constitution* in commission on 26 March, requested and received permission to sail for New York to complete manning. He departed the Yard on 16 April and cleared the Capes the next day. The trip northward was a miserable ten-day affair that began with a three-day gale which drove them out into the Gulf Stream before they could head for their destination. *Constitution* anchored off Castle Garden, near the Battery, on the 27th.

Captain John Percival, one of the Navy's genuine characters, was born in Barnstable, Massachusetts, in 1779, the same year that John Paul Jones defeated *HMS Serapis* off Flamborough Head. A midshipman during the Quasi-War with

*Captain John "Mad Jack" Percival.*

France, he entered merchant service when the peacetime cutbacks occurred in 1801. While so engaged, he was pressed into service in the Royal Navy and reportedly served in Lord Nelson's flagship *Victory,* as a topman, during the Battle of Trafalgar (1805). Later, while a member of the prize crew aboard a Spanish prize, he and other Americans deserted at Madeira and promptly sought asylum in an American ship, the *Washington.* Percival reentered the U.S. Navy in 1808 and was assigned to *Syren.* During the War of 1812, he served with dash and daring in a gunboat which captured a British liner's tender, and then in the war-brig *Peacock,* which captured 14 British merchantmen and two men of war. He was promoted meritoriously to lieutenant for his exploits — and also earned his nickname of "Mad Jack". After the war, he served in a series of routine assignments, including having been on duty at the Boston Yard when Elliott was Commandant.

*Constitution* spent more than a month in New York on this occasion. Recruiting went well; she soon had about 400 crewmen aboard. Unlike the early part of the century, a majority of the men were immigrants and aliens from

223

around the world: Canadians, Prussians, a Chilian, Russians, Chinese, and so on. There were a great many English and Irish. But it wasn't recruiting that kept the ship in port: it was waiting for a diplomatic passenger. This time, the frigate would carry Mr. Henry A. Wise to his new post as Minister to Brazil. He didn't arrive until 27 May, when he appeared with wife, four children (one just eight months old), secretary, and seven servants — plus baggage. Captain Percival turned over the entire cabin to the Wises and had an area on the gun deck partitioned off with canvas as a temporary cabin for himself.

## AWAY TO RIO

Percival at last was able to get underway at 10 A.M. on 29 May — towed down to Sandy Hook by the steamer *Hercules.* Enroute, the *Constitution*s exchanged "huzzas" with the inbound ship of the line *Columbus* (74), just coming home from the Brazil Squadron. They were on their way, with orders to check up on the safety of American merchants, survey new waters, seek potential sites for future stations, and show the flag around the world.

The wind was fair and the seas calm as the ship headed east for the Azores. (Prevailing wind patterns were — and are — such that it was more efficient to sail east, then south and southwest, than it was to beat directly for the Brazilian bulge.) On Sunday, 2 June, it was so peaceful that the ship sailed with her awnings fully spread, fore and aft. Promptly at ten, the church call was heard throughout all decks, and crew and passengers alike went to their assigned positions. Abaft the weather gangway in order were the warrant officers, midshipmen, lieutenants, and the Captain and passengers. Ship's company was mustered to leeward. After First Lieutenant Amasa Paine read the service, Captain Percival read the Articles of War, which applied to the passengers, too, as long as they were aboard. Then Purser Thomas M. Taylor called the general muster, and each man passed around the capstan individually under the close scrutiny of "Mad Jack." As Fifth Lieutenant John B. Dale noted, "Woebetide him with long hair or unshaven chin!" That has a modern ring to it.

Percival fumed through most of this leg of the voyage because it was taking longer than he wanted, even though the log showed the old frigate to be making fourteen knots on the 9th. Daily gun drills helped pass the time and kept the crew occupied, although no powder was expended. Flores, western-most of the Azores, was sighted on the 12th, but dying winds left them with another four days at sea before making the harbor of Fayal. This was the first such visit by an American frigate.

American Vice Consul Frederick Dabney called upon Ambassador Wise and Percival the next morning, and made his home available to the diplomat and the ship's officers. The Wise family took advantage of this opportunity to enjoy more familiar surroundings for a few days.

Dabney threw a ball for *Constitution* on the 18th which was well attended by the local Portuguese gentry. It lasted until two the next morning and all pronounced it a success despite the fact that few on either side spoke the other's language. Percival reciprocated with a reception and dance on the ship that afternoon.

*Constitution* was underway on the 20th, the Wises having reoccupied the great cabin. The American brig *Lycoming,* bound for Boston, was spoke the next day and took letters for the folks at home. In three more days, they were at anchor in Funchal, Madeira. Found in harbor were the English razee *America* (60), as well as a Portuguese frigate *(Diana)* and a war brig.

Madeira proved to be a pleasanter stay than the wretchedly poor Fayal. The Wises again moved ashore to the residence of our Vice Consul, a Mr. Baynim. He, too, threw a party in honor of the ship's visit. These diplomatic outposts were lonely places; the arrival of a countryman nearly always was cause for celebration. The major attraction of Funchal for one member of the crew, at least, was the opportunity to purchase a warm bath: luxury for the equivalent of 60 cents.

A brief, two-day sail brought *Constitution* next to Santa Cruz, on the island of Teneriffe, one of the Canary Islands, on 1 July. It proved to be a decaying society with beggar women and naked children in the streets, and soldiers of the Spanish garrison very much in evidence. The 4th of July was observed by a 21-gun salute at noon, an entertainment in the cabin for the officers, and the firing of some rockets in the evening. That such an occasion should have been marked with so little celebration is indicative of the indifferent relations found at Teneriffe.

Percival got underway once more on the afternoon of 6 July, followed out of harbor by the French corvette *Berceau,* also bound for Rio. For several days, the two warships kept informal company but on the 10th the Frenchman shaped a course to pass between the Cape Verde Islands and the African mainland while the Americans took a more westerly heading. Southward they went, out of the trades and into the equatorial doldrums. There were days when not fifty miles were made good. On the 22nd, when the ship happened to be making a rare eight knots, a seaman named Corbett fell overboard from one of the channels where he had been scraping paint. Quickly, a life buoy equipped with a red flag was cut away. It was a mile and a half farther on before the frigate could be brought to a stop and one of the quarterboats sent to pick him up. Happily, he had reached the buoy and was brought back aboard none the worse for his plunge.

The next evening, as the ship was nearing the Equator, an old seafaring ritual was begun: the "crossing the Line" ceremonies, when those who had never before ventured beneath the Southern Cross ("polliwogs") were initiated into its mysteries by those who had ("shellbacks"), generally with high jinks and hilarity — and some discomfort for the neophytes. It was just after the setting of the evening watch when a lookout sang out, "Light ho! Dead ahead!" From the bow head area there shortly appeared the "herald" of "Neptunus Rex, Lord of the Watery Domain." One of the officers present has left us a description of what transpired:

> ... his messenger... when, instead of being a stalwart Triton, covered with sea weed and dripping with brine, a little Forecastleman by the name of Fitzgerald was rig'd out more like a North American Indian than a Sea-God. Indeed, it was a laughable burlesque, for our little Forecastleman with his wiry legs developed in his white sheeting wrapper, which he drew around him in a tragedy style, and with a paper cap on his head, had lost his presence of mind and forgotten his part. However he managed to deliver a letter to the officer of the deck from Neptune to Capt. Percival an old acquaintance welcoming him back once more to his dominions, requesting the names of such of his children as had never been initiated, and also permission to come on-board to-morrow morning. This was graciously accorded by the Capt. with an appropriate speech, when Old Neptune was again heard hailing for his 'Postman'...

Fitzgerald disappeared back into the bow head, and shortly thereafter was seen Neptune's "flaming chariot" passing down the ship's side. It was, in fact, a half-barrel of tarred rope-yarns made up for the purpose. At nine the next morning, as *Constitution* lay hove to, King Neptune arrived. Our eye witness:

> ... Old Neptune soon after hailed us and was seen coming aft in the weather gangway in a *triumphal car* (a map chest mounted on trucks) drawn by four *sea-horses* (four negroes painted with red streaks across their faces and naked from the waist up-wards) with *Amphitrite* seated by his side and one or two boys dressed very queerly but whether they were to represent male or female gods was very doubtful, accompanied by Tritons and Constables with long spears and oakum beards. The barbers too performed their part in the strange procession flourishing their razors made of hoop-iron a foot or two in length. Father Neptune was personified by Kemp an old broken down boatswain now a quarter-gunner, and when he arrived on the quarter-deck he made, thro' his speaking trumpet a very complimentary speech to the Captain and Old Iron-sides with permission to initiate those of his children who had never before crossed the line. After a good deal of mummery of that sort, and some private cursing of Neptune *sotto voce* to his black sea-horses when they came near capsizing his Majesty in turning. The whole party took a glass of grog and returned to the Forecastle. Then was a platform raised and the starboard gangway occupied by a large tarpaulin triced up so as to hold water. The hose of the forcing pump was led into it, and the Carpenters set to in pumping. A band of oakum bearded constables came aft with a list of names and first pounced upon the Lieutenant of Marines who walked off with them most manful-ly. Soon he was seen striped of his coat, seated on the platform with his back to the tar-paulin reservoir of water, with the grotesque barbers flourishing in the air their huge razors and lather-brushes: many of them wore masks of canvas with painted faces pro-ducing a hideous effect; and there sat old Neptune in state, with his white flowing beard, red-robed, paper crown, and in place of his trident, a dolphin on a staff. Screams of laughter echoed from everybody as they proceeded with different in-dividuals, excusing none but the females, the sick, and Mr. Wise, who got off by mak-ing a stump speech (from the Jacob's ladder over the stern!) in which he claimed, as an Ambassador, privilege of free transit thro' neutral territories agreeable to the laws of Nations, offering at the same time to substitute all his children, his Secretary and his servants for the ordeal, adding some *spirited* promises which probably was the most favorable argument he could have used.
> Fast as the neophytes were lathered with soap suds and coaldust, shaved by these rough barbers with their rasping razors, with edges like sand, they were cap(s)ized over backwards into the water where they were received by four Tritons — the biggest, blackest, half-naked, woolly-headed Tritons — who sous-ed them under, washed them over, and held them for the engine hose to play on,

till they made their escape, half dead and half drowned by such rude handling.

Many were refractory and ran aloft where they were caught by the manhunting constables and lowered down by a bowline, only to get rougher treatment than the others. No place was sacred for a party came down to the Purser's room where he was engaged writing: he was obliged to put by his ledgers and go through the ordeal. The reefers were shaved and soused in the most unconscionable manner. One of Mr. Wise's boys was very refractory, but a drummerboy taking him by the head and shoulders, while another boy, both rigged out like imps, took him by the heels, and lugged him up to the dreaded platform. The spirit of fun was now rife. Shouts of laughter resounded from all parts of the ship. Little bye plays were going on, very ludicrous in themselves and especially on an occasion where every-body was disposed to laugh.

After two more hours frolic the boatswain piped belay. However it closed by a scene not soon forgotten. The Capt. among others had mounted upon the boats amidships to see the fun, when some of the midshipmen got hold of the hose, pointing at some particular person: in the *melee* which occurred our veteran Captain received a full charge from the force pump and there was such a scramble to get off the boats that some came off coatless or tailess, and all looking like drowned rats. The Capt. laughed as heartily as any of them with his yellow nankens clinging close to his legs, and the grey-head drenched with water.

Percival was 65 at this time, the oldest of any of *Constitution*'s Captains.

The days passed quietly as the ship moved southward. On the 27th, a strange sail was sighted astern and continued following along the same course. On the 30th, *Constitution* met and spoke the stores ship *Erie* (4), which had been with her for a part of her tour in the Pacific Squadron and was only now returning home. The mysterious stranger first sighted on the 27th was identified the next afternoon: it was *Berceau*. Captain's Clerk Benjamin Stevens wrote:

> ... Thus had we again met upon the Atlantic after an absence of nearly thirty days; probably the circumstance would not happen again in a lifetime of two vessels crossing each other's track so near the port of their destination.

With the coming of dawn on the 2nd, the famed Sugar Loaf was sighted. Percival came to anchor in Rio harbor that afternoon amid men of war from England, France, Genoa, Brazil, and Portugal. American frigates *Congress* (36) and *Raritan* (44) also were present, as well as brig *Pioneer*. A few days later, Minister Wise and his party were put ashore with all appropriate ceremony.

For a month, Percival remained in Rio readying his ship for the long voyage ahead. This was to be the last modern metropolis they would see for many months. The ship was deeply laden with supplies, eventually drawing 21'4" forward and 23'2" aft. Percival sought the finest foodstuffs he could obtain, recognizing their importance to the health and well-being of his crew. He also attempted to ameliorate the expected debilitating heat of the tropics with a new paint scheme: he had the hull painted with white lead to reduce absorption of the sun's rays. And he had the gun stripe done in red — "...somewhat to the wonderment of the Brazilians, who think we have put on *war-paint*." Passed Midshipman Isaac G. Strain joined the ship there, having had to abort an intended expedition into the interior when his civilian associates backed out. He became the

Constitution *and* Raritan (left) *in Rio de Janeiro in August 1844, as "Old Ironsides" was beginning her cruise around the world.*

ship's Sailing Master while Gough W. Grant, his predecessor, was promoted to Acting Sixth Lieutenant. Naturalist I.C. Reinhart was another new face on board, replacing a botanist named Chandler, who chose to return to the United States.

## ACROSS THE SOUTH ATLANTIC

Percival left Rio on 8 September, heading southeastward in fair weather. The days passed quietly, the crew sometimes diverting themselves with small amusements. On the 17th, for example, some "fished" for a trailing albatross by trolling astern a hook baited with a piece of fat pork. One finally struck and was snagged. He was hauled aboard, squawking and flapping. Tiring of the bird's efforts to rid itself of its snare, the sailors released it, but

> ... not until one of the sailors had by stealth cruelly cut off one of his feet to make use of the skin for a purse! It is to be hoped that the spirit of this unhappy albatross may not plague us as happened to the 'Ancient Mariner'...

Since leaving Rio, Percival had reduced the frequency of drills at battle stations to once weekly, although these were made more beneficial through the actual firing of the guns. On the 19th,

> ... An empty cask was taken off in a boat and then the guns trained upon them and discharged for practice. All the shots were good and some clearly proved that the old ship's Barkers had not forgotten their days of glory.

Gradually, the days grew cooler and the winds fitful. Some days, they lay becalmed; on others, moved right along at an eight knot clip. Rough, squally weather became their lot. Percival spent two days in the vicinity of Tristan da Cunha hoping to be able to secure water from the island, but continuing gales led him to head for the Cape of Good Hope.

> ... While before the wind the Frigate rolled tremendously, rolling the muzzles of her spar deck carronades, sometimes into the water; but always very easy and nothing of the jerking motion peculiar to many of our ships.

On the night of 3 October, the ship was struck by a ferocious gale whose winds snapped the crossjack in two places and tumbled the ship about in "hay cock seas." Swells from astern

> ... would now and then force (their) way through the *rudder-coat*, flooding the pantry of the Wardroom, the cascading, *slushing* noise of which added to that of divers(e) chairs, boxes, & materials adrift, the rattling of the wheel-ropes, and the agonizing scream of an ungreased leading block, rendered our apartments conducive to anything but sleep.

## IN THE INDIAN OCEAN

The gale abated the next day, and at noon the sailing master was able to fix their position as being on the edge of Agulhas Bank. They had rounded the Cape and entered the Indian Ocean. A new crossjack yard was fitted on the 6th, a Sunday. Bad weather, adverse winds, and confusing currents consumed eight days before the big frigate arrived in St. Augustine's Bay, on the southwest coast of Madagascar, a wood and watering stop for whalers.

Hardly had the anchor gotten wet before a gaggle of native canoes came out to the ship bearing a strange assortment of locals ready to do business — and steal the unwary blind. Somewhere along the line, probably from the whalers, these bandits had acquired some outlandish names: Prince Green (the head man), John Green (his "purser"), John Stouts, Captain Amber, Captain Martin, etc., etc. Their attire was as wild as their names, comprised as it was of castoff items of Western civilian and naval clothing. Some bore letters they supposed recommended their services to the newcomers, but which really called them out as rascals. The *Constitution*s of course, did nothing to disenchant them. The females accompanying these Malagasy "merchants" were "in the most primitive state of nudity." A lieutenant waxed eloquent in his journal entry, writing of "...the women with but little more covering (than) a strip of cloth around the middle, their figures shining in voluptuous and greasy contour..." It was going to be a *long* trip!

Water and wood stocks replenished, *Constitution* took five days to sail next to Mozambique, fading capitol of Portuguese East Africa, anchoring there on 25 October. Her entry into port proved to be a test of seamanship:

> ... us being to the Sd. & Wd. of the port the wind was now dead ahead, so we commenced beating up towards the town; the crew worked the ship beautifully, on the in shore tack we would sometimes come within about 2 cables length of the surf, and then we would go about with the surf under our stern, it was a beautiful sight; Captain P has...implicit confidence in his abilities to manage or work a ship...

Captain Percival paid an official call on the Governor General, accompanied by Clerk Stevens, on the 27th. It was a friendly meeting during which the Captain learned that the entire American trade with Mozambique consisted of an annual voyage by a brig from Salem and another from New York. Each brought in cotton and took out ivory, gums, and copal. There was an active slave trade between that coast and Brazil, but no Americans appeared to be involved. Percival sailed on the 28th.

Next port of call was back on Madagascar's west coast, to the adjacent towns of Majunga and Bembatooka, whence *Constitution* arrived on 1 November. There, American trade was dominant, and predominantly from Salem. There even was a commercial agent in residence in this out-of-the-way spot. A 9-gun salute was fired to the "Queen of Madagascar" the next morning with a plain white flag flying at the fore truck because "the Malagash flag appeared to be of this appearance."

The Americans were made to understand that thievery was considered to be the most heinous of crimes. Grisly evidence was pointed out on a nearby sand spit: a series of pointed poles, one of which carried the decaying head of a thief. The punishment for stealing was being burned alive and the corpse beheaded. Two other skulls seen laying near the poles subsequently were smuggled aboard ship by midshipmen who regarded them as exotic souvenirs of the cruise.

Heading north, Percival stopped for water at the island of Nos Bey, off Passandava Bay, on the 7th. During the two-day trip, the Captain dispensed justice to all those who had been unable to resist the temptations offered by the many bumboats which had hovered around the ship at each port, and had let demon rum lead them from the straight and narrow path. Philosophized Lieutenant Dale:

> ... At sea, sailors are the most obedient, respectable, and apparently happy of all laboring classes: their good conduct has inspired confidence, their uniform deportment the respect of their officers. But it is a sad truth that no sooner do they come within the spheres of spiritous liquors, then all their good resolutions give way before the besetting demon of strong drink. And in a Frigate crew there are always enough who are sure to make themselves far worse than brutes. Sailors are improving in this respect, but it is very, very slowly... Yet with all this temptation ashore is too strong for poor Jack, I am not clear on the utility of abolishing the spirit ration in the Navy. Sailors have but few sources of happiness: and one is the enjoyment of their meals seasoned by the small and regular allowance of whiskey now served out onboard men of war.

By this time, the influence of temperance movements and others had caused the Navy to cut the ration in half and, further, regularly to urge the men to a pennies-a-day increase in pay in lieu of the whiskey.

*Constitution* headed for Zanzibar on 12 November and anchored off the town of Metany on the morning of the 18th. There she found her old sailing partner, *Berceau,* busy surveying the harbor. In exchanging visits, the American officers found the Frenchman to be equipped with two innovations. *Berceau* had a still (evaporator) which, using the caboose's fire, was able to produce sufficient potable water from the sea to handle the normal daily needs of her crew — "a great improvement & which demanded our serious attention," noted one American. She also was built so that her anchor chain was led directly to the capstan, instead of having to use a "messenger" between chain and capstan as *Constitution* did. It was a safer, much more efficient system, demanding fewer men for the job.

While some of his officers were visiting the French, Captain Percival, who wasn't feeling too well, and some others dined with the Sultan of Zanzibar in the company of the American Vice Consul, Mr. Waters. It literally was a feast: roast goat, curried sheep, chicken, rice "enough for our ship's company", and other viands. Highlight of the meal was the sherbet, made of rose water and honey, and as clear as crystal. The Americans found it to be a delicious drink, but it left a "sickening taste in the mouth." Be that as it may, Percival seems to have survived the surfeit well, and was over his indisposition by the 23rd. Fully stocked for the first time in months with fresh meat, vegetables, and fruit, *Constitution* headed out across the Indian Ocean on 26 November.

It was a long haul in those equatorial waters. Some days, the ship made good 240 miles; on others, a wind couldn't be found, the sails slatting against the masts as the mercury went above 100 and the black hammock cloths became too hot to touch. Percival's repainting of the hull was believed to have been most beneficial. As the days went on, however, the sick list began to grow, some coming down with dysentery or a fever, others taken ill as a result of overeating unripe or unfamiliar fruits. Percival himself was forced to his cot by what variously was reported as gout or inflammatory rheumatism. At times, he was able to hobble about on crutches, but First Lieutenant Paine had to take on more and more responsibility for the operation of the ship. There were forty-three on the sick list on 18 December, and it was growing. The first death of the voyage occurred on the 20th, when Seaman Wester was found dead on the berth deck near sick bay. Two days later, bandsman Christian Fischer, a German in his fifties, succumbed. Burials were conducted as quickly as possible. On the 23rd, Percival ordered his day cabin converted into a hospital for the sick while he, himself, largely was confined to the after cabin.

Christmas 1844 was a dolorous day, given the nearly sixty sick on board and temperatures that never got below eighty. The wardroom had a dinner of shoulder of pork, ducks, and preserved (canned) soup, but no one had the spirit. The wine was "passed by as so much poison." A comet was visible on the southwest horizon that evening, but aroused very little interest. Seaman John Peters died of dysentery on the 30th and joined his two comrades in a watery grave.

## THE FAR EAST

The high land of Sumatra was a welcome sight at sunrise on New Year's Day, 1845. Light and adverse winds, however, continued to frustrate the debilitated crew until the 3rd, when they arrived at notorious Quallah Battoo. In February 1831, treacherous Malay pirates temporarily captured the American merchantman *Friendship* as she lay at anchor off the town, killing a number of her crew. In response, President Jackson had ordered *Potomac* (44) to apply suitable chastisement. One day shy of the first anniversary of the attack, retribution was delivered. It still was a vivid memory thirteen years later when still another American frigate appeared. Present in the port was the Salem merchant *Caroline Augusta*. Po Adam, a Malay who had been an ally in the earlier fracas, paid a call on the ship and was thought to be "not very prepossessing."

Captain Percival received Rajah Chedulah with his "tagrag and bobtail" abed in his cabin. His indisposition did nothing to improve his diplomacy, and he proceeded to tell the Rajah that peace between him and the Americans rested solely on the good conduct of the Malays. There were, he said, many American "big ships" ready to punish evil-doers. The Rajah knew he meant it.

Midshipman Lucius M. Mason of Virginia died on the morning of the 6th, of dysentery and "inflammation of the brain." *Constitution* got underway at four that afternoon with Po Adam as pilot, bound for Annalaboo and Wylah to look in on American traders in those ports. Midshipman Mason was buried enroute with full honors. Po Adam was put ashore at Wylah.

"Old Ironsides" departed Wylah late on 8 January, heading for Singapore and a recuperation period. It was an unbelievably difficult trip. Adverse winds and currents fought her all the way, turning each mile made good into a victory over Mother Nature. Forced northward, she first spent two days in sight of the Nicobar Islands. Then it took her until the 24th to pass Prince of Wales Island (Pulo Penang) and enter the Straits of Malacca proper. Once in that unfamiliar, relatively narrow gut, she anchored each night. On some days, only 20-30 miles were made good. Petty Officer Peter Wolfe died in the forward cabin on the evening of the 29th; he was buried the next morning. Singapore was sighted, at long last, on the last day of the month, but three more days were needed before anchors could be dropped.

The *Constitution* that arrived in Singapore on 3 February 1845 was but a sad shadow of the smart frigate decked out in black and white that had cleared New York so lightheartedly nearly nine months earlier. Her spars still stood tall, all right, and her yards were squared and rigging taut. But below she looked to be the scruffiest of merchantmen. The worn lead-white had splotches of old black showing through; the ribband of bright red had grown dim and was similarly mottled by its underlying coat of white. Rust streaks streamed down and aft from the chains. President Andrew Jackson, the figurehead, was more a mendicant, a tramp dressed in a millionaire's cast-off finery. Among her people, "Mad Jack" was bedridden, and more than sixty cases, mostly of dysentery, reposed about her decks. The time had come to "get well."

First aboard was the Consul, Mr. Balestier. He offered quarters at his house to Captain Percival who, once he was satisfied that the needs of his ship and crew were being attended to, accepted the invitation a few days later. His hostess, Mrs. Balestier, was a daughter of Paul Revere.

The next day, Percival received a call from the British Commodore whose broad pennant flew from the frigate *Cambrian*. He was a tall, erect gentleman of an age with the Captain, genial and relaxed. A curious expression was seen to cross his face as he paused on the quarterdeck, receiving the honors due his station. He seemed at once puzzled and a little surprised. Lieutenant Paine escorted him below to meet "Mad Jack," who managed to be up on crutches as his guest entered. The Commodore was quick to offer the services of his surgeon and any other facilities the Royal Navy had that might speed Percival's command back to health. Then he asked if this was the same *Constitution* that had fought so brilliantly in the War of 1812. When told that it was, the Commodore revealed his interest: he was Henry Ducie Chads, and he had had to surrender *Java* to Commodore William Bainbridge on these very decks, thirty-three years before and a half a world away! His very genuine assistance in Singapore thus was doubly appreciated. If this chance meeting weren't coincidence enough, there was, nearby, moored a large Indiaman named — *Java*.

Two more men died before the effects of the Indian Ocean finally were shaken: Charles Springer and Stephen Hoyt. Both were buried ashore.

With the crew once more healthy and the ship overhauled and replenished, Percival got her underway for Borneo. He, however, was little improved, and had to leave the ship's operation to his "Number One."

## BAD TIME IN BORNEO

*Constitution* took a week, working against head winds, to raise the Borneo coast. When she dropped anchor off the Sambas River on the 17th, she was believed to be the first American warship to have moored in those waters. A two-day boat expedition under Second Lieutenant William C. Chaplin was sent 40-odd miles upriver to the town of the same name to determine whether or not it was under Dutch administration and what conditions were. Chaplin returned on the 21st to report that the Dutch were there, and that trade for American cotton was desired. Such port taxes as there were, were minimal.

The big frigate proceeded north slowly on the 22nd, her officers well aware that the charts they had were neither correct nor complete. Cautiously, it was underway each morning and anchor each night until the northwest corner of Borneo (Tadjung Datu) was turned. On the 29th, a fair wind gave them a few hours of real progress before it failed them; still, it was safer to anchor at night, as heavy nocturnal rains further reduced any capability they had for finding their way along. Late on 4 April she very nearly grounded due to a twenty-mile error in the chart, and was saved only by Lieutenant Paine's quick action. A subordinate wrote in his journal later that night:

> ...I may as well remark here, that of all ships in the Navy, the Frigate *Constitutuion* is the last one which should have been sent in her old age on so perilous a voyage as this.

*Constitution* finally arrived safely off Brunei on 6 April, having been groping through some of the world's most hazardous waters for more than two weeks. Lieutenant Chaplin again headed a boat expedition ashore to the city of Brunei, but returned the next morning (9th) with little information and no supplies. Apparently, the British "white rajah," Brooke, saw to it that the natives would deal with none but his countrymen. The Americans departed on the 10th, pausing long enough off Labuan for Dr. Reinhart to determine that there were no coal deposits on the island. With short-range steam ships beginning to join the Service, the Department was anxious to determine where in the world fuel could be most readily available.

In standing north from Labuan, "Old Ironsides" came as close to defeat as ever she would, for Lieutenant Paine unwittingly was taking her into an extensive area of reefs and shoals that even today is known as the Dangerous Ground. The first near miss occurred at sunrise on the 12th, when she lightly scraped her keel on some coral about fourteen miles NNW of Labuan Island. A kedge anchor was lost in maneuvering her clear. Two more days were spent looking for leads north in much the same manner as an icebreaker in pack ice before Paine headed southwest once more — until he suddenly found himself blocked by a semicircle of coral reef. In kedging her out astern, a second anchor was lost and she again "touched lightly." On the 16th, another "perfect horseshoe of coral rocks;" another effort to tow her astern through the one passage out. By that evening, it seemed as if they might have found a safe channel. On the 17th, they made five miles, and so it went. A final scare — a near-miss on Luconia Shoal — and they finally were able to turn north on 23 April after an 11-day ordeal.

The next two weeks underway were uneventful except for the night of the 25th:

> ...We were astonished last evening at 11 by a severe squall which made the old ship reel before the sails could be taken off. We had scarcely gone to sleep after this interruption before the cry of 'man overboard! — cut away the life buoy!' started everybody to their feet. It seems a poor fellow (John Thompson #2) was furling the foretopgallant sail from whence he fell in some way, striking the belly of the foretopsail and thence overboard. The ship was instantly hove to, and a boat lowered. The buoy was found but the unfortunate sailor was nowhere to be seen.

## THE FIRST TIME

Land was sighted to the northwest as early as 2 May, but contrary winds prevented the ship from even closing the coast for six days, let alone enter port. After two days of battling contrary winds at the entrance, the great frigate was at last able to beat into the bay, the chopping seas spewing in froth from her bows. On the starboard hand, mountainous ridges, their roots in the sea, marched into the distance to the west and northwest. To port, the blunt abrupt knob that would become known to a later generation as Monkey Mountain gave way to low, flat land that made up the south shore of the bay. Rounding to smartly west of the knob, *Constitution* came to anchor, two months from Singapore and three weeks shy of a year since she had sailed out of New York. The date was 10 May 1845.

"Old Ironsides" was at Turon (now Danang), Cochin China (Vietnam), and the first order of business was to make arrangements for the burial of one Cooke, musician, who had died that day. Through the medium of one of the embarked Chinese servants, a plot was secured within the limits of a native burial ground at the foot of Monkey Mountain for the sum of two dollars — perpetual care included! When the burial ceremony was completed, the ship shifted berth deeper into the bay, and made preparations to water ship.

On the 13th, a recuperating Captain Percival sent the redoubtable Lieutenant Chaplin ashore to visit the Mandarin of the city, taking with him a small party of junior officers, sailors, and Marines. Guided by a Chinese from the crew, the group proceeded along city streets and through the bazaar, finally leading through a double line of soldiers to the courtyard of the principal Mandarin's house. Each soldier was dressed in a knee-length coat of red with a circular green emblem on the chest, and wore a conical wooden helmet sheathed in metal, and each bore a tall spear with a brightly colored pennant attached just below the head.

The lieutenant, his party grouped behind him, was seated at one side of the table set up in the open. The Chief Mandarin, with his umbrella bearer and other attendants, appeared shortly thereafter and took the seat opposite. Despite all the ceremonial, the meeting was but a short exchange of introductions and pleasantries, with the Mandarin agreeing to pay a call on board the American man of war.

The next day, Wednesday, 14 May, the Chinese, as they were termed, called on Percival and were received with appropriate ceremony, despite the fact that the crew had begun to repaint the ship in her familiar black and white scheme. All went well, and the Chinese left, apparently properly impressed with "Mad Jack" and his ship. As they were leaving, though, the Chinese party's interpreter returned to the cabin on some pretext and delivered a letter to the Captain, saying his life would be forfeit if his master found out. Upon opening, Percival found it to have been written by a French missionary, Bishop Dominique Lefevre, who stated that he was "surprised at not having heard from his former letter," and appealed again for help as his village had been "delivered over to pillage" and that he "with twelve Cochin Chinese, were then arrested and under sentence of immediate death."

The Americans were shocked into precipitate action. "Here," wrote Lieutenant Dale, "was an opportunity of a rescue from this semi-barbarous nation. It was enough for us to know that a fellow Christian was in danger of his life. The strongest and most instant measures must be taken. Humanity was to be our warrant than the law of nations."

Captain Percival quickly called for a party of sailors and Marines, all "armed to the teeth," loaded them into the ship's boats, and headed for the beach. Up the streets, across the market place, and through the double rank of soldiers went Percival. The natives acted as if nothing was going on, but the American skipper took the precaution of stationing an unbroken line of U.S. sailors and Marines in sight of one another all the way from the boats to the Chief Mandarin's house.

Help could be called at the slightest hint of trouble.

The Captain took his place at one side of the table, and the Oriental headman took the other. Some time was spent by Percival satisfying himself that he was, in fact, talking to *somebody*. That point settled, he demanded that the Mandarin dispatch immediately a letter he had prepared to the Frenchman, and that an answer be returned within twenty-four hours. Furthermore, the three known local native leaders would be held in *Constitution* as hostages. If the deadline was not met, Percival, warming to his mission, declared he would take possession of the three forts near the town and all the shipping he could lay his hands on. All of this announced despite the presence of numerous armed soldiers, the fact that the causeway along which the Americans had come could be enfiladed by two of the forts, and "a fellow who stood by the big gong with uplifted hammer ready to sound the tocsin." For reasons beyond the ken of the mystified American, "the tocsin did not sound" and they returned to the frigate with the three hostages and two attendant pipe bearers, no one having made a move to stop them.

Tensions mounted on board as the twenty-four hours ticked away. When the appointed time had passed without result, Percival directed the cessation of watering operations and cut all communication with the shore until the arrival of the Bishop's reply. *Constitution* again shifted anchorages to a position closer to town and just a half-mile from one of the forts, which was closely watched. Further to reinforce his demands, the Captain then directed that three men of war junks seen anchored a mile-and-a-half off be captured. The ship's three largest boats were armed and manned in short order, and underway with the sailors' valor "screwed up to the highest notch."

It soon became apparent that the three targets would not get away, being both anchored and moored to the shore. The wretched, half-naked people manning them offered no resistance to the hallooing Americans who came piling aboard, and all junks were moved and anchored off the quarters of "Old Ironsides." Sailing Master Strain was tasked to keep them under observation, and during the night alertly prevented one of the three from sneaking off.

The next three days passed uneventfully and then, on Monday the 19th, *Constitution* was kedged in still closer to the river mouth at the town and well within range of the forts on either side, springs being used to keep her starboard battery trained shoreward. Indications from the shore were that all of Captain Percival's threats had had no effect, except that the Cochin Chinese now were refusing even further negotiation until the hostages were released. The Captain went ashore again in the same manner as before, and again largely was ignored by the populace. Returning to the ship after a long and fruitless parley, he ordered the three hostages released and hoped thereby to break the stalemate.

In the excitement of kedging in closer to town and standing at battle stations while Captain Percival parleyed ashore, the Americans had ignored their three prize junks. When Sailing Master Strain inspected each of them that evening, he made an amazing discovery: with the Americans looking the other way, the hill fort commander apparently had managed to send a detachment out to the captured craft — not to retake them, but to punish the junk commanders for having been taken. Mr. Strain reported finding all three men had been whipped with bamboo wands and each yoked with two pieces of heavy wood four to five feet long. The bindings at the ends of the yokes bore the seal of the Mandarin. One of the skippers, possibly the senior of the trio, also had had his eyes cemented shut with a pitch-like substance likewise bearing the seal of authority. So great was the fear of these men for the Mandarin that they refused the American intention to relieve them, indicating by vivid signs that they would be beheaded. However, they willingly shifted the three junks to anchor again closer to "Old Ironsides" and further away from the hill fort.

Tuesday dawned, squally and nasty. Taking advantage of the cover provided by the wind-driven rain, the three men of war junks slipped their cables and ran with the wind, seeking escape from the Americans by dashing up-river. One shortly was retaken as *Constitution*'s opening broadside caused her crew to drop anchor and jump overboard, some probably drowning. The other two succeeded in crossing the bar and appeared to be making good their escape.

The American boat crews sent in pursuit, however, were not to be daunted by the tempestuous weather and seas, nor potentially hostile Chinese. Pulling boldly, the launch and four cutters surged past six or eight armed boats loaded with native soldiers, through waters covered by the guns of the forts on either bank. The native craft scattered without a shot fired. The second junk soon was retaken without opposition, and a small guard left on board.

Onward pressed the American force, leaving pacific red-coated troops to port and starboard. A mile upstream, the last escapee was found run aground and abandoned, its sails destroyed. After a quick inspection, the Americans completed preparation to refloat the junk before there appeared an "Indian file" of armed Chinese troops — 150 of them — who took up positions just thirty yards off. The boat crews gripped their cutlasses and leaped into the three-foot deep water, sent up "a real Anglo-Saxon shout" and charged pell-mell at the Chinese. These "took to their heels in a most precipitate manner" and were not seen again. The Marines busied themselves gathering coconuts on the way back to the boats, while an old Chinese watched the whole ludicrous affair impassively from his porch nearby.

The return of all three junks under the guns of "Old Ironsides" was accomplished uneventfully, the weather even moderating temporarily to make the long pull easier. A short time later, however, it kicked up again and one of the junks broke loose and broached. It took the Americans until late evening of their busy day to refloat her and return her to the anchorage. The Chinese ashore once again confounded their visitors by transporting a huge wooden anchor a mile-and-a-half on their backs to assist the Americans in their task.

As day dawned on the 21st, "the view was wild and grand. Heavy, lowering clouds were rushing onwards from the sea, and wreathing wildly about the mountain summits all magnified into gigantic spectres by the rainy atmosphere; while rollers were tumbling in upon the beach to leeward, and the long sand spit from the river, one drift of snowy breakers." It hasn't changed. And to the Americans' surprise, three ships wearing "the yellow flag of Cochin" were seen anchored below the hill fort on the side of Monkey Mountain. They apparently had come in quietly during the night. Did they portend overt counteraction to Captain Percival's threats and forays? Not that day, at least.

The weather moderated during the night that followed, and the thermometer, which had been as low as seventy-eight degrees during the gale, again rose to an oppressive level. Still no sign or word of the French priest. The junk that had broached was found to be leaking badly and was returned formally to the Chinese, who were perplexed that the others weren't returned also. Captain Percival attempted to visit the three newly-arrived brigs, but was refused permission to go aboard, his gig being pushed off "with oars & sticks."

Credulity concerning the situation was strained further on 23 May when trade was reopened for provisioning ship!

The next morning, two letters were received from the Mandarin and "from little officer". The former said nothing was known about the Frenchman and asked for the return of the junks; the other stated that the priest would be surrendered when the junks were returned. To reinforce the demand, provisions were stopped until the junks were freed. Percival bowed to this, and food and water again came to the ship — but no Frenchman.

On the 25th, Percival made a final try for the Bishop by sending a letter ashore to the effect that he would leave shortly for Canton where he would report the incident to the French authorities, who undoubtedly would wreak swift retribution. The response indicated that the threats were considered hollow, and that unless a "good letter" was drafted, no further communications would be forwarded to the king.

Threats had failed, bribes rejected, and, thus far at least, aggressive actions tolerated. But beneath the surface, the native leadership was marshalling its forces. There were the three brigs that had arrived. The junks had been refitted. And three ships that had been lying in ordinary were completing reactivation. Ashore, the forts were being refurbished and extended, their approaches being rendered more difficult. Percival recognized that the situation could only get worse and his solitary frigate, glorious record notwithstanding, insufficient to the task. After sunset on 26 May 1845, after sixteen hectic and fruitless days, *Constitution* departed quietly, leaving things much as they were before she arrived. "Mad Jack" vented his frustrations by firing six shots from his starboard Paixhans guns at an island off the harbor entrance. Only one reached the target.

Lieutenant Dale summed up this first Navy-Marine Corps experience in Vietnam thusly:

> ...it seems, I must say, to have shown a sad want of 'sound discretion,' in commencing an affair of this kind, without carrying it through to a successful issue.

Prophetic words.

## CHINA VISIT

Percival's next stop on this odyssey was to be China, but even before he arrived there he learned of what the next chapter was to be in the adventures of Bishop Lefevre. On 30 May, while some ten leagues off Hainan Island, he spoke the British ship *Duilius* from Singapore to Hong Kong. A French squadron had been at Singapore when she left fifteen days earlier, whose Admiral was in receipt of the Bishop's *first* letter. He planned heading for Turon to make the rescue. To put "finis" on this incident, the French squadron did just that. Subsequently, upon learning of *Constitution*'s efforts in the affair, King Louis Philippe — who, it will be recalled, had attended her launching — is said to have ordered that Percival and his crew be rewarded for their efforts. Political turbulence in France, however, forced him from the throne in 1848, and the matter was dropped. And, in any event, the Secretary of the Navy had disapproved of Percival's actions.

The frigate arrived at the anchorage about six miles below Macao on 5 June and received her first mail from the United States since leaving Rio nine months earlier. It was a great day. While Percival paid calls on the Portuguese authorities, the crew spent the day catching up with their loved ones at home. Some evidently celebrated in other ways, for on Monday, 9 June, "...Punished all the first Cutters for drunkenness and smuggling liquor (except 6)..."

*Constitution*'s was only the ninth visit of an American warship to China, and it came at a time when the relationship between the Celestial Kingdom and the United States was blossoming. Commodore Lawrence Kearney had arrived in China in 1842 with frigate *Constellation* and sloop *Boston* just as the First Opium War was concluding. In the Treaty of Nanking, which brought peace that summer, the British received Hong Kong and "most favored nation" trade considerations. In reporting these events to Washington and in discussions with the Chinese, Kearney had set in motion a chain of events which resulted in the completion of the Treaty of Wanghia in July 1844, which granted the Americans similar commercial arrangements. In fact, Commodore James Biddle in the liner *Columbus* (74) had just gotten underway from New York for China to exchange Treaty ratifications.

Having ascertained the political situation, Percival got underway and headed up the Pearl River on the 18th, just the third time an American man-of-war had done so. The trip did not begin auspiciously, for the big ship soon was on a mud bank. Floated off later in the day, the voyage was renewed the next morning. Blenheim Reach (Whampoa), some fifteen miles below Canton, was reached at noon on the 20th.

*Constitution* remained swinging at her hook deep in China for the next six weeks, while Captain Percival called on officials of the Kwangtung Government, dealt with complaints of American merchants, and had his portrait painted by a Chinese artist. For the crew, it was a period of growing boredom and increasing sickness. The ship had followed the summer season northward. Day after day, they had to endure stifling heat, high humidity, swarms of mosquitoes, and near-ly daily rain storms that only made the climate more oppressive. The men were no better able to withstand the conditions than they had been in the Indian Ocean; the sick list began to grow once more. Captain of the Foretop Charles Lewis died on 17 July and Ordinary Seaman Michael Fritt at about the same time. Both were buried ashore. Percival, considering he had accomplished everything that required him to be near Canton, began the return trip downriver on the last day of the month, a favoring breeze allowing him to set the royals and starboard stunsails. The sick list again stood at sixty, most suffering from dysentery.

Percival dropped down as far as the Wantong Passage, where he anchored near the French frigate *Cleopatra* on 3 August. The new anchorage proved to be somewhat cooler, improving the health situation, although Private Henry Lohman died of dysentery on the 13th. Seaman George Folcher's death was the last to occur in China — on the 24th. *Constitution* moved to her original berth below Macao on the 27th and began taking on stores in preparation for the next leg of her journey. Through all the long weeks inside China, drinking water had been secured by filtering the *river water* through charcoal. The result was said to be "very good," but probably was the cause of the return of dysentery.

China was left astern on 1 September, as Percival headed his heavy frigate for Manila, capitol of the Spanish Philippines. Luzon quickly was raised, but then head winds and calms left the ship drifting along at a snail's pace. At dawn one morning, the Americans awoke to find themselves nearly surrounded by a squadron of what obviously were European men of war — 6 of them. Who were they? Were they at peace or war with the United States?

> ...As a matter of precaution the *Constitution* — the favorite ship of our Navy — was got ready for action, or rather put in a state of defense; it would never have done in any event to give up 'Old Ironsides' to any other nation than the one which built her and had fought her."

A flag unfurled from what evidently was the flagship of the unknown squadron (a steamer) revealed they were English. A lieutenant from the steamer informed Captain Percival that the squadron was commanded by Admiral Sir Thomas Cochrane. The Admiral sent a request for any provisions that could be spared, because the adverse winds had extended his expected time at sea to the point where they were about to run out. Percival gladly complied, having so recently provisioned, and officer visits were exchanged while five tons of bread and 400 gallons of whiskey were transferred. With a final salute from the English, each side went on its own way. *Constitution* subsequently anchored near Corregidor on 11 September and finally made it to Manila on the 18th where she spent a week.

## ACROSS THE PACIFIC

*Constitution* paused briefly off Batan Island, one of the small specks dividing the Bashi Channel from the Balintang Passage north of Luzon, on 26 September. From the island, Percival was able to purchase a few bullocks for fresh meat, and to top off his water supplies. The Pacific Ocean was entered on the 28th, an event which seemed to the crew to mark the start of the voyage home.

Light winds sent the frigate to the southeast for three days and then northward to the vicinity of the Ryukyu Islands. From there, she was able to head roughly northeastward, on the great circle sailing for the Hawaiian Islands. This took her somewhat to the south of the coasts of Japan,

> ... that *terra incognita*, where no Western barbarian may dare to cast anchor, except one annual Dutch ship at a single port of Nangasaka (sic; Nagasaki)...

Perry's opening of Japan to the West still was eight years in the future. The last piece of Far Eastern territory seen by the American sailors was a solitary rock sticking out of the ocean, known as Lot's Wife.

The trans-Pacific crossing required 50 days, in all. Gales made shipboard life miserable on two occasions: 20-24 October and 3-5 November. The ship was leaking so badly that 10 to 18 inches of water were pumped from the bilges twice daily. Crossing the International Dateline at Latitude 35.5 North gave them two Sundays dated 2 November. On 9 November, a Marine private died after a long illness and was buried. He was, it was said, the son of a Purser in the Royal Navy who previously had served as a master in that Navy and as a First Lieutenant in the Ottoman Navy. *Constitution* arrived off Honolulu on 16 November, having come in from the *eastward*, where the winds had taken her. Because of her draft, she had to remain anchored outside the reefs.

A bad surprise awaited Captain Percival on Hawaii. He found there Commodore John D. Sloat of the Pacific Squadron in his flagship, *Savannah* (44). Sloat, aware that trouble was brewing at home over the "Texas affair," informed "Mad Jack" that he and his ship would be detained in Sloat's command as needed reinforcement pending resolution of the difficulties with Mexico. Percival was to stock for six months and proceed to join the squadron on the West Coast while Sloat remained in Honolulu as long as necessary to settle another minor diplomatic dispute. For the crew,

> ... This was a great disappointment to us who fully expected the ship would return almost directly to the United States. But such is life! especially *Naval* life! Little did we think the Texas question would so sensibly affect us in the Pacific Ocean!

There occurred during this Hawaiian stay an incident pregnant with implications for the future. It seems that two years earlier, a British man of war had appeared and had bull-dozed King Kamehameha III into ceding his kingdom to the British Empire. Shortly thereafter, Commodore Kearny of China fame showed up and, in defending American rights in the Islands, ultimately caused an end to British rule after five months. Recalling that unhappy situation and the reasonable course of action by the U.S. Navy, on the present occasion the

Hawaiian Foreign Minister approached *Constitution*'s Lieutenant of Marines, Joseph W. Curtis, to survey the Honolulu area quietly and recommend to him where fortifications might best be placed to thwart foreign aggressions. Curtis' secret report recommended Pearl Harbor.

*Constitution* sailed from Honolulu on 2 December, making for the California coast. The trip was a bad one of constant storms. As they neared the coast on 27 December, the rain began coming down incessantly and heavy fogs made navigation dangerous. A break in the weather on the last day of the year showed Percival that no one was in Monterey Bay, and the next day he filled away for Mazatlan, Mexico — again in squalls and rain. In a week, the weather improved. From whalers, they learned that the squadron was, in fact, at Mazatlan. The anchor was dropped there on the 13th. Commodore Sloat had arrived ahead of them. Also present were war sloops *Levant*, *Warren*, *Portsmouth*, and *Cyane*, schooner *Shark*, and stores ship *Erie*.

For more than three months, the big frigate swung on her hook. War did not come. Morale plummeted with the continued absence from home and lack of purposeful activity. Sloat was in a difficult position. Most of the squadron was in a deteriorating condition, including both frigates; and they were thousands of miles from home. Still nothing happened, although rumors ran rife. Finally, he acceded to Percival's repeated concerns for his aged command and permitted *Constitution* to sail for home. It was 22 April 1846. The crew partied all that first night at sea, the toast to "sweethearts and wives" being drunk to exhaustion.

## HOMEWARD BOUND

A week was spent in Valparaiso stocking up before the ship headed south once more, making preparations to double the Horn as they went. All guns forward of the foremast and aft of the mizzen were moved amidships and lashed down. Gun ports were shut and caulked. Hatches were battened down and tarpaulins secured over them.

Cape Horn was sighted on the Fourth of July in as wild a holiday as any of the crew ever would experience:

> ...hove to in SE gale — 34 degrees...here we are shivering... the Frigate rolled tremendously and...our 'Independence dinner' underwent marvellous transmutations and chaotic confusions, not to mention broken crockery, gravy capsized, and turkies that took wing even from under the carver's fork...

Sleet and snow squalls followed her into the Atlantic. By the 15th, however, they were enjoying beautiful weather and relishing every diminished mile home. In Rio, *Constitution* was greeted by Ambassador Wise and participated in salutes to the birth of the Emperor's second child. Mail and newspapers awaited them in profusion. There, it was learned that the war with Mexico had begun two months earlier, and many no doubt gave thanks that they had been able to leave the Pacific Squadron in the nick of time. Because of the war situation, when she sailed on 5 August, the big frigate had in convoy sixteen coffee ships bound for the

## A Most Fortunate Ship

United States.

The voyage to the Delaware Capes, where the convoy was to disperse, was uneventful until the coast was in the offing. Somewhere off Cape Hatteras, *Constitution* came upon a mastless hulk, all that remained of the brig *Washington,* which had been under the command of Lieutenant Commander George M. Bache, a descendant of Benjamin Franklin. She had been employed on coastal survey and had been cast on her beam ends by a hurricane on 8 September, rolling the masts out of her. Captain Bache had been one of the 10-12 swept overboard. The hulk was taken in tow and turned over to the Philadelphia pilot boat *Enoch Turley* when the convoy broke up.

In the waning days of this epic voyage, the old frigate's crew made every effort to restore her to spit and polish for her return home. Midshipman John E. Hart made his own unique contribution:

> ... The ships painter came to me just now for some vermillion to paint old Jacksons figure head I had a quantity that I purchased in China which was all that there was in the ship. The painter knowing that I took some interest in his 'hickory phiz' come and got it to *rouge* him up a little. The Old Gentleman looks hearty and hale as he did in his prime days I got the Painter to give his standing collar a 'dab' of red to make him look 'a la militaire'...

*Constitution* arrived home in Boston on Sunday, 27 September 1846, having sailed, by official reckoning, 52,370½ miles. She was towed to the Navy Yard the next day. "Mad Jack" Percival hauled down her commissioning pennant and went ashore on 5 October.

Midshipman Hart has left his parting sentiments:

> ...she is now come home like her aged Commander to lay her old bones up 'for a full due.' She has gone about like a 'Good Samaritan' and her life has been a tissue of benevolent actions from the time she first left the land that grew her timbers, until she returned to be stripped and her old war-worn and tempest-torn frame laid by a deserted hulk. Every old plank, bolt, spar and rope yarn in her has a share of my love... I can scarcely bear the idea of leaving her, but I must...

# 15 Mediterranean Finale

## WORK-UP

The principal reason for *Constitution*'s overhaul and recommissioning in 1848 was the widespread outbreak of revolutions in Europe. Beginning in France with the deposition of King Louis Philippe, rebellion caught on in Austria, Germany, and Hungary, and on into Italy, which then was yet a collection of petty kingdoms and city-states. Heavy American commercial interests in the Mediterranean Basin made it incumbent upon the Navy to take what steps it could to protect our people and trade in the unsettled region. The Squadron was built up to its greatest strength in decades. Thus it was that "Old Ironsides" came to be docked and readied for one more tour of duty in those waters she had come to know so well.

The most obvious change made in the old frigate was the replacement of the clumsy Jackson figurehead, which Elliott had installed in 1834 and which had weathered badly during the long trip around the world. A more flattering rendering of the late president was done by the Boston carvers, J.D. and W.H. Fowle. This new Jackson stood tall, with stern visage, and clad in well-fitting attire topped by a draped cloak. He carried a scroll in his right hand and his left was tucked into the front of his tailed coat, a la Napoleon. The Fowles also carved new trail boards for the ship; these were similar to those still to be seen on her today, but with a flower reminiscent of a Tudor rose in the position currently occupied by the national shield. The Fowles were paid $330 for their work.

Perhaps the most important change effected during the readying of "Old Ironsides" in 1847-8 was the major alteration of her gun batteries. In 1845, a "board of captains" had recommended that the Navy standardize its guns by using only 32-pounder smooth bore long guns and the 8-inch shell guns. The recommendation was approved and implemented. As a result, *Constitution* was re-armed with new, light-weight 32-pounder long guns on her spar deck and another, somewhat heavier new model of 32-pounder long gun on the gun deck, together with the four eight-inch Paixhans guns. Her total battery consisted of 46 32-pounders and the four shell guns.

Marylander John Gwinn, whose orders to command *Constitution* were dated 31 August 1848, had had an unusual career pattern for a naval officer of the day; one might say it was the antithesis to that of sea-going Jacob Jones. Gwinn received his warrant as a midshipman in 1809, and spent the opening months of the War of 1812 on a schooner in Chesapeake Bay. He had the misfortune to be assigned to the sloop *Frolic* (18), the first ship built at the Boston Navy Yard, which was captured by the British on her maiden voyage in 1814. He spent the

*Figurehead of Andrew Jackson.*

rest of the war as a prisoner. In the decade that followed, he made two Mediterranean deployments and one trip to Northern Europe in three different ships. Between 1828 and 1848, he spent a total of ten years at the Philadelphia Navy Yard, three more on leave, and five "awaiting orders"! Like Preble, it appears that his physical condition was not up to his ambition, and broke down at times. Before commanding *Constitution,* he had been Captain of *Vandalia* (18) and *Potomac* (44) — each for a year. He formally placed "Old Ironsides" back in commission at 2:30 P.M. on 9 October 1848. It took him exactly two months to complete her outfitting and manning. *Constitution* began what was to be her final cruise to the Mediterranean at 9 A.M. 9 December.

## BACK ON DUTY

The transit to the Straits of Gibraltar was made in the good time of twenty-three days, but instead of breaking the voyage there, Captain Gwinn headed her directly for his first port of call, Tripoli, where he arrived shortly after noon on 19 January 1849. For the next two days, the crew was busy loading aboard the personal goods and household effects of Consul D.S. McCauley, who was being transferred to Egypt with his pregnant wife, six children, and a servant. Gwinn set sail on the 22nd for Malta, where he remained for a little more than two weeks before heading west. Moderate gales made life uncomfortable for the travellers for two days, but the voyage was otherwise without event until on 24 February,

> At 9:30 Mrs. Frances Ann McCauley wife of D.S. McCauley U.S. Consul General of Egypt gave birth to a Son, who received the name of Constitution Stewart...

*Constitution* idled for more than a month in the Egyptian port as Gwinn and his officers took advantage of the opportunity to visit the famed pyramids. The Captain himself spent eleven days as a sightseer. He returned aboard with McCauley's predecessor, a Mr. Wells, whom he would carry to Spezzia. The winds came fair on the 27th.

The trip proceeded without incident: Candia sighted on the last day of the month and Cape Spartivento five days later, they rounded the west end of Sicily on 9 April, and arrived at (La) Spezzia on the 12th, to find the screw steamer *Princeton,* first propellor-driven warship in the world, and the old faithful stores ship *Erie* already there. Spezzia had become the Navy's principal base in the Mediterranean during the preceding year or so. The continuing notorious conditions ashore at Port Mahon had led the Spanish government, in 1846, to ask the Americans to close it down. In the present situation, the shift to Spezzia had both good and bad points. Proximity to the scenes of rebellion in Italy meant that American interests could be readily guarded; but that very proximity also made it viable only so long as the belligerents respected American neutrality. That there was turmoil in the area became obvious to the *Constitution*s after they had been in Leghorn, fifty miles south of Spezzia, for ten days. The 10 May log:

## A Most Fortunate Ship

> At 2:30 the Austrian Army made its appearance before the city and opened fire upon it with shot & shells... A party of Ladies & Gentlemen came on board to seek protection...

And the next morning:

> ...the Austrians Bombarding with shot & shells... White flags were shewn on the different Forts.

Nearly a dozen "Livornese" came aboard seeking protection during these hectic days. On the 13th, Gwinn transferred them to the steamer *Allegheny,* which, for nearly a week, was busy evacuating these displaced persons to refuge elsewhere on the coast. By the 21st, the city was quiet once more and liberty parties were permitted to land. *Constitution* went north again to Spezzia on the 27th.

During the eight months since Gwinn had taken command, the ship had become increasingly unhappy. Never before or since, has her log been so filled with notations of punishments awarded to crew members. Whether because of his professional attitude or the physical discomfort ulcers were giving him, Captain Gwinn caused men to be flogged at a spectacular rate: in fact, he averaged close to one flogging for every day he was in command. Punishments were laid on either with the cat-o'-nine-tails or with the "colt," nothing more than a knotted rope. Desertion and drunkenness were, of course, common offenses calling for discipline, but others noted in the log included such acts as "carelessly leaving an iron loose in the top," "letting a heaver fall out of the Top," "throwing soapsuds in the eyes of the Capt. of the Afterguard" (a petty officer), "smoking after 10 PM," and "for filthiness in cooking" (the wardroom cook). All of these latter offenses are examples of the sort of incidents which always have occurred in a command where, for whatever the reason, the crew feels its leaders are treating them unfairly. They could be fiercely loyal to a bastard of a Captain who was professionally competent while strictly enforcing official regulations; they found ways of demonstrating their protest of a bullying, incompetent, or erratic leader. Something definitely was wrong in *Constitution.*

Whatever the reason Gwinn had for using the cat so frequently, and however much the sailors considered it the proper punishment for genuine infractions, they were running contrary to the popular feeling back home. Since 1845, there had been a potent movement afoot to do away with the practice. In fact, while Gwinn was busily being a martinet, the House of Representatives voted to *prohibit* flogging for evermore. It would become the law of the land in 1850.

*Constitution* took on stores at Spezzia, then sailed south to Naples, arriving late on 7 June. Here, in the Kingdom of the Two Sicilies, was more political turmoil, for King Ferdinand II was contending not only with unrest in Sicily itself, but attempting to support Pope Pius IX maintain the integrity of the Papal States in his confrontation with the Austrians. The big frigate spent the rest of

June and all of July there, a potent reminder that American neutrals would be protected.

## POPE PIUS IX ABOARD

In the afternoon of 30 July, "Old Ironsides" got underway with U.S. Charge d'Affaires John Rowan aboard and proceeded to Gaeta, arriving in the early morning of 1 August. Near noon that day, King Ferdinand II and Pope Pius IX were received on board with yards manned and to the thunder of a 21-gun salute. Outwardly, this was nothing more than an official visit of pomp and ceremony; in fact, it was politically desirable that these two sovereigns be "out of reach" for a few hours. Whatever other importance may have been attached to the incident, it was the first time a Pope had set foot on American territory — and the only time until Pope Paul VI actually visited the United States during 1965. *Constitution* was underway again late that afternoon and returned briefly to Naples to drop off Mr. Rowan — and fire a 21-gun salute in honor of the "accouchement of the Queen of Naples", before proceeding southwest to Messina.

## CAPTAIN GWINN DIES

Following a 12-day stay at Messina, an ailing Captain Gwinn took his ship westward to Palermo. He dropped anchor there on the afternoon of the 21st, and later moved to the Trinacria Hotel in hopes that some time ashore would allow him to regain his health. On 1 September, in the evening, "...Capt. Gwinn being dangerously ill on shore assembled all the officers in the Cabin and offered up prayers for him." At 3:18 P.M. on 4 September 1849, Captain John Gwinn died of chronic gastritis with "severe cerebral complication." In memory "of our late beloved Captain, the officers of this ship will wear on the left arm for 30 days 'Crape' as a token of respect to his memory." First Lieutenant James H. Rowan took command in accordance with Naval Regulations and caused the flag to be lowered to half-mast.

The ship's carpenters spent much of the 5th making a coffin for the late skipper. After placing the remains in it, it was sealed in lead so that, some day in the future, it might be disinterred and returned to the United States. This was done in 1850. The body was reinterred in Philadelphia until 1931, when it was transferred from the then-abandoned graveyard to Arlington National Cemetery.

The funeral took place on the morning of 6 September. All the ship's boats were used to take all off-duty officers, 100 sailors, and thirty-seven Marines ashore for the procession to the Protestant burial ground near the Lazaretto and the graveside ceremonies. The solemn occasion was a shambles even before the marchers reached the site. Perhaps giving vent to their own bitter memory of their late Captain, at least fifteen men deserted along the line of march, while others got roaring drunk on wine purchased from roadside vendors. About a quarter of the participants either were dispersed or disheveled by the time the actual burial took place at 11:30, as nine minute-guns boomed out from the frigate in the bay. Now-Captain Rowan evidently believed wholeheartedly in the policies of his predecessor, for he had thirty-four men flogged the next day for their misdeeds during the funeral. This is the saddest human experience to be found in all of *Constitution*'s history.

## NEW CAPTAIN

Rowan made the short trip from Palermo to Naples during 8 and 9 September, and there reported Captain Gwinn's death to Commodore Charles W. Morgan, aboard his flagship, the razee *Independence* (54). Morgan drew upon the resources available to him in the larger ship and directed Captain Thomas Conover of the flagship to take command of *Constitution*. This he did on 18 September.

Thomas Conover hailed from New Jersey and had been in the Navy since 1 January 1812. He had served with David Porter in *Essex* during that frigate's epic operations in the Pacific, and later had commanded the galley-gunboat *Borer* in Macdonough's victorious squadron on Lake Champlain. On the latter occasion, he was voted a letter of thanks and a sword by Congress.

Captain Conover had little opportunity to show off his seamanship skills in command of *Constitution*, for between his arrival on board and the end of November, the ship was underway less than eight days — half of them spent moving northward from Naples to Spezzia late in September. Brief round trips up to Genoa and down to Leghorn were all that broke the monotony of swinging at the hook. At the end of November, "Old Ironsides" moved back to Genoa, where she wintered over. A happy fact for the crew through all these long months was that there were only half as many floggings as there had been under John Gwinn.

In the afternoon of 27 January 1850, a heavy squall struck the ships at anchor in Genoa. A Grecian brig dragged her anchor at the height of the blast, coming down hard across *Constitution*'s stem. The crash carried away the flying jib boom, the jib boom, and both boomkins, but Andy Jackson apparently escaped injury. The American sailors cut away the brig's foremast back stays, by which she was hung up, and "with great difficulty" moored her alongside until the blow was over. As if this weren't problem enough, the sloop *Jamestown* (20) also dragged her anchor and swung into *Constitution*'s starboard quarter gallery, smashing some window frames and shattering the boomkin above it. When the storm was over, the old frigate's boats were used to haul off her two assailants and see to it that they were reanchored well clear of her. Repairs occupied the carpenters until the first day of the new month.

The 1850 sailing season opened for *Constitution* on 3 March as she got underway for Toulon, France, for a visit that took up the latter half of that month. It was an all too brief break in the routine, however, for she was back in Spezzia on the last day of the month to resume the tedious round of duty "go's" at Leghorn and Genoa. In April, May, and June, she was once in Genoa, twice in Leghorn, and thrice in Spezzia.

"Old Ironsides' " people got another break in their routine in July, when she was ordered to Marseilles, where she spent an entire month, and then to Naples for another ten days. The 26th of August found her back in Spezzia for stores. She moved on to Genoa from 30 August through 17 September, then went back to Spezzia to make preparations for the voyage home. Throughout all of October, she lay in the Italian port, taking on stores, receiving personnel going back to the States, and transferring some of her people who were early in their enlistments to other units of the squadron. The last two men ever to be flogged in *Constitution* received their punishment on Saturday, 19 October 1850.

The anchor was weighed in Spezzia for the last time on 2 November at 1:20 in the morning. Following a farewell 3-day stay at Genoa, it was westward ho! Corsica was seen on the 12th, Minorca two days later, and Cabo de Gata on the 17th. At that point, head winds began to bedevil the ship; she didn't make Gibraltar until the early evening of the 27th. There, she waited four days with more than 200 other ships for a wind to carry them out into the Atlantic.

## A COLLISION

The wind came fair on 1 December. *Constitution* and all the others swarmed out of port, straining to take full advantage of Nature's benevolence. With her vast cloud of canvas towering nearly 200 feet into the sky, the old frigate showed her stuff as she overhauled slower craft and swept westward. By sunset, she had outdistanced all those who had left the Rock with her.

At one bell of the night watch, one of the cathead lookouts cried, "Light ho!" Only a brief flash, it was believed to have been about two points on the port bow. A dark object was next seen ahead, and although an attempt was made to miss it the big frigate smashed into a brig, hitting her starboard side right between the masts. Both sticks whipped and snapped off. *Constitution* had the tip of her flying jib boom split and half of her dolphin striker carried away. Captain Conover was called as the Officer of the Deck ordered the stunsails taken in and the ship hove to. Boats were put over to search for whatever it was they hit, but nothing was found: no wreckage, no people. Conover got under way once more.

A few minutes after moving on, a member of the crew appeared before the Officer of the Deck, a bedraggled young lad in tow. Upon questioning, he turned out to be the cabin boy of the English brig *Confidence* of Cowes, which had been taking coal to Barcelona when struck. There had been eight in the crew. The boy said he caught a cable at the bow and had managed to work his way up to and in through a gun port. As the minutes passed, other *Constitutions* showed up, escorting similarly drenched and dazed Englishmen, each of whom had caught onto *Constitution* as she crushed her way through their ship, and who had been found wandering about the gun deck and forecastle. Soon, all but the Captain and Mate were accounted for. The crewmen reported that a light from "Old Ironsides" had been seen, but that the officers had gotten into an argument as to whether it was a light on a ship or ashore, and had done nothing to avoid the col-

## A Most Fortunate Ship

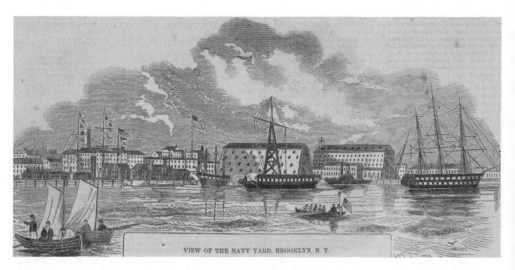

VIEW OF THE NAVY YARD, BROOKLYN, N. Y.

Constitution *in ordinary at Brooklyn Navy Yard in 1851.*

lision.

While these people were turning up on the quarterdeck, another *Constitution* in the duty section stepped from the forecastle into the head to relieve himself, and was startled to hear some of the most exquisite cursing he ever had heard. Peering curiously over the bulwark, he saw below him a man clinging to the wooden legs of Andrew Jackson and swearing at the statue for not doing a thing to help him get aboard! The American tar grabbed the highly vocal stranger by the collar and, calling for some of his mates to help, soon had the man on deck. He turned out to be the missing Mate of *Confidence*. In his stunned state, he had mistaken the figurehead for a real person and was understandably upset by the bloke's seemingly un-Christian attitude. When he calmed down, the Mate said he had seen the Captain knocked overboard when *Constitution* hit them, so there would be no further discoveries that night. These Englishmen ended up going all the way to the United States in the frigate because an eastbound English ship, spoke several days later, refused to take them.

The remainder of the trip home had but two further incidents to disturb the peace. On Christmas day, Seaman Joseph Bryson got in a fight with Captain of the Mizzen Top Peter Wilson and stabbed him. Placed in double irons, Bryson was dishonorably discharged upon arrival; Wilson survived. Early in the new year, a sudden squall carried away the crossjack yard in the slings — a two-day repair job for the carpenters.

A lookout sighted land in the vicinity of Barnegat, New Jersey on 10 January 1851. Shortly before noon the next day, steamer *Cinderella* took *Constitution* in tow and, aided by steamer *Wave,* brought her safely to the Brooklyn Navy Yard. Thomas Conover had his personal gear moved ashore on the 13th; he placed the ship in ordinary about two weeks later.

252

# 16 African Adventure

## BACKGROUND

America's initial action to end slavery was the passage of a bill, on 2 March 1807, which prohibited American participation in the African slave trade. Enforcement of the law, however, was left to moral suasion, rarely an adequate deterrent where material gain is to be had in such abundance. Slave trading continued unabated, and further pressure from then-President James Monroe caused Congress to pass another bill on the subject on 3 March 1819. In this one, the President was given the power to use American men-o'-war to "seize, take, and bring into any port of the United States, vessels of the United States unlawfully engaged in the transportation of any negro, mulatto, or person of colours."

The sum of $100,000 also was appropriated in the same bill to assist in the establishment of a safe haven for such slaves as were rescued somewhere "on the coast of Africa." This provision was the germ from whence came the establishment of a colony in the vicinity of Cape Mensurado on 15 December 1821. For more than a quarter-century, this colony was led by a Governor under the aegis of the Society for Colonizing the Free People of Colour of the United States. On 26 July 1847, the colony having reached an adequate level of self-sufficiency, it was declared the free and independent Republic of Liberia, and the last Governor, Joseph J. Roberts, himself a colonist, became its first President.

For its part in implementing the "police" aspect of the new law, the Navy promptly sent the corvette *Cyane*, *Constitution*'s prize, as escort for the transport *Elizabeth*, which carried the first group of colonists. Thereafter, it was customary for American warships to pay periodic visits to the African coast, but what little attention there was to the actual suppression of slave trading was done by the West Indies Squadron, which was established in 1821 and which also operated against Caribbean pirates. The African Squadron finally was organized in 1843, but most often was no more than two vessels — a token to insure that the British (who averaged nineteen units on that station) did not stop and board American ships. The suspicions of 1812 lingered long.

## "OLD IRONSIDES' " NEW LEADERS

Rhode Islander John Rudd recommissioned *Constitution* on 22 December 1852 at New York. He was the first officer of the rank of Commander regularly to be ordered to command the frigate, an indication of her advancing age and diminishing position in the mid-century Navy that was shifting rapidly from wind to steam propulsion. His ship would wear the flag of Commodore Isaac Mayo, commanding the African Squadron. Other units on the coast during 1853-6 included the sloops of war *Marion* (16) and *Dale* (16), and the brig *Perry* (8). As they never operated in company with *Constitution* — meeting only occasionally in port — they will not appear again in this narrative. Rudd had been appointed a midshipman in late 1814, and had been a commander for over twelve years. He previously had commanded the brig *Dolphin* (10), in the Home Squadron, and *Dale,* when she was in the Pacific Squadron.

Commodore Mayo broke his flag aboard on 23 December, making himself at home in the newly-installed flag quarters erected on the spar deck abaft the mizzen mast. This poop cabin included a central reception room, sleeping cabins for the Commodore and his clerk, a clerk's "office," a pantry, a wash room, and a head. Windows were installed in the three gun ports in the transom and in the two after gun ports on either side — gun ports which had long since ceased to be in regular use. It was a remarkably efficient use of the limited space available. Captain Rudd, of course, used the cabin on the gun deck.

Surprisingly, the Commodore's arrival on board did not presage an immediate departure. Indeed, so leisurely was the pace of preparation that it wasn't until two months later the *Constitution* spent a couple of days taking aboard powder and shot from Ellis Island. Finally, at 8:20 A.M. on 2 March 1853, steamers *Hector* and *Ajax* towed the frigate clear of New York harbor and she was off on a voyage that would keep her out of home waters for more than two years.

## TO AFRICA — THE LONG WAY

Before taking station off the west coast of Africa, however, Commodore Mayo headed first for the Mediterranean to confer with Commodore Silas H. Stringham, commanding the squadron in that sea, and to transport the new U.S. Consul to Tunis, J.H. Nicholson, to his post. Pausing at Gibraltar for five days, Mayo ultimately found Stringham and his flagship *Cumberland* (50) at Spezzia. He finished his official business with Stringham in short order, then spent nearly two weeks sightseeing the famous marble quarries at Cararra, next Pisa and Florence, and rejoined *Constitution* at Leghorn on 24 April, where it had arrived late that afternoon.

Mayo got underway again on 29 April, paid a three-day call at Tunis while disembarking Colonel Nicholson, and spent another four days at Algiers, considered by many on board as the finest visiting port on the entire littoral. Algiers, by this time, had been a French dependency for over two decades. While there, "thousands" of the local populace enjoyed touring the ship. Another leisurely sail brought the Commodore back to Gibraltar once more on 2 June, where he spent a further week.

*Constitution* stood to sea on 9 June and paid a brief call at Tangiers, where she first had brought her power to bear on the Barbary pirates a half-century earlier. Upon her departure the next day, adverse winds caused Rudd to return to the Rock, where five days passed awaiting favorable conditions. *HMS Sans Pareil,* propellor ship of the line, saluted the Commodore's broad pennant as she stood in on the 14th. Captain Dacres, the British skipper, was the son of the Captain of

*HMS Guerriere,* defeated by *Constitution* in 1812.

When she sailed on the 15th, *Constitution* was one of 168 sail to stand out, so long had a favorable wind been wanting. In five hours, she sailed them all out of sight.

## ON STATION

Funchal, Madeira, was reached on 18 June — 3½ months after leaving New York — and the African duties finally taken up with the act of officially relieving the sloop *John Adams,* with Commodore Elie A.F. LaVallette embarked. But not too arduously. For weeks, *Constitution* remained in port while the Commodore waited for cooler weather and exchanged pleasantries with the local gentry. The Civil Governor called on board on 27 June, followed by the Military Governor and his wife, the Count and Countess of Taverade, on the 30th. The next evening, Mayo gave a gala on board, with the ship's band providing music for dancing "until a late hour."

Underway from Funchal on 3 July, *Constitution* called briefly at Teneriffe before dropping anchor in Porto Grande, Sao Vicente Island, for two days. British General Hugh Wheeler, together with a Lord and Lady Russel, were feted at a gala on board on the evening of the 12th that included dancing and fireworks. The next morning found the ship underway once more.

In Porto Praya, also in the Cape Verde Islands, for a week (15-21 July), Commodore Mayo encountered the steamer *John Hancock* and storeship *John P. Kennedy,* vessels assigned to Commander Cadwallader Ringgold's squadron, enroute on a survey expedition to the "China Seas," the northern Pacific, and "Behrings Strait."

Just hours out of port on the 22nd, *Constitution* came upon the *George,* a British schooner in distress. To ensure the safety of the merchant's crew, Mayo directed Rudd to see the vessel safely into port. A slow, four-day trek saw *George* snug in Porto Grande and the frigate once again on her way, touching briefly again at Porto Praya for any late-arriving mail before calling at Monrovia, Liberia.

## PEACEMAKER

Underway from Monrovia on 25 August *Constitution* stopped at Sinow (Sinoe: Greensville today) and Cape Palmas. During the stop at Cape Palmas, in conversations with the Governor about slaving operations in the general area, that official asked Commodore Mayo to see what he could do to put an end to a tribal war that had been simmering on Liberia's southern boundary for some three years. At issue were the slave-raiding habits of the Barbo tribe vis-a-vis the Grebo people. Mayo consented, promising to look into the matter on his way south on patrol.

Arriving off the mouth of the Cavally River on 4 September, Mayo sent a lieutenant ashore in a ship's boat named *Water Witch* to scout the terrain and locate the disputants. The Grebo town soon was located and the people found ready and willing to secure an end to the unhappy situation. Across the river, however, the Barbos threatened the lieutenant with death and vowed to resist any force sent against them. Mayo reacted to his emissary's report decisively.

At 8:30 the next morning, five boats bearing Commodore and Captain, 200 sailors and Marines, a 12-pounder howitzer, and rockets put off from the frigate and pulled smartly toward shore. Holding the bulk of his force off for the moment, Mayo sent in one boat under a white flag to renew the mediation offer. This was rebuffed again. Equally determined, the Commodore commenced a bombardment of the Barbo town on the river's left bank with both the howitzer and the rockets. It required only the destruction of a few huts to convince the natives that negotiation was the only sensible course of action. One Barbo had been wounded: a woman (and they "are known for their curiosity") was singed on the arm by an exploding rocket as she attempted to see what was going on from behind a tree.

Before the sun was high in the sky, deputations from both tribes were brought to the poop cabin of the frigate for a "Grand Palava" with Commodore Mayo. By hand signs and pidgin English, the savage nobility in all their native finery conversed with the crusty salt in his blue and gold. In the end, after "going through various frantic actions," and accompanied by the "Spewing of Water & Shaking of Hands," a peace was agreed to. The "spewing of water" — literally, the same sort of performance required of us by a dentist — was meant to wash away the bad words and feelings; perhaps the shaking of hands was purely for the benefit of the Americans. Dinner for the deputations followed, and the former enemies returned ashore after the presentation of "dash" (trade goods gifts).

On 6 September 1853, the Barbo-Grebo Peace Treaty was ratified formally on board *Constitution*. With more "dash", the natives were put ashore. At that, the frigate weighed anchor for the Gulf of Guinea.

Ever since she called at Porto Praya in mid-July, *Constitution* had been signing on a growing number of natives to perform some of the more menial tasks in the ship. Little has been recorded about these 40-odd "Kroomen," as they were called, beyond the names given them by the regular crew. Those that have come down to us speak volumes concerning the prevailing American attitudes, assigned duty stations, and personal characteristics: Tom Coffee, John Grey, Jack Half-Dollar, Bottle of Beer, Second Cutter, Tom Two Glass, Prince Will, John Crow, Bean Soup, Pea Soup, Jack Everyday, Jack Frying Pan, Frying Pan 2nd, Tom Boston, and Jack Constitution.

*Constitution* visited four ports on the Gold Coast during the subsequent two weeks — "Dix Cove," near the Pra River; Elmina, which fort had been founded by the Portuguese in 1482 and was still in fighting trim; Cape Coast Castle; and finally, Accra. As has been noted earlier, "entertainments" often were held on board to bring some freshness into the lives of the people manning these perilous outposts and to provide an outlet for the ship's company's boredom and frustrations. Commodore's Clerk Edward Cobb has left us a description of such an event

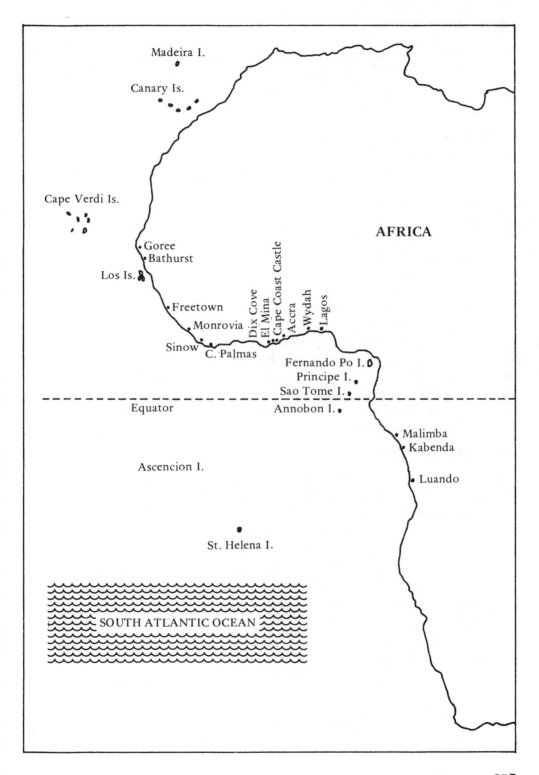

Madeira I.

Canary Is.

Cape Verdi Is.

**AFRICA**

Goree
Bathurst
Los Is.

Dix Cove
El Mina
Cape Coast Castle
Accra
Wydah
Lagos
Freetown
Monrovia
Sinow
C. Palmas

Fernando Po I.
Principe I.
Sao Tome I.

Equator

Annobon I.

Malimba
Kabenda

Ascencion I.

Luando

St. Helena I.

SOUTH ATLANTIC OCEAN

off Cape Coast Castle:

> The Gun Deck was handsomely decorated with Flags, and ornamental insignia, with tables spread, and heavily laden with choice viands, for the accommodation of the guests... Dined at 3PM, after which dancing commenced and was prolonged until 7PM at which time the entertainment was varied by the 'Musical and Dramatic' performances of the 'Associations' formed on board...

The embarked band undoubtedly provided adequate music, and the crew were enthusiastic if grossly amateurish thespians, but "choice viands"? From ship's stores? Perhaps market days along the African coast were remarkably good.

*Constitution* arrived at Fernando Po on 29 September, having stopped overnight at Lagos, then still under native rule. Here, calls were made on the local Spanish authorities and the ship was watered.

Leaving volcanic Fernando Po on 2 October, Mayo next ordered the frigate to the mouth of the Gaboon River (more probably Libreville, which had been founded only four years before) to touch base with the French authorities there before moving on to the Portuguese island of Sao Tome, where she anchored on the 14th in Man of War Bay.

*Constitution* crossed the Equator for the first time during this cruise shortly after leaving Sao Tome on the 15th. By the 26th, she had begun patrolling between "Malimba" (Mayoumba, Gabon) and the Angolan coast. And on that particular day, she spent six hours in a fruitless chase of a swifter, shallower-draft slaver. Not only was Commodore Mayo's squadron numerically insufficient to its task, his flagship was ill-suited for it.

## SLAVER CAPTURED

Continuing south, the frigate called at Kabenda, a Portuguese enclave north of Angola, before arriving off that shore. There on 3 November, through the use of false colors, she brought to the American schooner *H. N. Gambrill* of New York, a slaver. The boarding officer reported the evidence of her involvement as follows:

> On boarding the American schooner *H.N. Gambrill* this morning I found her papers apparently formal and correct, but I could find no list of cargo... I then proceeded to examine the vessel and on going to the Caboose (cook) house found it closed. The door was opened and I found a very large Copper boiler recently set in brick work, such a copper as would be required to cook the food for slaves.
>
> Upon opening the hatches I found a deck of loose hemlock boards, laid smoothly and carefully upon the tiers of casks, which upon examination were found to contain provisions, and several thousand gallons of water. The fore peak usually occupied by the crew had no bulk head to seperate it from the hold, but the crews quarters were next to the cabin...
>
> The cook at last told me the whole story of the voyage, as far as he knew it as follows: he had shipped to go in the Schooner on an honest trading voyage, to the coast of Africa... They sailed from the Congo on the evening of the 1st of November, and yesterday they k(n)ocked down the bulkhead which separated the forecastle from the

hold, broke up a part of the mens chests, threw overboard their old clothes empty barrels &c in order to make room, and laid the slave deck, ready for the reception of the
negroes. The crew moved their quarters from forward, aft, they then got up a big box,
took from it the Copper for Cooking, and set it in brick work in the caboose house. All
doubt was then removed as to the object of the voyage.

When the Constitution was discovered from the Mast head this morning, the Captain examined her with his glass, and declared she was a Brig he had seen in the
Congo. When he found out it was a Frigate, it was too late to run away...

... Every thing that I saw and heard stamped her inequivocally as a Slaver, on the
eve of receiving her cargo.

She quickly was declared a prize and placed under the command of Lieutenant
John DeCamp, who remained in company. This was *Constitution*'s last
capture.

Two days later, another schooner was overtaken, but she proved to be a
Portuguese war schooner, the *Conde De Jozal.* Later that same day, the Commodore brought his two ships to anchor at Ambriz overnight before proceeding
to Sao Paolo de Loando (Luanda, Angola), whence they dropped their hooks on
the 8th. Here, ten days were spent in rewatering and resupplying the ships and
making repairs. On the 13th, Mayo ordered DeCamp to return *Gambrill* to the
United States for adjudication.

## PATROL RESUMED

Refreshed and restored by this "break" in the voyage, "Old Ironsides" was
underway once more on the 17th, headed westsouthwest, bound for the British
island of Saint Helena. It took twelve days to cover the roughly 1200 miles direct
distance, hardly a memorable sailing.

A leisurely five days were passed at the friendly British colony. Here, Napoleon
had been exiled after Waterloo until his death in 1821. Some of the American
officers took advantage of the opportunity to visit the Emperor's final residence.
The Commodore and the ship staged one of their familiar "entertainments" on
board for their British hosts on 3 December, with dancing on the quarterdeck
"until a late hour." On the official side, Mayo succeeded in making
arrangements to have stores for American ships on the African Station warehous-
ed on the island at no cost. Henceforth, there would be supply bases at both
extremities of the Station, located in areas clear of the inimical African shore.

On 5 December, the day after leaving Saint Helena, the crew assembled to
hear of Commodore Matthew Calbraith Perry's initial successes in getting Japan
opened to Western trade. Three cheers were given to honor the event. Mayo had
written Washington in July 1853 suggesting he take *Constitution* across the
Indian Ocean to join with and reinforce Perry's efforts.

Pausing two days at Monrovia, "Old Ironsides" drove on northward for Porto
Praya, dropping her anchor there on 6 January 1854. And in the mail awaiting
him, Mayo found Secretary Dobbin's response to his proposal to join Perry: No.

For the next five months, *Constitution* idled among the Cape Verde and

Canary Islands, in April getting as far north as Madeira. Dignitaries were received on board, entertainments held, and minor diplomats transported from island to island. Late in January, she made a quick (5-day) trip to the Los Islands to pick up twenty-one survivors of the wrecked American merchant ship *Sylph* and return them to Porto Grande for onward transportation. Finally, on 22 June, she weighed anchor at Porto Praya and filled away for Monrovia, beginning her second tour of the station.

## MORE "DIPLOMACY"

Following eight days in Monrovia, *Constitution* proceeded to Cape Palmas, where the Governor requested the Commodore to exercise his proven powers of mediation, this time in settling a territorial dispute between the Grahway and Half Cavally tribes. He agreed, and the "palava" was held that day in his cabin. Mayo at this time was bed-ridden with a "severe sprain" — of what and how received is not recorded. The same sequence of talk, "frantic actions," the "spewing of water," and "dash" marked progress to another successful outcome. The cabin's low overhead must have strained diplomacy to the utmost, given the dynamic nature of negotiations! The frigate was underway quickly that evening.

The ship called again at Cape Coast Castle, and on the 23rd provided an anchor and cable to the American merchant ship *Winnegance* at Serra. Continuing eastward, she found a considerable amount of shipping off what is today the coast of Dahomey. In three days, sometimes under false colors, she stopped, inspected, and released as innocent one Spanish, one Dutch, one Hamburg, five English, and "several" Portuguese merchantmen. She anchored off the Lagos River on 28 July.

On 31 July, "King" Docemo of Lagos and his principal nobles called upon the Commodore and were received on board with full honors, including a 13-gun salute and the King's flag being flown at the fore truck. Sadly, no description of this banner has come down to us. After the usual amenities, a treaty was signed which granted "most favored nation" status to the United States in Lagos. Late in the day, the frigate was again on the move.

Standing to the southsoutheast, a five-day run was made to "Prince's Island" (Principe) where, in West Bay, the ship took on water and some provisions. On the 8th of August, a working party went ashore and disinterred the remains of M. H. Abbot, son of Captain Joel Abbot, USN, once captain's clerk in the "sloop" *Macedonian,* for return to his homeland. They were encased in canvas and pitch and brought to the ship.

Southward again on 9 August, Captain Rudd brought his ship to off "Anna Bona" (Annobon) Island in order to take on fresh fruits and vegetables before turning eastward to close the African shore once more.

On 19 August, the order "splice the Main brace" was heard, and all hands celebrated the forty-second anniversary of *Constitution*'s victory over *HMS Guerriere,* perhaps the most dramatic of her many successes, with an extra tot of grog.

The coastal patrol proved to be a difficult one as calms, capricious airs, and a northward-setting current all conspired to defeat progress. In the seventy miles between Mayoumba and Luanda, during the period 24 August-5 September, the ship was forced to anchor thirty-one times in order not to lose ground. On the latter date, she arrived in Luanda and Commodore's Clerk Cobb noted in his journal that the people there were "a fine race, and seem to be much more intelligent, than any other tribes we have heretofore visited."

An unintended diplomatic event occurred here as a result of normal ship's routine: It seems that on the day prior to *Constitution*'s arrival, the local "King" had decoyed two English traders to his village and taken them prisoner. The subsequent arrival of the frigate and the routine firing of her morning gun led him to believe that retribution was at hand and caused him to release his prisoners! At a subsequent "palava," a friendship treaty was agreed to between the King and the local white merchants. Lieutenant Christopher R.P. Rodgers was the official witness at the signing.

On 8 September, *Constitution* stood out of Luanda and turned northwestward, ending her last visit to those waters. Crossing the Equator at 6 A.M. on the 17th, she paused briefly at Cape Palmas before coming to anchor at Monrovia on the 22nd. A week later, Ordinary Seaman James Lee, while preparing a sternboat for lowering, was struck in the head by a parting block, knocked into the water, and drowned. His was the first fatality from any cause in the eighteen months since the ship had left home waters, a truly remarkable accomplishment in view of the terrible conditions of the station, and a testimonial to the attention given his crew by Captain Rudd.

While beating into Porto Grande more than two weeks later, a rapidly freshening wind caused the splitting of the jib, mainsail, and foretopsail, as well as the crossjack to be carried away. Prudently, Rudd stood away from land and effected necessary repairs. Porto Grande finally was entered on the 19th.

For the next five-and-a-half months, the easy cycle of trips amongst the islands, Cape Verde to Madeira, that characterized the first quarter of the year, was repeated. On 27 October, shortly after she began a three-week stay in Porto Praya, *Constitution* was rammed by the American whaling barque *Osceola* which missed stays while maneuvering into the harbor and struck her amidships. Damage in the frigate was limited to the loss of an accommodation ladder, but the whaler was "much damaged in the bows." *Constitution* returned to Porto Grande in November, where the Abbot remains were "temporarily" reinterred, and she was in Madeira for Christmas and the beginning of 1855 before returning to the Cape Verde Islands.

## A REUNION OF SORTS

During one of her calls at Porto Grande, there was in harbor the British mission yacht *Allen Gardiner*. The embarked missionary recalled the meeting:

> I found at St. Vincent the American frigate *Constitution*... I forwarded some

(newspapers) to the Americans, and had a message sent back in return that if they could be of service to me they would be glad to show it.

This offer, I thankfully accepted, inasmuch as I wanted a competent ship's carpenter to examine my pumps, and accordingly I went on board the *Constitution* to make the request in person. I was most courteously received by both the captain and the commodore, and in the course of conversation I learned to my surprise that the vessel I was standing upon the deck of was the very *Constitution* so well known in the War of 1812! And what to me appeared still more singular was the fact that she had happened to be the very ship on board of which my late father chanced to be a prisoner of war after the capture of the *Guerriere.*

A thrill of natural emotion ran through me when I was informed that this *Constitution* was the old vessel, for I had imagined she was another vessel bearing the name; but for me, the son, to be at the captain's table as a guest on board of the same ship in which the father had been a prisoner of war, produced a variety of thoughts and ideas that I am sure will be considered excusable. The result was that an especial invitation was given to me, my wife and passengers, to attend an evening entertainment on board of the *Constitution* the following day...

The vessel was covered fore and aft with awnings, and was gaily lit up with numerous candles, lamps and artificial fires. The poop was apportioned off for vocal and instrumental music, the principal musicians, however, forming the band of the ship being located on the quarterdeck.

At a given signal several rockets went up; the band played a well-known American national air, and then the commodore, taking my wife's arm in his, walked from the state cabin, where we had all been seated, to lead us where chairs had been placed for himself and visitors. As we passed through the door, and made our appearance on the quarter-deck, the band in an instant burst forth in our glorious national anthem, while some fireworks went off in various directions.

The effect was good; and we at once understood the graceful compliment conveyed by Commodore Mayo in acknowledging the presence of an English lady on board his ship. A flattering mark of respect to our beloved queen.

In February, *Constitution* made a swing eastward, looking in at the Gambia River, stopping at Gorée, Senegal, and reconnoitering the Los Islands one last time. During much of March, she sailed about the Cape Verdes until, at Porto Grande on the 31st, the crew heard the welcome order passed, "All hands up anchor for home." It was 6:30 P.M., and the main brace was "spliced."

## GOING HOME

The voyage westward was uneventful until the twenty-third day out — and just 3-400 miles from her destination — when *Constitution* met and spoke the American ship *Isaac Jeames* outward bound from the Delaware capes. The merchant captain passed on the news that a Spanish frigate, *Ferrolana,* recently had fired upon a U.S. mail steamer, the *El Dorado,* off the coast of Cuba. Commodore Mayo came to the conclusion that they might be needed in the Caribbean area and turned south accordingly. He put fifty-two of the crew in double irons for 28 hours when they protested his decision.

Mayo entered the Caribbean early in May, and it was while he was off the south shore of Cuba seeking to rendezvous with units of the West Indies Squadron, on the 5th, that Marine Private James Sherry died of dysentery, the only man lost to illness in the entire cruise.

Still seeking American units, Mayo circumnavigated Cuba and took *Constitution* into Havana on the 16th. Three days later, the screw frigate *San Jacinto* stood in, wearing the broad blue pennant of the Commander of the Home Squadron, Commodore Charles S. McCauley. Mayo, being junior to McCauley, caused appropriate honors to be rendered and substituted a red command pennant for the blue one previously flown, proclaiming his subordinate position. Knowing now that the *Ferrolana* matter was being dropped Mayo departed for home on 24 May, leaving Havana on the end of a steamer's towline.

*Constitution* arrived at Portsmouth, New Hampshire, on 2 June 1855. Her African adventure, which had seen her at sea 430 out of 822 days, and had covered 42,166 miles, was over. Commodore Mayo hauled down his flag, and the ship herself decommissioned, on the 14th. Her days of front-line service were at an end. She was almost fifty-eight years old.

# 17 Second Rate Ship

## A NEW ROLE

The training of young naval officers, as we have seen, had been left largely to "on the job training." Secretaries and senior officers of the Navy repeatedly had recommended the establishment of formal schooling for these youngsters before they regularly were assigned to shipboard duties. These recommendations were not acted upon, for one reason or another, until Secretary George Bancroft was able to convince the Congress to appropriate the monies needed for the Navy to acquire Fort Severn at Annapolis, Maryland, as the site for such a school. It had opened its scholastic doors for the first time in October 1845, with three students under the charge of Captain Franklin Buchanan. During 1850-51, the school was designated the "Naval Academy," and was reorganized with a four-year curriculum. Class sizes grew steadily in the years that followed.

By the middle years of the decade, it had become apparent to the staff of the Academy that the school needed additional space in which to house its students, as well as a place where the young mids could begin their education in rigging and shipboard routine. What better vehicle for both purposes than one of the old sailing ships? Since 1854, "steam ships" had been joining the Navy at an accelerated rate, making it possible to retire those pure square-riggers not already in reduced status. And what better sailing ship was there to teach and inspire the young salts than "Old Ironsides" herself — the undisputed champion of fighting sailing ships? Thus it was that *Constitution* was taken in hand in 1857 for leisurely restoration and outfitting as a school ship for the Naval Academy.

## CONVERSION

The big frigate was hauled out of the back water at Portsmouth and taken up on the ways at the Navy Yard for inspection and thorough overhaul of her hull. While she was high and dry, the earliest known photographs of the fabled frigate were taken, showing the sleek lines and great depth of her large hull dwarfing the men working around her. It is evident in these pictures that her waist no longer was open, and that the bulwarks on her forecastle and quarterdeck have been raised. Careful study has revealed that in both cases the shipwrights merely have boxed in the hammock stowage with wood, replacing the nettings with which she originally had been fitted. It is not known whether the "boxing" was new with this overhaul. It is possible that it could have been done as early as 1847-8, when she was being readied by Gwinn. Another obvious change made at this time was the replacement of the six windows in the stern with just three, and the planking up of the quarter galleries but for one centrally located single-pane window. The gun stripe was extended all the way to the after edge of the now-solid galleries.

*One of the earliest photographs of* Constitution, *taken in May 1858 at the Portsmouth, New Hampshire Navy Yard during her rebuilding as a school ship. The figurehead is the second one of Andrew Jackson carried by the ship. (White marks in the left portion of the picture are due to tears in the original print.)*

*Constitution* was returned to her usual element in May or June of 1858, where conversion to a school ship commenced in earnest. The poop cabin was gutted and rearranged as two recitation rooms. Forward, the main hatch area of the spar deck largely was decked over and a small house erected on it, containing two more recitation rooms. Down below,

> ... The three study rooms were on the gun deck, bulkheads having been run along parallel with the sides, and the gun ports serving as windows... (L)ockers, one for each midshipman, were fitted against the sides on the berth deck. Forward was the wash room, the number of basins averaging about one to five of the washers...

As for armament, "Old Ironsides' " batteries were reduced to six 32-pounders of 42-hundredweight and ten of 33-hundredweight — sixteen guns, in all. Her official classification was changed to "2nd rate ship," and she was recommissioned by Lieutenant David Dixon Porter on the morning of 1 August 1860.

## TAKING UP NEW DUTIES

After several days of sail drill, Captain Porter got his ship underway on 5 August and made the entrance to Chesapeake Bay a little more than a week

*David Dixon Porter as a Commander.*

*George W. Rodgers as a Commander.*

later. Several days of tacking northward in steadily more restricted waters brought him to anchor off the Annapolis Bar in the very early morning hours of the 18th. Her deep draft necessitated a delay of two days as she off-loaded stores and equipment and pumped water tanks so that the bar could be cleared. This was accomplished in the tow of steamers *Annacostia* and *Merchant* late on the 20th, and she came to anchor off the Academy at ten that evening. Shortly thereafter, the big ship was moved to a mooring at the end of a long, narrow walkway jutting out from the shore where she received all of the Fourth Classmen from the school. Lieutenant George W. Rodgers, nephew of the late Commodore, relieved Porter as Captain.

The Fourth Classmen were the newcomers to the Academy, the neophytes. Academy Commandant Captain George S. Baker decided it would be best to house and train all 127 of them largely in isolation from the distraction of the shore and the influence of the upperclassmen. Thus it was that these lads studied and worked all day in the frigate, and one-sixth of them were marched to the bath-house on shore each night. The lads got into all the normal sort of high jinks one would expect of teenagers, and "authority" reacted predictably: a common punishment for a boyish prank was three days locked in a blacked-out room in the wardroom area. But there seem to have been some things that were done

267

without retribution. As one Rear Admiral recalled many years later,

> ... I have seen Rear Admiral Harry Taylor, who was one of the little fellows in my class, sitting on the main truck of 'Old Ironsides' amusing himself by rolling up the pennant and letting it flow again. His only rival was 'Brick Top' English, who once got on his feet on the truck, aided a little by the lightning conductor, which projected about a foot above it...

## CIVIL WAR

The question of slavery in the United States had galled regional politics for decades, gradually moving opposing groups into positions from which only war could move them. The slide toward this internal holocaust had been accelerating steadily during the latter part of the 1850's; the election of Abraham Lincoln to the Presidency in November 1860 brought the country to the brink, and his inauguration the following March made it certain.

The Naval Academy was, geographically and socially, right in the middle of the confusion of the dividing country. Maryland was Northern economically and Southern in sympathies. Which way the State would go was unknown. In Baltimore, people were acting to disrupt the sole rail line to Washington from the North. Across the Severn River, what appeared to be a volunteer cavalry troop could be seen practicing formation maneuvers in preparation for joining Southern forces. The local citizenry outside the thin walls surrounding the Academy hurled threats and rocks into the compound — threats that included the capture of "Old Ironsides" to be flagship of the rebel fleet.

Local fears and rumors were heightened by news coming in from elsewhere in the country. The miracle of the telegraph not only helped government be more responsive, it disseminated information — and misinformation — as never before. Underscoring the concerns of those at the Academy was an awareness that the Pensacola Navy Yard already was in Confederate hands, that Fort Sumter had been evacuated (14 April), and that the moment of crisis was nearing at Norfolk. Secretary of the Navy Gideon Welles telegraphed on 20 April orders to defend *Constitution* "at all hazards. If it can not be done, destroy her." Similar orders went to Commodore Charles S. McCauley, Commandant of the Norfolk Navy Yard, relative to his Yard and the ships there. Shortly after 4 the next morning, McCauley directed the destruction of his command. One of those scheduled to die in the resultant flames was "Old Waggon," *United States* — *Constitution*'s lone sister. Would she follow?

At Annapolis on the 20th, all was a bustle of activity. Having only about twenty-five seamen regularly assigned to her, the Commandant ordered all mid-shipmen aboard *Constitution* to see to her defense. Internal bulkheads were knocked down as they had been in the glory days and four 32-pounders run out astern through the cabin windows to provide some firepower in the direction of the Bay. Scuttling charges were laid in the magazines. Watches were set with the midshipmen about the ship to detect anyone or thing approaching from the river

*From a contemporary newspaper, the imaginary spirited defense of "Old Ironsides" by the Eighth Massachusetts Regiment.*

or the opposite shore, while others patrolled the walled grounds to provide early warning of an attack from the town.

The situation remained tense but calm until two in the morning of the 22nd, when a midshipman on watch reported seeing a large steamer coming from the Bay. The ship beat to quarters and the green youths gathered at their guns, determined to do their best. Loaded with grape, the cannon were run out. Firing locks were double checked. Slow matches were blown on to make the coals glow red hot. They might only get off one salvo, but the Rebs would pay dearly in that blast of grapeshot at close range.

The steamer continued its approach, seemingly steering so as to avoid coming in way of the frigate's broadside. That she was heading for the mooring astern of "Old Ironsides" suited the defenders well, for it would mean the greatest damage from their fire. Captain Rodgers hailed the stranger when she was about 300 yards off, her decks seen to be packed with people. There was no answer. He hailed a second time with no better luck. One last time he called, "Ship ahoy! Keep off, or I'll sink you!" This time, he got an answer — from the familiar voice of the Academy's chaplain.

When the steamer moored, it was learned that she was the ferry *Maryland.* The chaplain explained that he had been returning from leave in the north when he found Colonel Benjamin F. Butler and his Eighth Massachusetts Volunteer Infantry Regiment at Havre de Grace, near the head of Chesapeake Bay, seeking a way to get his troops to Washington following the stoppage of the trains at Baltimore. The Colonel had commandeered the ferry and sailed to Annapolis, and planned to march his men the remaining miles to the nation's capital. The citizen-soldiers were a welcome reinforcement to the harried mids.

At daylight, all the midshipmen were withdrawn from *Constitution* and placed in a defensive perimeter toward the outer walls while Butler disembarked his troops and got them into some semblance of order. Butler next agreed to help the Navy get the old frigate clear of her moorings and to a position from which she could head seaward if necessary. Many of his Massachusetts troops hailed from towns along its coast, particularly the North Shore, and so had varying degrees of expertise in marine matters — many being more knowledgeable in such things than the midshipmen. Thus it was that "Old Ironsides" received a temporary crew made up of 107 soldiers from such units as the Salem Zouaves, Lynn City Guards, and the Beverley and Gloucester Light Infantry companies.

During the afternoon of the 22nd, three of the ship's anchors were slipped and the fourth taken to the cathead, and she was hauled clear of her berth by *Maryland.* Whether through miscalculation or design on the part of *Maryland*'s pilot, the frigate swung out of the channel and onto a mud bank shortly after getting underway. The grounding was of short duration, however, and she moved on down the Severn toward the Bay proper, ultimately coming hard aground on the bar off Greenbury Point Light. She had almost made it to deep water, but would have to wait now for the tide's assistance; it was 10 P.M.

At midnight, a report was received that the rebels would be making an effort to block the outer end of the channel before daybreak. This generated a new effort to get *Constitution* moving — tide or no tide. All hands were called and a kedge anchor run out with a ship's boat. Men strained at the capstan and actually got her moving, but just then a squall came up that set her still more firmly aground. As if this weren't problem enough, several ships were seen in the offing to the south, ships whose identities could not be determined in the overcast night. The ship beat to quarters, prepared for a desperate defense. Her crew might be a polyglot gang of midshipmen, militia, and Marines, but they would fight as fiercely as any crew "Old Ironsides" ever had known.

The alarm proved to be no more than that. The contacts disappeared. The guns, secured. And the kedging effort was resumed. Several hours of pulling finally broke the big frigate free. At about four that morning, the steamer *Boston* appeared, having on board the Seventh New York Regiment. With her help, *Constitution* was moved to the safety of a deep water anchorage. *Boston* then moved in toward Annapolis town to land her troops, joined by other transports bearing the First Rhode Island Artillery and other Army units bound to secure the town and go on to defend Washington.

## THE NAVAL ACADEMY RELOCATES TO NEWPORT

For the next couple of days, *Constitution* remained at her anchorage, taking on supplies and generally getting ready to go to sea. The guns removed to *Maryland* while getting over the bar were set back aboard and put in their ports. On the 25th, 140 midshipmen — those committed to the Union — came aboard with their baggage and some of the educational equipment from the school. It had been decided to move them and the old frigate farther north, clear of any possible Confederate action. At ten the next morning, more of her Army "crew" having been transferred to normal duties, *Constitution* got underway in tow of steamer *R.R. Cuyler* to get clear of Chesapeake Bay. Her journey to the Virginia capes was escorted by steamer *Harriet Lane,* which had been fired upon while attempting to get through to Fort Sumter earlier in the month. There was no trouble this time. *Constitution* cleared the capes still in tow on the morning of the 27th. She arrived off Governor's Island after dark thirty-six hours later, then moved to a berth at the Brooklyn Navy Yard on the 29th. There, the last two companies of soldiers left her, cheered by the midshipmen.

Secretary Welles had issued further orders concerning *Constitution*'s future as the frigate was clearing the capes: the Naval Academy was to be reestablishzd at Newport, Rhode Island. The steamer *Baltic,* which had been employed in taking troops south for Washington, was detailed to take aboard all remaining personnel and all the furniture, books, models, and apparatus she possibly could carry.

*Constitution* remained in New York about a week, not wishing to arrive in Newport much before *Baltic.* Such First Class Midshipmen as had not been ordered to Washington with the troops were detached for service in regular operational units. The remaining mids were permitted daily liberty ashore, by sections. An Admiral remembered:

> I think we must have received our allowance of spending money at this time — the sum of one dollar per month — for I remember our hurrying in large numbers to the restaurants of lower New York, which we invaded like a swarm of hungry locusts... A dollar must have gone far in those days, or else people were kind in giving us its full value, for even after this raid on the restaurants, we were able to take a ride in the Broadway omnibuses, ending up with a visit to Barnum's Old Museum...
>
> Sunday morning some one proposed going to hear Henry Ward Beecher, and after much noisy argument nearly all of us put our names down on the list as applicants for permission to attend the services at Plymouth Church...

The old frigate got underway in the early evening of 8 May, towed through Hell's Gate by steamers *Freeman* and *Resolute.* She arrived in Briton's Cove, off Fort Adams at Newport, at two the next afternoon. *Baltic,* with the naval and academic staffs aboard, pulled in 3½ hours later. *Constitution* announced her arrival on the morning of the 10th with a *34-gun salute* to the Union.

In the days that followed, the last of the First Classmen, and then the Second and Third Classmen, were transferred for war duty. Suddenly, the Fourth Classmen were the "old hands." For a few months, they continued to live aboard "Old Ironsides," but took their classes in Fort Adams and paraded on its grounds. By September 1861, the Government had leased the Atlantic House in Newport as Academy headquarters and residence for upper classmen. George Rodgers became Commandant of Midshipmen. Lieutenant Edward Phelps Lull succeeded him as the frigate's Captain. The ship herself had been warped into the channel between Goat Island and the mainland, and moored to the island's

*Lieutenant Commander Edward Phelps Lull.*

wharf. She became home to some 200 newly appointed midshipmen destined for accelerated training and assignment to a rapidly expanding Navy with more responsibilities than resources. Somewhat later that fall, the *Santee* (44), the last sailing frigate commissioned (1855), arrived to provide more room for the mids. She was moored just ahead of *Constitution.*

The late spring of 1862 found the Newport Academy further augmented by the assignment of sloops *John Adams, Macedonian,* and *Marion* as underway training ships. That summer, they took the midshipmen south to view Hampton Roads — site of the recent duel between *Monitor* and *Virginia* (formerly *Merrimack)* — and to Port Royal, North Carolina, site of a successful Union amphibious assault, before returning to Newport. *Constitution,* of course, remained at her wharf. Although it seems to have passed without note in the ship, during 1862 the grog ration was forever ended in the United States Navy.

While "Old Ironsides" was seeing service inspiring and training new officers for the Navy at Newport, a large ironclad steamer named *New Ironsides* was commissioned in August 1862 to carry her tradition of victorious combat into the thick of the Civil War. Displacing nearly 3500 tons, this powerful warship had wooden sides as thick as her namesake's, but sheathed for much of its length in 4-inch iron plates; her firepower consisted of fourteen 11-inch smooth bores and two 150-pounder Parrott rifles. From January 1863 until May 1864, she saw very

Constitution (left) *and* Santee *at Newport, Rhode Island in 1863.*

active service with the squadron blockading Charleston, South Carolina. Following a two-month overhaul, she was assigned to the attack force which ultimately took Fort Fisher, near Wilmington, North Carolina, in January 1865. She was considered by many to be the most powerful warship then afloat. *New Ironsides* and "Old Ironsides" never met; the former was destroyed by fire at Philadelphia in December 1865.

The months passed uneventfully for *Constitution* at Newport. During the spring of 1863, Lieutenant Philip C. Johnson, Jr., succeeded Edward Lull as her Captain. He was still in command at war's end in April 1865.

The end of the academic year in June 1865 signalled the beginning of preparations to return the Naval Academy to Annapolis. After so long at the wharf, the first requirement for *Constitution* was for an inspection and repairs to ready her for a sea voyage. Caulkers worked to make her hull and decks tight. Divers went down on 7 July to scrape four years' accretion of marine life from her bottom; at about the same time, her guns were brought back from a battery that had been established on Goat Island. Later in the month, a cargo of unbelievable variety was brought aboard: everything from mess chests and Academy furniture to eight *Army* howitzers. On 8 August, twenty-two women and twenty children, all dependents of Academy staff personnel, came on for the trip south, which began the next morning.

*Philip C. Johnson as a Commander.*

It had been planned to tow the old frigate back to Annapolis, using her sails to ease the strain of the tow when possible. The steamer *Mercury* was to be the tug. On the 10th, it was seen that *Constitution* was making good six knots with her sails and was overtaking *Mercury*. As a result, the tow was dropped near sunset to permit "Old Ironsides" to set her own pace. For the remainder of the voyage, she made good between seven and nine knots by the log, and arrived in Hampton Roads shortly before midnight on 12 August. *Mercury* came in, huffing and puffing, ten hours later! It was quite an achievement for the 68-year-old man-o'-war.

*Mercury* picked up its towing bridle once more at first light on the 14th. She was much more efficient in restricted waters. She got *Constitution* to the entrance to Annapolis on the 16th, where the frigate's great draft again preclud-

*Constitution at the Naval Academy after the Civil War. Note the "school house" built over her main hatch area.*

ed her ready approach to the wharf. Guns, anchors, and chains were landed the next morning before she was forced alongside her assigned pier — slicing three feet into the bottom mud at high tide. All her ammunition was landed on the 23rd to help get her out of the mud.

During September, workmen were aboard on assignments that indicated clearly there were no plans for the ship to move in the foreseeable future. First aboard were the pipefitters, busily making steam connections to the shore to provide heat to the ship through radiators. Later, the gas fitters came aboard to rig up gas lights in the classrooms, office, and berthing areas. A classroom "house" on her forecastle was made more weatherproof. *Constitution* had become a structure, a strange sort of building among a gaggle of randomly designed and built edifices dotting the Academy grounds.

Diminutive Lieutenant Commander Edmund O. Matthews succeeded Lieutenant Commander Johnson as Captain on 16 February 1866, and he, in turn, was relieved ten days later by Lieutenant Commander Thomas H. Eastman. One is tempted to call them "Super" rather than "Skipper," for their assignment was more nearly that of a building superintendent than ship's captain and they had additional administrative duties, as well. As time went on, *Constitution*'s Cap-

*Thomas H. Eastman as a Midshipman.*

tains also were made responsible for the maintenance of all the ships of the training squadron when they were in ordinary between summer cruises. All of the
caretaker crews eventually lived in "Old Ironsides," only working and standing
security watches in their nominal commands.

Steadily the months slipped into years in an almost unvarying routine. The
new class of midshipmen would report aboard in September. In October, hatch
houses would be placed aboard to cover the ladders giving access to the interior
of the ship during the winter season; in April, they would be removed. Midshipmen would be transferred to the units of the reactivated training squadron
in June to spend the summer at sea, usually with ports of call in the Caribbean or
northern Europe. While they were away, the 100-140 members of *Constitution*'s
crew would overhaul her and get set for the new cycle the following September.

On 19 October 1867, Vice Admiral David Dixon Porter, the same who had
commanded her as a lieutenant just seven years earlier, paid a visit to the old
frigate, coming aboard from the steam "yacht" *Albemarle*. A few moments after
*Albemarle* had cleared *Constitution*'s accommodation ladder, her boiler blew
up, killing the Admiral's Coxswain and two others, and injuring three more. Two
of *Constitution*'s boats were employed in rescuing survivors and retrieving the

*George Dewey as a Captain.*

bodies.

Captain Eastman was relieved on 6 November of that year by Lieutenant Commander George Dewey, relative of the infamous Samuel Worthington Dewey of the Jackson figurehead caper, and himself later to become famous as the "Hero of Manila Bay" in the Spanish-American War. Dewey remained in command until 1 August 1870.

During these quiet postwar years, there occurred two deaths which essentially marked the end of *Constitution*'s glory years in living memory. In Kendall's Mills, Maine, on 15 June 1867, died William Bryant, state representative, long-time town selectman, and one of the original crewmen to serve in "Old Ironsides." He probably was the last surviving "plank owner." His passing went without notice at the ship. Rear Admiral Charles Stewart, victor over *Cyane* and *Levant,* died at his home in Bordentown, New Jersey, on 9 November 1869. The frigate's colors were half-masted in his memory when notice was received two days later. He was the last of her hero-skippers: Preble had died in 1807, Bainbridge in 1833, and Hull in 1843.

Dewey's successor was Lieutenant Commander Henry Lycurgus Howison. For a year and a half, Howison continued the cycle followed by his predecessors.

*Henry Lycurgus Howison as a Commander.*

However somnolent the ship herself was, his was a fulltime job, for he was responsible for the readiness of the five units of the training squadron as well, and acted as an "administrative aide" to the Academy Superintendent. The opening and closing of each school year must have been periods of great pressure for him.

During the summer of 1871, the decision was made to end *Constitution*'s service as a school ship because of her deteriorated condition. Even as she rested at the wharf, ship's company began tearing down the recitation house over the main hatch and removing the study room bulkheads from the gun deck. Stores were transferred to *Santee;* lockers removed from the berth deck. On 13 September, she was hauled away from the wharf and provided with an anchor and 120 fathoms of chain from *Dale*. On the 16th, she received a gig and one whaleboat for her quarter davits. A temporary crew came aboard two days later command-

*Rear Admiral Alexei M. Kalinin* (left) *of the Soviet Navy pays a call on Rear Admiral Rex D. Snyder, Jr.* (right), *on board "Old Ironsides," 12 May 1975.*

Left: *The Commodore of the Continental Navy, a Bicentennial militia, and* Constitution's *Captain await opening ceremonies for the* Constitution *Museum, April 1976.* Above: *Mr. H. Robert Freneau, Special Assistant to the Secretary of the Navy, and* Constitution's *Captain dedicate* Constitution *Grove in Crane, Indiana on 8 May 1976.*

Top left: Constitution *in her berth in Boston, as portrayed by John Charles Roach.* Bottom left: *The ship's Master at Arms and an honored guest convene during the International Youth Bicentennial Salute Turn-Around Cruise, 17 June 1976. Above: John Charles Roach's portrayal of "Old Ironsides" leading the tall ships into Boston, 10 July 1976.*

**Above:** *"Old Ironsides"' cannon salute to the nation's 200th birthday.* **Left:** *Piping the side for the Queen of England.* **Top right:** *The 21-gun salute to England's Queen.* **Bottom right:** *Queen Elizabeth II, escorted by the Secretary of the Navy J. William Mittendorf II and the ship's Captain, receives official honors as she commences her tour of* Constitution.

*"Old Ironsides" and* Britannia *at peace.*

ed by Commander Augustus P. Cook.

Steamers *Phlox* and *Pinta* towed her away from Annapolis at 8:30 a.m. on 20 September, passing the returning training ships *Constellation,* the 1854 corvette which had succeeded to the name of the earlier frigate, and *Saratoga,* no doubt exchanging cheers with the embarked mids. After two days at anchor in Hampton Roads making final preparations for sea, *Pinta* cleared the Virginia capes on the 23rd with the frigate in tow. *Constitution* set her main spencer to ease the strain. The pair anchored off the Delaware capes the next evening, worked their way up to Newcastle on the day following, then completed the run to Philadelphia, arriving off the Navy Yard in the Southwark district of the city at noon, the 26th. Captain Cook hauled down the commissioning pennant before dark.

## ANOTHER RESTORATION

During October 1871, preliminary inactivation work was accomplished in the frigate: yards sent down, rigging taken ashore, remaining stores and equipage landed. In November, orders came to suspend all work in her and she was left in ordinary. Work of an unspecified nature was resumed in September of 1872, then suspended once more two months later.

There were many reasons behind these start-and-stop proceedings. Firstly, no money had been specifically appropriated for the overhaul of *Constitution.* Secondly, there were the invariable few in the hierarchy who proposed that she be scrapped, and the greater number who shouted "No!" Thirdly, no future employment had been determined upon; without a reason for being, monies should not be spent. And finally, the Philadelphia Navy Yard was on the verge of transferring its entire operation to League Island, but how soon this was to be accomplished and when ship work should be stopped at the old site had not been determined.

In the spring of 1873, it was decided that *Constitution* was to be thoroughly repaired and restored insofar as possible to her original appearance for the purpose of being exhibited to the public during the year of Centennial (1876). In August, work resumed with the removal of the old joiner work below decks, and the preparation of plans for the "restoration." In December, final preparations were made to take her out of the water.

It was intended to take her up on the sectional dock on 5 January 1874, but several days of high northwest winds had denied them sufficient water for the operations. Two more attempts, on the 12th and 13th, had to be stopped because of mechanical failures in the dock machinery. A successful docking was achieved at last on the 27th. The dock was grounded that same day in position at the end of one of the building ways where the old frigate would be hauled ashore. This was done in a six-hour operation on 5 March.

Work on the ship was slow and sporadic. Gradually, she was taken down to her live oak skeleton, shorn of everything. The closeness of her frames, however, might have caused the casual observer to miss the fact that he was seeing a ship stripped of all her planking. By late May of 1875, she had only been planked up to the vicinity of her waterline. More and more of the Yard's equipment and labor force was going to League Island — making the transition from wood and canvas to iron and steam in the process — until *Constitution* remained the sole major project uncompleted. Finally, in December, she was ready to be returned to the water. On 30 December, she was moved back into the sectional dock. She lay there until 12 January, when conditions were right to refloat her. Naval Constructor Philip Hichborn did the honors. The old Navy Yard had been formally decommissioned five days earlier.

Recognizing that working on *Constitution* to completion would delay further the final transfer of the Navy Yard, a contract to complete her outfitting, sparring, and rigging had been put out to bid during the latter months of 1875. Winner was Wood, Dialogue and Company of Kaighn's Point, New Jersey. During March of 1876, the old frigate was moved to that company's "works." Exactly how long she lay with the contractor has not been ascertained. It is known that she received two additional sets of boat davits in the vicinity of the main shrouds. A small boiler, operating at 10-20 pounds pressure, was installed on the forward orlop to provide heat through the radiators first emplaced at Annapolis. Much of the forward magazine became a coal bin. Centennial celebrations came and went as the contractor dawdled through the work.

There were a considerable number of visual changes to the ship during the course of this restoration that should be mentioned. The Andrew Jackson figurehead was removed and ultimately relocated at the Naval Academy. It had been hoped to return Hull's billet head to the ship in keeping with the directive requiring a return to her youthful appearance, but the Boston Navy Yard reported it too rotten for further use. The contractor then attempted to get the Jackson figurehead back, but its new masters refused, and so he carved a simple scroll similar to that worn a century later. The new trail boards differed from those emplaced in 1858 only in the substitution of the shield for the "rose," in keeping with the patriotic theme of the Centennial. Gone forever were the three busts on the transom — if, in fact, they ever really were installed — and the decor simplified to one emphasizing the eagle and six stars which she has worn ever since.

At the end of 1876, the Navy found itself with an old sailing frigate of great sentimental value on which it recently had spent a considerable sum of money and for which it had no planned function. What to do? As an expedient, it was decided to recommission her and use her as a barracks and school ship for apprentice boys right there in Philadelphia. Captain Henry A. Adams, Jr., was transferred from command of the receiving ship *Potomac* and did the honors on 13 January 1877. The ship was moored in the stream off the new Navy Yard at League Island. Recognizing that many boys in a restricted environment could be a problem, four brig cells were fitted to contain the obstreperous.

Constitution *"high and dry"* in the Philadelphia Navy Yard. All outer hull planking has been removed above the water line, permitting a view of her heavy ribbing of live oak.

*Captain Henry A. Adams.*

## BOYS' TOWN

From January until mid-December, *Constitution* was college and campus to young teenage lads enlisting in the Navy. There were almost daily drills in a wide variety of seamanship evolutions both on deck and in the rigging, as well as drills at the great guns remaining on board. Matches with single sticks allowed the boys to work off their energies in personal "combat" — and probably served to settle "scores," as well. Off the ship, the boys received periodic drill on the parade grounds; on other occasions, weather permitting, pulling races with the ship's boats were a happier part of their education. Quarterly examinations determined their progress and readiness to join the fleet.

During August and September, there was a flurry of command changes as the Office of Detail, later to be known as the Bureau of Personnel, shuffled skippers through "Old Ironsides" almost before their names could be learned by the apprentices. Captain James A. Greer relieved Henry Adams on 15 August and was himself relieved by Captain Reigart B. Lowry eight days later — giving him the record for shortest term in command of *Constitution* ever. Captain Lowry, in

Constitution *anchored off the Philadelphia Navy Yard shortly after the completion of her third restoration. Note the presence of two pairs of davits on either quarter and spencer gaffs on the fore and main masts.*

turn, was relieved by Commander Augustus P. Cook on 5 September. When Congress resolved to authorize the Navy to provide transportation for exhibits going to the 1878 Paris Exposition, Secretary Richard Thompson knew just the ship: who better than the fabled "Old Ironsides" to give prestige to the business?

Thus, in December 1877, the big frigate was placed back in drydock for eleven days to repair caulking and coppering on the ship's bottom. The "hatch house" that had been raised earlier in the year was torn down. All but two of her guns were landed to make room for cargo. Similarly, since she would be carrying deck cargo as well, her spencer rig also was set ashore.

## FREIGHTER TO FRANCE

Captain Oscar C. Badger, 55-year-old Connecticut Yankee and veteran of both Mexican and Civil Wars, relieved Captain Cook on 9 January 1878. For the next month, he and his crew of nearly 170 sailors and Marines loaded stores, landed unnecessary gear, and got ready to load a variety of cargo which con-

## A Most Fortunate Ship

*Captain Oscar C. Badger.*

stituted the exhibit materials. The ship was moved to Philadelphia's Walnut Street Wharf on 8 February where, for more than two weeks, the cargo was fitted into every nook and cranny in the ship. Last of the exhibits to come aboard were three pieces of railroad rolling stock which were carefully lashed and braced on the spar deck. Last to come aboard was the Marine detachment which would accompany the exhibits to Paris, and five tons of anthracite for the ship's little boiler. Bright and early on the last day of February, the tug *Pilgrim* towed the big frigate away from the wharf and down to the mouth of the Delaware, where "Old Ironsides" was anchored to await a fair wind. Her last trip to Europe began on 4 March, as she headed out into stormy seas.

The entire passage had only one or two days where smooth seas were noted in the log. More common notations were "stormy," "heavy squalls," "very rough," and "pumped out 1 foot of water." No doubt to everyone's relief, the ship rode well, and the train and other cargo stayed in place. On the 29th, an ordinary seaman named Young fell or was washed from the bowsprit while the ship was in a heavy gale, and was lost.

This particular gale — an easterly — struck the ship as she was nearing the western end of the English Channel. For several days, she tacked back and forth on long reaches trying to make headway in the adverse winds and steep seas. It seemed almost as if she couldn't gain an inch. With everyone approaching exhaustion from the continuous sail-handling and pumping, it was decided to take a chance and try sailing as close to the wind as possible, and into the seas, to see if they couldn't reach Carrick Bay at Falmouth without being beaten to pieces or driven on a lee shore. It was, in many respects, a gamble similar to that taken by Elliott in 1835 when, going west in these same waters, he drove her past Scilly. Once again, it was a cliff-hanger. And once again, she made it, her stout bows smashing through the swells, driven by more canvas than many would have dared to sheet home in those conditions. The sheltered peace of the bay allowed everyone the solid night's rest so sorely needed.

Conditions had improved sufficiently by early the next afternoon so that Badger weighed anchor and stood up the Channel for Le Havre, although he still had to do it by a series of tacks back and forth across the waterway. *Constitution* was greeted off Le Havre by the steamer *Jean Bart* at first light on 3 April, furled her sails, and was towed in. While attempting to get her alongside the Customs House Wharf, the pilot caused her to collide with the French naval steamer *Ville de Paris*, smashing the #4 cutter in the after port davits. Off-loading required a week, then the ship was shifted to a little-used berth where she could await the full run of the Exposition and the return of the exhibits later in the year.

In May, Badger made arrangements to have the ship drydocked to make a closer inspection of her port quarter. One plank was found to have been shattered by the collision, some caulking started, and sheathing ripped off. Additional caulking was replaced when it was found to have been poorly done either by the old Navy Yard or Wood, Dialogue. She was undocked and returned to her berth on 1 June.

The months that followed were a challenge, especially to Lieutenant Commander William H. Whiting, the Executive Officer, to keep the crew busy and out of trouble. In many ways, the days aboard recalled those off Philadelphia when the apprentice boys had been aboard, for there were frequent gun drills, cutlass drills, single stick bouts, and small arms practice. Still, liberty ashore and boredom worked their way with some men. Drunkards and deserters were common sights, being returned each morning by the French authorities. Fights occasionally broke out on board. There were at least two stabbings. Captain Badger ordered summary courts martial regularly to deal with these infractions, and they just as regularly awarded confinement and fines to the sinful. "Summary courts" had been established in 1855 as the replacement for the "cat." They continue to be a part of the system today.

Month followed month until 2 December, when *Constitution* moved back to the Customs House Wharf. Two days later, recrated exhibits began arriving from Paris and were taken aboard. The arrival of crates was an almost daily occurrence until 10 January 1879, by which time about a thousand had been received. With everything accounted for and the Marine Guard returned, the old frigate left Le Havre under tow of the tug *Neptun* late on the 16th. Badger's intention was to stand nearly northward across the Channel close hauled until he could change course to the west and let the easterly wind blow him straight into the Atlantic.

## AGROUND

The first few hours went well, the wind steady and the sky clear. The orders were to maintain this course until 2 A.M., then call the Captain and Navigator, and change course for home. The Navigator already was on deck when the appointed hour was tolled, exchanging small talk with the Officer of the Deck, when, high above and ahead of them, could be seen what appeared to be tree tops. Orders to change course were too late: smoothly and steadily, *Constitution* slid aground, the pale expanse of one of the famous chalk cliffs not more than a hundred yards beyond her flying jib boom. She had outsailed her Navigator's estimates by more than thirty miles in about ten hours.

Daylight came. Soon, a British coast guard boat appeared and informed the Americans that they had gone aground under Bollard Head — said to be the only spot on that entire English coast out of range of a lighthouse. Word of "Old Ironsides' " grounding quickly flashed all across southern England and to London. By ten in the morning, five tugs were in the area, together with myriads of lesser craft hoping there might be a windfall for them. But the big frigate had landed gently, remained upright, and was in no danger from the weather. Lighters were brought alongside to remove the guns and her anchor chain. The water tanks were pumped out, and an additional fifty casks were jettisoned. At 3:30 P.M., she was hauled off easily and towed into Portsmouth Naval Shipyard. Three days later, once preparations had been made, *Constitution* was moved into Drydock 11 to learn the damage. Careful inspection showed only that she had lost some sheets of copper and about eighty-five feet of her false keel — nothing serious. She was refloated on the 24th.

While the Americans were getting ready to sail, the owner of one of the tugs on the grounding scene, the *Admiral,* presented Captain Badger with a bill for ₤1500 for "salvage services." He responded with an offer of ₤200. The Britisher went to Chancery Court, seeking the arrest of the ship and her cargo. Counsel for both the American Embassy and the British Foreign Office went before Judge Sir Robert Phillimore to argue against the writ. Given the unity of both governments' lawyers, Phillimore could do little more than deny it. Badger had himself towed out of port by the tug *Malta* at first light the next day (30 January), eager, no doubt, to be clear of the shore.

## RUDDER LOST

It wasn't long before those aboard knew the voyage home was going to be as uncomfortable as the outward trip had been. The strong winds that let her bowl along at ten knots on 3 February became "strong squalls" on the 5th. The

Constitution *on shore at Swanage Point, 16 January 1879.*

barometer stood at 29.56 on the 6th (seas "rough"), dropped to 29.35 on the 7th (the ship "rolling deeply but easily"), to 28.97 on the 8th ("heavy squalls"), and to 28.70 on the 9th. But the 9th also was a day of strange peace; the proverbial calm before the storm. So rare was it that the log-keeper felt compelled to write, "A remarkable instance of pleasant weather with an exceedingly low barometer." The ship next was subjected to seas which caused her to lurch heavily. Winds were screaming out of the southeast at forty knots on the 10th as the barometer slid to a low of 28.36. Very heavy swells came barrelling down on *Constitution* from the northwest. Badger had her lying to on a starboard tack. Hailstones pelted the watch. So far, the cargo had held — but what if —? On succeeding days, the barometer began to climb, but the storm in the frigate's vicinity only grew worse. Badger tried running before the wind while mountain-high seas, oft-times clashing at cross angles, smashed at her stern. That the 80-year-old ship withstood them as well as she did is a testimonial to those who had built her those many years gone by.

During the morning watch on 13 February, the people on the quarterdeck noticed "frequent heavy thumps caused by seas striking stern and rudder." During the following watch, it was discovered that the rudder had been twisted from its head — it was flapping free. The helmsman was guiding a tiller no longer attached to anything. Badger used one part of his crew to trim sails and maneuver the ship as best he could by that means to get her as steady as possible. The carpenter and his gang began their struggle to recover the situation aft. Their first effort was to try and rig a spare topsail yard across the poop with a system of hawsers with which to control the rudder. It failed. Other men went over the side in boatswain's chairs or slings and secured lines to the rudder chains at great risk to their lives. These were led forward on either side and on deck through the gangway ports. By this means, the rudder was steadied for a short time until the chains broke and the hawser chafed through. A spare crossjack yard was sent down to be used as a fair leader for the rudder pendants, but these lines soon chafed through, too. On the men worked, sometimes dangling perilously over the side where they were struck and submerged in the angry sea, working with massive lines and spars that could snuff them out in a twinkling at the slightest error. They could see that the upper gudgeon on the rudder post was weakening; that it could give way and the rudder fall clear at any time. Their calm desperation and perseverance was rewarded after twenty-three hours of effort. The rudder was secured firmly at 8:30 the next morning, when the sea had fallen considerably.

Close to noon on 14 February, *Constitution* was hailed by the English barque *Sagitta,* which offered to take off the crew. Badger, not surprisingly, refused. He asked, instead, that they direct the first steamer she encountered to come to his assistance. *Sagitta* passed on. The *Constitution*s turned their attention to rigging a jury rudder. It took them all day and into the early evening to build their "raft rudder" and get it in place. The chains controlling it were led around both sides of the stern and into the Captain's day cabin where the Marine detachment provided the muscle power. Orders were passed to them by shouted relays down the companionway. Badger set course for Lisbon, the closest port under prevailing conditions.

With the weather abating and a measure of ship control restored, "Old Ironsides" made the 700 miles to Lisbon in four days. A pilot and three tugs got her safely moored up the Tagus River at the end of the second dog watch on the 18th.

Life in the Portuguese capital did not move at the same pace as it did in England. The local authorities were every bit as willing to provide assistance to the Americans, but in their own time. The damaged rudder was unshipped and sent ashore on the 24th, but not until 10 March were they ready to dock the frigate. In the two weeks she was high and dry, new fittings were provided on the stern post and the copper in the area refurbished before a healthy rudder was installed. While they were at it, the ship also received a new main topgallant yard. Later, during the course of back-loading ammunition and stores, one of the carpenter's gang discovered rot in the jib boom, and this, too, was replaced.

Badger happily cleared Lisbon on 11 April without assistance from any steamer and hoped for a fast voyage home. He didn't get it — but neither were there any more disasters. The ship pulled in to Martin's Dock in Brooklyn on 24 May. Offloading the "New York" cargo required only six hours, but the ship remained until the 30th, when she headed south. She off-loaded the "private" Philadelphia exhibits on 6 and 7 June at Philips' Wharf, then shifted to the Navy Yard where all the Government exhibits were taken off in less than eight hours. On the 21st, Badger brought her proper gun battery back aboard: eighteen 32-pounders (Model 1842) and two breech-loading 20-pounder rifles.

## APPRENTICE TRAINING SHIP — "THIRD RATE"

In July 1879, *Constitution* embarked on what was to be her final role as an active unit of the Navy, that of being the mobile school for apprentice boys. Captain Badger got her underway on 19 July and took her to New York, where she entered into a docking and overhaul while still training the youngsters. Captain Francis H. Baker succeeded Badger in command on 2 August.

The ship was in drydock on 7 September when Lieutenant Commander Theodore F. Jewell, the Executive Officer, presented Medals of Honor to Carpenter's Mate Henry Williams and the diminutive Captains of the Top Joseph Matthews and James Horton "for gallant conduct aboard this vessel the 13th Feb. last." It must be remembered that, at this period, the Medal of Honor was the sole personal decoration in use, not merely the highest.

Francis Baker was not a well man when he took command of the old frigate, and had taken himself off to the hospital on 21 August. After a month's absence, it was obvious that he could not retain the command. Jewell was ordered to take the ship until an officer of appropriate seniority could be ordered in. This he did, on 25 September. Commander Oscar F. Stanton, who would be promoted to the rank of Captain early in the new year, relieved Jewell on 1 October, as the overhaul was completing.

*Constitution* left New York on the 8th and was in Norfolk three days later. There, she took on another forty-eight boys. While still there on 15 November, she was again rated as "ship, second class, 20 guns." From the 24th on, she was ready to go to sea but was prevented from doing so by foul winds. She was finally able to clear on 11 December, displaying her "number" (identifying signal flags: G-Q-F-C) for the lookout tower as she passed Cape Henry, southbound for the Caribbean.

## WINTER IN THE SUN

This voyage began much more auspiciously than her last, the log frequently reeling off ten knots as she swiftly left winter behind and gave the youngsters their first taste of the sea. A brief call at Guadaloupe on Christmas Eve was followed by an 11-day visit to Fort de France, Martinique. Third Class Boy Albert Rathbun

*Captain Oscar F. Stanton.*

died and was buried there on 4 January 1880.

The stay in Frederikstadt seems to have been almost idyllic. The boys were most often involved in learning small boat handling, drills that were made fun by frequent pulling and sailing races. When there were infractions of the rules, the boys were punished by having to "toe the seam" (stand with one's toes carefully marking a particular caulk in the deck) for anything up to eight hours, or by missing the evening meal — a marked contrast to the "good old days" when the cat and colt ruled.

The school ship spent the entire month of February 1880 in or near Limon Bay, Colombia, an area near what later became the eastern terminus of the Panama Canal. There, the boys went through the school of the ship with few distractions.

Now-Captain Stanton got underway on 1 March for the return northward. Even before reaching the latitude of Cape Hatteras, Mother Nature reminded them that winter was not yet over, with strong gales, drizzling sleet, and heavy seas. Many a boy discovered a new aspect to being a sailor, and may have wished he hadn't signed on.

After a month and a half at Norfolk, "Old Ironsides" sailed on 16 May for New York, where she received a new draft of boys, and where Stanton had the experts do a survey of the ship to determine how badly she was ageing. She was approved for another training cruise.

This second cruise began on 8 July when, with the assistance of tugs *George L. Garlick* and *Mary A. Hogan,* the big frigate passed northward through Hell's Gate and sailed to Gardiner's Bay, at the east end of Long Island. Operating out of there for the next twelve days, the boys were provided with training at the great guns and with small arms. Fifty-five rounds were fired from the 32-pounders — what a thrill for those impressionable lads.

Following a few days at Newport, the ship went northward, visiting Bar Harbor, Maine, for a week beginning 31 July, then Halifax, Nova Scotia, for four days in mid-August before turning southward again. Brief stops at New Bedford, Massachusetts, Newport, and Lewes, Delaware, provided breaks in the trip deep into Hampton Roads and up the York River to Yorktown, where the old frigate and her young sailors provided some color to the shoreside celebrations marking the centennial anniversary of Cornwallis' surrender. As she was leaving that port, "carried away runner of Mizzen topsail halliards; the yard came down with a run carrying away the starboard yard arm at top-gallant sheet sheeve hole." She anchored for a day off Wormley's Creek to make repairs. She'd been underway again on 4 October for ten hours when "carried away maintopgallantmast four feet above the cap." She anchored again to remove wreckage and make repairs. It seemed that she was literally falling apart. Following a six-week stay in Hampton Roads, the ship returned to the Philadelphia Navy Yard for overhaul.

Test borings were taken throughout *Constitution*'s hull on 15 December which showed that the hull still was quite strong, even though it was showing signs of distortion. The rudder had to be taken ashore again for repair. She had to be thoroughly caulked throughout. And her bilge pumps and heating plant needed to be overhauled. On 4 April 1881, she was moved out to anchorage in the river, pronounced fit enough to resume her relatively undemanding duties.

## ACHES AND PAINS

Captain Stanton sailed his tired ship from Philadelphia on 9 April, under orders to proceed to Washington so that his ship and crew could participate in the dedication of a memorial to Admiral David G. Farragut. They were yet two days shy of Cape Henry when both the middle and lower bobstays carried away at the bowsprit. New ones were set up the next day, and on the 17th the frigate entered Chesapeake Bay, where the gunboat *Yantic* passed her a towline for the trip up the Potomac.

*Constitution*'s deep draft precluded a simple trip to Washington — a fact which appears to have had to be relearned on this occasion. As a result, the ship herself got no closer than the waters off Piney Point, where she anchored near the steam frigate *Tennessee.* Her Marines and sailors went on to the celebration on board *Yantic* and the steamer *Norfolk.* She departed on 7 May as the sun rose, the middle ship in a column with sloops *Saratoga* and *Portsmouth* bound for

*Edwin M. Shepard as a Rear Admiral.*

Norfolk. There, "Old Ironsides" was taken to the Yard where "yard birds" again busied themselves "hunting for rotten places." During the first week in June, iron braces were run through the ship athwartships beneath the gun deck at intervals throughout her entire length. These, it was hoped, would stop the tendency she was showing to sag outward.

The tug *Powhatan* towed her from Norfolk to Newport during the period 9-12 June. Two days after her arrival, Commander Edwin M. Shepard relieved Captain Stanton.

At two bells of the evening watch on 18 July, Third Class Boy C.W. Wheelock attempted to desert by swimming ashore from *Constitution*'s anchorage off Goat Island. He never made it.

## PARTING SHOT

Captain Shepard got his command underway for a short training cruise on 11 August. In a series of daylight runs, he worked his way up the Sound as far as New Haven (15 August), then turned eastward, coming to anchor at New London, Connecticut, on the 26th. For the next few days, there was a gradual increase in the "naval presence" until there were seven units in harbor. They had come to New London to participate in a final centennial observance. Sailmaker Charles E. Tallman was there for the 6 September event and has left this account

*The only known photograph of* Constitution *underway, taken in the summer of 1881 by a soldier at Fortress Monroe, Virginia, as the ship was standing in to Hampton Roads.*

of it:

> ... Today is the celebration of the Massacre of Fort Trumbull, at Groton Height. At noon all the saluting ships fired a salute of 21 guns. The scene was enacted as in 1781, when the British attacked Fort Trumble. At that time a preconcerted signal was made between the American Army & Navy, to fire 2 guns from the fort in the morning, & if all was right, to be answered from the flagship by one gun. The morning was foggy & the British came in, with Benedict Arnold (the traitor) on board the flagship. The two guns were fired from the fort, and Arnold being aware of the American signal, caused the answer of one gun to be fired from the British flagship thus misleading the Americans. The British immediatley landed on both sides of harbor, & moved on the fort thus easily securing its capture. On this day (Sept. 6 1881) the *Constitution* frigate took the part of the British flagship, in the drama and fired one gun & launched the troops & moved on the fort, same as the British did a hundred years ago. The day was foggy as it was then. The smoke of the firing mixing with the fog, made it quite dark and gave the sky the appearance of a copper color. A feeling of depression seemed to be upon everyone. It seemed that nature itself took part in the event of the day.

What irony, that the guns of the ship that had done so much to humble the Royal Navy should end their regular service reenacting the actions of a British attacker.

On 11 September, the tired old frigate resumed her daylight training routine, sailing to an anchorage off New Bedford, then off Cuttyhunk Island, and Bren-

*Midshipmen receiving gunnery instruction on board* Constitution *at Annapolis.*

ton's Reef Light, before returning to Newport. She made one more trip to New London on 2 October, remaining in that port for two weeks. The tug *Rocket* towed her back to Newport.

A few minutes after midnight on 3 November, *Constitution*'s career very nearly came to an end: fire was found in the beams beneath the boiler down on the forward orlop. Alert work by ship's company prevented the situation from getting out of hand, and brought the emergency to a happy conclusion within an hour.

During the dog watches the very next afternoon, the anchorage was struck by heavy squalls. *Constitution* began dragging her anchor; shortly thereafter, she went hard aground by the stern just off Goat Island. She was hauled off and reanchored as the sun rose the next morning. Not a leak.

As it turned out, "Old Ironsides'" moment of truth came on 14 November, in the form of a Board of Inspection and Survey under the leadership of Commodore A.C. Rhind. Their careful and thorough work resulted in what must have been an obvious conclusion: the ship was unsafe structurally to be used at sea. The quality of work at Philadelphia during 1874-6 evidently was so poor that, in 1881, it was almost as if it hadn't happened at all. The Navy of 1881 was at a low point — perhaps its lowest ever. There was no money available for the major overhaul of a ship that ostensibly only recently had had one — especially an obsolete wooden ship.

## END OF AN ERA

It didn't take long for the order to be issued to lay up the 84-year-old frigate. On the 22nd, forty-nine apprentices were transferred to the receiving ship *New Hampshire.* In another two days, fifteen crewmen and 135 more boys went to *New Hampshire* while her twenty-three Marines were taken into the steam frigate *Minnesota.* The ship's topgallant masts were sent down because rot and splitting had been found in the maintopmast head.

No record has been found of the scene when *Constitution* left Newport on 25 November 1881 at the end of a towline from *Tallapoosa.* In late November, the weather on Narragansett Bay almost certainly was sharply cold. The waters were slate gray and probably choppy, little curls of foam looking like rime ice. And there went the old "eagle of the sea," her masts no longer towering to the clouds, no longer supporting glorious billows of canvas in a fresh breeze. If there were any "huzzahs," they were echoes in some old salt's mind as he watched that damned chuffing, smoking gunboat haul that once sleekly free hull out of sight beyond Point Judith. Shed a tear, sailor-man.

Laying her up was done swiftly. Moored at the New York Navy Yard on 27 November, the powder was offloaded the next day; the rigging began coming down on the 29th. Sails and ordnance stores went ashore on 3 December. Anchors were landed and the boats sent to the boat shed on the 5th. Her yards came down on the 8th. A period of rainy weather began on the 12th. The following afternoon, she was "towed to Ordnance dock and secured under steam derrick," which began lifting out her guns that afternoon. The chore was completed before noon on 14 December. It began raining again as the ship was moved back to a backwater berth at the cob dock by the tug *Catalpa.* Shortly before 5 that afternoon, Edwin Shepard hauled down her commissioning pennant from what was left of the mainmast. The fifty-four remaining crewmen were formed up on the dock and marched off into the wet evening to their new home in the receiving ship *Colorado.*

## "GUARDO"

*Constitution* herself became a receiving ship a year or so after this dolorous scene at New York. Towed to the Navy Yard at Portsmouth, New Hampshire, she had an ugly, huge "barn" built above her hull and around her lower masts, making her over into a barracks and assembly hall for transient sailors. Thus she stayed as months passed into years, and years exceeded a decade. A familiar bulk in the skyline of the Navy Yard, the old ship lay there, getting older and weaker. If rot appeared in her planking, other boards were nailed over it. Cement was

**Above:** *Receiving ship at Portsmouth, New Hampshire.* **Left:** *"Guardo" in Boston. An additional layer of sheathing has been installed over decaying outer hull planking.*

used as patching in her bilges. How much longer she might continue to serve in that condition was anybody's guess.

As he himself later told it, Massachusetts Congressman John F. Fitzgerald happened to see a newspaper item sometime during 1896 which reported the old frigate was about to sink at her moorings in Portsmouth if something weren't done. Fitzgerald made a personal tour of inspection to the ship and found the report to be all too true. Upon his return to Washington, he called on Secretary of the Navy John D. Long to see what could be done. Maintenance funds being scarce, and receiving ships being recognized as obsolete ships which would continue to be of service so long as they didn't fall apart, Long could say only that if Congress would authorize it, the ship would be saved. Fitzgerald introduced a resolution in Congress on 14 June 1897 to authorize the repair of the ship sufficient to permit her return to Boston in time for her 100th birthday. That did it. Work was begun immediately to make her tow-worthy. Commander Samuel W. Very, who had made her last trip to Europe as a lieutenant, was placed in charge of the move and given a temporary crew. He brought her back to Boston on 21 September 1897 — one month before her centennial — to be greeted and saluted by major units of the modern Navy. The Boston Navy Yard became her home where, following the celebrations in October, she settled once more into quiet erosion.

# 18 The Long Road Back

## THE "HOUSE" IS LOST

*Constitution*'s return to Boston, and the resultant publicity about her centennial, sparked continuing interest in her well-being among a small number of historical and patriotic groups in the metropolitan Boston area, groups whose memberships included people belonging to famous families of the Revolution as well as those who could wield considerable power in the nation's capital when it was necessary. It was at the insistence of these people that Congress, on 14 February 1900, authorized the restoration of the frigate with non-governmental funds. The Massachusetts State Society of the United Daughters of the War of 1812 took the lead in this project by kicking off a campaign to raise the $400,000 thought necessary to do the job. The program, regrettably, failed despite protracted efforts on the ladies' part.

At the end of 1903, the Massachusetts Historical Society, through its Council, and representing similar bodies in New England, forwarded a memorial to the Congress asking that "the necessary steps forthwith be taken for preserving the 'Fighting Frigate' of 1812; that she be renewed, put in commission as a training ship, and at suitable seasons be in future stationed at points along our coast where she may be easily accessible to that large and ever-increasing number of American citizens who, retaining a sense of affection, ... feel also a patriotic and an abiding interest in the associations which the frigate *Constitution* will never cease to recall." First to sign this document was Charles Francis Adams, President of the Society and descendant of presidents. This was not to be his only involvement with "Old Ironsides," as will appear subsequently.

In his annual report of 1905, Secretary of the Navy Charles Joseph Bonaparte (grand-nephew of the Emperor Napoleon, for whose mother Isaac Hull had carried china for Baltimore on his return from France in 1811) audaciously suggested that the "frigate *Constitution*, 'Old Ironsides,' being old and no longer useful, be used as a target for some of the ships in our North Atlantic fleet and sunk by their fire." When the newspapers reported the Secretary's message, there was an outcry. One is particularly worthy of mention: Moses Gulesian, an Armenian immigrant who had worked his way to wealth in his adopted homeland, offered Bonaparte $10,000 for the frigate so that she would not be destroyed. The outcry was sufficient to restrain Bonaparte from implementing his proposal, and his menace to the old ship ended a few months later when he was transferred to the post of Attorney General by President Teddy Roosevelt. With "Lunchbox Charlie" out of there, an amendment quickly was tacked onto the 1906 naval appropriations act providing $100,000 "to repair the *Constitution* but not for ac-

298

*Inside the "barn," a view, looking forward on the spar deck. Note the four 32-pounder long guns stowed in the bows.*

tive service."

Work was put in hand as soon as the bill became law. Under the direction of Naval Constructor Elliot Snow at the Boston Navy Yard, carpenters went to work stripping away the ugly barn that had hidden the graceful lines of her hull for a quarter-century. Removed, too, was the extra wooden sheathing that had extended down the hull to the waterline. Once again the waist was open but for hammock nettings, just as it had been under Isaac Hull, and the spar deck bulwarks formed a smooth, flowing line with a cap rail enclosing the upper sides of the gun ports. Batteries of guns were cast to represent the cannon of an earlier day, but the design employed was not accurate. The caboose was relocated to its earlier position between the anchor bitts from its 1876 siting under the forward end of the main hatch. Masts were restepped to the topgallants, yards sent up, and the rigging rerove. A billet head, with a dragon in the design, and which was thought to reproduce the one carried in 1812, was installed in place of the "curlycue" model of 1876, but the stern decorations of that refit merely were refurbished. Once again, she took on the appearance of the "eagle of the seas."

*Restepping the mainmast.*

*The last vestiges of the "barn" come off, and the ship begins to look like her old self.*

Virtually no work was done below decks, however, the area of the captain's quarters continuing to be subdivided into individual staterooms. The limited amount of money available to work on her precluded any repairs to the underwater body and only those of a limited nature relative to the outer hull planking; neither was rebuilding of the decaying stern possible. Therein lay the seeds of future problems. Nevertheless, by June of 1907, *Constitution* had, outwardly at least, the appearance of her old self. During Boston's Old Home Week, 28 July - 3 August, Governor Guild of the Commonwealth hosted a reception on board the old frigate which was recalled as having been one of the highlights of the festivities. The total bill for this restoration came in within the budget: $99,996.00.

With the ship once more looking somewhat as she did in her halcyon days, and a celebration of the fact having been duly conducted, *Constitution*'s life settled into a quiet backwater of resting snugly against a pier in the Boston Navy Yard, changing locations from time to time within the Yard, and being taken notice of on holidays through the flying of flags from each of her masts and ceremonies on her spar deck. Sailors attached to the Yard were assigned duties aboard her as guides, touring visitors around topsides and perhaps the gun deck, regaling them with the popular sea stories about her. In the summer months, as many as 500 people a day paid her a call. Thus the years passed.

*"Old Ironsides" on the eve of World War I.*

## A NAME IS LOST AND REGAINED

On 29 August 1916, President Woodrow Wilson signed into law an authorization for the Navy to construct six battle cruisers. This type of warship, combining much of the fire power of a battleship with the lighter armor and greater speed of a cruiser, had gained considerable notice in the English and German navies — then at war — and the victory of the Royal Navy's *Inflexible* and *Invincible* over the crack German armored cruisers *Scharnhorst* and *Gneisenau* off the Falkland Islands in December 1914 appears to have made them desirable to the Americans and Japanese. This Act was of significance to "Old Ironsides," for the name initially assigned to the lead unit was *"Constitution."* Several reassignments of names were made as the contracts were awarded, however, and the name *"Constitution"* finally came to rest on the fifth hull, provided for in March 1917. In order to make the name available, the sailing frigate officially was renamed *Old Constitution* on 1 December of that year. No one appears to have objected. The keel for the battle cruiser was laid at the Philadelphia Navy Yard on 25 September 1920.

A conference was called in Washington in 1921 to bring together the principal naval powers of the world — England, France, Italy, Japan, and the United

*An artist's conception of the battle cruiser* Constitution.

States — to seek a limitation to the shipbuilding programs that then were burgeoning in these countries in what was supposed to be an era of peace following the "war to end all wars." A treaty was completed before the year was out which required massive cutbacks in the fleets and building programs of England and the United States and, to a lesser extent, Japan. Insofar as the American battle cruiser program was concerned, it was dead. The treaty permitted the first two hulls could be completed as aircraft carriers — then considered to be an auxiliary type — but the remainder were to be scrapped. With the final ratification of the treaty on 17 August 1923, the Navy Department took immediate steps to implement it; within eight days, the battle cruisers had been cancelled. The incomplete *"Constitution"* was sold "as is, where is" on the ways for $92,024.40 on 25 October 1923, missing being a present for "Old Ironsides' " 126th birthday by just four days. To get ahead of our story a little bit, the final act in this episode occurred on 24 July 1925, when *Old Constitution* was again named *Constitution*.

## ANOTHER RESTORATION

Exactly two weeks after the scrap sale, the Chief of Naval Operations, Admiral Edward W. Eberle, ordered the Board of Inspection and Survey to conduct a detailed inspection and provide a clear evaluation of *Constitution*'s condition, together with a recommendation for future action. The Board actually conducted its inspection on 19 February 1924. Its report made official the deteriorating conditions obvious to the most casual observer, and much more. She was shipping water at a rate which made it mandatory that a tug come alongside every evening and pump her out. The stern was so decayed that it nearly was falling off. She was badly distorted, so much so that her port side bulged out nearly a foot more than the starboard, the stem skewed nearly nine inches to port, and there was a 14½-inch hog in the hull. All the deck beams were badly decayed at the ends and many in the center section, as well. Virtually all knees and breast hooks were shot through with dry or wet rot. The keelson was broken

303

just abaft the foremast step. Patches of cement were present, filling rot holes in the hold ceiling planking. Nonetheless, perhaps recognizing the popular interest in the ship, the Board concluded that the ship should be "rebuilt and refitted, and preserved and put in condition for preservation for the greatest length of time practicable as a seaworthy vessel.". The preliminary cost estimate was $400,000, and an immediate request for the funding was recommended as the ship was assessed as being on the verge of total ruin.

Secretary of the Navy Curtis D. Wilbur made a personal inspection tour of the old frigate in July 1924 and returned to Washington convinced of the need for immediate action. It was his feeling, however, that the cost of her restoration should be borne by the American people in a popular subscription, thereby giving them the opportunity to participate personally in the restoration of the beloved frigate and also enhance her value to them on a more intimate basis. Accordingly, he included in his next report to Congress a request for authority to restore "Old Ironsides" with monies sought by a nationwide campaign. The authorization was granted in a bill passed on 3 March 1925. Soon, a National Executive Committee, composed of people in the Navy, Government, and the business world, was established to coordinate the effort.

At the Boston Navy Yard, passage of the authorization was the signal to begin all the preparatory work necessary before any actual work could start on the ship. A search was begun for plans on which to base the restoration, and when a set failed to turn up, further research was undertaken to develop the data necessary to fill in the gaps — and there were many. A search was begun for the materials that would be needed, for it was intended, if at all possible, to use those identical to the originals. Finding the massive white oaks, the live oak, and the myriad of natural knees needed was a gargantuan task that took searchers nationwide, much as had been the case in 1794. Lieutenant John A. Lord, Construction Corps, U.S. Navy, one of the few men remaining on the Navy's rolls who had a familiarity with wooden shipbuilding, was assigned to superintend the project. As he and his subordinates dug more deeply into the problems of the ship, the cost estimates rose sharply. Their costing of the Inspection and Survey Report came to $473,725. A more extensive examination of the frigate early in 1926 raised this figure to $650,654, and was upped again to $747,983 when suppliers began to submit bills for the unusual material requirements of the job.

This upward spiral must have been rather disheartening to the fundraisers as they arranged to get the campaign underway. One of the first elements of it was directed at the school children of the country during the last week of October 1925. This particular portion was under the sponsorship of the national Elks organization, and featured patriotic exercises and classroom instruction in *Constitution*'s history. In a year, the overall campaign raised $246,000, of which $148,000 had come from the children and $31,000 from the Navy, Marines, and Coast Guard — just one-third of the estimated requirement.

In September 1926, another major fund-raising effort was begun when Presi-

*The working replica of* Constitution *especially built for the Paramount Pictures film* Old Ironsides, *starring Wallace Beery, Esther Ralston and George Bancroft.*

dent Calvin Coolidge bought from Secretary Wilbur the first of more than one million lithographic copies of a painting of the ship done by the noted marine artist, Gordon Grant. Priced at fifty cents a copy, it provided an important boost to the effort. Often, companies purchased them in quantities as large as 10,000 copies and gave them out to their employees. So many prints were distributed that fifty years later they could be purchased quite readily at the many flea markets in New England — but not for fifty cents. Grant's original painting was hung in the White House.

Paramount Pictures assisted in bringing "Old Ironsides" into public consciousness by the production of the movie "Old Ironsides," starring Wallace Beery, Charles Farrell, George Bancroft, and Esther Ralston. A richly funded picture for the time, the Maine-built ship *Llewellyn J. Morse* was altered to take the starring role, and the city of Tripoli was recreated on Catalina Island off California as the setting of the principal action. Involving a cast of over 2000 and a fleet of nearly twenty vessels, the story was nonetheless only slightly related to the ship's history. It premiered on 6 December 1926.

Back in Boston, as the year 1927 opened, Lieutenant Lord was moving nearer to the actual commencement of the restoration. The problem of materials had begun to be resolved. Stocks of white oak had been located in southern Ohio and West Virginia, while white oak knees had been contracted for in Delaware. Douglas fir from the State of Washington was substituted for the long leaf yellow pine originally used in deck planking when stocks of the latter in the dimensions required were found to be inadequate. Fir similarly was substituted for white pine in the new masts. Live oak, which might have proved impossible to acquire, was found in Commodore's Pond on the Naval Air Station at Pensacola, Florida. It evidently had been cut in the 1850's for an unrealized building program when that site was a shipyard; some 1500 tons of the stuff was shipped northward.

John Lord also had to locate the men and the tools capable of doing the shipwright's work in the old manner. He scoured the East Coast to collect his resources. An old time futtock saw, for example, was found in Kittery, Maine, and brought to the Yard, as were a giant planer and a treenail machine from Bath, Maine. These and other esoteric equipment he located in sheds near Drydock #1 in the Yard. A steam box, built of steel plates and bars, was installed so that large timbers could be steamed and bent to shape.

The Secretary of the Navy authorized the commencement of the restoration on 13 April 1927, and Lord went to work immediately, removing bulkheads and such furniture as remained in the old ship, as well as the gun batteries. In accordance with a Congressional authorization of 3 March 1927, many of these materials were sold to add to the funds raised by the National Committee. The wood and metal was used to produce cigarette boxes, bookends, ashtrays, medallions, picture frames, and other memorabilia. Commodore Vanderbilt is said to have purchased $800 worth of old air port frames to install in a yacht he then was having built in Connecticut. Another man is said to have completely furnished a room of his house with furniture made from *Constitution* wood.

*Constitution* was moored in Drydock #2 during 25-27 April in order to remove her masts and bowsprit, and to check the ship's hog. From what he saw at this time, Lieutenant Lord concluded that the frigate was so weak, distorted, and hogged that there was a distinct possibility she would fall apart if the dock were pumped dry. Special plans were drawn up to insure against this disaster.

In the weeks that followed, the ship was shored thoroughly internally, using longitudinal x-bracing and slip joints worked into the cap pieces to permit adjustment as the ship came out of the water. A pyramid of heavy timbers was erected just forward of the mainmast on the spar deck, over which were run steel cables around the stem and to harpins across the stern in order to "lift" her drooping extremities and to counter the hog. About 150 tons of ballast also was embarked for this latter purpose. An 80-foot-long "crib" was constructed to fit around the ship's bottom to cradle the sagging hull as it settled onto the blocks on the drydock floor. And to brace the ship further, a whole forest of shoring timbers was prepared and stowed in appropriate places about the dock. A crowd of 10,000 people was on hand when John Lord carefully moved *Constitution* into Drydock #1 on 16 June 1927 — eight days short of the 94th anniversary of her first entry into the same dock. Slowly pumping down the dock and checking and rechecking the old ship at every step of the way, she was landed successfully on the blocks, well shored and braced, without collapse or further distortion. So far, so good.

The first phase of the actual restoration work consisted of removing all decayed wood in the ship. Because delays were being experienced in the delivery of large timbers, the work proceeded slowly and involved few men. Things began to move more dramatically in November when the white oak keelson timbers finally arrived — seven months late. Two large holes were cut in the frigate's bows, on either side of the stem below the berth deck level, to permit entry of these large timbers directly into the bowels of the ship. Through the ensuing

Constitution *enters Dry Dock #1 of Boston Navy Yard, in 1927. The cables supporting her sagging extremities can be seen crossing the pyramid of heavy timbers amidship.*

months, the keelson was replaced and assistant (or "sister") keelsons installed to increase the ship's longitudinal strength. Working upward, short-spliced futtock sections were replaced with full-length members, a new cutwater was installed above the waterline, and the big task of totally rebuilding the stern undertaken. It was for this latter job that the steam box was particularly important, for the timbers going into the "tuck" below the Captain's cabin had both to twist and bend to fit the shape; after being saturated with boiling linseed oil and steamed in the box, they were quite pliant. By January 1929, major internal structural work had been completed to the level of the gun deck port sills.

In February, the National Executive Committee reported that collections to date had reached $660,000 before deduction of fund-raising costs.

The work of rebuilding the hull's upper works commenced as winter turned to spring, the problem of eliminating the distortion of the one-foot skew to port demanding the best efforts of all those involved. Caulking of the underwater body was begun in mid-summer and went into the fall. On Navy Day (27 October), a large gathering watched as the newly constructed bowsprit was slipped into place. Nearly all the ceiling planking had been replaced by year's end; the outer hull planking was on to a point midway up the spar deck gun ports.

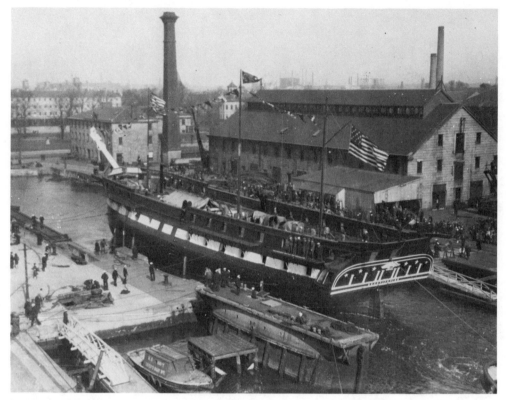

*A refurbished* Constitution *leaves Dry Dock #1 on 15 March 1930.*

If things were going well in the ship, they weren't with the fund raising campaign. After four years of trying, it was becoming apparent to those involved that they had gone as far as they could go, that they had entered the condition of diminishing returns. Faced with this fact, and having *Constitution* halfway to health, the Congress was prevailed upon to appropriate the monies needed to bring the project to completion. Reluctantly, in the face of the "Great Depression," an authorization for funding "up to $300,000" was approved. The national campaign had raised a total of $942,599.23, of which $296,364.97 was eaten up by expenses.

*Constitution* left Drydock #1 on 15 March 1930, her hull sound and freshly coppered, and subsequently spent a day moving across the harbor to Drydock #3 in South Boston to have her new masts stepped. In keeping with tradition and ancient sailor superstition, coins were placed beneath each one: a five-dollar gold piece under the fore, a silver dollar under the main, and a 1797 copper penny under the mizzen.

The emphasis of the project now shifted to the internal layout and the installation of fittings. Stylistically, the design of the cabins and furnishings was that prevalent during the mid-19th century, the earliest period for which Lieutenant

*The "Shipmate" stove installed inside the caboose to accommodate the modern crew, 1931.*

Lord seems to have had information. It was, therefore, less spartan than that present in the War of 1812 or earlier days. A "typical" brig was installed on the berth deck, although Lord said he had no evidence of one ever having been fitted in the ship.

The batteries of 24-pounder long guns and 32-pounder carronades cast for the ship, while far better representations than those of the 1906-7 they replaced, still were not completely accurate for the War of 1812: for example, firing locks were omitted.

President Herbert Hoover entered office in 1929 and with him came a new set of officials. The new Secretary of the Navy was Charles Francis Adams, the same Charles Francis Adams whose signature had been first on the Massachusetts Historical Society's petition more than a quarter century earlier. With Mr. Adams' advent in the Navy Department seems to have come the idea of having *Constitution*, once the restoration was completed, visit many ports around the United States so that the people who gave their money to her continued well-being could see what they had accomplished and take fresh pride in their heritage.

The prospect of voyaging in *Constitution* was taken into consideration in the internal fittings of the ship. Modern "head" facilities were adapted and installed in the bow head area, in "cabinets" forward on the gun deck, and in the quarter galleries. A modern stove was installed on the hearth of the old caboose so that a crew could be messed aboard. Water tankage and lines were installed, as was a

*Commander Louis J. Gulliver.*

lighting system. Provisions were made for mounting peloruses on the waist rails, port and starboard, to assist the Captain in maneuvering the ship in coastal waters.

On 8 October 1930, *Constitution* made her first ceremonial trip around Boston harbor. It came about as a part of the festivities surrounding the national convention of the American Legion in Boston, and for it she had the company of five cruisers, six destroyers, a submarine — and four tugs. The cruiser *Memphis* marked the occasion with a 21-gun salute as airplanes flew low overhead. This was, one might say, the first "turnaround cruise."

The remaining work went swiftly under the impetus of the forthcoming grand tour. Yards were swayed into place and rigging completed. A full set of sails was provided by a generous contributor, although there was no official intention to sail her. A crew of sailors and Marines was determined upon and orders for their transfer issued. On 14 March 1931, a set was issued for Commander Louis J. Gulliver, then Executive Officer of the cruiser *Rochester* in the Caribbean, to proceed and report as Prospective Commanding Officer, *USS Constitution*. Gulliver had no more than sixty days in which to become familiar with his unique command and prepare for the long voyage ahead.

During the latter part of June, the ship was opened to visitors, giving the people of metropolitan Boston an opportunity to see first-hand the transformation that had taken place in "their" ship, as well as the new crew an opportunity to practice handling crowds on board. A record 3595 came on board on the 15th. Two gentlemen visitors one day were seen conducting a "commissioning" ceremony of their own on the gun deck: checking first to see if any crew member was watching, each took a hip flask from a pocket and christened the grog tub with a few drops. Most fitting.

On 1 July 1931, after nearly a half-century in limbo, *Constitution* was recommissioned "in an inactive status for exhibition purposes only" in a ceremony that gave voice to the anticipation and enthusiasm engendered during the four years of her rejuvenation. As recorded by the Boston *Evening Transcript*:

> Thousands of persons, including a large number of school children, assembled for the exercises which were held on the athletic field near the pier where the historic frigate was moored. In honor of the occasion all the ships in the yard displayed all their pennants and many of the buildings nearby were decorated with signal pennants of many hues... The officers of the Yard and those attached to the various vessels were in full dress uniform, resplendent in cocked hats, gold braid and swords. On the athletic field had been erected a canopied grandstand for the speakers and special guests...
>
> After the speechmaking on the athletic field (by Rear Admiral Philip Andrews of the campaign committee, Boston's Mayor James J. Curley, Senator David I. Walsh, Governor Joseph B. Ely, former Secretary of the Navy Curtis D. Wilbur, and Assistant Secretary of the Navy Ernest Lee Jahncke) the second part of the ceremony, the actual commissioning of the vessel, took place on the afterdeck of the *Constitution*. There Rear Admiral Nulton (the Commandant) read the commission and Commander Gulliver received it and read his orders. At the moment the frigate was placed in com-

Constitution *awaiting recommissioning, July 1931.*

mission the commission pennant of blue, with thirteen white stars, and forked ends of
red and white, was hoisted to the afterpeak. At the same time the Navy Yard battery
fired the national salute of twenty-one guns.

The total cost of the restoration was reported as $987,000.

## GULLIVER'S TRAVELS

Hardly had the festivities ended than Captain Gulliver had his crew hard at
work, preparing for the morrow's sailing. There was the usual "organized confusion" of getting aboard last-minute stores, attending to late-breaking problems,
and making final checks of duty assignments for the crew of six officers, sixty
sailors, and fifteen Marines. Moored nearby was the mine-sweeper *Grebe,* under
the command of Lieutenant Emil H. Petri, which would provide the tow for
*Constitution* on this extended tour. This was decided upon, not because the ship
couldn't be sailed, but to ensure adherence to a tight schedule. The 950-ton
minecraft had been commissioned in 1919 and had participated in the unherald-
ed, but dangerous sweeping operation in the North Sea after World War I. For
the coming three years she again would be in a position of playing an important,
but largely unnoticed role. She would not only tow the old frigate from place to
place: at each port she would tie up alongside and provide power for her charge.

Quietly — no official ceremonies had been laid on — *Grebe* got *Constitution*
away from her berth at the Yard at about noon on 2 July. The departure time
was common knowledge, however, and soon the waters were churned by craft of
all sizes busy giving them a proper send-off. Outside Boston Light, the well-
wishers dropped away and the ships turned north.

First port of call was Portsmouth, New Hampshire. On hand to greet them the
next morning were destroyers *Breckinridge, Wilkes,* and *Barney,* and Coast
Guard cutters *Tampa, Ossipee,* and *Agassiz.* In a routine that would become all
too familiar, local dignitaries were the first aboard to welcome "Old Ironsides" to
their town, then the ship was opened to public visiting. That evening, a banquet
was tendered and the next day, being the Fourth of July, there was a mammoth
parade, followed by a variety of sports programs in and around the harbor, and a
dance in the evening. Civic and social groups vied with one another to do "Old
Ironsides" and her men honor. Boy Scouts helped control the crowds as they
waited to visit the ship and helped ensure they got up and down the often steep
gangways without mishap. Nearly 31,000 people boarded the ship in the nine
days of visiting during the stay, coming from miles around to take advantage of
the once-in-a-lifetime opportunity.

There followed brief stops at Bar Harbor and Bath, Maine (Lieutenant Lord's
home town), before spending a week in Portland. During this period, when she
had to get underway from anchor, *Constitution*'s crew learned that there was
something special about her mode of weighing anchor. Unlike modern ships, she
did not take the anchor chain directly to the capstan; instead, it was clamped to a
"voyol," or "lazy jack," by means of "nippers" (clamps), and the endless lazy jack

went 'round the capstan. It took a number of tries by the 20th century sailors before they learned to get a sufficient number of nippers securing the two to bear the weight of the hook as it came off the bottom. No one but those involved seems to have become aware of the several false starts which occurred.

*Constitution* and *Grebe* headed south on a daylight trip that brought them to Gloucester on the afternoon of 23 July. There, her arrival was announced by repeated blasts on the fire house siren, and she was escorted into the harbor by seven Coast Guard cutters as a 21-gun salute boomed out from French 75s stationed in Stage Fort. The usual round of exercises and social events followed. One night, small pleasure boats formed a ring around the old frigate and, on signal, lighted the waters around her with a circle of red flares. A barnstorming air show added to the excitement early on another evening.

*Constitution*'s greeting at Marblehead on the 29th was hardly less noisy, the guns of Fort Sewall providing the salute. This, of course, had been the port in which "Old Ironsides" had sought refuge from pursuing British warships in 1814, when the countryside had rallied in readiness to defend her. On this later occasion, the Marbleheaders made sure no one could doubt their continued affection. It was an event-filled two-day visit.

*Constitution* and *Grebe* next proceeded through the Cape Cod Canal to New Bedford, where whale boat races were an unusual feature of the festivities, and then on to Providence, Newport, New London, Montauk, and Oyster Bay, Long Island, site of Theodore Roosevelt's home. Insufficient water in the planned anchorage caused the frigate to anchor in a less accessible location, so that a mere 4000 people paid calls in three days.

Underway once more on 27 August, the travellers headed east around Montauk Point and then back west for New York City. This "long way 'round" was necessitated by the low bridges over New York's East River. A few hours were spent in Gravesend Bay as a "grand entrance" was organized, then destroyers *McDougal, Porter,* and *Upshur,* led the way into the Hudson River at 3:30 on the afternoon of the 29th. Three Coast Guard cutters were in column on either side, and hundreds of private and public small craft milled about the parade. *Constitution* was moored to Pier 113 at 79th Street, and one of the first to board was August F. Smith, who had been an apprentice on board a half century earlier. The cancellation of the scheduled visit to Newark — low bridges again — resulted in "Old Ironsides" remaining in the "Big Apple" until 14 September. During the extended stay, the firm of Abercrombie and Strauss, upon learning that Gulliver's crew was showering with a perforated bucket, donated "the very latest model in portable, outdoor free-standing showers" for their use. Over 102,000 people walked her decks in fifteen days.

Moving once more through the waters where she eluded an entire British squadron in 1812, the frigate rounded into Wilmington, Delaware, where Isaac Hull had scraped her bottom, welcomed aboard nearly 155,000 Philadelphians during her stay in the City of Brotherly Love, and then stopped at Newport News

*Armistice Day, 1931.* Left to right: *Secretary of the Navy Charles F. Adams, Mrs. Herbert Hoover, President Hoover, and Captain Gulliver.*

before anchoring off Yorktown, Virginia, in time to be the "star" of the celebrations commemorating the 150th anniversary of Cornwallis' surrender. Keeping her company in the stream were the battleships *Arkansas* and *Wyoming,* and the French cruisers *Suffren* and *Duquesne.*

Navy Day 1931 found *Constitution* in Daltimore where Secretary of the Navy Adams hosted a dinner for 50 on board. The Naval Academy Band provided musical entertainment. While these pleasantries were going on, the papers of that date were calling attention to reports that President Hoover intended to direct the Navy to bring the frigate to Washington and lay her up with a caretaker crew of twenty-five in order to save the costs involved in continuing the projected tour ($50,000 had been spent thus far). It required only four days for public outcry to cause officialdom to deny the proposal, whether or not there was any truth to it. *Constitution* would be visiting the federal capital, but then she would go on.

*Grebe* towed *Constitution* to the Washington Navy Yard on 7 November after having spent four days off Annapolis upon leaving Baltimore so that the Brigade of Midshipmen could tread the deck of the "eagle of the seas." President and Mrs. Hoover, together with Secretary Adams, paid an Armistice Day visit to the ship. She lay there for eleven days as over 35,000 people came aboard.

Leaving Washington on the 18th, *Constitution* visited Wilmington, North Carolina (where her departure was delayed a few hours by fog and the smoke

315

from nearby *forest fires!*), Charleston, and Savannah, before arriving at Brunswick, Georgia on 12 December. Because it was from this area that the live oak had been shipped to Boston in 1795, the local populace viewed the visit as a sort of homecoming. In fact, these Georgians were vying with the residents of Annapolis and Boston (the eventual winner) to have the ship homeported with them when the grand tour ended. Among the 27,000 who came aboard was the one millionth visitor since the start of the trip. It was here that the ship was "captured" by a bevy of twenty-five Georgia beauties costumed as pirates in an event that was a publicist's dream. Captain Gulliver managed to maintain a proper image throughout the high jinks and chose not to record his view of the proceedings for posterity.

Jacksonville was the next stop, and then Christmas was spent in Miami. While his crew enjoyed the resort city, Captain Gulliver took a few days of leave to spend the holiday with his family in Washington. New Year's Eve found the two ships at Key West for what must have been a very quiet celebration.

Pensacola was the first of the Gulf ports to be visited, the stay lasting from 6 to 11 January 1932. Here, a basketball team from *Constitution* was overwhelmed by a local five, 53 to 18 — due to "lack of training." The fact that live oak had been shipped to Boston for the recent restoration from Commodore's Pond piqued local curiosity, so that over 35,000 Pensacolans came to the ship.

Following a daylight voyage, *Constitution* and *Grebe* spent a week at Mobile, Alabama, and a whopping 120,000 visitors demonstrated that interest in the fabled frigate was high in the Deep South.

It was Mardi Gras week at New Orleans when the two travelers arrived following a short visit to Baton Rouge. Their compatriot at Yorktown, the battleship *Arkansas,* also pulled in, and the crews had a *grand time* in the pre-Lenten madness. Nearly 200,000 visitors were received in the frigate. The pet monkey Rosie, belonging to *Grebe*'s crew, was absent upon sailing on 12 February. The gloom felt by the crew was alleviated, however, as the ships reached the mouth of the Mississippi. While they watched in disbelief, a seaplane appeared on the northern horizon, circled the ships, and landed nearby. Taxiing close to *Grebe,* the pilot delivered the errant mascot to her delighted masters.

Between 14 February and 19 March, *Constitution* and *Grebe* made calls at the Texas ports of Corpus Christi, Houston, Galveston, Beaumont, Port Arthur, and Orange — a last-minute addition to the schedule. Captain Gulliver was marshal of the Texas Independence Day parade in Galveston and laid a wreath at the Texas Heroes Monument. In Beaumont, he was taken ill and had to be hospitalized. Lieutenant Commander John H. Carson, the Executive Officer, became acting captain in order that the schedule of port calls could be maintained.

Carson's first chore upon leaving Orange was to see his venerable charge forty miles across Calcasieu Lake and up the Calcasieu River to Lake Charles, Louisiana, on 19 March. The more than 37,000 visitors in the ensuing three days reflected the great local interest in the ship and must have made the effort seem all worthwhile.

Moving back into open waters on 22 March, the ships made short visits to Gulfport, Mississippi, and Port St. Joe, Florida, before arriving at the twin cities of Tampa-St. Petersburg, where Captain Gulliver again was in command. One of the people to come aboard here was Charles Nowack, who reported himself aboard as "gun Captain, Gun #11," which he had been many years before. Despite his seventy-six years, he flitted about the ship and even headed into the rigging. His exuberance led Gulliver to caution him against further efforts. Mrs. Arthur Drapeau became the two millionth visitor during this same port call, which marked the end of the Atlantic Coast/Gulf Coast phase of *Constitution*'s grand tour.

*Grebe* towed "Old Ironsides" back to the Washington Navy Yard, arriving on 16 April 1932. There they remained, but for one brief move, until 8 December, resting up and refurbishing the old frigate after the passage of over two million people across her decks. The one brief move came in mid-May when the ships moved to an anchorage off Alexandria for two days during the dedication of the Washington Masonic Memorial building. It was a time of high winds and drenching rains, and "Old Ironsides" gave everyone an unexpected thrill by dragging her anchor. *Grebe* brought her restless charge under control, however, before she could go aground down the Potomac, and returned her to her previous site. While resting at the nation's capital, there were many changes made in the crew. Captain Gulliver remained, but he received Lieutenant Commander Henry Hartley as Executive Officer, replacing Carson, together with other officer replacements. Hartley's young son, Henry, Jr., was christened on board on 26 June. Secretary Adams hosted a Bastille Day luncheon aboard on 14 July; the guest of honor was French Ambassador Paul Claudel. President Hoover also visited the ship again before she departed.

*Grebe*, now commanded by Lieutenant Andrew Simmons, picked up the towline once more on the morning of 8 December, she and her charge heading for the Pacific. A five-day call at the U.S. Naval Base at Guantanamo Bay, Cuba — "Gitmo," to the Navy — broke the voyage across the Caribbean to the Panama Canal. Christmas was spent at Cristobal in the Canal Zone. It seems strange that it should have been here that "Old Ironsides' " crew should have been hosted to a showing of the movie of the same name by Paramount Pictures, but thus it was. *Constitution*'s actual westward transit of the Canal occurred between six in the morning and 3:40 P.M. on 27 December, under the care of *Grebe* and the Panama Canal tug *Gorgona*. While at Balboa, on New Year's Day 1933, President Harmodio Arias of Panama and his wife, together with U.S. Ambassador Roy T. Davis and his wife, were received on board, attended by the Canal Zone authorities.

Following some minor repairs, *Constitution*, towed by the submarine tender *Bushnell* on most of this 2800-mile leg, and *Grebe* sailed into the Pacific waters

Constitution *passing through the Gaillard Cut of the Panama Canal, with the tug* Gorgona *alongside.*

on the morning of 7 January. The trip northward proved to be a rough one, a storm in the Gulf of Tehuantepec giving the ship a "severe wrenching" and opening many deck seams. San Diego was made safely, however, on the 21st. Here began the familiar sequence of port visits as the famed frigate moved steadily northward, her arrival sparking even more interest at each port than had been the case earlier in the tour. This first port call accommodated nearly 180,000, but the second, in San Pedro (harbor for Los Angeles) amassed an amazing 478,000 callers in three weeks. The highest single visitor day was the 3rd of March 1933, when 36,400 people crossed her decks! It is said that the waiting line was ten abreast and three miles long — an incredible sight! While succeeding port calls were similarly spectacular, none matched San Pedro's "human sea" — over 357,000 in San Francisco Bay (including the 3 millionth visitor) and more than 500,000 in the greater Puget Sound area. This northward trip required just five months.

Constitution and *Grebe* headed south once more on 19 July, generally visiting smaller ports previously bypassed, although a second call in San Francisco Bay netted another 67,000 callers, and a second stop at San Pedro another 100,000.

Bushnell *tows* Constitution *into San Diego, California, 21 January 1933. The aircraft carriers* Lexington *and* Saratoga *in the background were completed from two battle cruiser hulls.*

Arriving in San Diego once more on 3 November, the two ships paused to winter over and make routine repairs. It was in San Diego that Captain Gulliver's daughter, Grace, was married to Lieutenant Wells Thompson on the frigate's spar deck.

The final leg of this epic grand tour by the 136-year-old frigate began on 20 March 1934 when the tender *Bushnell* again picked up the tow for the voyage to Balboa. *Grebe* sailed with them and would resume her familiar role once the Canal was transitted. As it turned out, the voyage was without incident. The Canal was traversed on 7 April, and the next morning *Grebe* and *Constitution* moved out of Cristobal on the final leg. The trip essentially was over. The great enthusiasm engendered by the prospect of her visits was now but a memory. People were moving to new interests, no matter how sweet the memories were. Following two quick stops — at St. Petersburg and Charleston — home came the travellers to Boston on 7 May, fatigued from an epic towing operation of some 22,000 miles and the reception of 4,614,762 visitors into the ship's limited confines.

Captain Gulliver hauled down the commissioning pennant on 8 June and placed *Constitution* "out of commission" but "in service," turning over responsibility for her to the "senior officer on board," Lieutenant Harry St. J. Butler, who had been her Navigator throughout her travels.

# 19 Until The Bicentennial

## IN SERVICE

In placing *Constitution* "out of commission, in service," the Navy was, in effect, returning the old frigate to the status she had had when Isaac Hull was ordered to replace the resigned Silas Talbot in 1801: she would be assigned a small crew to oversee her day-to-day existence and to ensure that her most pressing material needs were attended to. This crew was established as consisting of one Lieutenant, one Lieutenant (junior grade), one Boatswain, one Gunner, and twenty-six enlisted men. Because she was not in commission, Lieutenant Butler was not the "Captain," but instead functioned more as a "project officer," keeping the Yard Commandant apprised of the ship's needs and pleading her case for money and materials. He also was responsible for the handling of visitors on board — comprising on the order of 100,000 annually in the 1930's — and for the support of ceremonies held on board.

One of the concerns of the people in the ship, now that she would be essentially immobile for the foreseeable future, was to provide better facilities for her safety than the few fire hoses available. The proposal to install an automatic sprinkler system was turned down by the Bureau of Construction and Repair in June 1934 because of funding limitations. The need was recognized, however, and Lieutenant Butler directed to bring it up again for the next funding period.

Looking ahead to the winter, the lieutenant also requested that a heating system be installed, as his men were living aboard and New England winters could be severe. He won this proposal: a system of steam radiators fed from the Yard boiler was installed in the living areas late in October. In February, he reported that the system would have to be changed as the steam heat was causing severe drying of the timber near the units. A humidifier subsequently was installed to ease this problem. A forced air system finally was installed in the mid-1950's.

An inspection report dated 27 September 1935 stated that the hull and sheathing were in excellent condition, with only about a 1-2-inch growth of mussels. Most coamings around the spar deck hatches were rotted and needed replacement, as did three on the gun deck. The sails, still stowed aboard, no longer were serviceable. On the "plus" side, the sprinkler system had just been installed, complementing the half-hourly rounds of the entire ship being made by the crew between sunset and sunrise, a practice that continues to this day. Six weeks later, a letter from the Yard said that deterioration in the ship was occurring more rapidly than had been estimated earlier when requesting funds for her maintenance, and indicated an additional $34,620 was necessary for caulking, replacing coamings, and renewing twenty knees and bulwark planking. Significantly, it also requested a statement of policy concerning whether just adequate repairs were to be made or was an effort to be made to ensure historical accuracy through proper restoration. The Bureau of Construction and Repair responded on 9 December that "… it is considered that the vessel should be, in general, maintained as an exact replica of the original ship, both in design and materials." In practice, this meant that the ship would be kept just as she had completed the previous restortion, which, as has been briefly noted, was not necessarily as the ship originally was, nor did it reflect any one period of service.

*Constitution* was docked briefly, 30 September-2 October 1936, while seventy-five sheets of copper were renewed along the water line. Electrolytic action had eaten them through. During the same season, considerable work was done on the port bow, where timbers around the bridle port and Number 1 gun port had rotted out. Nearly $30,000 was spent in these and other repairs.

As the years went by and insufficient monies were provided, "Old Ironsides" slowly deteriorated. Among other money-saving expedients, her yards and masts gradually were landed, and her rigging reduced. The sails, which finally had been stored ashore in December 1935, rotted away without replacement or were cut up for souvenir purposes. Many, many of her smaller and more portable fittings disappeared for many reasons: belaying pins rotted out or became mementos; muskets and cutlasses adorned offices and mantle pieces; paintings likewise went to offices and board rooms; silver went… With the limited crew and the pressures of the grand tour, there never had been the opportunity to inventory and control the many objects constantly coming aboard. The reduction in personnel at the decommissioning and the easy access afforded by her being berthed amidst the hustle and bustle of a navy yard combined to make such "requisitions" possible. In a sense, it was a price paid for being so popular with the citizenry; many wanted a part of her in their everyday lives.

On 21 September 1938, during the course of the great hurricane which struck New England at that time, *Constitution* broke loose from her moorings, taking Lieutenant (junior grade) Arthur Barrett and his crew on an unexpected voyage on the waters of Boston harbor. They didn't go far, however, as the winds rammed her into the destroyer *Ralph Talbot,* giving the latter a good gash. "Old Ironsides," true to her name, suffered nothing more than gouges in her hull. Crewmen from the "tin can" leaped across to help moor the errant frigate and keep her from further harm. For the rest of her career, *Ralph Talbot* bore a brass plate recalling the incident.

## BACK IN COMMISSION

During the Summer of 1940, President Franklin D. Roosevelt toured New England, warming up for his bid for a third term in the White House. In Newport, he saw the 1854 sailing corvette *Constellation,* and in Boston, of course, he saw *Constitution.* Being a long-time naval buff and a former Assistant

# A Most Fortunate Ship

*A* housed-over Constitution *without topgallant masts, and a bereft* Constellation *share a Boston pier in 1947.*

Secretary of the Navy, as well as an astute political leader who recognized that his country soon would be at war, Roosevelt ordered that these two veterans of the "Old Navy" were to be placed back in commission to serve as symbolic flagships in the fleet, and to inspire the citizenry to a higher sense of patriotism. For *Constitution,* the formal ceremony took place just two weeks later, on 24 August, with Lieutenant Commander Hermann P. Knickerbocker in command. At the same time, the gallant old frigate was assigned the unglamorous designation of "IX-21"; "miscellaneous unclassified vessel #21."

During 1941, as the war came closer, Captain Knickerbocker was ordered to more pressing duties, being succeeded in command by 58-year-old Clarence E. McBride, a retired Lieutenant recalled to active duty.

A melancholy duty assigned to *Constitution* during World War II was to be the place of confinement for officers awaiting courts martial. The several gentlemen for whom this was the case were maintained in the Captain's quarters, Marines from the Yard Barracks and members of ship's company providing the sentries at the cabin doors.

*Constitution,* under her new Captain, Lieutenant Commander Owen W.

Huff, was docked for the first time in nearly nine years during 28 July-2 August 1945. Test borings of the hull found it to be in very good condition. However, 210 sheets of copper, mostly at the water line, had to be replaced, and the stern under the cabin required caulking.

*Constellation* was moved up to Boston from Newport, in October 1946, and the two veterans existed side by side, *Constitution* the visited ship and the other providing quarters for the crews. In fact, the two ships began sharing a common Captain and crew. To ease maintenance, "houses" had been built over their spar decks. Unlike the one *Constitution* had borne at the turn of the century, the new one hardly extended above the line of the bulwarks.

As the armed forces were reduced following the end of World War II, so, too was the seniority of *Constitution*'s Captain: following Huff, there came a Naval Reserve Lieutenant (for a few months) and then two Chief Warrant Boatswains. Later, junior officers in the ranks of Lieutenant and Lieutenant (junior grade) completing their obligated service filled the billet.

The United States Post Office issued a stamp commemmorating "Old Ironsides' " 150th birthday in October 1947, the only U.S. warship so honored.

In 1949, a program was begun to refurbish the ship, set up her upper masts, and give her back her graceful lines. The *SS Kenyon Victory* arrived about 15 August and unloaded Douglas fir timbers from Oregon to be used in the new spars. For the next year or so, a small group of workers turned out spars, renewing almost every "stick" other than the lower masts, and the bowsprit, as well. The low "house" was removed during March 1950. In April, Chief Warrant Boatswain Knied Christensen relieved Louis Wood in ceremonies held on board *Constellation* so as not to interfere with the visitors. In September, crew members participated in the celebrations attending the Yard's 150th birthday in "early Navy" uniforms prepared by the Yard Sail Loft.

The early 1950's found maintenance efforts shifting from the spars to the hull itself. Many areas of outer hull planking were showing signs of rot after nearly twenty-five years. At this time, the Yard chose to experiment by substituting red oak for white in these planks; it was more readily available and was thought to be more easily treated with the approved preservatives of the day. Unfortunately, Time was to prove the experiment a failure, for severe conditions of deterioration were to appear within fifteen years, and it was seen that the preservatives had inadequately penetrated the wood. The shipwrights of 1797 had recorded that red oak was the poorest of the oak family, and they were proven right.

At about this time, some people in the Navy became concerned with the fact that several historic ships remained in the inventory, but were not specifically provided for in the budget. Monies supporting their continued existence were coming from other "pots" as skillful managers could make them available. In an effort to clarify the situation, the Congress was approached for a decision as to the future of these units and, if the Navy was to continue their maintenance, for the funds with which to do so. The ships in question were *Constitution,* the sole

*"Old Ironsides" at the beginning of January 1950.*

survivor of the original program; *Constellation*, the corvette constructed, in part, of timbers from the earlier frigate of the same name; *Hartford*, Admiral Farragut's flagship at Mobile Bay; *Olympia*, the flagship of Commodore Dewey at Manila in 1898; and the battleship *Oregon*, which had made a dramatic high-speed transit from the Pacific during the Spanish-American War. A bill signed into law by President Eisenhower on 23 July 1954 directed the Navy to retain *Constitution* and restore her, insofar as possible, to her "original appearance, but not for actual service." House Speaker John McCormack also had included a provision that Boston was to be her homeport: the only time Congress has directed the Navy on this subject. *Constellation* was to be turned over to a non-profit organization in Baltimore and *Hartford* was to go to a similar group in Mobile. If arrangements like these could be made for *Olympia* and *Oregon* within six months, they, too, were to be transferred. *Constellation* and *Olympia* did find new homes in Baltimore and Philadelphia, where they are moored today. *Hartford* was destroyed in a tragic fire at Norfolk before she could head south. *Oregon*'s remains finally became part of a breakwater, her passing mourned only by a few ship buffs. *Constitution*'s Captain, Lieutenant Charles W. Morris, was reduced to having just one ship.

In the post-World War II years, two events have come to be thought of as traditional in "Old Ironsides:" Easter sunrise services and the "turnaround" cruise. The earliest mention found of the religious service was on 16 April 1953, when Methodist Bishop John Wesley Lord officiated. Begun primarily for the naval personnel and their families then at the Yard, it gradually has come to include any of the general public wishing to attend; for more than ten years, the service has been broadcast locally by one of Boston's radio stations. The turnaround cruise likewise evolved from very modest beginnings when, in the 1950's, the ship randomly was turned around at her berth to weather evenly her wooden hull. Sometimes she was turned once a year, sometimes twice, and sometimes not at all — and never with passengers until November 1959. The Commandant of the First Naval District was the official host for the hardy few males who came. A note of that period in the headquarter's files has been found which recommended, "for the record," that if guests are to be invited again, a better season of the year be chosen for the cruise. The event evolved in the 1960's to where, by 1965, upwards of 400 men were invited by the Commandant for an annual trip under tow down Boston harbor and back, upon the completion of which each was issued a florid certificate attesting to the fact that they had been underway in "Old Ironsides." In 1971, the publicity given the presence of a female stowaway ended this demonstration of male chauvinism, and each subsequent cruise has sought to make the opportunity available to a wider number of people.

Backtracking for a moment, *Constitution* was drydocked in 1957 for most of the month of March in order to replace 390 sheets of deteriorated copper and inspect the hull, which required no work. She was docked again from 3 December 1963 to 25 March 1964 for similar work, although at this time it was found necessary to replace the cutwater, as well.

But if the spars and yards were holding up well, and the underwater body was, too, the outer and ceiling planking and the decks were not. The red oak employed in the sides, as noted earlier, was proving inadequate to the task. The steady flow of visitors across the decks, handling fittings and often climbing them, took a steady toll — in some ways, it was far harder service than fighting British frigates. *Constitution* had borne 175,000 visitors in 1950, 342,000 in 1960, and would nearly double that figure again in 1970. It was evident to Rear Admiral Joseph C. Wylie shortly after he became District Commandant in 1969 that the time for another major restoration was near. Through his efforts, the Navy's Board of Inspection and Survey was called in to do just that: inspect and report.

## ANOTHER RESTORATION

The inspection took place in August 1970 and the report issued on 1 September. The Board found that "the repairs and alterations... (needed)... are not disproportionate to the value of the ship" — no one expected them to say

# A Most Fortunate Ship

*Commander Thomas Coyne.*

otherwise — but that the routine maintenance of the ship had been "neither adequate nor effective." The sum of the report was that the ship should be refurbished from keel to main truck, and it was estimated that $4.2 million would be needed to do the job. Delays in getting Congressional authority for the money precluded a start on the work in 1972. With the nation's bicentennial coming up in 1976, consideration was given to dividing the work into two phases: the drydocking phase to be completed before the celebrations and the rest to be done afterwards. The steady diminution in the value of the dollar led those concerned to rearrange the plan so that all work would be done in a continuous effort in such a way as to minimize any limiting effect on the ship's availability for the big year.

Admiral Wylie also concluded that one of the reasons that *Constitution* had gotten into such condition was that she had not had an officer of sufficient experience and seniority in command, one who was sensitive to maintenance problems and who had the "horsepower" to get things taken care of. His campaign in this regard resulted in a policy change whereby henceforth "Old Ironsides' " Captains were to be officers of the rank of Commander, men with about two decades of service behind them.

*Constitution*, then commanded by Commander Thomas Coyne, was drydocked from April 1973 to April 1974. During that time, one-sixth of the outer underwater hull planking was replaced and the whole hull recoppered. The white oak used came mostly from the area around Piqua, Ohio, after a strenuous search for adequate stands of timber. A major problem for the modern shipwrights again proved to be the preparation of timbers to fit into the "tuck" at the stern — great timbers that had to be both twisted and bent in order to fit the lines. Repeated tries at steaming the wood in a modern steam box resulted in shattered timbers. Resort finally was had to the method set forth by Joshua Humphreys in 1794: boil them in salt water. It worked.

While this work was going on outside, another crew of craftsmen labored deep in the ship to restore her forward structure, which was settling badly. Sections of the keelson and nearby deck beams had to be replaced; an entire new step for the foremast was needed, as well. Having accomplished that, the team worked progressively up through the ship's bow structure, overcoming the sagging induced by the large weights exerting severe pressures through long lever arms in this area. Structurally, it was, perhaps, the most significant element of the restoration.

Ashore, in the nearby rigging loft, yet a third crew labored to refurbish or replace the miles of rigging required by the ship, and similarly renew the yards and spars. Only the lower mainmast, new in 1963, had been left in the ship as she lay in dock. On a floor below, other men worked over the ship's guns, replacing rotted carriages.

Amidst all this activity came the disconcerting announcement that the Boston Navy Yard, as an economy measure, was to be shut down as of 30 June 1974. Moving quickly, those concerned with *Constitution*'s welfare organized from the existing Yard work force an identifiable *"Constitution* Restoration Group" which would continue in being until the scheduled end of the restoration program two years later. In addition, equipments were consolidated into one building adjacent to the drydock so that the work of decommissioning the Yard would not conflict with or be delayed by the frigate's overhaul.

*Constitution* came out of drydock on 25 April 1974 and was moved to a fitting out pier. Many of the artifacts previously in her were set up in a temporary museum nearby and a viewing platform had been erected from which visitors could get a view of the ship and the work in progress. In July, the work of restepping her masts and restoring her top hamper began. In September, it was realized that virtually all the ceiling planking above the spar deck would have to be replaced, contrary to earlier evaluations. A special effort was made to accomplish both of these jobs before winter's bitter cold and snows came on. It was a very busy time for the work force and for the new Captain, Commander Tyrone G. Martin, who had taken over in August.

President Gerald R. Ford on 1 October signed into law a bill authorizing the creation of the Boston National Historical Park. Pertinent to *Constitution* was the provision transferring about thirty acres of the now-defunct Navy Yard to the National Park Service, including her normal berth, Drydock #1, and the

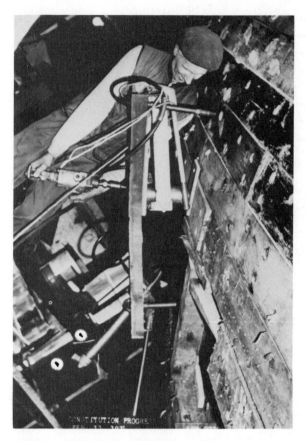

Left: *Replacing outer hull planking with the ship in dry dock, 1973.* Below: *Just out of dry dock, April 1974.*

Left: *Restepping the mizzenmast, July 1974.* Middle: *Returning the bowsprit, September 1974.* Below: *Replacing the outer hull above the water line, March 1975.*

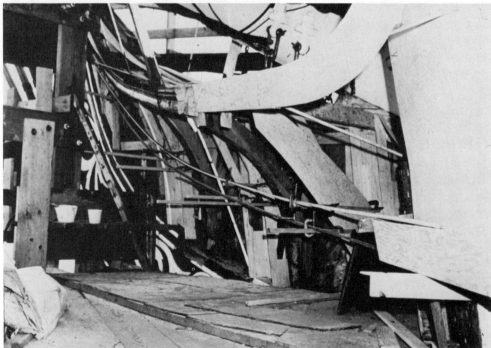

Top: *Building a new port quarter gallery, summer of 1975.* Bottom: *Rebuilding the bow to its 1812 appearance, spring of 1976.*

*The bow rebuilt, June 1976.*

building housing her artisans' shops. For the first time, she would be berthed in a setting with an historical theme, rather than existing amidst the conflicting priorities and programs of an operating shipyard. Other elements of the geographically dispersed Park include the Old North Church, Paul Revere's house, Faneuil Hall, the Old State House, and the Old South Meeting House. The ship remained a part of the regular Navy, her commission unimpaired.

By February 1975, most of the work was done per the schedule and the ship was returned without fanfare to her normal berth. Between then and 14 March, "Old Ironsides" was a beehive of activity. Her guns were swung back aboard and emplaced. Crewmen returned the bulk of the 6000 items removed two years earlier to their proper places about the ship and completely painted the ship's interior. Regular watches were resumed on board. On the March date, with Secretary of the Navy J. William Middendorf II and other dignitaries in attendance, *Constitution* formally reopened to visitors. Virtually all of the planned internal work had been completed.

The remainder of the month was spent erecting staging and making other preparations for what was then thought to be the last major job: replanking the outer hull above the water line. This would involve the removal of over 440 lengths of rotted red oak and replacing them with "custom-tailored" white oak — something like a giant jigsaw puzzle. Through the expertise and teamwork of the restoration work force, it all went smoothly.

The summer of 1975 was a time of some redirection in the restoration as Captain Martin, after nearly a year of study, concluded that more effort should be put into returning the ship to her earlier appearance rather than merely replacing decayed wood parts as found. In a detailed report to the Chief of Naval Operations, he recommended that a long-term, open-ended program be established to move in the direction of *Constitution*'s 1812 appearance (her most famous era) in the spirit of the oft-repeated Congressional directive. He included a listing of about two dozen projects within the scope of this theme, each one based on cited historical references. CNO ultimately approved the plan before the year was out and directed that the projected rebuilding of the bow head area be accomplished before the major restoration period ended.

A lesser project which came up during the summer of 1975 had to do with whether or not the ship's guns could be used for firing salute charges. The Captain arranged for an informal feasibility study to be done by the Navy's Ordnance Laboratory, and as the determination was positive, he was ready to get the necessary modifications made when it became known that the reigning monarch of England would visit Boston during the main Bicentennial celebrations the following summer.

On 1 September 1975, Secretary Middendorf issued a directive cancelling the nondescript "IX-21" hull number *Constitution* had borne for more than four decades. This he did in response to the suggestion from the Captain that a ship of her prestige needed nothing more than her famous name to identify her.

As the work force struggled with the hull replanking, the rebuilding of the head, and the construction of all-new quarter galleries, management was wrestling with the problem of what was to happen when the on-going restoration ended. After weeks of study, the proposal was made that a full-time restoration and maintenance group of a dozen artisans be established to insure "Old Ironsides' " material well-being for all time. The evident merit of the proposal almost completely precluded its disapproval, and the only real question was whether or not to begin the program as soon as the restoration period ended. After some discussion, it was decided to begin its operation the day after the restoration was over so that skilled men would not be lost and there would be no deterioration in the ship to "catch up" on. It happened just that way on 1 July 1976.

More than 895,000 people had visited *Constitution* during the 9½ months she was open in 1975. As winter 1976 turned to spring, it was obvious to all concerned that there would be at least that many in the new year. All of these people not only were able to tour the ship in the accustomed manner, they also could view the rebuilding of the ship at close range and, sometimes, talk directly with the craftsmen as they plied their traditional trades. Both sides seemed fascinated by the opportunity.

## THE BICENTENNIAL

The *USS Constitution* Museum opened its doors for the first time on 8 April 1976, and for the first time the fabled frigate had associated with her a facility dedicated to helping people know her as well as they wished. The Foundation which backed the Museum, a private non-profit organization, had been the inspiration of Admiral Wylie when he was Commandant, and after his retirement he and other dedicated citizens formally had incorporated themselves for the purpose in September 1972. With the help and cooperation of the Navy, the National Park Service, and many interested private individuals, it had been possible to remake the old (1833) machinery building for Drydock #1 into a pro-

*An impression of the* U.S.S. Constitution *Museum, by John Charles Roach.*

per museum.

Just one month after the Museum opened, there occurred another ceremony which looked to the frigate's future. On Navy-owned land near Crane, Indiana, a white oak grove numbering thousands of trees spread over some 25,000 acres formally was dedicated to the sole use of *Constitution,* when and as such timbers would be needed. The days of tedious searches for prime white oak appear to have ended with this act.

Events of the Bicentennial year were crowding in upon one another. On 17 June, *Constitution* conducted her first turnaround cruise since 1972 with youngsters from thirty-three friendly foreign countries as her special guests. On the nation's 200th birthday, *Constitution*'s newly-returned modified 24-pounders boomed out a 21-gun salute at high noon in honor of the occasion. Nearly ninety-five years had passed since last they had been heard, and a more appropriate occasion there never would be. On 10 July, "Old Ironsides" was the official host ship for the visit of many of the world's remaining "tall ships" to Boston and led them in a majestic sea parade up the harbor, her guns firing at one-minute intervals as hundreds of thousands of people watched and cheered from every possible vantage point.

*On the gundeck the Captain and Queen discuss* Constitution's *British-made long guns.*

The culminating event of the season — one which, in a sense, makes *Constitution*'s story come "full circle" — took place on Sunday, 11 July 1976. Underway promptly at eight that morning with her attendant tugs, the old frigate moved smartly to a position just inside the Boston Lighthouse where, at 20 minutes past 9, the 24-pounders roared out yet another 21-gun salute as a large, sleek, dark blue yacht slid swiftly past: the royal yacht *Britannia* was bearing England's Queen Elizabeth II and Prince Philip into Boston for a one-day visit. Flags snapping smartly in the wind, the royal craft appeared and moved on almost before anyone knew it — almost before "Old Ironsides," swinging smartly to keep the proper bearing, could complete the salute. The smoke still was heavy in the air when a message flashed between ships: "Your salute was magnificent — Britannia sends." The gunners were proud as peacocks.

Later that afternoon, the royal couple visited *Constitution* and spent nearly an hour in a private tour of the ship with Secretary Middendorf and Captain Martin. The crew wondered what it was going to be like, since the ship's reputation is based largely on victories over units of the Royal Navy. The royal visitors exhibited a keen interest in everything about the ship, including *Guerriere*'s mirror and the long guns bearing the monogram of King George III, and acknowledged that the two countries were not always as friendly as they were on the present occasion. A crew member later was heard to swear as gospel that, when the Queen was shown the King George guns she turned to the Prince and said, "I say, Philip, we really must talk to the Secretary about these foreign arms sales when we get home". Another story is born. Upon their departure from the frigate, the crew demonstrated their admiration for the royal visitor when they leaped into the shrouds and Master of Arms Walter R. Gross shouted, "Three cheers for the Queen, lads! Hip, hip!" "Hooray!" "Hip, hip!" "Hooray!" "Hip, hip!" "Hooray!"

"Hip, hip, hooray," indeed — and for *Constitution* and her men. While her Captain became the first skipper since Charles Stewart to be decorated for his performance in office, the ship herself received her first-ever official recognition for superlative performance of duty, in this instance for her contribution to the celebration of the nation's 200th birthday. The citation accompanying the Secretary of the Navy's award of the Meritorious Unit Commendation to the ship reads:

> For meritorious service in inspiring patriotism and making Americans more aware of their maritime heritage... Through their continuous display of professionalism and resourcefulness, the ship's crew inspired all their fellow Americans and to the visitors from more than sixty-five foreign countries exemplified America's determination to stand ready to defend freedom and democracy throughout the world, thus making a major contribution toward achievement of U.S. foreign policy objectives. By their superb performance and total devotion to duty, the officers and men of *USS Constitution* reflected credit upon themselves and upheld the highest traditions of the United States Naval Service.

Thus has it always been with this most fortunate ship; thus will it ever be.

# Afterword

Nearly every book written about *Constitution* has ended with a chapter or a piece on the theme of "what *Constitution* means to us," or something similar. One wonders why, after having read her incredible success story, such a passage should be needed. Should it be so now, Commodore William Bainbridge, who certainly had reason to know, may have said it best:

> "...the ship! Never has she failed us! Never has her crew failed in showing their allegiance and belief in the country they served, or the honor they felt, in belonging to the ship that sheltered them, and on whose decks they fought, where many gave their lives. To have commanded the *Constitution* is a signal honor; to have been one of her crew, in no matter how humble a capacity, is an equal one. Her name is an inspiration. Not only do her deeds belong to our Naval record, but she herself is possessed of a brave personality. In light weathers, in storm or hurricane, or amid the smoke of battle she responded with alacrity and obedience, and seemed ever eager to answer the will of her commander. May the citizens of this country, in gratitude, see that she, like her namesake and prototype, will never be forgotten. Her commanders in the future, as in the past, will see to it that her flag never shall be lowered. She was conceived in patriotism; gloriously has she shown her valor. Let her depart in glory if the fates so decree; but let her not sink and decay into oblivion..."

Amen, Commodore.

# Sources

## Chapter 1 The Quasi-War with France

Allen, Gardner W. *"Our Naval War with France."* Boston: Houghton, Mifflin Co., 1909.

Dow, Jesse Erskine. "Sketches from the Log of Old Ironsides." Burton's *Gentlemen's Magazine*, July 1839.

Dunn, CDR Lucius C., USN (Ret). "A Chapter from Genesis of the War of 1812." U.S. Naval Institute *Proceedings*, November 1939.

Fowler, William M., Jr. "The Non-Volunteer Navy." U.S. Naval Institute *Proceedings*, August 1974.

Grant, Bruce. *"Isaac Hull: Captain of 'Old Ironsides'."* Chicago: Pellegrini and Cudahy. 1947.

Journal of Midshipman James Pity, 22 July 1798 - 11 May 1799. National Archives.

Log of *USS Constitution* inscribed "Peter St. Medard", 1 December 1798 - 15 February 1800. *USS Constitution* Museum.

Log of *USS Constitution,* 6 December 1798 - 20 October 1800.

Navy Department. *"Barbary Wars: Personnel Data."* Washington: GPO. 1945.

Navy Department. *"Dictionary of American Naval Fighting Ships."* Vols. I-VI. Washington: GPO. 1959-76.

Navy Department. *"Quasi-War with France."* Vols. I-VII. Washington: GPO. 1935-9.

Tuckerman, Henry T. *"The Life of Silas Talbot."* New York: J.C. Riker. 1850.

## Chapter 2 The Ship and Life Aboard Her

Anonymous (probably Mercier, Henry). *"Life on a Man-of-War."* Boston: Houghton, Mifflin Co. 1927.

Anonymous (Nordoff, Charles). *"Man-of-War Life."* Cincinnati: Moore, Wilstach, Keys and Co. 1856.

Barrows, Colonel John S. "The Beginnings and Launchings of the United States Frigate *Constitution*." Paper read before the Bostonian Society on February 17, 1925.

Bass, William P. "Landlubber's Look at some special Square Rigged History." Unfinished monograph. Personal copy.

## Sources

Bell, Frederick J. *"Room To Swing A Cat."* New York: Longmans, Green and Co. 1938.

Brewington, M.V. *"Shipcarvers of North America."* New York: Dover Publishing Co. 1962. Appendix.

Brooks, George S., ed. *"James Durand: An Able Seaman of 1812."* New Haven: Yale University Press. 1926.

Cate, Margaret Davis. *"Our Todays and Yesterdays."* Brunswick, Ga.: Glover Bros., Inc. 1930.

Chapelle, Howard I. *"The History of American Sailing Ships."* New York: W.W. Norton and Co. 1935.

Chapelle, Howard I. *"The History of the American Sailing Navy."* New York: Bonanza. 1949.

Crumpacker, CDR J.W., (SC), USN. "Supplying the Fleet for 150 Years." U.S. Naval Institute *Proceedings*, June 1945.

Goodwin, LT J.F., USN. "Ship's Orders — 1815." U.S. Naval Institute *Proceedings*, January 1940.

Hazzard, William W. *"St. Simon's Island, Georgia: Brunswick and Vicinity."* Virginia Steele Wood, ed. Belmont, Mass.: Oak Hill Press. 1974.

Hollis, Ira N. *"The Frigate Constitution."* Boston: Houghton, Mifflin and Co. 1901.

Letter, Franklin M. Garrett, Atlanta Historical Society, to Virginia Steele Wood, April 23, 1976 (misdated August 23, 1977).

Letter, Secretary of War McHenry to George Claghorne, 27 July 1797.

Letter, Quartermaster General of Massachusetts to the State Senate and House of Representatives, 7 February 1800.

Letter, Quartermaster General of Massachusetts to the Govenor, 7 January 1805.

Letter, Secretary of War to the Governor of Massachusetts, 30 May 1798.

Maclay, Edgar S. *"A Youthful Man-O'-Warsman."* Greenlawn, N.Y.: Navy Blue Company. 1910.

Miller, Nathan. *"Sea of Glory."* New York: David McKay Co. 1974.

Morison, Samuel Eliot. *"The Oxford History of the American People."* New York: Oxford University Press. 1965.

Navy Department. *"Navy Regulations (1802)."*

Navy Department. *"Quasi-War with France,"* Volume I. Washington: GPO. 1935.

Navy Department. *"Barbary Wars,"* Volume I. Washington: GPO. 1939.

Oliver, CAPT Frederick L., USN (Ret.). "Prize Money." U.S. Naval Institute *Proceedings*, October 1946.

Paullin, Charles Oscar. *"Paullin's History of Naval Administration, 1775-1911."* Annapolis, Md.: U.S. Naval Institute. 1968.

Peterson, Mendell L., ed. *"The Journals of Daniel Noble Johnson (1822-1863), United States Navy."* Washington: Smithsonian Institution. 1959.

Reilly, John C., Jr. *"Ships of the U.S. Navy: Christening, Launching and Commissioning."* Washington: GPO. 1975.

Skillman, CDR J.H., (SC), USN. "Eating Through The Years." U.S. Naval Institute *Proceedings*, March 1941.

Smelser, Marshall. *"The Congress Founds The Navy."* University of Notre Dame Press. 1959.

Snow, Elliot, and Gosnell, H. Allen. *"On the Decks of 'Old Ironsides'."* New York: MacMillan Co. 1932.

Stanton, Elizabeth Brandon. "Builder of the First American Navy." *Journal of American History* (1908).

State Department, *"American State Papers,"* Volume I. Washington: Gales and Seaton. 1834.

Tourtellot, Arthur Bernon. *"The Charles."* New York: Farrar and Rinehart. 1941.

Tucker, Glenn. *"Dawn Like Thunder."* New York: Bobbs Merrill. 1963.

U.S. Frigate Constitution General Harbor Regulations. Undated. *USS Constitution* Museum.

Valette, Henry M. "History and Reminiscences of the Philadelphia Navy Yard." Potter's *American Monthly Magazine*, January 1876.

## Chapter 3 The Barbary War: September 1795 - July 1804.

Cooke, Mary Lewis, and Lewis, Charles Lee. "An American Naval Officer in the Mediterranean, 1802-7." U.S. Naval Institute *Proceedings*, November 1941.

Cooper, James Fenimore. *"Naval History."* Mason, Baker, & Pratt. ca. 1866.

Frost, John. *"The Pictorial Book of the Commodores."* New York: Nafis & Cornish. 1845.

Howland, LT Felix, U.S. Marine Corps Reserve. "The Blockade of Tripoli, 1801-1802." U.S. Naval Institute *Proceedings*, December 1937.

Log of *USS Constitution,* 16 August 1803 - 6 March 1804. National Archives.

McKee, Christopher. *"Edward Preble."* Annapolis, Md.: Naval Institute Press. 1972.

Navy Department. *"Barbary Wars,"* Volumes II-IV. Washington, D.C.: GPO. 1940-42.

Paullin, Charles Oscar. *"Paullin's History of Naval Administration, 1775-1911."* Annapolis, Md.: U.S. Naval Institute. 1968.

Paullin, Charles Oscar. *"Commodore John Rodgers."* Annapolis, Md.: U.S. Naval Institute. 1967.

Pratt, Fletcher, *"Preble's Boys."* New York: Wm. Sloan Associates. 1950.

Preble, Edward. Memorandum Book, 1803.

Smith, Wright. Diary, 14 July 1803 - 19 August 1805. *USS Constitution* Museum.

# Sources

Sparks, Jared. *"The Library of American Biography."* Boston: Charles C. Little and James Brown. 1846.

Tucker, Glenn. *"Dawn Like Thunder."* New York: Bobbs-Merrill Co., Inc. 1963.

## Chapter 4 The Barbary War and Aftermath: July 1804-October 1807

Chappelle, Howard I. *"The History of The American Sailing Navy."* New York: Bonanza Books. 1949.

Cooke, Mary Lewis, and Lewis, Charles Lee. "An American Naval Officer in the Mediterranean, 1802-7." U.S. Naval Institute *Proceedings*, November 1941.

Cooper, James Fenimore. *"Naval History."* Mason, Baker, & Pratt. ca. 1866.

Daly, Robert W. "Richard Somers." U.S. Naval Institute *Proceedings*, September 1948.

Frost, LCDR Holloway H., USN. *"We Build a Navy."* Annapolis, Md.: U.S. Naval Institute. 1940.

Maclay, Edgar S. *"History of the Navy."* Vol. I. New York: D. Appleton and Company. 1895.

McKee, Christopher. *"Edward Preble."* Annapolis, Md.: Naval Institute Press. 1972.

Miller, Arthur P., Jr., LTJG, USNR. "Tripoli Graves Discovered." U.S. Naval Institute *Proceedings*, April 1950.

Navy Department. *"Barbary Wars,"* Volumes IV-VI. Washington, D.C.: GPO. 1942, 1944 (2).

Paullin, Charles Oscar. *"Paullin's History of Naval Administration, 1775-1911."* Annapolis, Md.: U.S. Naval Institute. 1968.

Paullin, Charles Oscar. *"Commodore John Rodgers."* Annapolis, Md.: U.S. Naval Institute. 1967.

Smith, Jay D. "Commodore James Barron: Guilty as Charged?" U.S. Naval Institute *Proceedings*, November 1967.

Smith, Wright. Diary, 14 July 1803 - 19 August 1805. *USS Constitution* Museum.

Snow, Elliot, and Gosnell, H. Allen. *"On the Decks of 'Old Ironsides'."* New York: The MacMillan Company. 1932.

## Chapter 5 Prelude to Glory

Allen, Gardner, W., ed., *"Papers of Isaac Hull,"* Boston Atheneum, 1929.

Drury, CAPT C.M., CHC, USN. "Famous Chaplain Teachers of Midshipmen, 1800-1845." U.S. Naval Institute *Proceedings,* May 1946.

Grant, Bruce. *"Isaac Hull, Captain of 'Old Ironsides'."* Chicago: Pellegrini and Cudahy. 1947.

Hollis, Ira N. *"The Frigate Constitution."* New York: Houghton, Mifflin Co. 1901.

Journal of Midshipman Frederick Baury, 5 July 1811 - 21 June 1812. Massachusetts Historical Society.

Log of *USS Constitution*, 17 June 1810 - 31 January 1812. National Archives.

Log of *USS Constitution*, 1 February - 9 December 1812. National Archives.

Navy Department. *"Barbary Wars."* Volume VI. Washington, D.C.; GPO. 1944.

Paullin, Charles Oscar. *"Commodore John Rodgers."* Annapolis, Md.: U.S. Naval Institute. 1967.

Rodgers Collection of Papers. Pennsylvania Historical Society.

State Department. *"American State Papers."* Volume I. Washington, D.C.; Gales and Seaton. 1834.

Todd, Charles Burr. *"Life and Letters of Joel Barlow, LL. D."* New York: G.P. Putnam's Sons. 1886.

### Chapter 6 The Great Chase

Forester, C.S. *"The Age of Fighting Sail."* Garden City, N.Y.: Doubleday and Co., Inc. 1956.

Grant, Bruce. *"Isaac Hull: Captain of 'Old Ironsides'."* Chicago: Pelligrini and Cudahy. 1947.

Hollis, Ira N. *"The Frigate Constitution."* Boston: Houghton, Mifflin, and Co. 1901.

Journal of Midshipman Frederick Baury, 5 July 1811 - 21 June 1812. Massachusetts Historical Society.

Journal of Midshipman Frederick Baury, 24 June 1812 - 27 October 1812. Massachusetts Historical Society.

Letter, Hull to Hamilton, 21 July 1812. National Archives.

Log of *USS Constitution*, February 1, 1812 - December 9, 1812. National Archives.

Maclay, Edgar S. *"History of the Navy."* Volume I. New York: D. Appleton and Co. 1895.

Mahan, Alfred T. *"Sea Power in its Relation to the War of 1812."* Volume I. Boston: Little, Brown, and Co. 1905.

Navy Department. *"Dictionary of American Naval Fighting Ships."* Volume V. Washington, D.C.: GPO. 1970.

Roosevelt, Theodore. *"The War of 1812."* 3rd edition. New York: G.P. Putnam's Sons. 1910.

Smith, Moses. *"Naval Scenes of the Last War."* Boston. 1846.

### Chapter 7 "The Americans Were Our Masters"

Boston *Gazette*, 31 August 1812.

Claxton, Lieutenant C., R.N. *"The Naval Monitor,"* 2nd ed. London: A.J. Valpi. 1833.

## Sources

Forester, C.S. *"The Age of Fighting Sail."* Garden City, N.Y.: Doubleday and Co. 1956.

Frost, LCDR Holloway H., U.S.N. *"We Build a Navy."* Annapolis, Md.: U.S. Naval Institute. 1940.

Frost, John. *"The Pictorial Book of the Commodores."* New York: Nafis and Cornish. 1845.

Grant, Bruce. *"Isaac Hull: Captain of 'Old Ironsides'."* Chicago: Pellegrini and Cudahy. 1947.

Hollis, Ira N. *"The Frigate Constitution."* Boston: Houghton, Mifflin and Co. 1901.

Journal of Midshipman Frederick Baury, 24 June 1912 - 26 October 1812. Massachusetts Historical Society.

Journal of Surgeon Amos A. Evans, 11 June 1812 - 15 February 1813.

Journal of Lieutenant Charles Morris (extracts).

Letter, Hull to Rodgers, 2 September 1812. National Archives.

Letter, Hull to Benjamin Silliman, 29 October 1821.

Log of *USS Constitution*, 1 February 1812 - 9 December 1812. National Archives.

Maclay, Edgar S. *"History of the Navy."* Volume I. New York: D. Appleton and Co. 1895.

Mahan, Alfred T. *"Sea Power in its Relations to the War of 1812."* Boston: Little, Brown, and Co. 1905.

Paullin, Charles Oscar. *"Commodore John Rodgers."* Annapolis, Md.: U.S. Naval Institute. 1967.

Pratt, Fletcher. *"Preble's Boys."* New York: William Sloane Assoc. 1950.

Roosevelt, Theodore. *"The Naval War of 1812."* 3rd edition. New York: G.P. Putnam's Sons. 1910.

Smith, Moses. *"Naval Scenes of the Last War."* Boston. 1846.

Thomas, R. *"The Glory of America."* New York: Ezra Strong. 1834.

## Chapter 8 Lightning Strikes Twice

Cooper, James Fenimore. *"Naval History."* Mason, Baker, & Pratt. ca. 1866.

James, William. *"Naval Occurrences."* London: T. Egerton. 1817.

James, William. *"The Naval History of Great Britain."* London: Baldwin, Cradock, and Joy. 1824.

Journal of Midshipman Frederick Baury, 24 June 1812 - 26 October 1812. Massachusetts Historical Society.

Journal of Midshipman Frederick Baury, 28 October 1812 - 16 February 1813. Massachusetts Historical Society.

Journal of Surgeon Amos A. Evans, 1812-13 (excerpts).

Letter, Bainbridge to John Bullus, 23 January 1813.

Letter, Bainbridge to Hamilton, 2 September 1812. National Archives.

Letter, Bainbridge to Hamilton, 14 September 1812. National Archives.

Letter, Bainbridge to Hamilton, 24 October 1812. National Archives.

Letter, Hamilton to Bainbridge, 8 September 1812. National Archives.

Letter, Hamilton to Bainbridge, 2 October 1812. National Archives.

Long, David F. "Bainbridge and His Navy." Ms. 1978.

Maclay, Edgar S. *"History of the Navy."* Volume I. New York: D. Appleton and Co. 1895.

Mahan, Alfred T. *"Sea Power in its Relations to the War of 1812."* Volume II. Boston: Little, Brown, and Co. 1905.

Roosevelt, Theodore. *"The Naval War of 1812."* 3rd edition. New York: G.P. Putnam's Sons. 1910.

## Chapter 9 Overhaul, Change of Command — and a Sea Story

Brewer, Lucy. *"An Affecting Narrative of Louisa Baker, A Native of Massachusetts ... and enlisted, in disguise, on board an American Frigate as A Marine."* 3rd ed. Boston: Nathaniel Coverly, Jr. 1816.

Cooper, James Fenimore. *"Naval History."* Mason, Baker, & Pratt. ca. 1866.

James, William. *"Naval Occurrences."* London: T. Egerton. 1817.

Letter, Bainbridge to William Jones, 21 February 1813. National Archives.

Letter, Bainbridge to William Jones, 14 March 1813. National Archives.

Letter, Bainbridge to William Jones, 3 May 1813. National Archives.

Letter, Bainbridge to William Jones, 23 June 1813. National Archives.

Letter, Jones to Bainbridge, 8 March 1813. National Archives.

Maclay, Edgar S. *"History of the Navy."* Volume I. New York: D. Appleton and Co. 1895.

Nau, Erika, *"Angel in the Rigging."* New York: Berkly Publishing Corp. 1976.

Pratt, Fletcher. *"Preble's Boys."* New York: William Sloan Associates. 1950.

Walker, Raymond J. "The Masquerading Marine." U.S. Naval Institute *Proceedings,* August 1938.

## Chapter 10 Stewart's Trials and Triumph

Chapelle, Howard I. *"The History of American Sailing Ships."* New York: Bonanza Books. 1935.

Cooper James Fenimore. *"Naval History."* Mason, Baker, & Pratt. ca. 1866.

Hollis, Ira N. *"The Frigate Constitution."* Boston: Houghton, Mifflin and Company. 1901.

Letters, Bainbridge to Massachusetts Adjutant General Brooks, 12 June 1814 & 13 June 1814. National Archives.

Letter, Bainbridge to Major General Dearborn, 27 Sep 1814. National Archives.

Letters, Bainbridge to Secretary of the Navy Jones, 21 Aug. 1813, 2 June 1814, 23 Jun 1814, 1 Jul 1814, 3 Jul 1814, 6 Jul 1814, 7 Jul 1814, 29 Jul 1814, 15 Aug 1814, 6 Sep 1814, 13 Sep 1814. National Archives.

## Sources

Letter, Boston Selectmen to Adjutant General Brooks, 19 Apr 1814. National Archives.

Letters, Secretary of the Navy Jones to Bainbridge, 24 Jan 1814, 16 Jul 1814, 1 Aug. 1814, 14 Aug 1814. National Archives.

Letter, Commodore John Rodgers to Bainbridge, 16 Jun 1815. National Archives.

Log, *USS Constitution*, 31 Dec. 1813 - 16 May 1815. National Archives.

Log, *USS Constitution*, 4 Jan 1814 - 16 May 1815. National Archives.

Mahan, Alfred Thayer. *"Sea Power in its Relation to the War of 1812."* Boston: Little, Brown and Company. 1905.

Maclay, Edgar S. *"History of the Navy."* New York: D. Appleton and Company. 1895.

Napier, LT Henry Edward, RN. *"New England Blockaded 1814."* Salem, Ma.: Peabody Museum. 1939.

Preble, George Henry. "History of the Boston Navy Yard." Manuscript. New England Historical Genealogical Society.

Roosevelt, Theodore. *"The Naval War of 1812."* New York: G.P. Putnam's Sons. 1910.

Turner, Lynn W. "The Last War Cruise of Old Ironsides." *American Heritage,* April 1955.

## Chapter 11 Mediterranean Sojourn

Frost, John. *"The Pictorial Book of the Commodores."* New York: Nafis & Cornish. 1845.

Journal of the Charlestown Navy Yard, March - May 1821. *USS Constitution* Museum.

Journal of Private William Fleming, 22 September 1824 - 4 July 1828. *USS Constitution* Museum.

Journal of Midshipman Philip Augustus Stockton, 29 October 1824 - 31 December 1826. *USS Constitution* Museum.

Letter, Sailing Master Briscoe Doxey to Commodore John Rodgers, 1 June 1821. National Archives.

Letter, Midshipman Samuel F. Dupont to his father, 19 April 1821. Eleutherian Mills Library.

Letters, Midshipman Samuel F. Dupont to his mother, 19 April 1821, 28 July 1821, 12 April 1822. Eleutherian Mills Library.

Letters, Midshipman Samuel F. Dupont to his brother Charles, 5 June 1821, 10 December 1821, 18 March 1822. Eleutherian Mills Library.

Letter, Commodore John Marston to Mrs. Samuel F. Dupont, 21 July 1866.

Log, *USS Constitution*, 10 April 1821 - 19 January 1822. National Archives.

Log, *USS Constitution*, 10 April 1821 - 22 May 1824. National Archives.

Log, *USS Constitution*, 28 October 1824 - 6 May 1826. National Archives.

Paullin, Charles Oscar. *"Commodore John Rodgers."* Annapolis, Md.: U.S. Naval Institute. 1967.

Paullin, Charles Oscar. *"History of Naval Administration, 1775-1911."* Annapolis, Md.: U.S. Naval Institute. 1968.

Pratt, Fletcher. *"Preble's Boys."* New York: William Sloane Associates. 1950.

Snow, Elliot, and Gosnell, H. Allen. *"On the Decks of 'Old Ironsides'."* New York: The MacMillan Company. 1932.

## Chapter 12 Rebirth and Brouhaha

Bass, William P. "Landlubber's Look at some Special Square Rigged History." Unfinished monograph. Personal copy.

Grant, Bruce. *"Isaac Hull, Captain of 'Old Ironsides'."* Chicago: Pellegrini and Cudahy. 1947.

Hollis, Ira N. *"The Frigate Constitution."* New York: Houghton Mifflin Co. 1901.

Jarvis, Russell. *"Life of Commodore Elliott."* Philadelphia: Howes. 1835.

Letters, Constructor Josiah Baker to Commandant Jesse Elliott, 30 August 1834, 24 December 1834. National Archives.

Letters, Secretary of the Navy Branch to Commodore John Rodgers, 17 August 1830, 30 August 1830. National Archives.

Letter, Commodore John Downes to Commodore Rodgers, 11 August 1829, 10 April 1835, 19 April 1837. National Archives.

Letters, Commandant Elliott to Commodore Rodgers, 24 June 1833, 23 November 1833, 6 December 1833, 8 January 1834, 14 February 1834, 1 March 1834, 21 March 1834, 2 May 1834, 8 May 1834, 23 June 1834, 26 October 1834, 22 December 1834, 27 December 1834, 5 January 1835, 13 January 1835, 26 January 1835, 9 February 1835, 14 February 1835. National Archives.

Letter, Constructor Samuel Humphreys to Commandant Elliott, 16 September 1833. National Archives.

Letter, Ebenezer Lester to Commandant Elliott, 13 February 1834. National Archives.

Letter, Commodore Charles Morris to Commandant Elliott, 3 September 1834. National Archives.

Letters, Commandant Charles Morris to Commodore Rodgers, 19 July 1828, 1 November 1828, 28 August 1830, 27 September 1830, 24 February 1831, 4 April 1831, 14 December 1831. National Archives.

Letters, Commodore Rodgers to Commandant William Bainbridge, 15 September 1832, 4 December 1832, 4 April 1833, 17 April 1833, 23 April 1833. National Archives.

Letters, Commodore Rodgers to Secretary Branch, 20 September 1830, 31 August 1833. National Archives.

## Sources

Letters, Commodore Rodgers to Commandant Elliott, 28 May 1833, 23 June 1833, 16 August 1833, 19 August 1833, 9 September 1833, 20 September 1833, 5 December 1833, 24 February 1834, 13 March 1834, 24 March 1834, 9 April 1834, 21 April 1834, 7 May 1834, 2 July 1834, 20 September 1834, 9 December 1834, 15 December 1834, 19 December 1834, 27 December 1834, 8 January 1835. National Archives.

Letter, Commodore Rodgers to Commandant Morris, 18 August 1830. National Archives.

Letters, Master Commandant John Smith to Commodore Rodgers, 19 April 1833, 28 April 1833. National Archives.

Letter, Commodore Charles Stewart to Commandant Morris, 22 September 1830. National Archives.

Letter, Master Commandant Thomas W. Wyman to Commodore Rodgers, 28 December 1832. National Archives.

Snow, Elliot, and Gosnell, H. Allen. *"On the Decks of 'Old Ironsides'."* New York: MacMillan Co. 1932.

### Chapter 13 The Mediterranean, Pacific, and Home Squadron

An Eye-witness. "Old Ironsides on a Lee-Shore." *The Parlor Annual and Christian Family Casket,* Volume 4, 1846.

Anonymous. *"Life in a Man-of-War."* Boston: Houghton Mifflin Company. 1927.

Brewington, M.V. *"Shipcarvers of North America."* New York: Dover Publications, Inc. 1972.

Hollis, Ira N. *"The Frigate Constitution."* Boston: Houghton Mifflin Co. 1901.

Johnson, Robert Erwin. *"Thence Round Cape Horn."* Annapolis, Md.: U.S. Naval Institute. 1963.

Log, *USS Constitution*, 2 March 1839 - 16 May 1841. National Archives.

Log, *USS Constitution*, 17 May 1841 - 12 November 1841. National Archives.

Log, *USS Constitution*, 22 June 1842 - 16 February 1843. National Archives.

Maffitt, Capt. John N. *Nautilus.* New York: U.S. Publishing Co. 1872.

Mitchell, Dr. Donald W. "Abel Upshur, Forgotten Prophet of the Old Navy." U.S. Naval Institute *Proceedings,* December 1949.

Morison, Samuel Eliot. *"The Oxford History of the American People."* New York: Oxford University Press. 1965.

Paullin, Charles Oscar. *"Paullin's History of Naval Administration, 1775-1911."* Annapolis, Md.: U.S. Naval Institute. 1968.

Peterson, Mendel L., ed. *"The Journals of Daniel Noble Johnson (1822-1863), United States Navy."* Washington, D.C.: Smithsonian Institution. 1959.

Snow, Elliot, and Gosnell, H. Allen. *"On the Decks of 'Old Ironsides'."* New York: The MacMillan Company. 1932.

## Chapter 14 Around the World

Dunn, CAPT Lucius C., USN(Ret). "The United States Navy and the Open Door Policy." U.S. Naval Institute *Proceedings,* January 1949.

Hanks, CAPT Robert J., USN. "Commodore Lawrence Kearny, the Diplomatic Seaman." U.S. Naval Institute *Proceedings,* November 1970.

Howell, LCDR Glenn F., USN. "Neptunus Rex." U.S. Naval Institute *Proceedings,* December 1926.

Johnson, Robert Erwin. *"Thence Round Cape Horn."* Annapolis, Md.: U.S. Naval Institute. 1963.

Journal of Lieutenant John B. Dale, 29 May 1844 - 27 September 1846. New England Historical Genealogical Society.

Journal of Midshipman Meriwether Patterson Jones, 20 May 1844 - 5 July 1846. National Archives.

Journal of Midshipman Lucius M. Mason, 8 August 1844 - 14 December 1844. National Archives.

Journal of Midshipman Colville Terrell, 1 October 1845 - 16 September 1846. National Archives.

Journal of Carpenter Henry G. Thomas, 1844-6 Cruise.

Letter, Midshipman John E. Hart to his sister, 7 September 1846.

Ludlum, David M. *"Early American Hurricanes, 1492-1870."* Boston: American Meteorological Society. 1963.

Paullin, Charles Oscar. *"American Voyages to the Orient, 1690-1865."* Annapolis, Md.: U.S. Naval Institute. 1971.

Ponko, Vincent, Jr. *"Ships, Seas, and Scientists."* Annapolis, Md.: U.S. Naval Institute. 1974.

Snow, Elliot, and Gosnell, H. Allen. *"On the Decks of 'Old Ironsides'."* New York: The MacMillan Company. 1932.

Stevens, Benjamin F. "A Cruise on the Constitution." New York: *The United Service Magazine.* 1904.

## Chapter 15 Mediterranean Finale

Brewington, M.V. *"Shipcarvers of North America."* New York: Dover Publications, Inc. 1962.

Emmons, LT George F.W. *"The Navy of the United States from the Commencement, 1775 to 1853",* Washington, D.C.: Gideon and Co., 1853.

Log, *USS Constitution,* 9 October 1848 - 12 October 1849. National Archives.

Log, *USS Constitution,* 13 October 1849 - 16 January 1851. National Archives.

Paullin, Charles Oscar. *"Paullin's History of Naval Administration, 1775-1911."* Annapolis, Md.: U.S. Naval Institute. 1968.

Smith, CAPT Horatio D., USRCS. "On the Deck of 'Old Ironsides'." Unpublished manuscript. *USS Constitution* Museum.

## Sources

### Chapter 16 African Adventure

Duke, CDR Marvin L., USN. "The Navy Founds a Nation." U.S. Naval Institute *Proceedings.*

"Hospitality on the 'Constitution'." *The Youth's Companion* (New England Edition), June 13, 1907.

Journal of Edward Cobb, Commander's Clerk, *USS Constitution,* 22 December 1852 - 2 June 1855. *USS Constitution* Museum.

Log, *USS Constitution,* 22 December 1852 - 23 December 1853, National Archives.

Log, *USS Constitution,* 24 December 1853 - 21 September 1854, National Archives.

Log, *USS Constitution,* 22 September 1854 - 14 June 1855, National Archives.

Paullin, Charles Oscar. *"History of Naval Administration, 1775-1911."* Annapolis, Md.: U.S. Naval Institute. 1968.

Ponko, Victor, Jr. *"Ships, Seas, and Scientists."* Annapolis, Md.: U.S. Naval Institute. 1974.

### Chapter 17 Second Rate Ship

Brewington, M.V. *"Shipcarvers of North America."* New York: Dover Publications, Inc. 1962.

Clark, RADM Charles E., USN. *"My Fifty Years in the Navy."* Boston: Little, Brown, and Company. 1917.

Davis, William H. " 'Old Ironsides' in Chancery." U.S. Naval Institute *Proceedings,* June 1941.

Evans, RADM Robley D., USN. *"A Sailor's Log."* New York: D. Appleton and Company. 1901.

Journal of John Hazlett, January - May 1879.

Letter, Mrs. Willard E. Mattson to author, 15 May 1978.

Log, *USS Constitution,* 1 - 25 August 1860. National Archives.

Log, *USS Constitution,* 22 April - 11 May 1861. National Archives.

Log, *USS Constitution,* 1 March 1865 - 14 February 1866. National Archives.

Log, *USS Constitution,* 15 February - 8 April 1866. National Archives.

Log, *USS Constitution,* 9 April - 14 October 1866. National Archives.

Log, *USS Constitution,* 15 October 1866 - 31 March 1867. National Archives.

Log, *USS Constitution,* 1 April - 15 September 1867. National Archives.

Log, *USS Constitution,* 16 September - 18 December 1867. National Archives.

Log, *USS Constitution,* 19 December 1867 - 29 December 1868. National Archives.

Log, *USS Constitution,* 30 December 1868 - 14 January 1870. National Archives.

Log, *USS Constitution,* 15 January 1870 - 16 January 1871. National Archives.

Log, *USS Constitution,* 17 January - 26 September 1871. National Archives.

Log, *USS Constitution,* 19 July 1877 - 19 January 1878. National Archives.

Log, *USS Constitution*, 20 January - 25 July 1878. National Archives.

Log, *USS Constitution*, 26 July 1878 - 31 January 1879. National Archives.

Log, *USS Constitution*, 1 February - 15 July 1879. National Archives.

Log, *USS Constitution*, 16 July 1879 - 21 January 1880. National Archives.

Log, *USS Constitution*, 22 January - 24 July 1880. National Archives.

Log, *USS Constitution*, 25 July 1880 - 4 February 1881. National Archives.

Log, *USS Constitution*, 5 February - 21 August 1881. National Archives.

Log, *USS Constitution*, 22 August - 14 December 1881. National Archives.

Mager, CHCARP Philip T., USN(Ret). Undated statement concerning grounding. *USS Constitution* Museum.

Magruder, P.H. "The U.S. Naval Academy and Annapolis During the Civil War." U.S. Naval Institute *Proceedings,* August 1945.

Navy Department. *"Official Records of the Union and Confederate Navies in the War of the Rebellion."* Washington, D.C.: GPO. 1921.

"Old Ironsides." *Harper's Weekly* (Supplement), July 10, 1875.

Paullin, Charles Oscar. *"Paullin's History of Naval Administration, 1775-1911."* Annapolis, Md.: U.S. Naval Institute. 1968.

Vallette, Henry M. "History and Reminiscences of the Philadelphia Navy Yard." Potter's *American Monthly Magazine,* July 1876.

## Chapter 18 The Long Road Back

Albright, Charles Leonard. *"The East Coast Cruise of the U.S. Frigate Constitution."* Richmond, Va.: Press of The Dietz Printing Co. 1934.

Andrews, RADM Philip, USN. "The 'Old Ironsides' Campaign." U.S. Naval Institute *Proceedings,* October 1926.

"An SOS from 'Old Ironsides'." Brochure published by the National Save "Old Ironsides" Committee. 1929.

Brewington, M.V. *"Shipcarvers of North America."* New York: Dover Publications, Inc. 1962.

"Ceremonies Incident to the Commissioning of the U.S. Frigate Constitution." Brochure distributed at the commissioning ceremony, 1 July 1931.

Downin, CDR Jack, USN(Ret). " 'Lunchbox Charlie' Bonaparte." U.S. Naval Institute *Proceedings,* August 1976.

Goodwin, Katharine Calvert. "The Spirit of 1812 Returns to the Sea." Daughters of the American Revolution *Magazine*, August 1931.

Hollis, Ira N. *"The Frigate Constitution."* 2nd ed. Boston: Houghton, Mifflin Company. 1931.

Krafft, Herman F. "New Lease on Life for Old Ironsides." U.S. Naval Institute *Proceedings,* October 1925.

Logs (monthly), *USS Constitution*, 1 July 1931 - 8 June 1934. National Archives.

Lord, LT John A.,(CC) USN. "U.S.S. Constitution Restoration, 1927-1930." Typed, duplicated report. n.d.

## Sources

Martin, CDR Tyrone G., USN. "The New *Constitution*." Unpublished manuscript.

Melling, George. *"Laws Relating to the Navy - Annotated, Supplement - 1929."* Washington, D.C.: GPO. 1929.

"Memorial to the Senate and House of Representatives of the United States" from the Massachusetts Historical Society. 30 December 1903.

Navy Department. "History of United States Frigate Constitution." 13 August 1970.

Norris, Lowell Ames. "Notes - Volume Five." Scrapbook. *USS Constitution* Museum.

Paramount Pictures. "Old Ironsides." Souvenir movie program. n.d.

Scrapbooks maintained by ship's company during the 1931-4 tour. *USS Constitution* Museum.

Snow, Elliot, and Gosnell, H. Allen. *"On the Decks of 'Old Ironsides'."* New York: The MacMillan Company. 1932.

*The Youth's Companion* (New England Edition). June 6, 1907.

*The Youth's Companion* (New England Edition). August 8, 1907.

### Chapter 19 Until the Bicentennial

Boston Naval Shipyard *News* (numerous issues, 1949-67). In files of the Boston National Historical Park.

Correspondence and/or conversations with CPO Jerry P. Knickerbocker, (nephew of LCDR Herman P. Knickerbocker, Captain, 1940-41), CDR Owen W. Huff (Captain, 1945-7), CDR Louis E. Wood (Captain, 1947-50), CW04 Knied H. Christensen (Captain, 1950-2), CDR Albert C. Messier (Captain, 1952-4), LCDR Charles W. Morris (Captain, 1954-7), David G. O'Brien (then LTJG; Captain, 1957-9), CAPT Edward J. Melanson, Jr. (Captain, 1959-60), CDR Victor B. Stevens, Jr. (Captain, 1960-3), John C. Kelleher (then LT; Captain, 1963-5), CDR Hugh A. Moore (Captain, 1969-70), CDR John D. McKinnon (Captain, 1971-2), CDR Thomas Coyne (Captain, 1972-4), and the men of the *USS Constitution* Restoration and Maintenance Facility: Donald A. Turner (Head), Joseph Brodeur, Clarence Gaudet, John McLean, John Paula, Daniel Scully, Domenic Silvaggio, Frank Stachowski, Anthony Vitale, Richard Wallace, Iggy Wencek, and Ralph Yarn.

Files of the Public Affairs Office, First Naval District (Boston, Massachusetts).

Letter and photograph files at *USS Constitution.*

Martin, CDR Tyrone G. " 'Old Ironsides:' Relevant Relic." U.S. Naval Institute *Proceedings,* September 1976.

Martin, CDR Tyrone G. *The Rejuvenation of "Old Ironsides."* Paper presented to the New England Section, Society of Naval Architects and Marine Engineers, January 1977.

Martin, CDR Tyrone G. *Maintaining "Old Ironsides."* Paper presented at the Bath Marine Museum Symposium on American Maritime History, May 1977.

Martin, CDR Tyrone G. "Ain't Necessarily So." Quincy (MA) *Patriot-Ledger*, 6 July 1977.

Personal recollections and memorabilia of ship's company, *USS Constitution*, August 1974 - October 1976.

*USS Constitution* Restoration and Maintenance Facility. *Record of Work Accomplished by Shop 64 on USS Constitution, January 1927 - June 30, 1972. Unpublished report in Facility files.*

# Supplementary Reading

Bell, Frederick J. *Room To Swing A Cat.* New York: Longmans, Green and Co. 1938.

Brewington, M.V. *Shipcarvers of North America.* New York: Dover Publications, Inc. 1962.

Brooks, George S., ed. *James Durand: An Able Seaman of 1812.* New Haven, Ct.: Yale University Press. 1926.

Chapelle, Howard I. *The History of American Sailing Ships.* New York: W.W. Norton and Company, Inc. 1935.

Chapelle, Howard I. *The History of the American Sailing Navy.* New York: Bonanza. 1949.

Forester, C.S. *The Age of Fighting Sail.* Garden City, N.J.: Doubleday and Co. 1956.

Grant, Bruce. *Isaac Hull: Captain of Old Ironsides.* Chicago: Pellegrini and Cudahy. 1947.

Johnson, Robert Erwin. *Thence 'Round Cape Horn.* Annapolis, Md.: U.S. Naval Institute. 1963.

Maclay, Edgar S. *A Youthful Man-O'-Warsman.* Greenlawn, N.Y.: Navy Blue Company. 1910.

Mahan, Alfred Thayer. *Sea Power in its Relation to the War of 1812.* Boston: Little, Brown, and Co. 1905.

McKee, Christopher. *Edward Preble.* Annapolis Md.: Naval Institute Press. 1972.

Napier, LT Henry Edward, RN. *New England Blockaded 1814.* Salem, Ma.: Peabody Museum. 1939.

Paullin, Charles Oscar. *Commodore John Rodgers.* Annapolis, Md.: U.S. Naval Institute. 1967.

Paullin, Charles Oscar. *Paullin's History of Naval Administration, 1775-1911.* Annapolis, Md.: U.S. Naval Institute. 1968.

Paullin, Charles Oscar. *American Voyages to the Orient, 1690-1865.* Annapolis, Md.: U.S. Naval Institute. 1971.

Pratt, Fletcher, *Preble's Boys.* New York: William Sloane Associates. 1950.

Reilly, John C., Jr. *Ships of the U.S. Navy: Christening, Launching and Commissioning.* Washington, D.C.: GPO. 1975.

Roosevelt, Theodore. *The Naval War of 1812.* 3rd ed. New York: G.P. Putnam's Sons. 1910.

## Supplementary Reading

Smelser, Marshall. *The Congress Founds the Navy.* University of Notre Dame Press. 1959.

Tucker, Glenn. *Dawn Like Thunder.* New York: The Bobbs-Merrill Company, Inc. 1963.

# Glossary

## A

ABAFT (or AFT or AFTER) — In or toward the rear part of the ship.

ANCHOR PORT — An opening in the spar deck bulwark abaft the cathead where an anchor was stowed.

## B

BARQUE (or BARK) — A three-masted vessel, square-rigged on the two forward masts, but fore-and-aft rigged on the mizzen.

BEAR UP — To alter a ship's course so that she runs more nearly *with* the wind.

BEAT TO QUARTERS — The drummer's particular signal for all hands to go to their battle stations and prepare to fight.

BERTH (or BIRTH) DECK — In *Constitution*, that full deck below the gun deck set aside for the crew's habitation.

BILLBOARD — A small, heavy platform outboard of and below the anchor port (q.v.) on which a stowed anchor largely rested.

BILLET — Office; position.

BILLET HEAD — Bow ornamentation other than a figurehead.

BINNACLE — A stand in which the compass is suspended, usually in gimbal rings, so that it remains in the horizontal.

BITTS — Strong wooden paired uprights used for securing heavy ropes, such as anchor cables.

BLISTER — To apply a strong poultice which will cause the skin to blister, thereby drawing the bad "humors" from the body.

BLOW ON YOUR MATCHES — Blow on the burning coal at the end of the slow match to bring it to white heat.

BOARDED HIS FORETACK — Hauled in the tack (q.v.) of a square sail in order to sail close to the wind.

357

# Glossary

| | |
|---|---|
| BOBSTAY | A rope used to confine the bowsprit of a ship downward to the cutwater (q.v.). |
| BOOMKIN | A short boom at either side of the bow or stern used to take either a foresail tack or a main brace (q.v.). |
| BOWER ANCHOR | The large anchor normally used in anchoring; the best bower on the starboard bow and the bower anchor to larboard. |
| BOWLINE | The line attached to the leech (q.v.) rope of a square sail, and leading forward; used to hold the weather side of a close-hauled sail forward and steady, enabling the ship to sail as close to the wind as possible. |
| BOWSPRIT | The large boom assembly projecting forward over a ship's stem (q.v.); also, the innermost, largest section of that assembly. |
| BRACE | Rope attached to a yard; used to adjust the yard in the horizontal plane. |
| BREAST HOOK | A thick, curved timber fastened across the inside of the stem holding the bows and sides together. |
| BREECHING TACKLE | A rope used to secure the cannon, and to prevent them from recoiling too much when fired. |
| BRIDLE PORT | The first square opening in either bow at the gun deck level through which a towing bridle could be taken in and secured to the ship, and from which handling an anchor could be facilitated. |
| BRIG | A two-masted vessel, square-rigged on masts of nearly equal height; also, a ship's jail. |
| BROADSIDE | The whole discharge of all guns on one side of a man-of-war. |
| BULKHEAD | A vertical partition between two decks; a wall. |
| BULWARK | Planking around the edge of the upper deck to provide the crew working there with some protection from the sea. |
| BUMBOATS | Small craft used to bring vendors of all sorts to the vicinity of a ship at anchor in port. |

# C

| | |
|---|---|
| CABLE'S LENGTH | 100 fathoms (200 yards). |
| CABOOSE (or CAMBOOSE) | The galley, the cook's stove. |
| CAP RAIL | The rail topping the bulwark (q.v.). |
| CAPSTAN | The apparatus used to raise an anchor. |
| CAREENING | To haul a ship over on one side in order to expose a portion of the underwater body for repair or maintenance. |
| CARLINGS | Short, fore and aft timbers placed for reinforcement between deck beams. |
| CATHARPINS | Ropes under the fighting tops (q.v.) bracing the lower ends of the futtock shrouds. (q.v.). |
| CATHEAD | A short, strong boom on either bow used to suspend an anchor clear of the bow for letting go, or upon weighing. |
| CEILING | The inner, horizontally laid layer of timber in a ship's hull. |
| CENTERLINE | The ship's longitudinal axis. |
| CHANDLER | A supplier of stores to a ship. |
| CHANNEL (or CHAIN WALES) | Broad, thick platform projecting from the ship's side abreast of, and somewhat behind, each mast. |
| CHARLIE NOBLE | Nickname for the galley smokestack. |
| CHOCKS | Wedges used to hold an object in a particular position. |
| CLAMPS | Thick beams on the inside of a ship's hull used to support the ends of the deck beams. |
| CLEAR FOR ACTION | Make preparations for battle short of actually stationing the men at their posts. |
| CLOSE REEFED | Said of sails when all the reefs (q.v.) have been taken in and the sails can be reefed no further. |
| COAMINGS | The raised edges around openings (hatches) in the deck. |
| COCKPIT | A compartment deep in the ship where battle casualties were attended to by the surgeon and his mates. |
| COME TO | Bring the ship's head nearer to the wind carefully. |
| COOPER | A barrelmaker. |
| COPAL | A hard, transparent resin; used in varnishes. |
| CORDWAINER | A worker in leather. |
| CORSAIR | A Mediterranean privateer. |

| | |
|---|---|
| CORVETTE | A warship carrying its guns on one deck only, next smaller in size to a frigate; sometimes called a "ship-sloop." |
| COXSWAIN | The petty officer in charge of a boat. |
| CROSSJACK | The lowest spar (q.v.) on the mizzenmast (q.v.). |
| CROSSTREES | Timbers laid across the trestletrees (q.v.) at the head of a mast to support a fighting top (q.v.) or spread the supporting shrouds of the upper masts. |
| CUTTER | A broader, shorter, deeper boat than the pinnace (q.v.), also with a square stern; among a warship's medium-size boats, usually identified by number, but sometimes by color or name. |
| CUTWATER | The foremost part of the stem (q.v.), forming a curving leading edge which parts the water as the ship advances. |

## D

| | |
|---|---|
| DAVITS | Curved pillars on a ship's side from which are suspended a ship's boat. |
| DEADEYE | A round or pear-shaped block pierced with three holes, used mainly in standing rigging (q.v.) to set up shrouds. |
| DOG WATCH | Either the watch from 4 to 6 PM, or that from 6 to 8 PM. |
| DOLPHIN STRIKER | A spar pointing downwards from the end of the bowsprit to spread rigging counterbalancing the upward pull on the jibboom end; in *Constitution*, it has *two* arms sloping down and out to the sides. |
| DOUBLING | The overlap of two sections of mast. |
| DRAFT (or DRAUGHT) | The depth of water necessary to float a ship. |
| DRAWING SAILS | Sails catching, or filling with, the wind. |
| DRESS SHIP | A full display of flags to honor a person or event; sometimes called a "rainbow." |

## F

| | |
|---|---|
| FATHOM | A linear measure of 6 feet. |
| FIDDED | Held in place with a shouldered, square-section pin, as a topmast with the trestletrees. |

| | |
|---|---|
| FIGHTING TOP | A platform mounted near the head of a lower mast from which snipers could fire down on an enemy. |
| FILL AWAY | Set sail. |
| FINE | In terms of direction, a small amount; a few degrees of bearing; less than a point (q.v.). |
| FISH | A long, convex piece of wood designed to reinforce a damaged mast or spar; a splint. |
| FISH HOOP | The iron band used to bind together the segments of a "made" mast. |
| FLYING JIB BOOM | The outermost section of the bowsprit assembly projecting forward over the ship's stem. |
| FORCING PUMP | A pump mounted on a channel (q.v.) and drawing water directly from the sea. |
| FORE (or FORWARD) | In or toward the front part of the ship. |
| FORECASTLE | Usually, a short deck uppermost in the forward part of a ship; in *Constitution*, that portion of the spar deck (q.v.) from the head to the main hatch. |
| FOREMAST | The forwardmost mast assembly in the ship; also, the lowest section of the three which comprise that assembly. |
| FORE YARD | The lowest spar (q.v.) crossing the foremast. |
| FREEBOARD | The height of the upper deck above water. |
| FRIGATE | A man of war carrying from 28 to 50 guns on one covered gun deck as well as on its forecastle and quarterdeck, fast and maneuverable. |
| FUTTOCK | One of the middle sections making up a frame, or ship's "rib." |
| FUTTOCK SHROUDS | The short shrouds running downward and inward from a fighting top. |

## G

| | |
|---|---|
| GAFF | The spar to which is attached the upper edge of a four-sided fore-and-aft sail. |
| GALLEY | The caboose (q.v.); also, a long, low craft propelled by a single bank of oars and a sail. |
| GALLEY WEST | Died. |
| GALLIOT | A small, speedy sailing vessel with oars for auxiliary power. |

361

*Glossary*

| | |
|---|---|
| GAMMONING | Rope or chain lashing staying the bowsprit to the knee of the head to hold the bowsprit down against the up-ward pull of the forestay. |
| GIG | The ship's boat particularly reserved for the Captain's use. |
| GREAT CABIN | The Captain's cabin. |
| GUARDO | A receiving ship; a floating barracks. |
| GUDGEON | Metal clamp bolted to the sternpost. *Pintles* on back of the rudder fit into corresponding holes in the gudgeons, hinging the rudder to the sternpost. |
| GUNBOAT | A small, light naval craft carrying perhaps only one gun. |
| GUN DECK | A frigate's main deck, supporting its battery of heavy long guns. |
| GUN PORT LIDS | The "doors" or "shutters" closing the gun ports in a ship's hull to the weather. |
| GURNET | A small narrow channel dangerous to navigate owing to current and numerous rocks. |

# H

| | |
|---|---|
| HALYARD (or HALLIARD or HAULYARD) | A rope or tackle used to hoist or lower a sail, yard, gaff, or flag. |
| HARNESS CASK | The large cask kept on deck near the caboose from which the daily meat ration is issued. |
| HAWSE PIPE | The opening through which an anchor cable runs from the anchor to the capstan (q.v.). |
| HAWSER | A three-strand, right-hand twist rope. |
| HEADSAILS | Collectively, those sails supported between the bowsprit and the foremast, i.e., the flying jib, jib, and fore topmast staysail. |
| HEAVING THE LEAD | Using a weighted line to determine the depth of water. |
| HOG | The result of stress on a ship's hull, causing it to droop fore and aft. |
| HOGSHEAD | A barrel of 60-65 gallon capacity. |
| HOVE TO | Trimming the sails so the ship is making no headway; stopped. |

362

| | |
|---|---|
| HULL DOWN | On the horizon with only masts and sails showing. |
| HULLED | Shot in the hull, usually at point-blank range. |
| HUNDREDWEIGHT | 112 pounds. |

## I

| | |
|---|---|
| IN ORDINARY | A ship essentially ready for use, but with only a caretaker crew aboard. |
| IN STAYS | A ship headed directly into the wind; usually a transitory condition when going from one tack (q.v.) to another and not one to be desired otherwise. |

## J

| | |
|---|---|
| JIBBOOM | The spar forming the middle third of the bowsprit assembly extending forward over the ship's stem. |
| JOINER | A craftsman who makes furniture and installs cabins and other light wood structures in a ship. |
| JORUM | A drinking bowl. |
| JURY RIG | A temporary repair. |

## K

| | |
|---|---|
| KEDGING | To move a ship, usually in harbor, by taking a light anchor out ahead with a boat, dropping it, and winching up to it; repeating the process in succession using two anchors in order to move the ship when wind and tide are adverse or non-existent. |
| KEELSON | A timber bolted to the keel above, or on either side, of that timber to strengthen it. |
| KENTLEDGE | Pig iron ballast. |
| KETCH | A small, two-masted vessel wherein the forward mast is taller than the after mast, and wherein the rig is relatively compatible with the employment of mortars firing high-angle projectiles, as in the case of Preble's bomb ketches, or mortar boats. |
| KID | A container in which rations are carried to the mess (q.v.). |
| KNEE | A large angled piece of timber with one arm bolted horizontally to a beam and the other |

KNIGHTHEAD     to the ship's side, for the purpose of strengthening the sides against sudden shock.

The heavy baulks of timber on either side of the stem which support the bowspirt.

## L

LAID UP     A ship not in use, unrigged and dismantled.

LANDED     Put ashore.

LARBOARD     The left-hand side of a ship as one stands on deck facing the bow.

LARBOARD TACK     Sailing with the wind striking the sails from the larboard side.

LATEEN YARD     A long spar hoisted obliquely to a mast, usually with the shorter, lower end forward of the mast.

LAY TO     Underway with no motion through the water.

LEDGE     A piece of timber place athwartships between beams to provide additional support.

LEECH     The edge of a sail.

LEE SHORE     Land toward which a wind is blowing.

LEEWARD     Downwind.

LET FLY     Releasing the sheets completely, as quickly as possible.

LIFTING     A sail bellying upward in the wind with its sheets slacked.

LOG     The ship's "diary," its official operating record; also, a device used to measure a ship's speed through the water.

LONG IN THE TOOTH     Old.

LUFF     To come closer to the wind; also, a tackle comprised of line, a single block, and a double block.

## M

MAGAZINE     A compartment deep in a ship used to store gun powder; kept locked with the keys in the Captain's possession.

MAINMAST     The middle mast assembly in the ship; also, the lowest section of the three which comprise that assembly.

MAIN YARD     The lowest spar crossing the mainmast.

| | |
|---|---|
| MESS | A group of 6-8 persons eating together. |
| MISSED STAYS | When a ship fails to complete tacking from one side to another. |
| MIZZENMAST | The rearmost mast assembly in the ship; also, the lowest section of the three which make up that assembly. |
| MOLE | Usually a stone structure which is at once a breakwater and, on the shoreward side, mooring space for ships. |
| MOULD | A pattern made of thin, flexible wood. |

## O

| | |
|---|---|
| OAKUM | A substance made by unravelling old rope, and used principally for caulking seams. |
| ON A TAUT BOWLINE | Sailing close-hauled to the wind. |
| ORLOP | Lowest deck in a warship; often a partial, or platform deck. |

## P

| | |
|---|---|
| PARTNERS | Timber framework strengthening the deck where it is pierced by a mast or other structure. |
| PINNACE | A heavy boat whose oars are powered by two men each, i.e., "double banked." |
| PLANK OWNER | Member of the original crew. |
| PLANK SHEER | The uppermost plank running along the top timbers outside of a ship's frame. |
| POINT | An arc of $11\frac{1}{4}$ degrees. |
| POLACRE (or POLACCA) | A Mediterranean three-master, square-rigged on the fore and main masts, but with a lateen yard (q.v.) on the mizzen mast with a square topsail above it. |
| POOP | Highest and aftermost deck in a ship. |
| POOPED | Having taken water over the stern. |
| PORT | Word officially substituted for "larboard" (q.v.) in the U.S. Navy in 1846 to end confusion with "starboard." |
| PRESS OF CANVAS | All sails set and drawing well. |
| PURCHASE | The mechanism by which mechanical advantage is gained. |
| PUT DOWN THE HELM | Pull the helm down to the leeward side to direct the ship toward the wind. |

# Q

QUARTERDECK — Usually, a partial deck located aft in a ship and above the main deck; in *Constitution*, that portion of the spar deck (q.v.) from the main mast to the stern.

QUARTER GALLERY — A small, windowed "balcony" located on either side of a ship at the stern.

# R

RAZEE — To cut down the spar deck of a vessel, reducing her freeboard; a small ship of the line might be converted into a fifth rate "ship" or heavy frigate in this manner.

REEF — To reduce sail area by gathering up a portion of the sail and securing it by means of reef points (short tie lines fitted in two or three rows across the face of a sail).

REEFER — A Midshipman; also, an officer's pea coat.

REEVE — To pass a rope's end through any sheave or block.

RELIEVING TACKLES — Adjustable rigging used to ease or offset stresses temporarily induced in a structure or rigging.

ROYAL YARD — The spar next above the topgallant yard.

RUDDER PENDANTS — Lengths of rope or wire by which the rudder chains can be connected to the rudder tackles, if necessary.

RUNNER — A rope used to increase the mechanical advantage of a tackle (pulley).

RUNNING RIGGING — Those ropes used to adjust yards and sails to suit wind conditions.

# S

SAILS — Square sail beneath the bowsprit: Spritsail
Fore-and-aft sails forward of the bowsprit (going out the bowsprit):
Fore topmast staysail, jib, flying jib
Square sails on foremast (from bottom up): Foresail (or course), fore topsail, fore topgallant sail, fore royal sail, fore skysail.
Square sails on mainmast (from bottom up): Mainsail (or course), main topsail, main topgallant sail, main royal sail, main skysail.

Square sails on mizzen mast (from bottom up): (Nothing below crossjack), mizzen topsail, mizzen topgallant sail, mizzen royal sail, mizzen skysail.

Fore-and-aft sails on after side of mizzen mast (from bottom up):

Spanker (or driver), gaff topsail

In addition, there were various fore-and-aft staysails between the fore and main masts, and main and mizzen masts, as well as studdingsails (q.v.). For *Constitution,* a set of some 37 sails amounting to 42,720 square feet of canvas.

| | |
|---|---|
| SALVO | The simultaneous discharge of a number of guns. |
| SCANTLING | Any piece of timber of a particular standard square-section. |
| SCARPH (or SCARF) | A method of joining the ends of two pieces of timber in a line by tapering an overlapping joint so that there is no increasing thickness at the joint. |
| SCHOONER | A fore-and-aft rigged sailing vessel having anywhere from two to seven masts. |
| SCOW | A rectangular, shallow vessel most frequently used for transporting cargo around harbors. |
| SCUTTLE | To sink intentionally a ship by opening the hull to the sea. |
| SCUTTLEBUTT | The barrel used to issue the daily fresh water ration. |
| SHEARS (or SHEER LEGS) | A triangular structure composed of two upright spars lashed together at their tops, the lower ends spread, and the whole guyed so that the structure can be moved and held at any desired angle (like a crane); hoisting tackle is rigged at the apex to handle masts or other heavy loads. |
| SHEET | A rope fastened to one or both of the lower corners of a sail. |
| SHEET ANCHOR | Often, the heaviest anchor carried, and kept ready for emergency use, as when a storm in port caused the ship to drag her bower anchor(s) (q.v.). |

367

## Glossary

| | |
|---|---|
| SHINGLE | Round beach stones used for ballast. |
| SHIP OF THE LINE | The sailing battleship; a ponderous ship having two or three full gun decks mounting from 64 to over 120 cannon. |
| SHOAL WATER | Shallow water. |
| SHOE | False keel; a protective strip on the lower surface of the keel. |
| SHOWING COLORS | Hoisting a national flag. |
| SHROUDS | Heavy rigging supporting a mast from its head to either side of the ship. |
| SKID BEAMS | Those beams spanning the main hatch on which were stowed ship's boats, spare spars, spare planks, etc. |
| SKY POLES | Short, light masts affixed to the after sides of the topgallant masts to accommodate the skysails. |
| SKYSAIL YARD | The spar next above the royal yard; in *Constitution*, the highest ever carried. |
| SLIPPING ANCHOR | Getting underway rapidly by cutting or releasing the anchor cable; the buoyed (marked) anchor could be retrieved when the emergency had passed. |
| SLOOP | A single-masted vessel carrying a large mainsail and a single head sail. |
| SLOW MATCH | A wick, often made of cotton, which was made to burn slowly and which was used to ignite a cannon's powder charge. |
| SPAR | Any rounded piece of wood, such as yards, gaffs, and booms. |
| SPAR DECK | *Constitution*'s uppermost deck, open to the weather. |
| SPLICE THE MAIN BRACE | Issue an extra ration of grog, usually in celebration. |
| SPOKE | Exchanged information. |
| SPRITSAIL YARD | The spar crossing the bowsprit; in *Constitution*, the sail associated with this yard was discarded within a year of her first voyage as being inefficient and unnecessary. |
| STANDING RIGGING | Those ropes used to support the masts. |
| STARBOARD | The right-hand side of a ship as one stands on deck facing the bow. |
| STARBOARD TACK | To sail with the wind striking the sails from the starboard side. |

368

| | |
|---|---|
| STAYSAIL | Any triangular sail hoisted on a stay abaft the foremast or mainmast. |
| STEERAGE | That area of the ship containing the Midshipmens' berthing. |
| STEERAGEWAY | Just sufficient speed through the water to make the rudder effective. |
| STEM | The upright component of the frame rising from the forward end of the keel. |
| STEPPED | Installed a mast in its seat ("step"). |
| STRAKE | A line of planking running along a ship's side. |
| STREAM ANCHOR | An anchor about one-third the size of a bower anchor used from astern in narrow waterways where a ship cannot safely swing with the tide. |
| STUDDINGSAILS | Light sails extended in light or moderate breezes, beyond the skirts of the principal sails. |
| STUDDINGSAIL BOOMS | Extensions to the yards run out to accommodate the studdingsails (q.v.) |
| STUNSAILS | Studdingsails (q.v.) |
| SUPERCARGO | An officer charged with the commercial affairs of a merchant ship. |
| SWEEPS | Long, heavy oars used in large ships' boats and in some smaller men-of-war. |
| SWIVEL | A small, light cannon mounted in a swivelling yoke on a ship's bulwarks. |

## T

| | |
|---|---|
| TACK | To work a ship to windward by alternately taking the wind from one side and then the other; also, a rope used to confine the foremost lower corners of the courses (fore or main sails) in a fixed position. |
| TAFFRAIL | An ornamental rail along the upper edge of the stern. |
| TAKEN ABACK | Stopped short, as by an unexpected, sudden shift of the wind. |
| TATTOO | A drumming sound, as when caulkers hammered oakum into a ship's seams. |
| TENDER | Any small vessel or craft used in support of a man-of-war. |
| TINKER | A sheet metal worker. |

## *Glossary*

| | |
|---|---|
| TOMPION | A plug used to stop the mouth of a cannon when not in use. |
| TOPGALLANT MAST | The third section up in a mast assembly. |
| TOPGALLANT YARD | The spar next above the topsail yard. |
| TOP HAMPER | Masts, yards, rigging, and sails, collectively. |
| TOP MAST | The second section up in a mast assembly; that section rising immediately above the fighting top. |
| TOPSAIL YARD | The spar next above the fore or main yard, or the crossjack. |
| TOUCH HOLE | A small hole leading down through the wall of a cannon to the rear of the bore through which the charge was fired. |
| TRAFFICKER | A ship carrying on a trade in a particular item, usually contraband. |
| TRAILBOARDS | The curved, decorative woodwork immediately below and aft of the figurehead or billet head topping a ship's cutwater (q.v.). |
| TRANSOM | The vertical face of a ship's stern. |
| TRESTLETREES | Two strong pieces of timber placed fore and aft at the head of a mast to support crosstrees (q.v.) and higher masts. |
| TRIED ON A BOWLING | To sail as close to the wind as possible. |
| TRIM | The difference in draft readings at the bow (or head) and stern; the attitude of a ship as she rests in the water: *Constitution* normally rode deeper aft as did most of her kind. |
| TRUCK | The circular wooden cap on the uppermost masthead. |
| TUMBLEHOME | The inward slope of a ship's side above its widest breadth. |

### U

| | |
|---|---|
| UNSHIP | To remove something from the place in which it was fixed. |

### V

| | |
|---|---|
| VEER | See WEAR. |

### W

| | |
|---|---|
| WAIST | That part of a ship between the forecastle and quarterdeck; roughly, the middle. |
| WAIST NETTINGS | Nettings in the waist (q.v.) in which the crew's rolled hammocks were stowed. |

370

WALES — Heavy fore and aft timbers in the side planking of a ship, particularly beneath the gun ports.

WARDROOM — The common room for officers, both lounge and dining room; first known as the "gun room."

WATERWAYS — Gutters along the outer edges of a deck.

WAYS — The supporting structure from which a newbuilt ship is launched.

WEATHER GAGE — The upwind position relative to an enemy.

WEAR (AROUND) — To put a ship on the other tack (q.v.) by turning her away from the wind.

WIND SHIP — (Rhymes with "mind.") Pivot her end for end, usually with a system of anchors and cables.

WOOLDING — To reinforce a mast or spar by tightly winding a rope around it; a fish (q.v.) is woolded to a damaged mast or spar.

## X

XEBEC — A craft native to the Barbary pirates, characterized by an unusually long overhang, fore and aft, by low freeboard, and employing a mix of square and lateen sails (q.v.).

## Y

YARD — A long piece of timber suspended across a mast to spread a sail to the wind.

# Index

# Index

# Index

# Index